Broadcast Advertising

Broadcast Advertising

A Comprehensive Working Textbook / Third Edition

Sherilyn K. Zeigler
University of Hawaii

Herbert H. Howard
University of Tennessee

Iowa State University Press / Ames

Sherilyn K. Zeigler is a scriptwriter and public relations director for one of Hawaii's premier entertainers, and she is an adjunct professor in the Department of Marketing at the University of Hawaii.

Herbert H. Howard, a professor of broadcasting, is assistant dean in the College of Communications at the University of Tennessee.

First Edition © 1984 John Wiley & Sons, Inc.

Second Edition © 1988 Iowa State University Press
Third Edition © 1991 Iowa State University Press, Ames, Iowa 50010
All rights reserved

Manufactured in the United States of America

⊛This book is printed on acid-free paper.

Library of Congress Cataloging-in-Publication Data

Zeigler, Sherilyn K.
    Broadcast advertising: a comprehensive working textbook / by Sherilyn K. Zeigler and Herbert H. Howard.–3rd ed.
        p.   cm.
    Includes bibliographical references.
    ISBN 0-8138-0072-2 (alk. paper)
    1. Broadcast advertising — United States. I. Howard, Herbert H. II. Title.
HF6146.B74Z44   1991
659.14'0973–dc20

90-33584

CONTENTS

Preface, ix

1 America's "World" of Broadcast Advertising, 3

An Overview of the Advertising Process, 3
The Broadcast Media, 4
Historical Perspectives, 4
The Scope of Broadcast Advertising Today, 11
Elements of the Broadcast Advertising Industry, 11
Types of Broadcast Advertising, 13
Types of Broadcast Advertisers, 14
Types of Campaigns, 15
Radio and Television: A Comparison, 16
A Look Ahead, 20
Study Questions, 21
Assignments, 22
Notes, 22
Suggested Readings, 22

2 Broadcast Stations and Networks, 24

Station Regulations, 24
Ownership of Stations, 25
Television Stations, 27
Radio Broadcasting, 29
Organization of Broadcast Stations, 30
Radio and Television Networks, 32
Cable Television: The Newest Mass Medium, 38
The Advertiser's Concern, 40
Study Questions, 40
Assignments, 40
Notes, 41
Suggested Readings, 41

3 Coverage, Circulation, and Facilities, 43

Station Coverage, 43
Coverage and Circulation, 50
Production Facilities, 52
Study Questions, 53
Assignments, 54
Notes, 56
Suggested Readings, 57

4 The Advertising Agency Business, 58

Functions of the Modern Agency, 58
Choosing an Agency, 63
Agency Payment, 64
The Station Representative, 66
Alternatives to the Full-Service Agency, 67
The Barter Alternative, 69
Study Questions, 70
Assignments, 71
Notes, 72
Suggested Readings, 72

5 Regulation of Broadcast Advertising, 73

Federal Regulation, 73
State Regulation, 81
Self-Regulation, 82
Study Questions, 86
Assignments, 87
Notes, 87
Suggested Readings, 88

6 Commercials and Social Responsibility, 89

Practicing Advertising Ethics, 89
The Advertiser/Agency Side, 90
The Question of Truth, 91
The Advertising Council, 93
Combined Campaigns: Public Service and
   Commercial Advertising, 95
The Issue of Violence, 100
Commercial Portrayals, 100
Political Concerns, 101
Looking Behind the Scenes, 102
The Challenge, 102
Study Questions, 103
Assignments, 103
Notes, 104
Suggested Readings, 105

v

7 Broadcast Media Audiences, 106

Growth of Television Households, 106
Characteristics of U.S. Television Households, 107
Growth of Radio Households, 107
Location of Radio Sets, 108
Radio and Television Set Usage, 109
Audience Composition, 113
Study Questions, 118
Assignments, 118
Notes, 118
Suggested Readings, 119

8 Television and Radio Programming, 120

Television Programming, 120
Radio Programming, 133
Study Questions, 136
Assignments, 136
Notes, 137
Suggested Readings, 137

9 Writing Radio Commercials, 138

The Nature of the Task, 138
The Elements of Radio Communication, 138
The Copy Platform, 142
The Commercial Message, 147
Study Questions, 158
Assignments, 159
Notes, 161
Suggested Readings, 161

10 Writing Television Commercials, 162

The Nature of the Task, 162
The Elements of Television Communication, 163
The Commercial Message, 165
The Copy Platform, 175
Television Commercial Formats, 175
Content Specifics, 184
Use of Children, 188
Developing a Recognizable Style, 188
Study Questions, 189
Assignments, 189
Notes, 191
Suggested Readings, 191

11 Broadcast Commercial Production, 192

Who's in Charge, 192
Commercial Production Equipment, 197
Costs, 211
Study Questions, 214
Assignments, 215
Notes, 216
Suggested Readings, 217

12 Commercial Copy Testing, 218

Defining the Problem, 218
Proceeding in Stages, 219
Validity and Reliability, 220
Surveys, Experiments, and Observations, 220
When to Test, 222
Pitfalls in Question Structuring, 227
National Commercial Testing Organizations, 228
Using Test Results, 237
Study Questions, 238
Assignments, 238
Notes, 239
Suggested Readings, 239

13 Audience Research, 240

Audience Measurement Techniques, 240
Terminology, 244
Audience Measurement Services, 254
Study Questions, 264
Assignments, 264
Suggested Readings, 265

14 Time Buying, 267

Sources of Information, 267
Preliminary Client Analysis, 272
Selecting the Network Schedule, 273
Selecting the Broadcast Market, 277
Selecting Specific Stations, 278
Television and Radio Station Rates, 281
The Station Sales Effort, 285
Study Questions, 289
Assignments, 290
Notes, 293
Suggested Readings, 293

15 Selling Television Time, 295

Calling on the Local Advertiser, 295
Calling on the Advertising Agency, 296
Maintaining Good Relations with
  Established Accounts, 297
Selling the Station and Its Inventory, 298
Selling the Independent Station, 300
Assistance from TVB, 300
Study Questions, 301
Assignments, 302
Suggested Readings, 302

16 Broadcast Advertising at the Retail Level, 303

Functions of Retail Advertising, 303
Successful Retail Broadcast Campaigns, 309
Cooperative Broadcast Advertising, 313
Research, 315
Study Questions, 315
Assignments, 315
Notes, 316
Suggested Readings, 316

17 Broadcast Advertising Plans and Campaigns, 317

The Master Marketing Plan, 317
The Advertising Application, 318
The Broadcast Advertising Plan, 319
The Broadcast Advertising Budget, 322
Ad Campaigns and Program Fare, 326
In Retrospect, 328
Study Questions, 329
Assignments, 329
Notes, 329
Suggested Readings, 330

Glossary, 331

Index, 341

PREFACE

As we approach the twenty-first century, the possibilities for exciting breakthroughs in the field of broadcast advertising stagger the imagination. Technological achievements, advancements in managerial and research techniques, and examples of creative genius abound, and more are waiting to be discovered — by today's students, tomorrow's practitioners.

But there is much to learn, and the third edition of *Broadcast Advertising* is packed with information and exercises designed to shed light on all facets of the business. Like its predecessors, it's conversational in style and laced with practical applications of theoretical principles. Examples are current, factual material has been updated, and input from industry personnel has been incorporated.

Whether you're interested in station and network operations or in broadcasting from the point of view of advertising agencies, this book will give you an in-depth look at day-to-day procedures and career possibilities. You'll learn how to write and produce television and radio commercials, how to test them, and how to check them for compliance with legal requirements and ethical concerns. In addition, you'll gain insight into the complexities of time buying and selling, as well as audience analysis, and you'll discover the differences between local and national campaign planning and execution.

Whatever your interest, we hope you'll find your study of these chapters an enlightening and challenging experience, and that you'll find therein at least a small part of the fascination your authors feel for this business.

Broadcast Advertising

1

America's "World" of Broadcast Advertising

One of the principal differences between advanced and primitive societies is the presence of well-developed mass media systems. During most of the nineteenth century in the United States, consumers and producers often met at the butcher's, baker's, and candlestick maker's establishments where sellers told buyers personally about product benefits. Then, as American society grew more sophisticated, more economically integrated, and more job-specialized, mass media all but took over the task of communicating information about products, services, and stores.

One result of the separation between suppliers and customers was the growth of brand-name merchandise that facilitated product-marketing through advertising channels; the emergence of radio broadcasting as an advertising medium in the 1920s thus filled an important rapid-communication need. Television's development as a mass medium, some three decades later, coincided with the self-service revolution in marketing, now a very prominent system in America. As a substitute for much of the personal salesmanship formerly found in retail establishments, TV helped bridge the gap between mass producers and individual product users. Today, both radio and television have become giant sales tools for twentieth-century merchandisers. Furthermore, New York State led the rest of the country in declaring these media "legal necessities of life." That means they are considered so vital to a family's total life-style that neither can be lifted from a household in order to satisfy debts.[1]

With increased complexities in both marketing and communication processes, America's population explosion has been matched by explosions in the number of goods and services available, the amount of information needed about products and stores, and the variety of media outlets and combinations from which to choose. Hence, broadcast advertising has become a world unto itself, but one which permeates and influences the lives of us all. And only if we understand thoroughly its values and shortcomings—the problems with which it must cope and the rewards it has to offer—can business and society as a whole hope to profit from its existence. Properly utilized, broadcast advertising holds great potential for socioeconomic advancement and for improvements in the efficiency and effectiveness of daily decision-making tasks.

Let us start by examining advertising and broadcasting independently and then see how they operate together.

An Overview of the Advertising Process

Consumers often confuse advertising with its marketing "parent" to the extent that they believe advertising's basic objective is to sell. Think back, however, to a purchase you made recently and ask yourself whether any commercial—by itself—could have sold you. If the product or service had not been (1) available where and when you wanted it, (2) packaged and priced appropriately, (3) offered with an

3

attractive service policy or warranty, or, perhaps, (4) tied in with a coupon, premium, contest, or other merchandising appeal, it is unlikely that the sale would have occurred. The objective of the entire marketing process is to *sell;* advertising's job is to *communicate*—to a defined audience—information and a frame of mind conducive to the buying action. The actual purchase may occur long after exposure to a given commercial and only after the intervention of other sales forces and influences.

Behavioral science is advertising's second parent. Now consumer predispositions come into play: wants and needs, likes and dislikes, experiences and beliefs. Commercials are successful in their roles as informer/persuaders only when they utilize words and pictures, sounds and music, and personalities and actions that audiences can understand and believe, with which they can identify, and through which meaningful, relevant sales messages can be delivered.

Finally, advertising, as referred to in this text, is paid for (with the exception of public service announcements), includes sponsor identification, and is controlled in terms of content, timing, and media placement. Hence, it is set apart from certain forms of publicity, propaganda, and personal selling. At its present rate of growth, advertising volume in the United States should reach the astounding figure of $200 billion per year by A.D. 2000.

The Broadcast Media

Basically, broadcasting in the United States consists of two systems: (1) commercial stations and networks and (2) public broadcasting. The commercial segment is supported by advertising. Public broadcasting is supported by educational institutions, nonprofit foundations, government and corporate grants, and other sources, including donations from viewers/listeners.

Commercial broadcasting was well established in the United States long before the proliferation of public radio and TV stations that followed passage of the Public Broadcasting Act of 1967. As a result, U.S. broadcasting is dominated by the commercial system that is supported by advertising revenue. Although public networks and stations carry no commercial advertising as such, they do identify prominently—through courtesy announcements—businesses that underwrite programming expenses. These now-familiar underwriting announcements closely resemble institutional advertising and usually include company slogans and logos.

Traditional over-the-air broadcasting is supplemented by a multitude of cable-originated program services, or networks, that provide an alternative means for advertisers to reach the public through the electronic media. The advertiser's ability to select networks that appeal to narrowly defined target audiences, a process called "narrowcasting," is a principal advantage of cable. Many advertisers now schedule commercial messages on national cable networks and, in many communities, on local cable systems.

While the public itself has an immense investment in radio and TV receiving equipment (billions of dollars are spent annually on color TV sets alone), it is the sponsors who defray the cost of programs that inform, entertain, and provide service to the public. At the same time, advertising keeps the broadcast media relatively free from governmental control. In the final analysis, however, all programs broadcast by radio and television stations in the United States succeed or fail on the basis of public acceptance.

Historical Perspectives

Broadcasting officially began in the United States in 1910, when Dr. Lee DeForest, the "father of radio broadcasting," transmitted a live performance direct from the stage of the world-famous Metropolitan Opera House in New York City.[2] His invention of the audion tube, in 1906, enabled wireless transmissions of electromagnetic energy to carry the energy patterns of sound. Guglielmo Marconi, an Italian inventor, however, had discovered the secret of wireless communication even earlier and went on to build a global business in wireless telegraphy.

Experimental sound broadcasting continued prior to 1920 as stations were built by other inventors, amateur enthusiasts, newspapers, and educational institutions. But, while enthusiasm for wireless communication was high, few people foresaw uses beyond such purposes as distress calls because it was impossible to limit reception to preselected audiences. What function, they asked, could "open broadcasting," available indiscriminately to anyone, serve? And on what economic foundation could a "wireless" industry be developed?

In 1916, four years after serving as a Marconi wireless operator during the *Titanic* disaster, David Sarnoff, then an employee of the American Marconi Company, wrote the following suggestion to his superiors:

> I have in mind a plan of development which would make radio a household utility. The idea is to bring music into the home by wireless. The receiver can be designed in the form of a simple "radio music box," and arranged for several wave lengths which should be changeable with the throwing of a single switch or the pressing of a single button. The same principle can be extended to numerous other fields, as for example, receiving lectures at home which would be perfectly audible. Also, events of national importance can be simultaneously announced and received. Baseball scores can be transmitted in the air. This proposition would be especially interesting to farmers and others living in outlying districts.[3]

Sarnoff's plan also called for the establishment of radio stations that would be supported by revenues from the sale of home receiving sets. Furthermore, he suggested, a great amount of goodwill would accrue to the owners of such stations who could advertise their names over the air.

KDKA: THE BEGINNING OF COMMERCIAL BROADCASTING

In 1919 and 1920, Pittsburgh's experimental station 8XK, owned by Dr. Frank Conrad, assistant chief engineer of the Westinghouse Electric and Manufacturing Company, scheduled regular music and talk programs. A local music store provided Conrad with records in exchange for announcements stating that the recordings were available at the Hamilton Music Store of Wilkinsburg.[4] Although it was in barter (trade) form, the Hamilton *plugs* probably constituted the world's first radio advertising.

Then, in 1920, the Joseph Horne Company, a Pittsburgh department store, attempted to capitalize on listener interest in 8XK by advertising through the newspaper the sale of amateur wireless sets which, at a price of $10, could pick up Dr. Conrad's station. A Westinghouse official concluded that if Conrad's broadcasts were received so enthusiastically as to prompt a well-known store to advertise receiving sets, there might be a promising future for radio. Shortly afterward, Westinghouse began regular broadcasting to the public on KDKA, the first commercially licensed U.S. station. KDKA was founded to stimulate a market for radio receiving sets and to serve as a public relations device for Westinghouse. Advertising was not sold on KDKA until a number of years later when it became necessary to sustain operation.

WEAF: AT & T AND THE START OF "TOLL BROADCASTING"

The American Telephone and Telegraph Company had been interested in wireless communication since its beginning. A holder of numerous important patents involving electronics, AT & T established a public radiotelephone broadcasting station in New York in 1922, and with it began a new philosophy of broadcasting. WEAF (later WNBC and now WFAN), operated by AT & T's Long Lines (toll) Division, was intended to carry messages that were paid for by senders, much like the company's long-distance service and calls from pay telephones.

In August of 1922, WEAF broadcast its first income-producing venture—a 10-minute message from the Queensboro Corporation promoting the sale of apartments in Jackson Heights. This first paid radio *commercial* cost its sponsor $50; by December of that year, WEAF had thirteen advertiser/clients.

The early pattern of toll broadcasting established by WEAF consisted entirely of program sponsorship; each client provided an entertainment program that included a nominal amount of low-key institutional advertising. *Spot* announcements (from other advertisers) were not permitted, and copy restrictions were quite rigid. For example, the mention of price was forbidden, as were descriptions of packages and offers of free product samples. Despite the restrictions, however, advertisers soon wanted their programs heard outside New York City; in 1923, AT & T began operating a network of about eighteen stations, mostly in the Northeast.

Sponsored programs of the early commercial era usually included advertiser names in their titles, for instance, the "A&P Gypsies" and the "Cliquot Club Eskimos." Soon, the duet of Billy Jones and Ernie Hare introduced the singing commercial or jingle. Known professionally as the "Happiness Boys," they performed for their sponsor, the Happiness Candy Company.

Radio group stations—those built by receiver manufacturers such as Westinghouse, General Electric, Philco, and Crosley—soon found it difficult to compete with the high-budget sponsored programming carried by WEAF and other stations licensed by AT & T. By 1926, it was obvious that advertising was the most logical means for supporting the radio industry. In that year, under governmental pressure, AT & T withdrew from its broadcasting activities, selling both its network and station WEAF to a new firm called the National Broadcasting Company (NBC). Initially, NBC was owned jointly by the Radio Corporation of America (RCA), General Electric, and Westinghouse.

THE FORMATION OF NATIONAL NETWORKS

The new network organization began regular service early in 1927 with two separate, but complementary, networks providing programs to a growing number of affiliated stations across the country. NBC's Red network, the former WEAF network, carried the most popular programs and the greater share of advertising. The NBC Blue network, fed from WJZ, New York, emphasized cultural and public affairs programs but also was used to launch new entertainment shows.

Later that year, a second network organization was formed to serve the programming needs of stations unable to secure affiliation with NBC. That network, known first as United Independent Broadcasters, soon became the Columbia Broadcasting System (CBS) and was the third network actually on the air. In 1934, a fourth radio network, the Mutual Broadcasting System (MBS), was established.

Advertising on NBC and CBS basically followed the program-sponsorship pattern set by WEAF. However, during the late 1920s, local stations began to accept spot announcement commercials as well as program sponsorship. By 1932, the practice of selling short spot commercials, which originated with station-break ads scheduled between network shows, had become widespread on local stations.

NAB CODE OF ETHICS

During the predepression years, network advertising remained essentially institutional in character, while advertising on local stations varied from institutional to more direct selling. Then, because some local stations permitted blatant selling and accepted the advertising of questionable and/or personal products, the National Association of Broadcasters (NAB) adopted its first Code of Ethics in 1929. The noncompulsory code recommended high standards of advertising acceptance and distinguished between daytime and nighttime hours in terms of advertising appeals. Code-subscribing stations were expected to maintain an institutional tone in their advertising after 6 P.M., while more overt salesmanship was accepted during the daytime, or business hours.

THE DEPRESSION YEARS: CHANGING PATTERNS

Radio advertising grew steadily during the 1930s as the public increasingly turned to radio for entertainment and information. By 1935, more than 22 million households, or two-thirds of the total number, had radios, and advertisers spent $79.6 million for radio commercials.[5] By the mid-1930s, program offerings included radio dramas, comedies, and variety shows, which regularly featured nationally known talent. One important innovation in programming was that of the daytime serial drama, which came to occupy several hours of the daily NBC and CBS schedules; because soap producers sponsored most of the serials, the shows were dubbed *soap operas*.

Two classes of advertisers came into prominence on radio during the 1930s: (1) those that produced low-priced, frequently purchased items, such as soap, cigarettes, toothpaste, and cereals; and (2) manufacturers of durable goods, such as automobiles and household appliances. Furthermore, advertising acceptance standards were altered during the harsh depression years. The ban on price-mention was lifted by CBS in 1931 and by NBC in 1933. Direct, hard-sell advertising messages and exaggerated claims also became common on both the networks and local stations.

Numerous production firms began to specialize in creating and producing complete radio programs for sale to advertising agencies and their clients. Such packaged shows included the talent (performers), script, sound effects, and production and virtually eliminated the need for networks to create programs at all. As radio time costs increased, advertisers began seeking evidence of audience reach. At first, stations substantiated their programs' audience levels by counting and analyzing listener fan mail. In 1930, however, the first national program rating service, the Cooperative Analysis of Broadcasting (CAB), was established for the Association of National Advertisers by Archibald Crossley.[6] The CAB system, like the "Hooperatings" of the C. E. Hooper organization (prominent from 1935 through the 1940s) was based on telephone interviews. Additional developments in sophisticated research methods followed.

WORLD WAR II: HEIGHTENED RADIO ADVERTISING

When the United States entered World War II, approximately nine hundred AM radio stations were authorized by the federal government, of which about seven hundred were affiliates of the national networks. By 1940, advertising revenues had nearly doubled from the 1935 level (from $79.6 million to $155.7 million)[7] and set ownership was approaching 90 percent of the nation's households. During the war, radio kept the public informed on a battle-by-battle basis, and the level of advertising remained high. In fact, expenditures for radio commercials increased to $310.5 million by 1945.[8]

Instead of discounting their advertising efforts during the era of scarce consumer goods, producers advertised to maintain brand awareness and customer loyalty. Numerous manufacturers engaged in wartime production used some of their profits to support prestige radio broadcasts, such as symphony concerts and war-oriented dramas. Institutional advertising became prominent again, as did advertising that supported the war effort.

POSTWAR BROADCASTING: EXPANSION

Radio set ownership became almost universal during post-war years, and radio advertising continued to expand. (Further data on broadcast advertising revenues appear in Table 1.1.) Between 1945 and 1950 three important changes occurred: (1) hundreds of new standard broadcast (AM) radio stations were established; (2) frequency modulation (FM) radio was launched; and (3) commercial television made its debut.

Table 1.1. Radio and TV gross advertising revenues

Year	Radio (million $)	Television (million $)
1935	79.6	...
1940	155.7	...
1945	310.5	...
1950	453.6	105.9
1955	456.5	744.7
1960	591.8	1,456.2
1965	827.8	2,265.9
1970	1,256.8	3,242.8
1975	1,892.3	4,722.1
1980	3,702.0	11,424.0
1985	6,490.0	21,290.0
1988 (est.)	7,500.0	25,000.0

Sources: *Television Factbook*, No. 50 (Washington: Television Digest, Inc., 1981), 71-a, 73-a; *Television & Cable Factbook*, No. 56 (Washington: Television Digest, Inc., 1988), C-307 (used with permission from Warren Publishing, Inc.).

Note: Gross advertising revenues are the total amounts paid by advertisers for the use of broadcast facilities, including commissions, facilities, and services provided by stations and networks. They do not, however, include production costs.

Expansion of Standard (AM) Broadcasting

The expansion of AM radio after the war was dramatic. There were nearly nine hundred authorized stations in 1945 when the war ended, but approximately six hundred new stations were either on the air or under construction sixteen months after the Federal Communications Commission (FCC) resumed peacetime licensing. An additional seven hundred applications were still pending on February 7, 1947,[9] and by 1950 the number of stations had doubled again (see Table 1.2). Most of the new stations were low-power outlets, but they succeeded in increasing the level of competition in large communities and in introducing local radio to small towns.

During this period, radio became an important local advertising medium, as well as a national one, and provided small business establishments at grass-roots levels with their first opportunities to advertise over the air. In 1947, for the first time, income from local advertisers surpassed that from network sponsors.

Table 1.2. Growth of AM and FM radio stations (commercial and noncommercial)

Year	AM Stations on the Air	FM Stations on the Air	Total Stations on the Air
1946	913	48	961
1950	2,045	728	2,773
1955	2,662	549	3,211
1960	3,456	677	4,133
1965	4,044	1,205	5,249
1970	4,292	2,468	6,760
1975	4,445	3,299	7,744
1980	4,523	4,043	8,566
1985[a]	4,973	5,106	10,079
1988[a]	4,902	5,342	10,244

Sources: *Annual Reports*, Federal Communications Commission; *Television & Cable Factbook*, No. 56 (Washington: Television Digest, Inc. 1988), C-309 (used with permission from Warren Publishing, Inc.).

[a]Licensed and authorized stations.

Introduction of Frequency Modulation

The introduction of frequency modulation (FM) radio, a superior form of audio transmission, created little enthusiasm among listeners and advertisers during the 1945-1950 era. In fact, FM continued to languish as a broadcast medium until the 1970s, when its listenership and advertising volume increased sharply.

The Beginning of Commercial Television

The introduction of commercial television marked the beginning of the most powerful and successful advertising medium ever created. Between October 1945 and September 1948, the FCC authorized the construction of 108 TV stations. No further station authorizations were made until 1952 while the Commission worked out a permanent frequency (channel) allocations plan. However, television became a mass medium as early as 1948 in cities where early stations were located, attracting both viewers and advertisers in substantial numbers. After 1953, TV stations were established throughout the rest of the country. As shown in Table 1.3, the number of stations has grown steadily for four decades. Most of the recent growth in television has occurred in the UHF band.

Table 1.3. Growth of commercial television stations in the United States

Year	VHF	UHF	Total
1946	7	...	7
1950	98	...	98
1952	108	...	108
1955	297	114	411
1960	440	75	515
1965	481	88	569
1970	501	176	677
1975	514	192	706
1980	516	218	734
1985	520	363	883
1988	539	489	1,028

Sources: *Annual Reports,* Federal Communications Commission; *Television & Cable Factbook,* No. 56 (Washington: Television Digest, Inc., 1988), C-299 (used with permission from Warren Publishing, Inc.).

Note: The grand total for on-the-air TV stations, including 334 noncommercial educational licensees, was 1,362 as of January 1988. Translators and low-power (LPTV) stations are not included.

Television broadcasting essentially followed the patterns set by radio. TV networks, however, maintained rigid control of their program schedules, whereas radio networks had allowed advertisers to buy time periods and fill them with their own programs. From 1948 to about 1960, network TV shows were sold to sponsors, while local stations accepted both sponsorship and spot commercials. Frequently, to save money, two advertisers would share a given network program through alternate-week sponsorship.

Ultimately, after networks began scheduling feature-length motion pictures around 1960, the 60-second spot became the basic advertising unit on network and local television. Multiple-product advertisers quickly realized that two 30-second commercials could be incorporated into a 60-second time slot, giving impetus to the practice of *piggybacking,* which was prominent during the 1960s. Today, advertisers have virtually abandoned program sponsorship except for *specials,* and for many years the 30-second spot has been standard. During the late 1980s, both stand-alone and piggybacked 15-second commercials also became widely accepted on television.

During the early years of television, commercials and programs were produced live and incorporated both the excitement and the hazards inherent in live performances. Today, live production has all but vanished in favor of filmed and videotaped material, and commercial production techniques, which are discussed in Chapter 11, have improved immensely.

With the growth of TV households and the universal use of color transmission, television advertising rates have increased steadily during the past four decades. Network advertisers paid an average of about $125,000 for 30-second participations in primetime network programs during the late 1980s, compared with approximately $50,000 for similar messages a decade earlier. Some primetime network shows of the 1989-90 season commanded even higher 30-second spot rates: "The Cosby Show" ($400,000 to $450,000), "Cheers" ($350,000), "Night Court" ($310,000), and "The Golden Girls" ($230,000). Corresponding costs per minute were $30,000 in the early 1960s and $65,000 by 1970.

As rates increased, audience research became a vital necessity—a tool to facilitate wise decisions in allocating advertising budgets. The two most widely employed TV research firms are the Arbitron Ratings Company, New York, and the A. C. Nielsen Company, Northbrook (Chicago), Illinois. The principal radio research firms are Arbitron Radio and Birch Radio, Inc., Coral Springs, Florida.

RADIO'S ALTERED ROLE

Because TV programming so closely resembled traditional radio broadcasting of the pretelevision era, the two services became direct competitors when TV was first introduced. With a significant decline in radio listenership during the 1950s, particularly during evening primetime hours, radio was forced to modify its role to retain its viability. From 1953 to about 1960, radio underwent a transition from a primary home entertainment medium to a personal companion medium. Stations emphasized music, news, and service rather than the lavish entertainment shows of the past. Many converted to format programming featuring unique sounds and mental images that followed a sequence or rotation pattern throughout the broadcast day. Specialization in audience appeal came to characterize modern radio.

The ownership of radio receiving sets continued to expand long after television's emergence as the dominant electronic medium. Although radio sets in automobiles and stationary radios in homes and offices predominate, literally millions of transistorized receivers, including pocket portables and "walkman" sets, are used daily by our mobile population. Table 1.4 provides historical data on radio ownership in the United States.

Despite the high usage of radio, few, if any, individual radio stations can deliver the mass

Table 1.4. Growth of radio sets owned by the U.S. public

Year	All Radios Other Than Automobile Sets	Radio Sets in Automobiles	Total Radio Sets
	(thousands)		
1950	67,200	18,000	85,200
1955	92,000	29,000	121,000
1960	116,007	40,387	156,394
1965	171,408	56,871	228,279
1970	240,200	80,500	320,700
1975	301,200	100,400	401,600
1980	341,000	112,000	453,000
1985	380,000	127,000	507,000
1990 (est.)	420,000	140,000	560,000

Source: *Television Factbook*, No. 55 (Washington: Television Digest, Inc., 1987), A-18 (used with permission from Warren Publishing Inc.).

audience. Instead, radio has become a segmented medium in which each station usually chooses which demographic audience it will serve. Advertisers may select individual stations to reach one or more specific, but narrowly defined, target audiences. Or, they may achieve broad audience coverage by selecting several radio stations within a market, each for its own listener appeal. Thus, radio has become a very flexible, often inexpensive advertising medium, with the capacity to complement and supplement other media as part of an advertiser's media mix.

REGULATORY CHANGES

Finally, public opinion, led by consumer groups, has focused on such aspects of broadcast advertising as commercials on children's programs, portrayal of women and ethnic groups in commercials, and general message clutter. Federal regulation has eliminated cigarette advertising from radio and television, prescribed maximum rates for political advertising, and established new standards for truth in advertising. Regulation of broadcast advertising is discussed in detail in Chapter 5.

The Scope of Broadcast Advertising Today

By the end of the 1980s, advertisers were spending about $32.5 billion annually to reach target audiences through radio and television. TV's gross advertising revenues, including cable, amounted to approximately $25 billion, or about 75 percent of broadcasting's total. Cable advertising, including both national cable networks and local systems, accounted for about one billion dollars, while broadcast TV networks garnered more than $8.5 billion of the total. Radio attracted another $7.5 billion, or about 25 percent, of the industry's advertising revenues. Media organizations sharing in this income included more than 10,000 radio stations, about 1,000 TV stations, and the television, cable, and radio networks.

Although TV continues to rank second to newspapers in total advertising volume, television with its powerful combination of sight, sound, color, motion, and emotion has long been the number one national advertising medium in the United States. (It is exceeded slightly by the amorphous direct mail form of advertising.) Local advertisers continue to prefer newspapers, with television now second and gaining steadily during recent years. Radio places fourth in total advertising revenues and third in the local category, drawing its greatest strength from local retail and service advertising. Approximate percentages of national and local advertising placed in various media are shown in Table 1.5.

Table 1.5. Annual U.S. advertising expenditures

	Percentage of National	Percentage of Local	Percentage of Total U.S. Advertising
Newspaper	5.9	52.1	26.4
Television	28.0	14.8	22.1
Direct mail	30.2	...	16.8
Radio	3.1	11.4	6.8
Magazines	9.3	...	5.2
All other	23.5	21.7	22.7
Total	100.0	100.0	100.0

Source: Derived from McCann-Erickson estimates for a recent year, which were prepared by and are used with permission from J. Coen, Senior Vice President, McCann-Erickson, Inc.

Elements of the Broadcast Advertising Industry

Modern broadcast advertising is a highly complex activity that draws from the interrelated work of a variety of organizations. For example, since 1949, when the first filmed commercial was aired, television commercial production has become its own industry. (Interestingly enough, some of the special effects, lighting, and camera techniques now seen in motion pictures were first used in commercials.)[10] The following are major elements of the industry.

Advertisers. Generally speaking, advertisers are business firms that use communications media to persuade consumers to buy their products or services, support their activities, or approve their goals.

Advertising agencies. These are organizations that advertisers hire to plan and execute advertising campaigns. Major responsibilities include media buying, creation and production of advertising messages, and research.

Television and radio stations. When licensed by the FCC, TV and radio stations broadcast to cities and regions throughout the country and serve as vehicles for transmitting commercial messages to the public.

Television and radio networks. Networks exist whenever two or more stations are interconnected to carry simultaneous programming. National networks provide programs on a regular basis to affiliated stations throughout the country, selling commercial time slots within those programs to national advertisers.

Cable television. Cable TV (CATV) systems deliver television programs to homes by cable as opposed to wireless, over-the-air transmission. Cable programming usually includes local cable productions, local or area TV stations, distant imported stations, and cable networks. Both national and local commercials run on cable systems.

Cable networks. National cable networks provide cable systems and their subscribers with a variety of program services, both general and specialized. Most cable networks are supported by a combination of advertising revenues and payments from affiliated cable systems. Others, not included in a cable system's basic service, are offered to subscribers for additional monthly payments. The latter are commonly called "pay cable" services. Program delivery of cable networks to local CATV systems is handled through satellite transmission.

Superstations. The broadcast signals of a few large city independent TV stations also are transmitted via communication satellites to cable systems throughout the United States. Although these stations are authorized primarily to serve their cities of license, their importation into large numbers of additional markets has given them national audiences.

Broadcast sales representative firms. Advertising is sold by these firms to national and regional advertisers on behalf of station clients. Stations handled by *national rep* firms customarily are noncompetitive with each other.

Time-buying services. These services specialize in negotiating with and purchasing time on stations and networks on behalf of advertisers and/or their agencies.

Program producers. Program producers are production organizations that create and produce programs for sale to broadcast networks and stations.

Program distributors. The job of selling and distributing syndicated programs to individual stations is handled by program distributors. Types of programs offered include movie packages, shows that were formerly carried by national networks, and new or "first-run" programs produced especially for television and radio.

Production studios. Facilities and staffs for the production of both commercials and programs are maintained by production studios. TV studios usually specialize in either film or videotape recording. Radio commercials, as well as the sound (audio) tracks for many television commercials, are produced at sound recording studios. Other production houses specialize in such techniques as animation and special-effects photography.

Library services. These services make available stock production materials, such as recorded music, sound effects, and visual aids suitable for use in commercials and programs. Stock commercials may require only the insertion of an advertiser's name.

Research organizations. Research organizations are employed to determine radio and TV audience size and demographic composition, to pretest commercial messages, and to measure the overall sales effectiveness of broadcast advertising.

Talent agencies. Agencies represent the talent (performers) who deliver and/or otherwise participate in commercials. Normally, they are located in major broadcast production cities.

Trade associations. The American Association of Advertising Agencies (AAAA), American Advertising Federation (AAF), Association of National Advertisers (ANA), Broadcast Promotion Association (BPA), National Association of Broadcasters (NAB), and similar organizations are devoted to furthering the business, ethical, and overall professional interests of advertisers and broadcasters. Their concerns cover national, regional, and local areas of operation.

Types of Broadcast Advertising

The three principal types of radio and television advertising are (1) network, (2) national or regional spot, and (3) local or retail. Each has its own distinct characteristics.

NETWORK ADVERTISING

Through network advertising, a company beams its messages to the audiences of two or more stations that carry the same broadcast simultaneously (or, perhaps, on a time-delayed basis). The most common form is national network advertising that uses one or more of the coast-to-coast radio, broadcast TV, or cable television networks for audience reach throughout the country. However, as Chapter 2 will discuss, other types of networks may be arranged to meet specific needs.

NATIONAL/REGIONAL SPOT ADVERTISING

Through *spot* advertising, a national or regional advertiser may select the individual markets needed to accomplish campaign goals. Also, individual stations may be chosen within specified markets regardless of their network affiliation. Thus, spot advertising provides greater flexibility than does the network approach; however, time-buying may become very complicated. Spot campaigns, which may involve program sponsorship and/or spot announcements (either within or between programs), normally are placed through *national sales representative firms,* which work for local stations in New York and other major advertising centers. Advertisers that use the spot broadcasting approach must provide commercial materials, such as videotape recordings (VTRs), and radio tapes and transcriptions, along with scheduling information, to each station selected (since stations carrying a spot campaign are not interconnected in any way).

LOCAL/RETAIL ADVERTISING

Local advertisers, such as retail stores and local service establishments, use stations in their own or nearby communities. Although such advertisers have no decisions to make with respect to market selection, they must choose from among competing stations and programs those most suitable for achieving their advertising objectives.

A special form of local advertising known as *cooperative* or *co-op* advertising involves joint payment for broadcast time by a national advertiser and a local dealer outlet. For example, a retail appliance dealer may be reimbursed a specified percentage of the cost of local broadcast advertising used specifically to promote appliances manufactured by a company such as White-Westinghouse or Whirlpool. Retail advertising is discussed more fully in Chapter 16.

Types of Broadcast Advertisers

Advertisers who use radio and television media generally may be classified as (1) national, (2) regional, or (3) local, depending on their sphere of operation. Most broadcast advertisers present consumer-directed messages that relate to (1) products, (2) services, (3) retail establishments, and/or (4) other activities. Some typical broadcast advertising clients are listed in Table 1.6.

Table 1.6. Typical broadcast advertisers by category

Scope	Product	Service	Retail	Other
National	Chevrolet Budweiser Maxwell House	Prudential American Air. Hertz Rental	J.C. Penney McDonald's Ace Hardware	National political, religious
Regional	Olympia beer JFG coffee Regional meat packers	Regional insurance, brokers, banks	Lazarus (Ohio) Rich's (SE) Goldwater's (SW)	State tourism, political
Local[a]	Local beers, bakeries, packers	Local banks, insurance, real estate, travel agents	Local retail stores	Local political, religious

[a]Local advertising may involve co-op deals between local firms and national companies.

NATIONAL ADVERTISERS

A national advertiser is a marketer whose products or services are available throughout most, if not all, of the United States. Examples include products such as Crest toothpaste, Pepsi, and Coke and companies such as Chevrolet and Ford, Goodyear Tire, Prudential Insurance, and American Airlines. In addition, certain large retail chains and nationally franchised concerns often function as national advertisers, even though they also may buy advertising on a regional or local market basis. Examples include J. C. Penney, Sears, K Mart, McDonald's, Burger King, Wendy's, and Pizza Hut.

REGIONAL ADVERTISERS

There is little difference between regional and national advertisers other than their geographical scopes of operation. The regional advertiser may distribute products in a portion of a state, an entire state, or a combination of several states. Normally, these advertisers avoid using national networks because of wasted excess coverage; however, under some circumstances, regional advertisers may buy time on part of a network through a *regional feed.* Spot advertising is the most common approach used by the regional advertiser because it allows the purchase of schedules in precisely those markets that coincide with distribution patterns.

LOCAL ADVERTISERS

The local advertiser usually is engaged in selling products and/or services at the retail level. The emphasis in commercial messages usually is focused on attracting customers to places of business and influencing them to buy advertised merchandise. In many instances, local merchants receive monetary rebates from the national companies whose products/services they advertise locally through a practice called cooperative, or "co-op," advertising. Chapter 16 will discuss this topic more fully.

OTHER ADVERTISERS

An endless variety of other clients also use the broadcast media from time to time. For example, political candidates rely on TV and radio to build their public images and to communicate their positions to voters. Other purchasers of broadcast time include religious groups, educational institutions, tourism organizations, trade associations, and labor unions. In addition, a multitude of noncommercial organizations use advertising's persuasive techniques during *public service* time granted them by networks and stations. Air time worth hundreds of millions of dollars is contributed annually by radio and TV broadcasters for such causes as AIDS education, warnings of the dangers of drunken driving, and solicitation of funds for medical research on various diseases.

Types of Campaigns

Broadcast advertisers may choose one or both of two basic approaches used in campaign planning: (1) program campaigns and (2) announcement campaigns. We will mention these options here and discuss them in more detail in Chapter 17.

PROGRAM CAMPAIGNS

Program campaigns are built around the sponsorship of programs carefully selected to match audience characteristics needed by the advertiser. Here, the advertiser pays both network or station time charges and the cost of producing or providing the program itself. In turn, the sponsor is entitled to a number of commercial messages within the show, as well as close identification with the program and its talent. And, as was true in the early days of radio, the sponsor may incorporate its company name into the program title (for example, the Bell System Family Theater and the Hallmark Hall of Fame). A principal advantage of program sponsorship is that it allows frequent repetition of advertising messages to regular listeners and viewers. Program sponsorship has declined markedly in recent years, however, because of costs and now is used most often in television specials or one-time broadcasts. Opportunities for program sponsorship also exist on radio and on cable networks at modest cost.

ANNOUNCEMENT CAMPAIGNS

An announcement campaign relies on the use of short advertising messages known as *spot announcements,* which may be broadcast within programs or during station-break intervals between shows. Most of today's commercial TV programs, regardless of type, are designed to accommodate clusters of advertising messages. Although the 30-second spot is the basic unit sold in television, other lengths are commonly available, particularly the 15- and 60-second announcements. On cable networks, even longer announcements, or "infomercials," may be scheduled. Most radio programs also serve as vehicles for spot announcements, and 30- and 60-second commercials are most common. Stations usually attempt to provide adequate separation between commercials for competing clients.

The vast majority of broadcast advertising campaigns use the announcement approach. One principal reason is that, with given budgets, advertisers may spread their messages over a number of different programs to achieve broader audience reach than is possible through program sponsorship; and advertisers may still select programs that cater to desired audience characteristics. Hence, the benefits derived from exclusive sponsorship must be waived in favor of increased reach.

Advertisers who use announcement schedules are charged for network or station time, which also covers program talent and production expenses. Rates for spot announcements vary from program to program depending on the size of audiences reached.

Radio and Television: A Comparison

Because radio and TV belong to the same electronic media family, they are usually grouped together. But, while the two have much in common, they differ in a number of significant ways. This section explores the advantages and disadvantages of each and compares radio and television in terms of their practical usage. Throughout the book, emphasis will be given to the ways in which advertisers can use both media effectively and efficiently by maximizing their strengths and minimizing their shortcomings.

Fundamental to understanding the characteristics shared by radio and television is the fact that all of broadcasting is time-based; listeners and viewers receive all programs and commercials simultaneously with their transmission, regardless of whether they are carried in live or recorded form. Hence, radio and TV claim the unique media attributes of immediacy and timeliness, while they lack permanence and tangibility, which are assets of space-based media such as newspapers and magazines. The widespread use of home videocassette recorders (VCRs), however, provides the possibility of permanence for television programs. The VCR also has allowed viewers to fast forward ("zap") through commercials of time-shifted programs to avoid advertisements.

ADVANTAGES OF BOTH RADIO AND TV

The basic advantages of both radio and television as advertising vehicles may be summarized as follows:

Universality. More than 98 percent of all U.S. households have at least one TV set in working order, resulting in a potential audience of approximately 92.1 million families in 1990. Seventy-one percent can receive 9 or more TV stations, compared with only 8 percent that could tune in that many stations in 1964. When cable channels are included with over-the-air station signals, 86 percent can receive 9 or more channels and 31 percent can receive 30 or more channels.[11]

Approximately 66 percent of the nation's households had two or more television sets, and color-set penetration had reached 96 percent by January 1988.[12] More than 52 percent of all U.S. television households subscribe to basic cable service, and about two-thirds (65 percent) have purchased home videocassette recorders.

Radio also claims its share of dramatic figures. Virtually every home in the country (99 percent) has at least one working radio. Estimates for 1990 place the number of sets in use by the American public at 560 million, or 5.9 sets per household. This number includes portables and automobile sets, as well as fixed-position radios in homes, offices, work areas, and other locations. In a recent year (1986), the U.S. public bought more than 41 million radio receivers. In comparison, 23 million TV sets were sold that year.[13]

Popularity. Ownership of TV and radio receivers in America, as we have seen, is virtually universal. We spend more time using the broadcast media than in any other activities except working and sleeping. The average adult spends about three hours daily with radio. Listening takes place practically everywhere, with in-home listening ranking first, followed by in-car and other out-of-home listening.

Turning to television, A. C. Nielsen Co. research indicates that the average American family uses its TV set, or sets, more than seven hours daily. Usage is greatest among three types of households: those with nonadults, larger households, and those with pay cable service.[14]

A more detailed discussion of broadcast audiences will be provided in Chapter 7. It is important to note here, though, that TV and radio are popular not only with the public but also with advertisers. The McCann-Erickson advertising agency estimates that a record-breaking 22.1 percent of all advertising dollars were placed in TV during 1986 alone. Radio accounted for another 6.8 percent.[15]

Immediacy and timeliness. The instant a radio or TV program or commercial is broadcast, whether by a nationwide network or by a single local station, it is received by its audience. With certain exceptions, there is no delay in reception as there is in the printed media. Among those millions of home VCR owners, some programs are watched later, at more convenient times. Although most viewers *still* watch their favorite TV shows when they are broadcast, home video recorders make TV more convenient, or "user-friendly," for busy people who cannot always be present at a show's broadcast time. Such time shifting by VCR users obviously affects audience levels, boosting viewership for some programs (most likely the already highly rated shows) and depressing the ratings of others. However, since most people watch programs at or shortly after their normal broadcast time (via time shifting), commercial messages almost always are fresh and timely. In some instances, even last-minute copy changes can be accommodated.

Use of sound. The transmission of sound permits full utilization of the human voice for persuasive salesmanship. This personal quality may enhance both the credibility and the interest level of commercials. In addition, music and sound effects may be used to augment selling messages.

Integration of commercial messages into program content. In time-based media situations, the audience receives only one message at a time (program, commercial, or whatever), and that message is selected by the broadcasters rather than by consumers. (On the other hand, readers may examine printed matter at their own convenience.) Advertisers benefit because the integration of commercials into the fabric of programming helps insure acceptable attention levels; each commercial is presented in its entirety before another begins. In addition, valuable lead-ins to commercials may be provided by program personalities. Radio and television work so well together, too, that programs on one medium are often advertised on the other—right up to the moment of broadcast.

Choice of program content. Programming on both radio and television is varied, permitting the choice of commercial positions that best match an advertiser's target audience.

Flexibility in coverage and schedules. As advertising vehicles, radio and television have become extremely flexible.

1. National advertisers may choose to have their commercials aired on network programs, thereby attaining national coverage; or they may select individual markets and stations to coincide with marketing goals.
2. Any advertiser may sponsor a program or use spot announcement schedules.
3. Broadcast advertising campaigns may vary in length. It is possible to schedule short commercial *flights*—only a week or two in duration—as well as campaigns lasting for months, a season, or a year.
4. Advertisers may select the level of advertising exposure desired. For example, a saturation campaign might be used to launch a new product, while a lower-intensity maintenance campaign reminds users of an established product.

Well-researched media. The audiences for both radio and television stations and programs are being studied continually by reputable and impartial research firms. Data on audience levels, composition, and flow may be used to guide advertisers and their agencies in planning effective campaigns.

UNIQUE ADVANTAGES OF TELEVISION

In addition to the characteristics shared with radio, television has certain distinct advantages as an advertising medium. The most important, of course, is its visual component, which permits the transmission of sight, motion, and color on an instantaneous basis. Through TV, advertisers may demonstrate products, focusing attention on their most visually appealing attributes and emphasizing packages and corporate logos through close-up camera shots. With both visual and sound capabilities, television comes closer to the ideal of person-to-person salesmanship than any other mass medium.

Furthermore, even with some decline in network audiences due to cable and other broadcast competition, the national television audience is still relatively unfragmented, including 65 to 70 percent of all primetime viewers. Therefore, with appropriate programming, reaching a dominant share of the mass audience continues to be possible through network TV. On the other hand, specific programs on network and nonnetwork stations, as well as on cable, allow advertisers to beam their messages to specialized target groups whenever that approach is desired.

Finally, whether television is watched in group or individual situations, the medium is a compelling one. Involvement levels for programs and commercials do vary, but on an overall basis they tend to be quite high.

UNIQUE ADVANTAGES OF RADIO

Despite the fact that TV has overshadowed radio as the most powerful of all communications media, radio broadcasting continues to have certain unique advantages of its own:

1. Because there is no predetermined picture, radio stimulates the imagination. Furthermore, the type of listening situation most common with radio (the individual who has tuned in for information, service, and companionship) is especially conducive to the power of persuasion inherent through voices of trusted announcers.

2. Radio is more pervasive than television because of its portability and mobility. Listeners may be reached at almost any time and in almost any location; automobile drive-time is a prime example of out-of-home listening. A Simmons research study indicates that five demographic groups use radio more than TV every day: professional/managerial men (42 percent more); adults aged 18-24 (40 percent more); single working adults (34 percent more); upper-income men (33 percent more); and adults in upper-income households (14 percent more).[16]

3. People may listen to radio while they are engaged in other activities. Despite the fact that resulting attention levels may sometimes be low, advertisers have found that frequent repetition of messages on radio can be a successful means of communicating product information. Especially helpful are commercials that incorporate catchy, highly recognizable musical elements and those closely resembling, and therefore reinforcing, TV messages.

4. Radio is an extremely flexible medium. In many cities there are one or two general service stations that attract large heterogeneous audiences; most, however, offer specialized programming to well-defined target groups. Advertisers may use radio stations in any combination that delivers a desired reach.

5. In both AM and FM radio, there are important differences among stations with respect to geographical coverage. These differences, which will be discussed in Chapter 2, provide a measure of geographical flexibility for advertisers.

6. Radio is a low-cost medium. Thirty-second national radio network commercials generally cost from $500 to $4,000. Local 60-second spots rarely exceed $1,000, even in the largest markets. In contrast, 30-second primetime network TV spots average about $125,000 each, but often are priced at $200,000 to $300,000, and sometimes much more. Local TV commercials during prime viewing hours range from $20 in small markets to $15,000 or more in large cities.

7. Because FM radio listening has surpassed AM listening, these characteristics peculiar to the FM service should be noted: (a) high fidelity sound reproduction, (b) stereophonic broadcasting, (c) static-free, nonfading reception, and (d) constant coverage patterns during both daytime and nighttime hours.

PROBLEMS INHERENT IN BROADCAST ADVERTISING

Despite the numerous advantages of radio and television as advertising media, certain inherent handicaps exist. First, and probably most important, is the lack of permanence and tangibility that are present in other media. Advertisers accustomed to using their ads for extended display or as point-of-purchase exhibits, for example, find the fleeting, intangible nature of broadcasting a severe limitation.

A second problem, related mainly to television, is high cost. Traditional TV is a high-investment medium, which often limits its use to firms with large advertising budgets. The recent influx of independent stations, however, has opened up substantial inventories of TV time at relatively low cost. In fact, availabilities on UHF independent stations often are competitive with radio rates. The fact that most television ad rates are high in no way suggests that TV is an expensive medium. On the contrary, when measured by the cost required to reach 1,000 households (CPM), television often is an extremely efficient buy. A large number of advertising dollars are obviously required, though, to make this efficient purchase.

Third, a problem with radio advertising lies in the low attention levels given to many types of programs. Additional research is needed on the effectiveness of advertising on a variety of radio formats. It is widely accepted, however, that commercials placed within informative programs and other types of foreground radio achieve the highest levels of attention from listeners.

Finally, the large number of different messages carried by many radio and TV stations is regarded by some advertisers as a ("clutter") problem. Because all commercials are intended to convince audiences to take some action, each one is, in effect, in competition with all others. During recent years, many radio stations have limited the number of commercial minutes per hour.

RADIO AND TELEVISION AS ADVERTISERS SEE THEM

Although both TV and radio are electronic media and possess many common characteristics, they differ noticeably in practical usage. Television is the most important single advertising medium for national advertisers. National network and national spot combined account for about two-thirds of all TV advertising revenues. (At the same time, local ad sales for television are growing dramatically.) In a recent year (1986), according to Broadcast Advertising Reports, Inc., 638 different advertisers bought network time for 2,837 different brands. In the same year, 2,155 different advertisers used national spot advertising on behalf of 10,697 different brands.[17]

On a total basis, television ad revenues (1986) in the United States were distributed as follows: network (37.1 percent), national/regional spot (29.8 percent), local (29.8 percent), and national (barter) syndication (3.3 percent).[18]

In contrast, radio's principal revenue source is local advertising, which accounts for about 75 percent of its total income. Radio frequently serves as a back-up medium to TV and/or newspapers in the advertiser's media mix; however, there are numerous instances in which radio is used as a primary medium.

Table 1.7 shows the approximate breakdown of broadcast revenues by sources for TV and radio stations. The data for individual stations, of course, vary widely.

Table 1.7. Average distribution of broadcast revenues for TV and radio stations

| | Network Compensation | Nonnetwork Revenue | | |
		National/ Regional Spot	Local	Total
		(percent)		
Television	3.9	50.0	46.1	96.1
Radio	1.0	24.0	75.0	99.0

Television's involvement capabilities and audience reach give it major responsibilities for communicating advertising information. TV has risen to the forefront as a primary advertising vehicle for large national marketers, and it also is being used more extensively by large retail organizations.

Radio has become a useful secondary medium for national advertisers. Its flexibility and low cost permit its use as a reminder medium by those who use TV, magazines, and/or newspapers for primary advertising purposes. At the same time, radio continues to be useful to numerous small business establishments as a primary means for communicating with the public.

Once strictly competitive, radio and TV actually function quite differently today. Their complementary nature makes them ideal media partners for countless advertisers.

A Look Ahead

From its beginning, broadcasting has been a dynamic, rapidly changing industry—in terms of technology, programming, and advertising. But through it all, Americans have continued to depend on both radio and television to satisfy their instant communication needs and desires. Recent years, however, have witnessed such an accelerated pace of change that the very nature of telecommunications is different from its form only a few years earlier.

Broadcast television no longer is the only source of TV programming. Advertiser-supported cable networks are drawing increasingly larger audiences each year. Within broadcast television, independent and public stations also have gained viewership at the expense of networks and their affiliated stations. And in radio, with the surge in FM's popularity, the long-dominant AM service has been left with only about one-fourth of the listening audience in most areas.

The number of radio and television networks also has increased, and "occasional" program services, including barter program syndication, have proliferated. Some cable networks, at times, even provide programs to broadcast TV stations. Much of this expansion has resulted from a dramatic increase in the number of new stations across the country. Advertisers, of course, have been delighted as greater price competition has developed for advertising time.

We cannot be sure exactly how broadcasting will change in the future. The following, however, are some developments that seem likely:

1. Given the long-term growth trend of the economy, as well as the continued presence of inflation, broadcast advertising expenditures are expected to rise each year.
2. In television, the greatest gains are likely to be from local sources, while modest increases are foreseen for network TV and national spot advertising. Radio's growth will come primarily in FM because of the steady shift of listenership to that band.
3. The increase in the number of networks—cable, broadcast TV, and radio—has provided advertisers with an efficient means for delivering messages to demographic and psychographic audience segments. For the foreseeable future, however, the number of fully programmed radio and TV networks is likely to remain stable.
4. The decline of mass audience numbers for network television is likely to continue as competition intensifies from cable, pay television, independent stations, and public television. The trend will result in increased frustration for those who wish to reach a large percentage of households with their (relatively few) traditional TV buys. Television will become more like radio and magazines as it is forced to serve segmented audiences.
5. The number of cable subscribers will continue to increase, though at a slower rate of growth, making cable an increasingly attractive means for beaming commercials directly to segmented audiences

attracted to specialized program channels. By 1995, more than 60 percent of the nation should be receiving cable, and advertising on cable networks and local systems should increase in step with subscriber growth. In the late 1980s, 30-second spots on cable networks cost less than 5 percent of the rates asked for primetime spots on ABC, CBS, and NBC. However, despite the ascendancy of cable and other forms of competition, broadcast TV should continue to thrive and expand.

6.   Radio will continue to reach the masses, with individual stations providing advertisers with a means to reach narrowly targeted audiences. Advertisers may achieve broad reach by combining several stations in any given media plan.

7.   Because of increased financial need and a lower level of government support, public TV and radio will become increasingly aggressive in soliciting program underwriting support from the business community. Already, the required "courtesy" announcements provided by public broadcasters approach the presentation style of generic commercials, including slogans, logotypes, corporate graphics, and mention of business locations. Ultimately, public stations may sell time for commercial messages, provided the FCC approves.

8.   An increase in *direct-response* advertising has occurred on television during recent years. In this advertising form, viewers are solicited to order advertised items direct from marketers by calling a telephone number or writing to an address mentioned in the ads. In addition to direct-response ads, a number of home shopping cable services also have proliferated. These services, such as Home Shopping Network, are analogous to mail-order catalogs, presenting a continuous showing of products from which viewers may choose. Although the future of direct-response advertising is uncertain, present indications suggest further growth.

With this overview of the industry behind us, we can turn now to specific considerations of the stations and networks that carry broadcast advertising daily to individuals and groups across the country.

Study Questions

1.   When did radio broadcasting begin in your state and city? When was the first commercial television station established? (Possible references: *Broadcasting Yearbook, Television Factbook*)

2.   Explain how American broadcasting became a synthesis of the concepts of radio set manufacturers and the telephone company. Identify other industries that have influenced U.S. radio and television broadcasting.

3.   How have broadcast networks contributed to the development of American broadcasting and advertising? In what ways have the networks affected the marketing of products? Have they had any negative effects on broadcasting and marketing?

4.   Why do national advertisers generally prefer television to all other media?

5.   Why is the bulk of radio advertising for local establishments rather than national ones?

6.   Radio underwent a major change in its role as a communication and advertising medium when television became prominent. The development of cable and other new signal delivery systems have brought about changes in television itself. Why is cable a satisfactory alternative to broadcast television for some advertisers? What are cable's major advantages and disadvantages? Are the roles of broadcast and cable television competitive or complementary for the advertiser?

7.   What future developments do you foresee that could alter the role or the form of broadcast advertising?

ASSIGNMENT 1-A

Broadcast advertising involves the productive output of many different organizations. Identify those that are involved in a typical national campaign. Then, diagram the relationships among them to show who works with whom and at what point in time during campaign development.

ASSIGNMENT 1-B

Given an assigned nonbroadcast advertiser, prepare on outline showing the points you would cover in a presentation made to convince this advertiser to use radio, TV, or both.

ASSIGNMENT 1-C

Select one of the elements of broadcast advertising discussed in this chapter. Prepare a paper on its role in the industry today. By listing possible section headings, show how your paper will be organized. You may want to work with a classmate in presenting opposing views or multiple sides of a particular topic.

ASSIGNMENT 1-D

Consider the effectiveness of (1) program sponsorship and (2) spot announcement advertising. List the strengths and weaknesses of both and assign what you feel are appropriate "weights" to each factor. Finally, total the points and see which side comes out ahead.

Notes

1. *Broadcasting* (June 1, 1981), 133.
2. Curtis Mitchell. *Cavalcade of Broadcasting* (Chicago: Follette, 1970), 39.
3. Irving Settel. *A Pictorial History of Radio* (New York: Bonanza Books, 1960), 31-32.
4. *Ibid.*, 35.
5. *Television Factbook*, No. 50 (1981) (Washington, D.C.: Television Digest), 73-a.
6. Erik Barnouw. *A Tower in Babel: A History of Broadcasting in the United States*, vol. 1 (New York: Oxford University Press, 1966), 270.
7. *Television Factbook*, No. 50 (1981), 73-a.
8. *Ibid.*
9. Sydney W. Head. *Broadcasting in America: A Survey of Television and Radio* (Boston: Houghton Mifflin, 1956), 150.
10. H. Ted Busch and Terry Landeck. *The Making of a Television Commercial* (New York: Macmillan, 1980), 3.
11. *1988 Report on Television* (Northbrook, Ill.: A. C. Nielsen), 2.
12. *Ibid.*, 3.
13. *Television & Cable Factbook*, No. 56 (1988) (Washington, D.C.: Television Digest) C-305, 311.
14. *1988 Report on Television*, 7.
15. *Estimated Annual U.S. Advertising Expenditures 1977-1986* (New York: McCann-Erickson, June 1987), 1.
16. *Broadcasting* (February 23, 1981).
17. *Trends in Television* (New York: Television Bureau of Advertising, June 1987), 15.
18. *Trends in GNP Ad Volume, TV Ad Volume (1960-1995)* (New York: Television Bureau of Advertising, May 1988), 2.

Suggested Readings

Barnouw, Erik. *A Tower in Babel: A History of Broadcasting in the United States*, vol. 1. New York: Oxford University Press, 1966.

_____. *The Golden Web*: *A History of Broadcasting in the United States*, vol. 2. New York: Oxford University Press, 1968.

_____. *The Image Empire*: *A History of Broadcasting in the United States*, vol. 3. New York: Oxford University Press, 1975.

Barr, David Samuel. *Advertising on Cable: A Practical Guide for Advertisers*. Englewood Cliffs, N.J.: Prentice-Hall, 1985.

Bergendorf, Fred L. *Broadcast Advertising and Promotion: A Handbook for Students and Professionals*. New York: Hastings, 1983.

Bogart, Leo. *The Age of Television*. New York: Ungar, 1972.

Busch, H. Ted, and Terry Landeck. *The Making of a Television Commercial*. New York: Macmillan, 1980.

Campbell, Robert. *The Golden Years of Broadcasting*. New York: Scribner, 1976.

Czitrom, Daniel J. *Media and the American Mind: From Morse to McLuhan*. Chapel Hill: University of North Carolina Press, 1982.

Eicoff, Al. *Eicoff on Broadcast Direct Marketing*. Lincolnwood, Ill.: NTC Business Books/National Textbook Co., 1988.

Fornatale, Peter, and Joshua E. Mills. *Radio in the Television Age*. Woodstock, N.Y.: Overlook Press, 1980.

Foster, Eugene S. *Understanding Broadcasting*. Reading, Mass.: Addison-Wesley, 1978.

Frankl, Razelle. *Televangelism: The Marketing of Popular Religion*. Carbondale: Southern Illinois University Press, 1987.

Geis, Michael L. *The Language of Television Advertising*. New York: Academic Press, 1982.

Head, Sydney W., and Christopher H. Sterling. *Broadcasting in America: A Survey of Electronic Media*. 5th ed. Boston: Houghton Mifflin, 1987.

Heighton, Elizabeth J., and Don R. Cunningham. *Advertising in the Broadcast and Cable Media*. 2d ed. Belmont, Calif.: Wadsworth, 1984.

Kaatz, Ronald B. *Cable Advertiser's Handbook*. 2d ed. Lincolnwood, Ill.: Crain/National Textbook Co., 1985.

MacDonald, J. Fred. *Don't Touch That Dial! Radio Programming in American Life, 1920-1960*. Chicago: Nelson-Hall, 1979.

McGee, William L. et al. *Changes, Challenges & Opportunities in the New Electronic Media*. San Francisco: Broadcast Marketing, 1982.

Meyer, Martin. *About Television*. New York: Harper & Row, 1972.

Pattis, S. William. *Opportunities in Advertising*. Lincolnwood, Ill.: National Textbook Co., 1984.

Percy, Larry, and Arch G. Woodside, eds. *Advertising and Consumer Psychology*. Lexington, Mass.: Lexington Books, 1983.

Reed, Maxine, K., and Robert M. Reed. *Career Opportunities in Television, Cable, and Video*. 2d ed. New York: Facts on File, 1986.

Smith, F. Leslie. *Perspectives on Radio and Television: An Introduction to Broadcasting in the United States*. New York: Harper & Row, 1979.

Sterling, Christopher. *Stay Tuned: A Concise History of American Broadcasting*. Belmont, Calif.: Wadsworth 1978.

Summers, Harrison. *Broadcasting and the Public*. Belmont, Calif.: Wadsworth, 1978.

Ulanoff, Stanley M. *Advertising in America: An Introduction to Persuasive Communication*. New York: Hastings, 1977.

Warner, Charles. *Broadcast and Cable Selling*. Belmont, Calif.: Wadsworth, 1986.

2

Broadcast Stations and Networks

Chapter 1 noted that nearly every home in America receives television and radio programming from a variety of sources. In fact, broadcast station towers dot the entire landscape, sending entertainment, information, advertising, and service to vast daytime and nighttime audiences. These stations make up a diverse collection of more than 11,500 radio and television outlets licensed to serve communities of all sizes and characteristics. Approximately 10,000 of them operate as commercial, advertiser-supported media. Most of the TV and nearly half of the radio stations are affiliated with network organizations that provide programs and solicit advertising for airing on local outlets across the country.

Radio's two different aural services are identified as frequency modulation (FM) and amplitude modulation (AM). FM and AM stations transmit signals on separate bands within the electromagnetic spectrum, and both types are classified to reflect the geographical coverage provided.

Television stations are designated as *very high frequency* (VHF) and *ultra high frequency* (UHF) facilities. There is little difference between VHF and UHF from a transmission standpoint (as there is between FM and AM radio); but the two TV services vary considerably in effective coverage because of wavelength differences in the two portions of the electromagnetic spectrum. Because of the disadvantages inherent in UHF broadcasting, stations on that band tend to depend upon cable carriage for much of their audience reach.

Radio stations exist in small towns (some with less than 1,000 population), cities, and major metropolitan areas. In contrast, because of television's more costly operating requirements, TV stations are usually located in or near metropolitan population centers (though some exceptions exist, notably in the rural West). The Federal Communications Commission (FCC) also authorizes low-power (LPTV) stations for limited-range broadcasting in both small and large communities. Such stations usually provide local service to the former and specialized programming to minority audiences in the latter.

Station Regulations

Under the American system of broadcasting, the license to operate a radio or television station is a public trust. The FCC, chartered by the Federal Communications Act of 1934, regulates station operations "in the public interest, convenience, and necessity."[1] The FCC represents the public in awarding licenses to individuals, companies, and corporations who pledge to serve their respective coverage areas. Revenue from the sale of advertising enables commercial stations both to fulfill public obligations and, it is hoped, to earn profits.

The commission assigns each station to a specific channel or frequency and specifies power output, type and location of transmitter and antenna system, and hours of operation.

Control of such technical factors is necessary to ensure efficient use of the limited spectrum and to prevent unnecessary interference between stations. Although the Federal Communications Act of 1934 specifically prohibits the FCC from censoring programming, the courts have allowed the commission to review past program performance to determine how well each licensee has served the public under its trusteeship.

Since 1980, the FCC has eliminated many of its former restrictions on broadcast stations, particularly radio; but these deregulatory actions do not reduce the broadcaster's obligation to serve the public interest.

The FCC exerts little influence over advertising. Since radio and television are not regarded as common carriers or public utilities, stations set their own rates in response to supply and demand considerations. Furthermore, they may accept or reject any advertising offered to them, provided they do not discriminate against competitors within an industry.[2] The FCC sometimes becomes concerned with broadcast advertising when it believes a station is carrying an excessive amount of commercial material; it is the Federal Trade Commission (FTC), though, that scrutinizes radio and TV spots for false and misleading claims.

Ownership of Stations

The FCC limits station ownership in several important ways. First, under new multiple-ownership rules adopted in 1985, each owner may hold up to 12 television stations provided the total audience reach does not exceed 25 percent of the nation's TV households, as determined by Arbitron market data. Similarly, for radio, each owner may hold licenses for as many as 12 FM and 12 AM stations.

Second, the FCC restricts ownership within broadcast market areas. For example, the common ownership of two stations of the same type (FM, AM, or TV) that overlap substantially in coverage is forbidden. With rare exceptions, the Commission will not authorize ownership of both radio and TV stations by the same entity in a given market. Neither will the FCC approve the licensing of broadcast stations to daily newspaper publishers in the city of publication.[3]

The three principal forms of station ownership include network owned-and-operated (O&O) stations, group-owned stations, and independently owned (single-ownership) stations.

NETWORK OWNERSHIP
The national network organizations, which are not licensed as such, are permitted to own stations subject to the multiple-ownership rules given above. Each of the three largest networks—ABC, CBS, and NBC—owns a group of major market television stations. The Fox Broadcasting Company, which established a fourth TV network in 1986, also owns an impressive array of television stations. Collectively, these network O&O stations are among the most valuable broadcast properties in the industry.

For example, each of the four networks owns a local TV outlet in the nation's three largest markets—New York, Los Angeles, and Chicago. Approximately 16.5 percent of all U.S. TV households are located within these three areas. Additional markets vary with each network. As of July 1, 1989, the number of television stations owned by each network was ABC-TV, 8; CBS-TV, 5; NBC-TV, 7; and Fox, 7.

GROUP OWNERSHIP
Group ownership exists wherever a licensee owns two or more broadcast stations situated in different market areas. Some 190 television and 300 radio station groups currently operate under the FCC's multiple-ownership rules.

A group operation may function as a highly integrated business enterprise, or it may be a loose federation of stations owned in common. Although group owners usually strive to obtain the maximum number of stations permitted by the FCC, the average number of TV stations owned per group is 4.1.[4]

Broadcast groups own approximately 77 percent of all TV stations in the top-100 markets and have become a powerful force in the industry, second only to the networks. Some major groups such as Westinghouse (Group W), Tribune Broadcasting, and Multimedia also engage in program production and syndication. Some groups maintain their own national sales offices instead of using independent representatives. Table 2.1 lists the 20 largest group owners in rank order of weekly circulation as of January 1989.

Table 2.1. Twenty largest television station groups, January 1, 1989

Rank	Group	Number of Stations	Net Weekly Circulation	Percentage of TV Households (ADI Basis)
1	Tribune Broadcasting	6	22,204,000	18.7
2	Capital Cities/ABC	8	20,109,000	23.4
3	GE/NBC	7	18,483,000	22.4
4	CBS	5	15,780,000	20.8
5	Fox	7	15,613,600	19.5
6	Gillette	12	11,003,600	11.3
7	MCA	4	10,403,500	11.6
8	Westinghouse	5	9,069,500	10.0
9	Gannett	10	8,737,600	10.0
10	Cox	8	8,546,300	9.0
11	United/Chris Craft	7	7,594,400	10.7
12	Scripps-Howard	9	7,088,800	7.6
13	Hearst	6	6,444,100	6.8
14	TVX Group	9	6,117,000	5.8
15	Gaylord	5	4,883,900	5.3
16	Belo	5	4,755,000	5.7
17	Post-Newsweek	4	4,423,200	4.8
18	Lin	7	4,277,000	4.6
19	Knight-Ridder	9	4,189,900	4.8
20	Great American	5	3,982,200	4.8

Source: Herbert H. Howard, "Group and Cross-Media Ownership of TV Stations: A 1989 Update," *Journalism Quarterly* (Winter 1989). Also see *Group and Cross-Media Ownership of Television Stations,* annual series from 1979 through 1990 (Washington: National Association of Broadcasters).

Note: Percentage of audience reach for groups is calculated by the FCC as the sum of the percentages of each group's ADI markets (percentage of U.S. TV households) rather than percentages based on weekly or daily circulation.

INDEPENDENTLY OWNED STATIONS

Independently owned stations are those whose owners have no financial interest in broadcast properties located in other markets. Such single-station ownership is most common among small-market radio stations and secondary radio stations in metropolitan markets. Independently owned television stations, though rare, are most numerous in smaller metropolitan centers.

A company that operates both radio and TV stations licensed to one city, with no other station ownership elsewhere, is regarded as a single-station owner. Among the small number of examples at the beginning of 1989 were WWL AM-FM-TV, New Orleans, and WNDU AM-FM-TV, South Bend, Indiana.

A distinction must be kept in mind between an independently owned station and an *independent* station. The latter term designates a station that has no affiliation with a national network, while an independently owned station may or may not be a network affiliate.

Television Stations

Commercial and educational television stations in the United States, numbering nearly 1,400 in 1989, operate on 82 different channels. Channels 2 through 13 are situated in the VHF portion of the spectrum, while channels 14 through 83 occupy space in the UHF band. Of these 1,400 stations, about 1,060 are commercial outlets (540 VHF and 520 UHF). Of the remaining 337 noncommercial stations, about two-thirds operate in the UHF band.

Three methods are commonly used for classifying television stations: type of channel assignments, size of market, and network affiliation or independent status.

CHANNEL ASSIGNMENT
Although a more detailed explanation will be given in Chapter 3, it is important here to recognize a critical difference between VHF and UHF television. The wavelengths of the UHF band are much shorter than those of VHF, resulting in critical reception problems for ultra high frequency stations. A number of attempts have been made by Congress and the FCC to reduce the disparity; these include (1) a requirement that all TV sets sold in interstate commerce be equipped with both UHF and VHF tuners and (2) a provision for UHF broadcasting at super power levels of up to five megawatts. In addition, the FCC has designated certain cities for all-UHF broadcasting in an attempt to equalize local TV competition. Although these measures have assisted UHF licensees, they almost always operate at a competitive disadvantage to VHF outlets.

Nearly 200 new UHF stations were established during the 1980s, and the number of new outlets continues to grow. The majority of these recently established UHF stations are located in the top-100 markets and operate as independent outlets or as affiliates of the Fox network. These stations, and indeed all UHF outlets, must rely heavily on cable carriage to maintain competitiveness with VHF stations. Since practically no unoccupied VHF channels remain, the future growth of over-the-air television will continue to be in the UHF band.

MARKET RANK
The more than 200 U.S. television markets are classified by the two principal audience research organizations according to the number of TV households within each market. The Arbitron Ratings Company identifies and ranks television markets by "Areas of Dominant Influence" (ADI), as shown in Table 2.2, while the A. C. Nielsen Company uses the term "Designated Market Areas" (DMA). The market rankings produced by both services usually are quite similar. Table 2.2 indicates the number of TV households in each of the 25 largest markets (1988), with the percentages of all U.S. television households for these markets.

Television stations in the top-50 markets generally are regarded as major-market outlets. Those located in markets 51 through 100 are considered secondary-market stations, and those located in smaller communities with ranking above 100 are classed as small-market stations.

Great significance is attached to market rank because the advertising potential of a TV station correlates closely with the size of its market area. Stations in large population centers have a decided economic advantage because advertising rates are based primarily on the number of viewers reached. To illustrate the point, the ten largest markets account for 31 percent of all U.S. TV households and

Table 2.2. ADI Television market rankings (based on Arbitron estimates of U.S. TV households on January 1, 1989)

Rank	Market	ADI TV Households	Percentage of U.S. TV Households
1	New York	6,944,400	7.72
2	Los Angeles	4,807,700	5.34
3	Chicago	3,068,600	3.41
4	Philadelphia	2,642,500	2.94
5	San Francisco	2,164,100	2.40
6	Boston	2,045,100	2.27
7	Detroit	1,712,600	1.90
8	Dallas-Fort Worth	1,676,700	1.86
9	Washington, D.C.	1,638,900	1.82
10	Houston	1,447,800	1.61
11	Cleveland	1,420,100	1.58
12	Atlanta	1,315,900	1.46
13	Minneapolis-St. Paul	1,307,200	1.45
14	Miami	1,259,900	1.40
15	Seattle-Tacoma	1,255,000	1.39
16	Pittsburgh	1,186,800	1.32
17	Tampa-St. Petersburg	1,161,600	1.29
18	St. Louis	1,104,700	1.23
19	Denver	1,032,200	1.15
20	Phoenix	959,700	1.07
21	Sacramento-Stockton	957,400	1.06
22	Baltimore	916,300	1.02
23	Hartford-New Haven	883,100	.98
24	San Diego	836,300	.93
25	Orlando-Daytona Beach-Melbourne	827,500	.92

(Used with permission from Arbitron Ratings.)

achieve about 44 percent of all national and regional television advertising income. Similarly, the top-50 markets contain 67 percent of the nation's television households and receive about 79 percent of the U.S. national and regional advertising. Eighty-six percent of the TV households are located within the 100 largest markets, and the stations there attract an estimated 91 percent of the advertising. In contrast, only 14 percent of the TV households are located in the television markets ranked 101-212; national and regional advertisers commit only about 9 percent of their budgets to those small-market stations.

NETWORK AFFILIATION OR INDEPENDENT STATUS

Television stations may be classified further depending on their status as network affiliates or independent outlets. Affiliation with one of the three major networks (ABC, CBS, or NBC) is highly desirable because of access to first-run network programming and advertising revenues. In contrast, independent stations must bear the full cost of programming their schedules. More than 100 independent stations are affiliated with the Fox Broadcasting Company (established in 1986), which programs a partial schedule, to gain similar network advantages. Other limited-time networks have been proposed by Turner Broadcasting and other firms. In rare instances, an independent station may secure some network programming that has been declined by a primary affiliate.

Independent stations usually feature movies, children's programs, sports, and reruns of off-network shows. In addition, first-run syndicated programming and special (occasional) networks have become increasingly available, resulting in higher quality fare and a more competitive stance for most independent outlets. An example is "Independent Network News" (INN), fed each evening by WPIX (TV), New York, to more than 50 stations across the country.

TELEVISION PROGRAMMING POLICIES

The prevailing programming philosophy of commercial TV stations is to attract as many viewers as possible during every broadcast period. Program directors seek not only to attain dominant shares of the audience, but also to attract specific viewers regarded as the most "demographically desirable" by advertisers. As a result, many programs are chosen because of their appeal to 18- to 49-year-old adults, the principal purchasing segment in our society.

In addition, TV networks, their affiliates, and most independent stations try to maintain a balanced program schedule to satisfy all viewers at some time during the week. Varied schedules also help stations and networks serve many types of advertising clients.

Radio Broadcasting

The commercial segment of U.S. radio broadcasting includes more than 10,400 stations, consisting of about 5,500 FM and 4,900 AM outlets, as of January 1, 1989. Despite the long period of AM dominance, listening to FM stations now exceeds AM listening by a wide margin. Reasons for this shift include the adoption of competitive formats by most FM stations, greater awareness of FM's superior sound quality, availability of FM radios for use in cars, and sometimes lighter commercial loads on FM compared with AM radio. FM garnered 73 percent of the listening audience in 1989, according to *American Radio*, published by James H. Duncan, Jr. The percentage, however, varies widely from market to market.

AM RADIO

The AM, or standard, band consists of 107 channels, each ten kilohertz (kHz) wide. These channels are identified by their *center* or *middle* frequencies and range from 540 to 1600 kHz on the dial. Each frequency is designated for a specific level of service, with power assignments ranging from 250 to 50,000 watts. The AM frequencies are divided into *clear channels*, intended primarily for service to broad coverage areas; *regional channels,* used by stations with middle-range coverage; and *local channels,* designated for low-power, local-service stations. Furthermore, AM stations are divided into four classes:

Class I: 50,000 watt "dominant" stations assigned to clear channels.
Class II: "secondary" stations assigned to clear channels.
Class III: stations assigned to "regional" channels, which operate with power ranging from 500 to 5,000 watts.
Class IV: stations assigned to "local" channels, operating with power output of 1,000 watts during daytime and at night.

FM RADIO

The FM broadcast band consists of 100 channels, each 200 kilohertz in width, extending from 88 to 108 megahertz on the dial. Stations are divided into four classifications, which reflect the extent of geographical coverage. Class A stations, which serve small communities and the surrounding rural areas, are roughly comparable to Class IV AM stations. Class B and Class C outlets serve larger cities and their surrounding regions. FCC limitations restrict the effective radiated power (ERP) of Class A stations to 3,000 watts, Class B stations to 50,000 watts, and Class C stations to 100,000 watts. The FCC also authorizes low-power educational FM stations to be used for teaching purposes. These Class D stations typically operate with about 100 watts.

RADIO PROGRAMMING POLICIES

Program policies vary widely among stations in both the AM and FM bands. With large numbers of outlets operating in most cities, stations tend to specialize in distinctive formats intended to attract specific target audiences. Most radio broadcasters must be satisfied with relatively small shares of the total listening audience because of the large number of signals available (for example, there are approximately 45 FM and 35 AM signals in the Los Angeles market). In every market, however, a few—perhaps five to ten—radio stations capture significant shares. Advertisers may select stations of various demographic appeals in any combination suitable to their needs; in the sense of program diversity, radio is a highly flexible advertising medium.

It is interesting to note that an Arbitron major market survey found a very small amount of radio dial-switching in markets across the country. The average number of stations used per person per week ranged from 1.8 in Mobile, Alabama, to 2.8 in San Francisco. The number of stations available to persons in these cities, however, was 13 and 42, respectively.

Organization of Broadcast Stations

Radio and television stations vary considerably in size and number of employees, but are usually organized into six major functional areas: engineering, programming, news, sales, promotion, and general office.

A general manager or other administrative executive is responsible for coordinating the efforts of all departments. A typical broadcast station organization chart is shown in Figure 2.1.

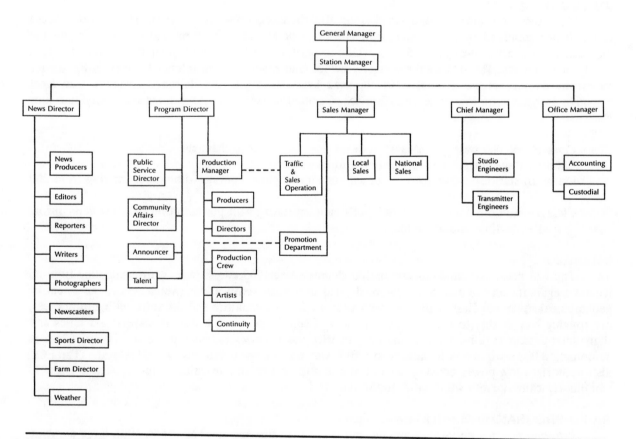

Fig. 2.1. Television station organization chart.

The average TV station today has a staff of approximately 80 persons, with many outlets having more than 100 employees. A decade earlier, only stations in the largest markets employed as many as 100 people. Much of the increase in television employment has occurred in the news area since TV has taken on a much more significant role as a news medium. A few large-market stations employ as many as 250 persons. In contrast, radio stations are relatively small employers, with only one station out of ten having as many as 25 employees. In fact, half of all radio stations have fewer than a dozen fulltime employees.

Every station is a functional organization in the sense that the activities of each department are closely integrated with those of other units. Fundamentally, broadcasting is made possible through electronic technology. Before a radio or TV station can be successful as a advertising medium, therefore, it must have solid engineering to deliver a usable signal to its audience, as well as attractive programs to win attention.

MAJOR DEPARTMENTS

Engineering department. This department is headed by a technical director or chief engineer and is responsible for both the station's physical plant and its broadcast facilities. Maintaining these facilities, so as to provide the audience with the best possible broadcast signal, is a major engineering function. Engineers also provide production facilities needed to meet program requirements and operate technical facilities at both the studio and the transmitting plant.

Program department. The program director, who is head of this department, is expected to obtain and present programs that will satisfy needs of the audience, sponsors, and management. Programming for a local TV station may be produced live by using the station's production facilities, staff, and talent, or it may be obtained from syndication sources and networks. The latter arrangement provides the backbone of programming for network-affiliated stations.

In radio, recorded program material predominates except for those stations that engage in all-news and all-talk formats. Selecting and developing a format suitable for a station's target audience becomes a primary consideration for radio program directors. Major program decisions, however, at both radio and television stations usually involve station managers, program directors, and sales managers.

News department. Headed by the news director, the news department prepares newscasts and other public-affairs programs. Because of the importance of news on both radio and television, this activity has been given the status of a top-line department throughout much of the broadcast industry.

Sales department. While engineering and programming functions are essential if a station is to attract a substantial audience, the sales department generates the vitally important advertising revenue needed to defray costs of operation. This department is usually divided into national sales and local sales. The national sales manager coordinates the solicitation of national advertising through the station's sales representative organization, ordinarily based in a major metropolitan area. The local sales effort is planned and supervised by a local sales manager, and the number of local salespersons employed varies depending upon market size and competition.

Promotion department. Broadcasting is a highly competitive business. For this reason, most radio and television stations engage in both audience and sales promotion to gain the largest possible number of listeners/viewers and as much advertising revenue as possible. The promotion department, in effect, is the station's own advertising unit. It promotes the station's programs and personalities on the station itself and through other media. TV stations have been known to use more than $2.5 million worth of their own air time annually to advertise themselves and their programs.[5]

National TV networks often obtain matching funds from affiliates for newspaper cooperative ads announcing the new fall lineup of programs and may secure trade-offs with *TV Guide* (exchanges of advertising time and space to promote the network's programs and the magazine's features).

A radio station may spend $100,000 on an image campaign—on-air jingles and announcements supported by TV spots and other media ads. Promotional personnel also assist the sales department by preparing sales materials for presentation to prospective clients and by planning advertisements for the trade press. Trade ads typically acquaint media buyers with a station's advantages as an advertising vehicle.

Recent years have seen a massive multimedia radio promotional campaign staged by the Radio Advertising Bureau. "Radio: It's Red Hot," claim the ads, and a survey among advertisers and advertising agencies found a 65 percent awareness level of this theme. By comparison, TV, magazine, and newspaper campaigns were pulling between 42 and 46 percent levels.[6]

General office department. This department of a television or radio station handles such diverse activities as bookkeeping, billing, payroll, preparing tax and corporate forms, general secretarial work, reception of guests, and custodial functions.

OTHER DEPARTMENTS
In addition to the six principal departments, a number of lesser-ranking units perform other vital functions, such as copy preparation, traffic or scheduling, merchandising, and research.

Continuity. The continuity department assists advertisers with preparation of commercials. Since most large advertisers rely on advertising agencies for this service, most of the commercial copy prepared by a station is for local, nonagency clients. At many stations, this department also writes program material and public service messages.

Traffic. The traffic unit prepares daily operating schedules that list each program, commercial, public service announcement, or other types of material to be broadcast. Included also are the sources and times of broadcast for all items. Figure 2.2 presents a typical operating schedule for a large television station.

Merchandising. Many stations go beyond the mere promotion of programs to assist advertisers directly with the merchandising of their products. Aids may include direct mail pieces and other forms of inducement to dealers encouraging them to stock merchandise advertised on the station, as well as point-of-purchase displays to remind shoppers of commercials they may have heard or seen. On-air contests also are popular. Figure 2.3 is an example of a direct mail merchandising item.

Research. Every station does research related to its audience and marketing area, though many studies are informal and limited in scope. Most stations in competitive markets subscribe to audience studies conducted by national research firms, such as Arbitron and A. C. Nielsen. Usually, only large stations and major broadcast groups have research departments of their own. When done well, a research project may produce results far greater than its cost by uncovering useful data on consumers and products as well as programs and audiences.

Radio and Television Networks

Networks have been integral to U.S. broadcasting since 1923, when the AT & T Company began linking distant stations to its New York outlet to rebroadcast the programs of WEAF. Today, TV networks occupy a commanding position in the industry, while radio networks play a lesser, but growing and still important role.

AIRTIME		INIT	SCHED-TIME			√	LINE NUMB	WMC/TV MEMPHIS **PROGRAM – SPONSORS** 05/24/88 CENTRAL DAYLIGHT TIME PG# 19		TYPE		VIDEO SOURCE	AUDIO SOURCE	FILM NUMBER	TUESDAY — REMARKS
START	FINISH		H	M	S										
			06	58	28			4 PILLSBURY/BURGE PSD – DAILY SPECIAL		CA	30	T	T	082	PBBK-8155-30
			06	58	58			4 MEMPHIS TOYOTA MAY PRE SELL/EVENT		CA	30	T	T	628	TCAM-1561-30
			06	59	28			4 WAL-MART PD#27 PAINT DEPT.		CA	30	T	T	991	530-88-27-30
			06	59	58			ANIMATED NEWS ID		ID	2	T	T	P-102	(NEWS) 1-05
			07	00	00			** MATLOCK	N	E					
			07	30	00			4 BMW OF NORTH AM AUTOMOTIVE EST 8533		CA	30	TS	TA	1050	YWWJ-8217-30 W/143
			07	30	30			ANIMATED NEWS ID		ID	2	T	T	P-103	(WEATHER) 2-05
								** NBC NEWS DIGEST	N	N					
			07	58	58			4 PONTIAC LEMANS		CA	30	T	T	851	GMPT-9938-30
			07	59	28			3 WRVR FM-104 WRVR-FM		CA	30	T	T	568	SPK-25-43-30
			07	59	58			ANIMATED NEWS ID		ID	2	T	T	P-104	(NEWS) 3-05
			08	00	00			** NBC MOVIE OF THE WEEK	N	E					DESPERADO AVALANCE @ DEVILS RG
			08	28	58			2 KFC-MEMPHIS CO- CHICKEN		CA	30	T	T	058	9914-30
			08	29	28			ANIMATED NEWS ID		ID	2	T	T	P-105	(SPORTS) 4-05
								** ACTION NEWS 5 UPDATE (COVER NBC NEWS DIGEST)	L	N			T	T	P-106	–
			08	58	28			7 DILLARDS DEPT. CORPORATE GENERIC E		CA	30	T	T	646	DIL-121771/ZDL8023-30
			08	58	58			2 ST. FRANCIS HOS OPTIFAST		CA	30	T	T	708	132-11-87-30
			08	59	28			2 MATA PUBLIC TRANSPORTATI		CA	30	T	T	071	3864-DISC-30
			08	59	58			OPRAH WINFREY WKDYS		ID	2	T	A	P-037	1-05

LEGEND SOURCE		PROGRAM CLASSIFICATIONS				NON-PROGRAM CLASSIFICATIONS	VIDEO/AUDIO SOURCE CODES	
		BASIC TYPES		SUB-CATAGORIES				
LOCAL	L	A-AGRICULTURAL	R-RELIGIOUS	D-EDITORIALS		CA-COMMERCIAL ANNOUNCEMENTS	FILM	F
RECORDED	R	E-ENTERTAINMENT	I-INSTRUCTIONAL	L-POLITICAL		CC-COMMERCIAL CONTINUITY	VIDEO TAPE	T
NETWORK	N	N-NEWS	S-SPORTS	U-EDUCATIONAL		PS-PUBLIC SERVICE	SLIDE	S
SPECIAL NETWORK	SN	P-PUBLIC AFFAIRS	O-OTHER			ID-STATION IDENTIFICATION	STUDIO (LIVE)	L
OTHER	O					PR-PROMOTION	REMOTE	R
SATELLITE	S						ANNCR	A
							AUDIO TAPE	C

Fig. 2.2. Sample television station program operating log. (Courtesy of WMC-TV, Memphis)

Dear

It's Northwest Cherry Time again in the Knoxville area.

Beginning June 29 and running through July 26, WIVK Radio
will be building consumer demand for those big, beautiful
Bing and Lambert Cherries...with a powerful advertising schedule.

Tennessee Valley housewives will be hearing a broadside of
60-second announcements morning, mid-day, and night...to
keep their level of awareness high during this prime selling
season for Northwest Cherries.

They'll be looking for these fresh Bing and Lambert Cherries
at your produce counters, too, because Northwest is including
your store name in the tags to these announcements. So, order
now to insure a plentiful supply when these shoppers come calling.

Sincerely,

James A. Dick
President and General Manager

JAD/ah

Fig. 2.3. Direct mail merchandising message. (Courtesy of WIVK AM-FM, Knoxville, Tennessee)

Behind every network operation is a central control point from which programming (including commercials) is fed to distant stations for transmission through their local facilities. Programs may originate at a network production center or at a remote point (such as a football stadium), or they may be produced on film or tape, either video or audio, ready to be fed from the network control center to outlying stations.

Historically, TV network signals have been distributed to affiliated stations across the country by microwave relay, while radio network feeds have been accomplished by microwave and/or special telephone lines. During the 1980s, however, network interconnection shifted to distribution by communication satellites. A typical TV station now uses from four to six satellite-receiving (downlink) dishes to pick up network feeds and other program sources. Network-affiliated radio stations usually operate one or more satellite-receiving dishes to obtain network and news feeds.

In the pre-satellite era, networks were limited to a single national programming feed with time-zone adjustment. But using satellites, networks can provide two or more simultaneous feeds from which affiliated stations may choose. The flexibility of satellite transmission also allows the networks to schedule a limited amount of regional advertising along with traditional national network advertising.

In addition to *live* interconnected networks, a limited amount of tape networking exists in the United States. It is feasible, for example, to provide common programming to a number of distantly located stations by shipping duplicate audio or videotapes to the respective stations.

CLASSIFICATION OF NETWORKS

A radio or TV network may be national, regional, or custom-made. Each has its own distinct characteristics.

National Networks

National networks broadcast on a regular and continuous basis through affiliated stations in all or most parts of the country. In TV, networks provide a variety of programming, including entertainment, news, sports, and special events, while in radio, networks offer mainly news and special events coverage. Various radio program services, fed by satellite, also emphasize format music programming and sell advertising on a network basis.

Each of the major national television networks—ABC, CBS, and NBC—has about 200 affiliated stations. These outlets vary to some extent from market to market, but overall the three networks are comparable and fully competitive. The newer Fox TV network serves about 100 affiliates, many of which are UHF stations that are not fully competitive.

In 1988, some ten organizations were involved in national radio networking, providing nearly 40 different program services. The most significant thrust, as shown in Table 2.3, has come from demographic and "life-style" programming.

Interconnected networks, however, are not the only ones that cover the nation. Several national radio sales representative firms (Katz, for instance) personally package groups of stations to sell on a spot basis as *rep* or *nonwired* networks.

Regional Networks

More than 100 regional radio networks exist in the United States. Ordinarily these organizations function as state news networks, providing frequent newscasts oriented toward listeners in a given geographical area. Affiliated stations also may be outlets for one of the national radio chains as well as the regional service, and they may receive programs through a combination of telephone links, off-the-air pickups (from other stations), and in some cases, from satellite feeds.

Table 2.3. Radio networks and program services

Network Organizations and Program Services	Type of Programming	Number of Affiliates (1988 est.)	Demographic Appeal
ABC Radio			
1. Contemporary Network	News (Top 40)	250	(12-34)
2. Directions Network	News (AC)	425	(25-44)
3. Entertainment Network	News (Personality)	580	(18-54)
4. FM Network	News (FM Contemp.)	140	(12-34)
5. Information Network	News-Talk (MOR)	620	(18-54)
6. Rock Radio	News (AOR)	95	(15-34)
7. Talk Radio	Talk/commentary	125	(25-54)
CBS Radio			
1. CBS Radio Network	News/sports	400	(18-54)
2. RadioRadio	AOR/contemporary	150	(18-34)
National Black Network	Black-oriented	115	Black
National Public Radio	Public stations	350	Adult
Satellite Music Network (Ad sales: ABC Radio)	Eight formats	960	Various
Sheridan Broadcasting Network	Black-oriented	130	Adult
Transtar Network	Six formats	1000	Various
Westwood One Networks			
1. Mutual Broadcasting System	News	700	(18-54)
2. Mutual PM	Talk		(25-65)
3. NBC Radio Network	Talk	375	(18-54)
4. NBC/The Source	News (AOR)	125	(15-34)
5. NBC Talk Network	Talk	290	(25-65)
6. NBC Radio Entertainment[a]	Music/rock/jazz		(18-35)
7. Westwood One[a]	Music/rock/jazz		(12-34)
	Big bands		(35-65)
United Stations Radio Network			
1. U.S. One	News	200	(18-49)
2. U.S. Two	News	330	(25-54)
3. U.S. Entertainment[a]	Music	1800	(18-34)

[a]Specials and other one-time programs predominate.

The largest regional network, the Texas State Network, has some 110 affiliated stations located throughout Texas. A list of regional radio networks appears annually in *Broadcasting and Cablecasting Yearbook*.

Custom-made Networks

Other specialized networks are set up to broadcast specific programs such as sporting events, political speeches, and occasional entertainment shows. Two such organizations, Mislou Network and Great American Independent Football Network, provide extensive regional coverage of collegiate athletic events not carried by national television networks. Custom-made networks also engage in entertainment programming, including movie showings, at times. Such ad hoc networks, whether they emphasize sports or entertainment, usually operate on a barter basis, selling a portion of the advertising availabilities while offering a telecast at no cost to selected stations. Stations using special network feeds may be independent outlets or network affiliates, preempting regular programming for the special one-time broadcasts.

Custom-made radio networks include a long list of college and professional baseball, basketball, and football networks. Others include networks assembled to carry auto races and other sporting activities. One of the few custom-made radio networks outside the sports realm is the Texaco-Metropolitan Opera Network. Functioning annually during the opera season (December through April), this network feeds live Saturday afternoon performances of New York's Metropolitan Opera to both commercial and public radio stations throughout the country, under the auspices of Texaco, Inc.

NETWORK AND STATION RELATIONS

Network affiliation is highly advantageous to TV stations for several reasons. First, major portions of an affiliate's programming needs are met with network offerings, and as noted before, affiliates normally obtain network broadcasts with no direct outlay of funds, while independent stations must defray programming costs via direct purchases or by bartering advertising time for syndicated shows. Second, attractive network programming enhances a station's appeal to its viewers, thus improving the station's viability as an advertising medium. Third, with rare exceptions, network affiliation is a revenue-producing arrangement whereby TV affiliates receive payment for carrying commercial network broadcasts.

Each affiliate has a contract that defines its relationship with its network. Major contractual items include the type of affiliation, the compensation plan, delivery of the network signal, and contract duration.

Affiliation. TV stations may be either primary or secondary network affiliates. A primary affiliate has first-call rights for all network programs within its market area. Although a station licensee has the legal right to reject any given show, it is presumed that a primary affiliate will accept most, if not all, of the network's commercial program schedule. In cities where independent stations exist, networks frequently contract with secondary affiliates to provide clearance for programs not broadcast by a primary outlet. These affiliations are also common in markets where only two TV stations operate; in such cases, two networks obtain primary affiliation agreements while the third may obtain a secondary contract with one or both of the stations.

Compensation plan. Television networks depend on their affiliates for clearance of time sold to advertisers and normally compensate them on a monthly basis. (A few small-market TV stations are *bonus* affiliates that receive no payment for network programs.) The value of an affiliate to its network depends on such factors as the size of the market, the station's circulation and share of audience, and the competition for affiliation within the market.

The most important factor in determining the amount of revenue an affiliate receives is the network base rate for primetime hours. This rate, which is subject to negotiation, varies from $50 to $10,000, depending on the station's value. Three other elements involved in establishing compensation are (1) the number of hours (primetime and primetime equivalent) of network commercial programs carried, less (2) a stated number of "free" hours for which the station gets no return, plus (3) a specific percentage of the applicable revenue (often 30 percent) granted to the affiliate. Network base rates for some TV affiliates may be found in the *Television & Cable Factbook.*

Although each network has its own standard contract, special concessions may be made to highly desirable stations to win and maintain their affiliation, and in rare cases, some affiliates even pay the networks for its program service. In effect, revenue generated from network advertising is divided between networks and their affiliates. The retained portion defrays network program costs, station-interconnection charges, and general administrative overhead, as well as profits, while the remainder is distributed to affiliated stations in approximate proportion to their importance as network outlets.

Network compensation is a significant source of income for the majority of TV stations, and a major expense item for networks. In contrast, the primary value of being a radio affiliate is added program quality from the network source.

Signal delivery. Generally speaking, television networks arrange for delivery of their programming to affiliates under terms of standard contracts. In rare cases, however, affiliates are required to provide their own means for obtaining the feed from the nearest network station. Such instances usually involve small-market stations.

Contract duration. Contracts normally are written for a two-year period, the maximum length permitted under FCC rules. However, shorter-term contracts may be used either when a network considers changing affiliates or when a station plans to switch to another network.

Although network affiliations are generally useful to radio stations because of their extensive coverage of national news and special events, many prefer, for economic reasons, to operate as independent outlets. In large markets, radio affiliates usually receive only a small amount of income for broadcasting network programs; in contrast, most small-market affiliates pay for the network as a program service. In any case, the amount of income derived from network affiliation in radio is almost negligible.

ADVANTAGES AND DISADVANTAGES OF NATIONAL NETWORK ADVERTISING

Advertisers who use the national radio and/or television networks to carry their messages benefit from:

Simultaneous coverage of the entire national market. Radio network programs, essentially hourly newscasts, are fed to the country on a simultaneous basis. For television, a practice of *comparable-time scheduling* is followed so that viewers in the various time zones can see shows at the most desirable hours. For example, West Coast stations broadcast most network TV programs three hours later than East Coast stations to adjust for time differences.

Simple administration. The process of administering network advertising, in contrast to national spot advertising, is extremely simple. An advertiser works with only one contract and one billing statement per network. Thus, advertisers who buy time on all three television networks reach viewers through some 600 stations, but the administrative details involve only three organizations.

Low effective net cost per station. Not only is paperwork simplified through network advertising, but the pro rata cost per station is also lower than if comparable times were bought on individual stations.

Reduced number of commercial copies. Instead of the large number of taped or filmed commercials required to supply each individual station, only a few copies are needed for network transmission. Furthermore, the quality control over network transmission of commercials is excellent.

Late changes in copy. When necessary, commercial copy substitutions can be made up to a short time before broadcast on network radio and television (thanks to the centralized control aspect of network broadcasting). The networks are unique as the only national media that can permit last-day changes in advertising messages.

In contrast to these advantages, however, there are some limiting factors in national network advertising:

Mixture of affiliates. National TV networks are composed of different types of local affiliates; each has weak, as well as strong, stations. Shortcomings are especially prevalent in network radio, even to the extent that some major markets are missing altogether in radio network rosters. Cable networks, too, are limited by the channel capacity of local systems and by the national subscriber base, approximately 57 percent of the nation's households in 1990.

Inability to split feeds. Another problem arises from the fact that networks are nationally oriented and, with rare exceptions, cannot easily handle regional advertising on an economical basis. However, the networks have attempted to serve regional clients in some instances, such as during regional feeds of sporting events. Such opportunities probably will increase in future years with proliferating satellite technology.

Long lead-time. Commitments for network schedules often must be made months in advance of usage because of heavy demand for network time. However, network schedules (flights) may be bought for long or short durations, as well as for light, moderate, or heavy (saturation) exposure levels.

Cable Television: The Newest Mass Medium

Cable television has become an increasingly valuable medium for broadcast advertisers. In the late 1980s, there were nearly 8,000 cable systems in the country. In turn, some 30 advertising-supported cable networks have emerged, providing programming to viewers of cable systems throughout the country.

Cable TV systems, located in thousands of communities, range in size from more than 240,000 households (such as San Diego, Calif., and Woodbury, N.Y.) to some systems with less than 100 subscribers. Altogether, more than 48 million homes, approximately 57 percent of the nation's television households, subscribed to basic cable service at the time of this book's publication. Even so, cable's growth continues, particularly in large cities, as an increasing number of homes become wired for cable communications.

Although most older cable systems offer only 12 channels, newer systems usually have the capacity to carry 35 or more program channels. In addition, many older systems have upgraded their capacity to permit carriage of more services. Cable operators typically fill their channels to capacity with programming obtained from local/area broadcast TV stations, local cable origination, and satellite transmissions. The latter is responsible for today's proliferation of cable network services, both advertiser-supported and subscriber-supported pay television.

A full-service cable system usually delivers the following types of programming:

OFF-AIR SIGNALS
Local and area stations

SATELLITE SIGNALS
Superstations: Large-city independent TV stations.
Cable networks: Program services supported by a combination of advertising and basic subscriber fees.
Pay TV networks: Program services supported by subscribers' add-on fees in addition to basic service fees.

LOCAL CABLE ORIGINATION
Community programming
Local movie channels
Automated channels (weather, time,
markets, community bulletin boards)

More than half of the nation's top 100 advertisers now use cable TV. A list of the top cable network advertisers closely resembles a similar list of broadcast network clients, including such companies as Procter & Gamble, General Mills, Kraft, Philip Morris, RJR Nabisco, Anheuser-Busch, Chrysler, and many more.

Advertisers may choose from a variety of national cable networks to reach narrow target audiences across the country. Table 2.4 presents a list of the most prominent advertising-supported cable networks and superstations. Although cable operators pay a small monthly fee per subscriber (typically 10 to 25 cents) to carry these services, annual advertising revenues for all cable networks have grown to more than one billion dollars annually. National cable network advertising should continue its rapid growth well into the 1990s.

Table 2.4. Major advertising-supported cable networks and super stations, 1988 estimates

Cable Network	Cable Household Subscribers	Est. Average Primetime Household Reach
1. ESPN	46,500,000	600,000
2. Cable News (CNN)/	44,000,000	600,000
Headline News	30,000,000	
3. TBS-TV, Atlanta	44,000,000	1,400,000
4. USA Network	43,000,000	700,000
5. CBN Cable Network	40,000,000	250,000
5. Music TV (MTV)	40,000,000	250,000
5. Nashville (TNN)	40,000,000	450,000
8. C-Span	38,000,000	
8. Nickelodeon	38,000,000	
10. Univision	37,000,000	
10. Lifetime	37,000,000	440,000
12. Weather Channel	30,000,000	
12. Arts & Entertainment	30,000,000	200,000
16. Financial News	28,000,000	
17. WGN-TV, Chicago	25,000,000	
18. Black Ent. Network	18,000,000	

Source: Compiled from various trade publications.

A growing percentage of the country's cable systems also solicit advertising locally. With special format arrangements, commercial messages are inserted into feeds from cable networks, as well as local cable origination programming. In large metropolitan areas, numerous cable systems frequently link together on an *interconnect basis* to enable advertisers to purchase simultaneous market-wide cable advertising.

In addition to its potential as a competitor for advertising revenues, cable undoubtedly will continue to affect the broadcast TV industry in other important ways, such as:

A leveling effect between TV stations. Stations that have experienced coverage problems due to channel assignments, especially UHF outlets, can enjoy reception quality through cable equal to any other TV station. With signal equality come direct benefits to some broadcasters and added competition for others.

Increased competition for audiences. Evidence of audience fragmentation from cable-originated programs is clear, although broadcast television continues to dominate overall viewing patterns, even among cable subscribers. At this date, no one can foretell the degree to which CATV programs will dissipate over-the-air station viewing as cable continues to expand.

A decreasing supply of certain types of entertainment programming. Major sports events and movie packages may not be so readily available to television stations as the cable industry derives increasing amounts of income from pay-TV operations. (NOTE: In the late 1980s, about 36 percent of the nation's homes subscribed to pay-TV services, the largest of which was Home Box Office.)[7]

The Advertiser's Concern

In selecting any station or group of stations for a particular campaign, advertisers generally strive for four basic elements:

1. Cost efficiency—getting the best station and air time for the dollars expended.
2. Maximum coverage—reaching the most prospective customers as often as possible.
3. Image enhancement—obtaining ideal commercial positions that contribute to favorable company and/or brand reputation and prestige.
4. Communication effectiveness—affecting listeners or viewers in the manner intended; laying the groundwork of information and persuasion necessary to stimulate sales.

Sometimes the most powerful stations are selected, sometimes specific network offerings are most appropriate, and sometimes an arrangement wherein both radio and TV stations work together proves most expedient. Program popularity and overall program environment must be considered, and once in a while it is a station's advertiser services—in terms of merchandising or research—that tip the scales in terms of station choice. Affiliation status, regulatory involvements, and general economic stability of a station may also have a bearing.

In short, advertisers and their agencies look to stations and networks as communication partners in reaching the "right audience" at the "right time," in the "right place," with the "right message." It is a tall order, but one that broadcasters fulfill anew each day. Chapter 3 will discuss some of the factors that help media buyers evaluate competing stations.

Study Questions

1. Explain the FCC's ownership rules for the broadcast media. (a) Do you think they are fair? Explain. (b) What changes do you believe these rules will have to undergo in the future as the number and types of media outlets increase?

2. Differentiate clearly between independent stations and stations that are independently owned.

3. If the manager of a TV station contemplating network affiliation came to you for advice, what kinds of information would you request before making a recommendation? (Remember that there are several types of networks.)

4. Under what circumstances would the station with the lowest rates in a given area be an unwise buy for an advertiser? What about the station with the most power? And the one with the largest audience?

ASSIGNMENT 2-A
List the radio stations in an assigned area, classifying them in the following categories: (a) AM or FM; (b) classes of stations: I, II, III, IV, A, B, or C; (c) network affiliation; (d) ownership; (e) basic program format; and (f) apparent target audience.

ASSIGNMENT 2-B

List the television stations in an assigned area, classifying them in the following categories: (a) VHF or UHF; (b) network affiliation; (c) ownership; and (d) any notable program emphasis.

ASSIGNMENT 2-C

List ten prominent advertisers on network TV and ten prominent advertisers on leading local radio stations. Indicate what types of products and services are most evident and whether the advertisers follow the patterns typical of the industry as mentioned in Chapter 2. If the approaches seem different, explain how.

ASSIGNMENT 2-D

Given an assigned cable network, indicate its type of programming, its likely target audience, and the types of advertisers who use the network.

ASSIGNMENT 2-E

Interview an official of a local broadcast station to determine its organizational structure. List your questions.

ASSIGNMENT 2-F

Given an assigned cable system, determine its number of subscribers; stations carried (local and imported); cable networks carried; local origination channels, with relative popularity of each; acceptance of advertising; and local ad rates.

Notes

1. The Communications Act of 1934, 45 U.S.C. § 5, §§ 1, para. 151 et seq. This act, Pub. L. No. 416 (1934), is reprinted in Frank J. Kahn, ed., *Documents in American Broadcasting*, 4th ed. (Englewood Cliffs, N.J.: Prentice-Hall, 1984).

2. Although broadcasting is regulated by the FCC, it is not regarded as a common carrier, such as the telephone and telegraph industries, which may not discriminate among prospective customers in the use of their facilities.

3. FCC, *Second Report and Order* (Docket 18110), 32 R.R. 2d 954 (1975).

4. Herbert H. Howard, *Group and Cross-Media Ownership of Television Stations: 1989* (Washington: National Association of Broadcasters, 1989).

5. *Broadcasting* (April 6, 1981): 14.

6. *Ibid.* (February 2, 1981): 52.

7. Home Box Office, Inc., initiated the first national satellite interconnected pay network on September 30, 1975, by using transponder time leased on the RCA Satcom satellite.

Suggested Readings

Baldwin, Thomas F., and D. Stevens McVoy. *Cable Communication*. 2d ed. Englewood Cliffs, N.J.: Prentice-Hall, 1988.

Bunce, Richard. *Television in the Corporate Interest*. New York: Praeger Publishers, 1976.

Grant, William. *Cable Television*. West Nyack, N.Y.: Reston, 1983.

Hamburg, Morton I. *All About Cable: Legal and Business Aspects of Cable and Pay Television*. Rev. ed. New York: Law Journal Seminars-Press, 1985. Updated 1986.

McCavitt, William E., and Peter K. Pringle. *Electronic Media Management*. Boston: Focal Press, 1986.

Marcus, Norman. *Broadcast and Cable Management*. Englewood Cliffs, N.J.: Prentice-Hall, 1986.

Newcomb, Horace, ed. *Television: The Critical View*. 4th ed. New York: Oxford University Press, 1987.

Pember, Don R. *Mass Media in America*. 5th ed. Chicago: Science Research Associates, 1987.

Sherman, Barry L. *Telecommunications Management: The Broadcast and Cable Industries*. New York: McGraw-Hill, 1987.

Singleton, Loy A. *Telecommunications in the Information Age*. 2d ed. Cambridge, Mass.: Ballinger, 1986.

Webb, G. Kent. *The Economics of Cable Television*. Lexington, Mass.: Lexington Books, 1983.

ALSO: Check recent issues of *Broadcasting*, *CableVision*, *Television/Radio Age*, and the *Journal of Broadcasting and Electronic Media*.

3

Coverage, Circulation, and Facilities

Although a station's programming policy and network affiliation may be considered major assets, three other elements are vitally important both to prospective advertisers and to station representatives who sell and service advertising clients. Station *coverage* refers to the geographical area in which a station's signal can be received by viewers or listeners if they wish to tune it in. The *circulation* of a station represents the estimated number of people, or households, that view or listen to the station on a regular basis. Station *facilities* consist of the equipment available for production and transmission of programs, as well as the buildings that house broadcast studios.

Although advertisers need not be concerned with detailed technical information, the knowledgeable media buyer understands basic factors that determine station coverage and is aware of the production capabilities of various stations, particularly when unusual production requirements are involved in an advertising campaign.

Station Coverage

A fundamental need in ad campaign planning is that of achieving appropriate geographical coverage. Two questions involved are: Does the coverage area afforded by a station or network coincide with the client's distribution or service area? To what extent is there either a coverage deficiency or excess? Obviously, although national networks are generally suitable for advertising universally marketed products, they may be a poor choice for regional advertisers because of wasted coverage.

Local stations vary somewhat with respect to coverage. Most TV stations tend to be area stations, effectively reaching out from 65 to 75 miles. (Because of inherent technical problems, however, UHF stations rarely blanket the totality of such areas.) Radio stations, both AM and FM, may be categorized into local, regional, and area broadcast outlets.

In terms of practical usage, large-area TV and radio stations are appropriate vehicles for businesses that need advertising reach throughout a metropolitan center and its marketing or trading area. For example, major retail outlets and chain stores, large banks, and regionally distributed products frequently use such stations. Those same large-area stations, however, are usually uneconomical for small business establishments that cater to customers in limited geographical sectors. The latter, typified by the small dress shop, corner drugstore, or local bake shop, may advertise more efficiently on low-power radio stations whose coverage and programming are concentrated in the community where customers live.

TELEVISION
The propagation of television signals is characterized by line-of-sight or direct-wave transmission, utilizing the very short wavelengths of VHF and UHF frequencies. The coverage attained results from

43

a combination of factors, including channel assignment and power radiated, antenna height, and obstructions in the signal path.

Channel assignment and power. Three different portions of the electromagnetic spectrum are used by U.S. TV stations. VHF stations assigned to channels 2 through 6 are identified as low-band stations, and those on channels 7 through 13 are high-band outlets. Beginning with channel 14 and extending through channel 83, TV stations use the ultra-high frequencies (UHF).

Wavelengths become progressively shorter and reception becomes increasingly critical with higher channel numbers (higher frequencies); consequently, the signals from high-band VHF stations are less effective than those on low-band channels. UHF channels, with their extremely short wavelengths, are far less effective than either high- or low-band VHF channels. To compensate for varying degrees of effectiveness, the FCC permits high-band VHF stations to use three times as much radiated power as low-band operations, and UHF stations may operate with up to 5 million watts to overcome severe coverage problems.

In 1952, the FCC established a nationwide television allocation system, designating specific channels for specific cities so as to promote the most effective use of limited frequency space. Stations on a given channel are separated from each other by 160 to 200 airline miles (depending on channel/frequency) to prevent mutual (co-channel) interference while maximizing the number of stations that may be operated. In only a few isolated cases has the FCC allowed TV stations at substandard mileage separations. During the 1980s, however, the Commission began authorizing low-power television stations (LPTV) to serve small communities and urban minority populations wherever their operation can be conducted without interference to full-power stations. Several hundred LPTV stations are now on the air.

Antenna height. Television antennas must be placed high above surrounding terrain to deliver audio and video signals effectively over a large area. Generally, they are located atop towers on high buildings and mountain peaks to take advantage of existing height. When such favorable sites are unavailable, ground-based towers are constructed; some approach 2,000 feet in overall height.

Obstructions. Since television signals are relatively inflexible, any obstruction in the path of propagation may prevent a signal from reaching homes. Thus, both natural barriers, such as mountains, hills, and ridges, and manmade obstructions, including tall buildings, bridges, and monuments, may limit TV coverage. Having the highest possible antenna height above average terrain (HAAT), therefore, enables TV stations to overcome most physical barriers.

Figure 3.1 depicts the propagation pattern for a television station with and without the presence of obstructions. (Coverage maps for all commercial TV stations in the United States and Canada are published annually in *Television Factbook.*) A sample coverage map, including Grade A and Grade B coverage contours (to be discussed later), is presented in Figure 3.2.

Extending TV Signals

Four methods are used to extend TV signals beyond the areas reached by their transmitting facilities. These include two special types of stations—translators and satellite stations—plus cable television and satellite communication. Each performs a different function.

Translator stations. A translator station is a low-power repeater station (typically 10 watts VHF or 100 watts UHF) used to fill in *shadow areas,* or gaps, in the normally expected coverage area of a television station, or simply to extend its reach. A translator rebroadcasts the signal of its parent station on a different channel, beaming the converted signal to a relatively small area. Such repeater facilities are

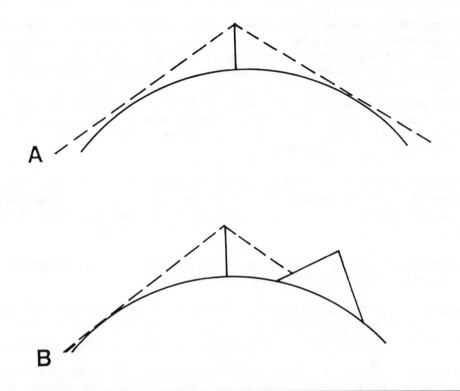

Fig. 3.1. Television propagation pattern. A. Television (and FM radio) signals, behaving as direct waves, do not follow the curvature of the earth. Instead, they are normally receivable to the horizon. The coverage area attained relates positively to antenna heights; that is, the higher the transmitting antenna, the larger the area in which the signal may be received. In the absence of intervening obstructions, TV (and FM) signals may be usable for a distance approaching 100 airline miles. B. Obstructions in the path of TV (and FM radio) signals interrupt the propagation path, preventing the signal from reaching its potential outer destination. Wherever this occurs, TV and FM stations sometimes use additional transmitting facilities to overcome signal-disrupting obstacles.

especially useful in mountainous sections and sparsely populated regions. For example, station WBIR-TV, Knoxville, Tennessee, uses 26 translator stations to supplement its coverage in a mountainous area, and each of the three network affiliates in Salt Lake City uses 100 or more translators to expand coverage throughout a sparsely settled region.

Satellite stations. In contrast to translators, satellite stations use full power and repeat the programming of key stations to coverage areas beyond the range of the originating stations. Although the term is similar to communication satellites, which transmit to earth from space, satellite stations are terrestrial, or ground-based, differing from regular stations only in that they originate little, if any, programming of their own. Satellite stations are most prominent in sparsely settled rural areas of the West; examples may be found in such states as Nebraska, Montana, Colorado, and the Dakotas. Advertising on TV stations that operate satellite transmitters is usually sold in a single package, using a combined rate card.

Cable television. Cable television represents a third means of extending a station's coverage. The original purpose of cable TV, or community antenna television (CATV), was to enable residents in poor reception areas to receive TV service. As noted in Chapter 2, the cable industry has expanded far beyond its humble beginnings. Cable now offers subscribers not only broadcast signals, but also cable-originated programming and other telecommunications services.

Today, cable tends to improve reception for all TV stations, but especially for UHF and high-band VHF outlets. Independent stations perhaps receive the greatest benefit because their signals may be imported without regard to distance; however, under FCC rules, the signals of network affiliates may not be imported into the immediate markets of other stations affiliated with the same network. Particularly favored are a select group of independent stations whose signals are delivered to cable systems through satellite transmission. These outlets are known, of course, as *super stations*. On the other hand, signal importation into a broadcast market means added competition for viewers, resulting in some dilution of market impact from local stations, as well as copyright and program exclusivity problems for the stations and program distributors.

Most cable systems also offer programming (especially movies) under a pay cable arrangement that requires payment of an additional monthly fee above the basic subscription rate. (Recall from Chapter 1, however, that cable systems that beam programs to homes by wire themselves receive these programs by satellite.)

The transmission of audio services to homes by cable is on the rise, too. Hook-ups to high-fidelity receivers bring subscribers musical programming in full stereo.

Satellite communication. Communication satellites are similar to ordinary broadcasting antennas—but they are situated some 20,000 miles above the earth. More than a dozen of them now serve North America, and they transmit both television and radio signals, telephone calls, and computer-data transmissions.

In 1982, the FCC authorized a direct satellite broadcasting service (DBS) to the public for the first time. Options include advertiser-supported as well as subscriber-supported (pay-TV) broadcasting. Although several companies made plans to enter this exciting new TV venture, only one actually launched a DBS service. The failure of that project, which depended on subscriber fees, discouraged others so much that all DBS plans were quickly abandoned. Apart from the possible usage of DBS to transmit the much heralded high-definition television (HDTV), there appears to be little likelihood that a separate DBS broadcasting service will be undertaken anytime soon in the United States.

One of the reasons for the failure of the first DBS effort was that, during the same era, several hundred thousand potential customers installed satellite receiving antennas (backyard dishes) and began picking up cable network interconnect feeds for which they paid no fee. Most cable networks signals are now transmitted in a scrambled mode and are made available for a monthly fee to satellite dish owners. As a result, cable network services unwillingly became a form of direct satellite broadcasting that was particularly valued by viewers in remote, noncabled locations.

A typical coverage map for a television station is shown in Figure 3.2. The inner circle denotes the Grade A, or primary coverage area, while the outer circle indicates the station's Grade B, or secondary coverage.

The effective coverage of competing TV stations may be compared by examining published maps, such as those found in *Television Factbook* and illustrated in Figure 3.2. Additional insight into comparative station coverage may be gained by examining channel assignment/power, antenna HAAT, the number of satellite and translator stations, and cable carriage of individual stations.

The chart shown in Table 3.1 provides such a comparison. Note that the lower channel stations tend to have greater total coverage areas than those of stations on high-band channels. In contrast, the high-band stations, utilizing more power, generate larger primary coverage zones.

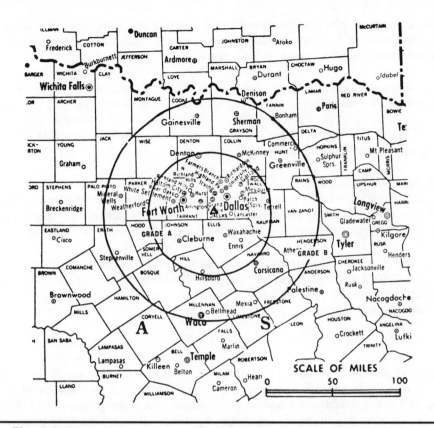

Fig. 3.2. Television station coverage map, KDFW-TV, Channel 4, Dallas-Fort Worth. (*Television Factbook* No. 56, 1988. Washington, D.C.: Television Digest. Copyright American Map Corporation, New York, No. 18256-C.)

Table 3.1. Television station comparison market: Metro City, USA

Station	Channel	Power (kw)	HAAT (feet)	Grade A Radius (miles)	Grade B Radius (miles)	Translators	CATV Subscribers
KAAA-TV	10	316	850	50	70	45	160,000
KCCC-TV	7	316	1010	48	70	32	78,000
KVVV-TV	5	100	1480	38	75	24	45,000
KZZZ-TV	3	100	1050	40	75	6	225,000
KUUU-TV	30	1,800	1100	35	65	10	205,000

FM RADIO

The FM broadcast band consists of 100 channels (200 kHz wide), extending from 88 to 108 mHz in the very high frequency (VHF) range. Frequency modulation broadcasting uses direct wave transmission, which, like television propagation, requires high antenna heights for effective coverage. In contrast to AM's ground-wave and sky-wave propagation, FM signals cover a constant service area during daytime and nighttime hours. Most FM stations transmit stereophonic signals, taking advantage of high-fidelity sound reproduction.

The FCC allocated FM channels to specific communities in order to utilize the spectrum as fully and as efficiently as possible. Thus, because of the high predictability of FM coverage, both daytime and nighttime, co-channel FM stations were spaced apart at optimum mileage intervals. The first 20 channels were designated for noncommercial stations, while three classes of commercial stations—A, B, and C—were authorized on the remaining 80 frequencies.

Twenty channels were established for use by Class A stations, which are intended to serve relatively small communities, cities, or towns and their surrounding rural areas. These stations generally are restricted to 3,000 watts of effective radiated power (ERP) and a 300-foot antenna height above average terrain (HAAT). Class A FM stations equate roughly in coverage with Class IV local AM outlets, which will be discussed in the next section.

The remaining 60 commercial FM channels are designated for Class B and Class C stations. A Class B station provides service to a sizeable community or town or to the principal city or cities of an urbanized area. Class B stations, which are mainly located in the urban Northeastern region, normally are restricted in coverage to the equivalent of 50,000 watts ERP, with 500-foot antenna HAAT.

Class C outlets provide the greatest coverage of the three types of FM stations. They may operate with as much as 100,000 watts ERP and antenna HAAT of 2,000 feet. Intended to serve a central city or town and large surrounding area, a Class C FM station may provide effective coverage for a distance of 75 or 80 miles from its transmitter.[1]

AM RADIO

Standard broadcast or AM radio operates in the medium frequency range; waveforms transmitted range from 600 to 1,800 feet in length, compared with VHF television wavelengths of 4.7 to 18 feet and UHF lengths of 1.2 to 2.1 feet. As a result of the longer and, consequently, more flexible waveforms propagated, AM broadcasting effectively travels much greater distances than does television or FM radio.

The propagation of AM radio consists of ground-wave and sky-wave signals, as shown in Figure 3.3. Ground waves tend to follow the curvature of the earth and establish the primary service area of an AM station. Sky-wave signals, which are lost in space during the daytime, are reflected to earth at night, often at great distances, by the ionosphere. The usefulness of sky-wave signals is limited largely to 60 clear channel frequencies that are kept free from nighttime interference. Service areas of stations other than dominant clear channel (50,000 watt) outlets are generally reduced after sunset due to ionospheric reflection; coverage deterioration results from mutual interference between stations assigned to the same regional or local frequency.

Overall coverage of AM radio stations is determined by a combination of factors, including the type of frequency (clear channel, regional, or local); the frequency itself (high, middle, or low position on the dial); the power radiated; the soil conductivity; and the type of antenna used.

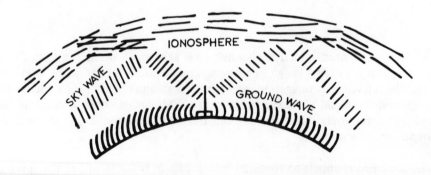

Fig. 3.3. AM radio propagation pattern. The AM ground-wave signal remains close to the earth, following its curvature. AM sky waves radiate outward into space. At night, however, these waves are reflected back to earth by the ionosphere.

Frequency and power. Frequencies on the AM radio band are divided into three classes for local, regional, and large-area service. The extent of coverage by any given station depends largely on the type of frequency to which it is assigned, as well as the amount of authorized power. In addition, technical characteristics are such that low radio frequencies provide greater coverage for any given amount of power than do high frequencies. Classes of stations and frequencies will be discussed shortly.

Soil conductivity. The ground-wave signal radiated from an AM station hugs the earth as it moves outward from the station's antenna. The conductivity of the soil in the signal's path significantly affects the distance it can travel and, therefore, the extent of effective coverage. Heavily mineralized soils absorb much of the radiated signal, thus restricting its ability to traverse the land. In contrast, soils high in loamy content and relatively free from mineral deposits facilitate movement of the ground-wave signal.

The FCC has categorized soil types throughout the country to assist engineers in predicting station coverage. In general, soil conductivity is most favorable in the Midwest and areas adjacent to the seacoasts and usually poorest in mountainous regions. Even local soil conditions affect the strength of a station's ground wave. The most favorable sites for AM radio transmission are moist, low embayments and riverbottoms. High, well-drained locations rarely prove as effective.

Type of antenna. The principal concern with respect to a station's antenna is whether the station transmits a directionalized or a nondirectionalized signal. If the propagation pattern is nondirectional, the signal radiates with equal strength in all directions, usually resulting in a circular coverage pattern (although sometimes the circularity is distorted by extraneous factors). When an AM signal is directionalized, the resulting coverage become something other than circular (see Figure 3.4). Directional

KIRO Newsradio 71

DAYTIME COVERAGE

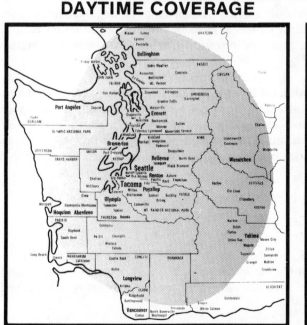

NIGHTIME COVERAGE

Fig. 3.4. Typical nondirectional and directional coverage patterns in AM radio. As the daytime and nighttime coverage patterns of KIRO, Seattle, indicate, a nondirectional antenna normally produces a circular coverage pattern, but a directional antenna system produces an irregular pattern. Such directional systems are used to prevent or minimize interference between stations on the same frequency. (Courtesy of KIRO NewsRadio 71, Seattle)

antennas, which function through use of multiple towers (antennas), are used primarily to prevent interference between stations operating on the same or adjacent frequencies. The daytime nondirectional and nighttime directional coverage patterns of KIRO, Seattle, are shown in Figure 3.4.

Classes of AM Stations

Three types of AM frequencies and four classes of AM stations are involved in radio broadcasting. Frequencies are identified as clear, regional, and local, and stations are designated as Class I, Class II, Class III, and Class IV.

Clear channel. Clear channel frequencies were established by the FCC to provide dependable radio service to large areas of the country by a limited number of high-power (50,000 watt) radio stations. Such stations may be heard for up to 200 miles during the daytime, depending on soil conductivity, and for much greater distances at night due to ionospheric signal reflection. Thus, clear channel AM stations are particularly effective in providing nighttime service to remote rural areas.

Two types of 50,000 watt stations are accorded dominance on clear channels. Class I-A stations usually provide the only fulltime service on clear channels in the continental United States. Typical Class I-A 50,000 watt stations include KFI, Los Angeles (640 kHz); WSM, Nashville (650 kHz); WLW, Cincinnati (700 kHz); WGN, Chicago (720 kHz); and WCCO, Minneapolis (830 kHz). Class I-B clear channel stations differ from I-A only in that two stations share the dominance of a frequency. Such codominant stations are widely separated geographically to prevent mutual interference. For example, WCKY, Cincinnati, and KFBK, Sacramento, share the dominance of 1530 kHz as Class I-B stations. In addition, numerous Class II, or secondary, stations operate on many of the clear channels, although their operations are restricted, usually by limited hours of service, to prevent interference with dominant stations.

Regional channels. Class III stations occupy regional channels and serve principal population centers and their rural neighbors. Class III stations may operate with power outputs of 500, 1,000, 2,500, or 5,000 watts and may provide either fulltime or daytime-only service. Assignments on regional frequencies range from 25 to as many as 80 stations, but because of the number of stations operating on each of the 41 regional channels, most Class III stations must use directional antennas to minimize mutual interference.

Local channels. Class IV stations, which operate with 1,000 watts daytime and nighttime, occupy the six local channels (1230, 1240, 1340, 1400, 1450, and 1490 kHz). Service is restricted to localized areas, such as a small town and its immediate environs, a medium-size city, or a portion of a metropolitan area. Because of their limited coverage, Class IV outlets are closely spaced, frequently at intervals of 60 to 80 miles; thus, the proximity of local stations to each other has permitted the assignment of nearly 200 stations to each of the six local channels.

Coverage and Circulation

The strength of a broadcast signal declines, or *attenuates,* progressively with distance from the station's transmitter. The FCC has established criteria for measuring the signal of radio and television stations sufficient to provide three levels of service—principal city service, grade A (primary) service, and grade B (secondary) service.

Each TV station is expected to deliver satisfactory picture quality at least 90 percent of the time for at least 90 percent of the receiving locations within its principal city. Grade A service contours are based on satisfactory reception at least 90 percent of the time for at least 70 percent of the receiving locations, and grade B contours represent satisfactory service at least 90 percent of the time for at least 50 percent of the receiving points. Similarly, both AM and FM radio signals can be measured for city grade, primary, and secondary levels of coverage. (Again, refer to Figure 3.2 for a sample TV coverage map.)

The potential audience for any station is the total number of households (or people) able to receive a usable signal from the station. Normally, this audience is considered to be the households (or population) located within grade A and grade B coverage zones.

A station's *circulation* is the estimated number of different (unduplicated) households in which persons tune to the station regularly. Some households within a station's coverage area watch or listen to a given station daily, others less frequently, and still others not at all. While a station's circulation is likely to be concentrated within its primary and secondary coverage areas, some audience members may be attracted from beyond the grade B contour. For example, television set owners in remote locations may use high-gain receiving antennas to pull in distant signals. Also, cable subscribers, in both remote communities and urban centers, frequently watch distant stations. And nearly everyone has had the "freaky" experience of pulling in a very remote radio station at night, particularly on a car radio while traveling from state to state. Although such listening may occur, because it is outside grade A and B areas, it is not of much interest to advertisers.

CIRCULATION DATA: SOURCES AND DEFINITIONS

Circulation data for TV stations are produced by the Arbitron Company, which derives its information from the sampling of viewing behavior in every county in the United States. As one of the country's leading audience research organizations, Arbitron provides information on total station reach, on both a weekly and a daily basis, as well as county-by-county circulation for each station. These data are published in the annual editions of *Television Factbook*.

Net Weekly Circulation (NWC) is defined as the estimated number of unduplicated households that view a station for at least five continuous minutes at least once a week during the rating season. Average Daily Circulation (ADC) refers to the estimated number of different television households reached by a given station for at least five continuous minutes each day of the week.

Media buyers interested in comparing two or more TV stations can use NWC and ADC information as general indexes to overall station reach.

The following example illustrates such circulation data for four hypothetical stations in a television market.

Station	NWC	ADC
WWWW-TV	600,300	425,800
WXXX-TV	561,000	376,700
WYYY-TV	582,900	404,400
WZZZ-TV	263,700	147,900

NWC data may be used to determine the location of a TV station's audience on a county-by-county basis or to compute the regular audience of networks and station groups (by combining the data for all of the individual stations).

The best compilation of radio audience data is in *American Radio*, published twice each year, spring and fall, by James H. Duncan, Jr.[2] This reference book provides summary data on radio audiences in all metropolitan U.S. markets and ranks each market's radio stations in both cumulative (cume) and average-quarter-hour reach.

FACTORS AFFECTING CIRCULATION

A number of factors influence the extent of a station's circulation or regular audience reach. Two of the most important are the strength and quality of the broadcast signal and the attractiveness of the station's programming to a diverse audience. The public, of course, may alternately choose programs that entertain, inform, or provide useful service. However, the technical ability of a station to deliver its programming with a dependable signal is also a strong determining factor in the selection process.

Other factors include the amount and quality of promotion used by a station, the strength and dependability of competing stations, and even a station's dial position. It is more advantageous, for instance, for a station to be located between or near other stations than it is to be isolated at a distant end of the dial.

Although circulation and cume data are useful indexes of a station's reach, more detailed information on the size and demographic composition of audiences for specific programs is needed in planning an advertising campaign. Audience measurement is discussed more fully in Chapter 13.

Production Facilities

Advertising carried by television and radio stations may take the form of commercial messages produced outside the station or those produced through the station's own facilities. (In practice, it is extremely rare for a commercial to be produced by a radio or TV network.)

National commercials are generally produced at independent production centers under supervision of the advertising agencies that handle the accounts. Television commercials may be recorded either on videotape (VTR) or on film, with duplicate copies of completed commercials delivered to each station and/or network in the media schedule. Instead of physical shipments, satellite transmissions are widely used today to deliver commercial material to TV stations. Radio commercials produced by agencies are delivered to stations and networks on audio tape or electrical transcription (disc) recordings. In some cases, satellite feeds also are used for delivery of radio commercial matter.

Commercial messages for local advertisers, both agency and nonagency clients, frequently must be produced at local radio and TV stations, where technical capabilities may vary considerably. Advertisers and agencies need to be familiar with both the equipment and the production expertise available at various stations under consideration.

Radio production facilities normally are quite simple and consist of a microphone, perhaps a turntable for playing music or sound effects, and audio tape recording equipment. The last item includes both reel-to-reel and cartridge recorders. Some radio stations, however, house sophisticated equipment such as that shown in Figures 3.5 and 3.6.

In contrast, television production considerations are always complex and include a number of studio cameras (color and/or monochrome); videotape facilities (monochrome, high-band, and low-band color); film chains (monochrome and color); and mobile facilities (electronic cameras, videotape recorders, film and microwave equipment). Much progress has been made during recent years in the improvement of TV production facilities, including more sensitive, lightweight cameras, which are highly portable and usable under low-light conditions; electronic character generators for on-screen graphics; video cartridge (videocart) tape systems; computerized program switching devices; and sophisticated special-effects generators.

Fig. 3.5. Harris 9003 program automation system. This is a revolutionary development in program control in radio broadcasting. It displays the name of the song or commercial currently on the air, plus the names and starting times of upcoming scheduled events. Also, this system lets the station's traffic director punch up a nationally packaged commercial and "match" it with one of a number of local copy tags. (Courtesy of Harris Corporation, Broadcast Products Division)

We will look more closely at equipment in Chapter 11, which discusses commercial production. At this point, however, we need to consider the other half of broadcast advertising's organizational team—the advertising agencies that write many of the commercials aired every day and that place them on the stations and networks just described. These agencies are discussed next in Chapter 4.

Study Questions

1. Differentiate clearly and specifically between station coverage and circulation in terms of their values to prospective advertisers.

2. Explain why all stations with the same amount of power are not as "powerful" in terms of signal outreach.

3. What is a satellite station? What are its values to advertisers? To viewers?

Fig. 3.6. IGM Communications Program Automation System. This is an ultramodern automation program control system for radio broadcasting. Although the system is computer-driven, the operator can make programming changes easily through keyboard commands. Other features include music rotation files with random selection, perfectly matched cartridge playback deck for announcement material, and floppy disk memory backup during operation. (Courtesy of IGM Communications, Bellingham, Washington)

4. Describe and analyze the types of audience promotion employed by the radio and TV stations in your market. During what times of the year do they promote most heavily? Is there an obvious reason for the seasonal patterns you detect?

ASSIGNMENT 3-A

Using data in *Broadcasting Yearbook* and *Television Factbook*, compare and analyze the coverage of the TV stations in an assigned area. Specifically, determine the following:

(a) Are there significant differences in station coverage?

(b) What factors contribute to the differences found?

(c) Do any of the stations use translators or satellite station facilities? If so, how many and where located?

(d) To what extent are the TV stations carried by CATV systems?

(e) Using the form below, prepare a comparative station chart similar to Figure 3.3, ranking the stations in order of extent of coverage.

Television Station Comparison

Market: _____

	Station	Channel	Power	HAAT	Grade A Radius	Grade B Radius	Translators	CATV Subscribers
1)								
2)								
3)								
4)								
5)								
6)								
7)								

ASSIGNMENT 3-B

(a) Determine the NWC and ADC of the TV stations in assignment 3-A.

(b) Rank-order the stations in terms of circulation on the chart below.

(c) Explain the differences in terms of facilities and programming.

Television Station Comparison

Market: _____

	Station	Net Weekly Circulation	Average Daily Circulation
1)			
2)			
3)			
4)			
5)			
6)			
7)			

ASSIGNMENT 3-C

Using data in *Broadcasting Yearbook* (and any obtained from personal contact with stations), analyze the coverage of the major radio stations in the market used in assignment 3-A. Specifically, determine the following:

(a) Are there significant differences in coverage?

(b) What factors contribute to such differences?

(c) Using the following form, prepare a comparative station chart, ranking the radio stations in order of extent of coverage.

Radio Station Comparison

Market: _____

Station	Classification	Power	Frequency	Antenna (Directional or Nondirectional)	Hours of Operation
1)					
2)					
3)					
4)					
5)					
6)					
7)					
8)					
9)					
10)					

ASSIGNMENT 3-D

Visit a local radio or TV station and observe the production of commercials or programs. Outline the procedures that were followed.

Notes

1. A few stations that operated with more than 100,000 watts before the limit on FM power was established were allowed by the FCC to continue using high power. Two such "grandfathered" stations

are WMC-FM, Memphis (300,000 watts), and WRVQ (FM), Richmond (200,000 watts).

2. James H. Duncan, Jr., *American Radio* (Indianapolis, Ind.: Duncan's American Radio). Published semi-annually.

Suggested Readings

Baldwin, Thomas F., and D. Stevens McVoy. *Cable Communications*. 2d ed. Englewood Cliffs, N.J.: Prentice-Hall, 1988.

Etkin, Harry A. *AM/FM Broadcast Station Planning Guide*. Blue Ridge Summit, Pa.: Tab Books, 1970.

Fornatale, Peter, and Joshua E. Mills. *Radio in the Television Age*. Woodstock, N.Y.: Overlook, 1980.

Head, Sydney W., and Christopher H. Sterling. *Broadcasting in America: A Survey of Electronic Media*. 5th ed. Boston: Houghton-Mifflin, 1987.

Kenecht, Kenneth. *Designing & Maintaining the CATV and Small TV Studio*. Blue Ridge Summit, Pa.: Tab Books, 1972.

Pelton, Joseph N., and Marcellus S. Snow, eds. *Economic and Policy Problems in Satellite Communications*. New York: Holt, Rinehart & Winston, 1977.

Smith, F. Leslie. *Perspectives on Radio and Television: An Introduction to Broadcasting in the United States*. New York: Harper & Row, 1979.

ALSO: Check recent issues of *Broadcasting*, *CableVision*, *Multi-Channel News*, *Television/Radio Age*, and the *Journal of Broadcasting and Electronic Media*.

4

The Advertising Agency Business

Whereas commercial broadcasting stations date back to the 1920s, it was as early as the mid-1800s when Volney Palmer, an enterprising newspaper space broker, established himself as this country's first advertising agent. His job was to convince a manageable number of advertiser/clients to run ads in the local press, and his payment took the form of media commissions.

Today's complex marketplace, of course, features an almost endless number of products and services, and all must compete for consumer attention and purchase. Likewise, sales communication occurs through an infinite number of media vehicles and vehicle combinations, and at all hours of the day and night. Obviously, individual agents could not begin to handle these work loads on a direct basis as Volney Palmer did; hence, large, intermediary organizations have become an absolute necessity for the advertising industry to operate efficiently on a large scale.

Functions of the Modern Agency

The modern advertising agency helps advertiser/clients develop and maintain successful, profitable businesses by providing them with well-designed and -executed ads and commercials delivered to target audiences (key buying prospects) at the time, in the place, and with the degree of frequency most beneficial to the stimulation of sales. Also, by keeping a close eye on competitors' advertising efforts, the agency makes expert decisions on how and when to change existing campaigns so clients get the most communication good out of dollars invested.

Another agency function is to supply an objective viewpoint in terms of the advertising problems and opportunities facing each client. Consumers who feel too close to their own situations sometimes call on counseling services in areas of marriage, religion, and career planning. Likewise, advertisers regard the advertising agency as an expert counseling staff with a wealth of experience and talent in creating and delivering the best messages to the best prospects and, generally, serving all aspects of an advertising account. On the other hand, advertisers themselves must be concerned with the packaging and pricing of goods and services; with their overall development, distribution, storage, and maintenance; and with any personal sales demonstrations and brand/trademark/corporate identity programs appropriate at a given time. Advertising is a concern, of course, but can hardly be expected to receive full-time company support.

Finally, through the years, advertising organizations have established valuable working relationships with the broadcast media and with production companies, research establishments, and retail outlets. In addition, many have their own legal staffs, or at least access to legal counsel. Agency personnel represent a wide range of expertise—in marketing and sales, behavioral sciences, English and the humanities, art and graphics, cinematography, and mathematics and computer science. In short, borrowing a line from Midas Muffler Shops, advertising agencies may justifiably claim "We're specialists; we have to do a better job."

In the late 1980s, the nation's 100 leading national advertisers accounted for 76 percent of total network TV expenditures, 61 percent of network cable expenditures, and 44 percent of all spot TV expenditures. In radio, these advertising giants spent 61 percent of all network dollars and 39 percent of spot dollars.[1] In terms of growth, motion pictures (an industry that once considered television a mortal enemy) have become the fastest-growing major advertising category on network television. Reasons cited include both TV's effectiveness in pre-selling customers and cost efficiencies.[2] A 16 percent increase between 1985 and 1986 resulted in a total expenditure of $278.5 million. One picture industry giant alone, MCA, spent $33.6 million in 1986 to tout its films.[3]

At this writing, the top U.S. ad agencies (in terms of broadcast billings) are spending more than $2 billion dollars annually in TV and radio. In terms of network versus spot buys (to be discussed more fully in Chapter 14), these organizations spend about twice as much in network TV as they do in spot TV; in radio, however, the network sum is only a fraction of the spot total.

The American Association of Advertising Agencies (AAAA), established in 1917, is the national trade organization of the advertising business. More than 530 member agencies operate more than 1,625 offices in hundreds of cities both here and abroad. They employ more than 51,000 persons in the United States and are responsible for some 75 percent of all U.S. advertising placed through agencies. AAAA members speak out for advertising self-regulatory efforts and do their best to foster, strengthen, and improve the advertising agency business.

In terms of annual billings, this country's largest agency is Young & Rubicam, with more than $2.3 billion in U.S. billings and more than $4.1 billion in world billings. Its U.S. employees total more than 4,900 and more than 10,800 worldwide. All of the top U.S. agencies are headquartered in New York, with the exception of Foote, Cone & Belding, and Leo Burnett (both Chicago), and Campbell Ewald (Detroit).[4] On the other hand, High Plains Advertising, a successful agency in Dodge City, Kansas, has total billings of only $54,700 and seven employees.[5]

Before moving inside an actual agency to examine its management structure, it should be mentioned that local area advertisers do not often hire agencies. Rather, most of them deal directly with local media (which, in turn, often serve as miniadvertising agencies, performing some of the same functions as the full-scale agency). Obviously, the needs of these advertisers are very narrow in scope and usually can be handled more simply. Chapter 16 will discuss retail advertising in detail, including more specific reasons for avoiding contact with an advertising agency or, in certain instances, for hiring one. For the present, however, we will assume a national advertising situation as we proceed through this chapter.

SPECIFIC AGENCY JOBS

In looking at some specific ad agency jobs, it should be noted that they are not always set up in exactly the same way; however, the following seven departments cover the activities most important to the majority of large broadcast advertisers.

Account Management

Account executives serve as liaisons between their agencies and advertiser/clients, thereby representing one to the other. These people are accounting coordinators, creative critics, planner/strategists, and talented salespersons who are well acquainted with all aspects of individual campaigns. In effect, they must relay and interpret clients' needs and wishes to the rest of the agency team, and they must sell the team's efforts and ideas to client management. These client representatives are most often referred to as product managers or brand managers. They coordinate all marketing activities for specific items, not just advertising. Often, therefore, in their contact with agency executives, the subjects of packaging, pricing, and channels of distribution are discussed.

Creativity

Copywriters and their partners in art (who have important broadcast roles in the creation of television storyboards) interpret sales messages in words and pictures, music and song, sound effects and motion. A unique creative flair is their long suit, but all efforts are channeled (or disciplined) to fulfill specific advertising objectives and to suit available resources—time, money, talent, and production facilities. Increasingly, they are working with in-agency computer graphics systems, too, thereby giving "life" to TV storyboards for purposes of critique and review.

Commercial Production

Commercials may be prepared in prebroadcast form by commercial production teams—for example, for purposes of preview and testing. These teams are experts in technical achievement and quality, and they combine a good grasp of staging, casting, and delivery with equipment and editing know-how. In addition, they are well versed in commercial costs and time requirements.

In effect, the teams are liaisons between writer/artists and ultimate outside producers; they assist with idea communication, on the one hand, and negotiate, on the other. Frequently, they then accompany other account representatives to production centers (notably Los Angeles, New York, or Chicago) to supervise final filming and recording activities.

When actors and actresses are involved, a number of local forms may come into play. For instance, Figure 4.1 shows an agency's advertising release form, which performers must sign before a commercial can be released for broadcast.

Media

Constantly assessing the nature of products, audiences, distribution systems, and competitive offerings, along with available dollars, media planners make vital time-purchasing decisions. The greatest commercials ever written are created in vain if they fail to reach their intended audiences. Furthermore, prospects must be reached at the specific time and with the specific degree of frequency deemed right to stimulate purchase behavior. In the broadcast area, media departments work closely with station representatives, who will be discussed later in this chapter.

Research

Measuring what, when, where, how often, and how much people buy is a well-established activity in marketing and advertising. In recent years, however, ad agencies have increased efforts toward determining the reasons behind specific brand preferences, selective store patronage, and individual choices among competitive service offerings.

Behavioral scientists know that with increased understanding of these reasons comes increased accuracy in predicting marketplace activity. Since attitudinal responses are extremely difficult to deal with, a fair amount of agency research effort may go toward simply developing appropriate measurement methods. Chapters 12 and 13 will consider research procedures and activities in detail. We should note at this point, though, that major agencies may undertake three different types of research:

1. *Market or consumer research:* target market demographics, along with shopping and purchasing habits, product usage patterns, and attitudes toward brands and stores.
2. *Media research:* audience preferences and loyalties in terms of both media classes (television versus radio) and specific media vehicles (soap operas, newscasts, and the like).
3. *Message research:* copy appeals, talent (performer) credibility, and effects of various production techniques.

Seigle Schiller Rolfs & Wood, Inc.

Advertising, Public Relations and Marketing Services.

Financial Plaza of the Pacific, Honolulu, Hawaii 96813, Telephone (808) 531-6211

Advertising release

(Individual)

...., 19......

SEIGLE SCHILLER ROLFS & WOOD, INC., Agents, and

(Client) ....

Dear Sirs:

I certify that I am at least 18 years of age, by birth date being ...., 19..........., and have the right to contract in my own name and to the extent herein set forth.

For good and valuable consideration received by me from you, the receipt whereof I hereby acknowledge, I hereby irrevocably grant to you and to your respective officers, employees, nominees, customers, agents, licensees, successors and assigns (collectively called the "grantees"), the absolute, unrestricted and unlimited license, right, permission and consent to use and reuse, disseminate, copyright, print, reproduce, publish and republish, for any and all trade purposes or commercial or other advertising purposes, and in any and all media, my name, signature and likeness, and any portraits, pictures, photographic prints, (motion pictures, television), or other representations of me, or in which I may appear, or any reproductions or sketches thereof or parts thereof, photographic or otherwise, with such additions, deletions, alterations or changes therein as you in your discretion may make, either separately or together with my name or a fictitious name, or the name of another person, with or without any advertising statements or testimonials made by me, or authorized by me which you may, in your discretion, prepare for use in connection therewith.

WITNESS my hand and seal the day above written.

Name .... (L.S.)

Address ....

Witness ....

Address ....

Talent Agent ....

(Note: If the person signing the above release is under eighteen years of age, the parent or legal guardian of such person must sign this document in the space provided below.)

I, the parent or guardian of the person who executed the foregoing release, for good and valuable consideration received by me from you, the receipt whereof I hereby acknowledge, hereby join in and consent to the above release and the execution thereof by my child (ward).

I hereby agree to indemnify the above-mentioned grantees and hold each of them harmless from and against any claim hereafter made by said child (ward) as a result of any disaffirmance by him or her of the foregoing release.

....

Parent or Guardian

....

Address

Witness ....

Address ....

Talent Agent ....

Fig. 4.1. Agency's advertising release form. (Courtesy of Seigle, Schiller, Rolfs, and Wood, Inc., Honolulu)

Actual *product* testing and research is normally conducted by the manufacturer. Obviously, though, creative teams do make use of the results in developing copy themes and sales propositions.

In all of these cases, agencies are often as concerned with competitive data as they are with data related specifically to their own clients.

Merchandising

In Chapter 2, it was noted that broadcast merchandising activities tie radio and TV stations (and their programming) in with sponsors' products—often at the point of purchase and sometimes as a means of bidding for additional sponsor dollars by capitalizing on successful campaigns. Advertising agencies may find it profitable to use client success stories to attract new accounts, but the public is not at all interested in which agency does which commercials. In the stores, therefore, agency merchandising activities involve coordination of advertising messages with actual products—their packaging, pricing, and availability, along with coupons, door-to-door sampling, and premium offers where they exist.

Obviously, agency merchandising departments work very closely with retail stores and are well acquainted with competitors' merchandising and advertising efforts. Finally, some agencies hire full-time merchandising personnel to develop and test new product ideas for clients.

While a separate department handles agency publicity—advertising columns and programs in major newspapers and on the air, promotions in trade publications, and guest appearances by key personnel—station promotion departments have no counterpart in advertising agencies. While stations compete with each other for a share of the listening and viewing audience as well as a share of the advertising dollar, agencies are not greatly concerned with public acceptance. They naturally put their clients first, and in the process they become, and remain, largely anonymous themselves.

On the other hand, an advertiser's sales promotion activities should not be confused with merchandising efforts either. As one ad agency executive puts it, sales promotion (coupons, refunds, premiums) moves a *product,* and merchandising (point-of-sale materials such as package flyers and brochures) sells the *idea* that moves the product.

Of all the available media, radio has often been considered the most effective and efficient for stimulating consumer action in terms of coupon redemption.[6] Recently, however, Product Movers, one of the largest printers and distributors of free-standing inserts (FSIs) in Sunday newspapers, launched an "electronic FSI" program. Coupon drops are preceded by TV spots. The 30-second spots, which open with a shot of the front cover of the upcoming FSI, air on Thursday nights before a Sunday insertion. Tests have already shown a 10 to 15 percent increase in consumers' intentions to look for and clip coupons for the products shown in the TV commercial.[7]

Account Service

Finally, account service personnel are liaisons between account management and production operations. They order graphics, mail prints and recordings, pay commercial performers, and generally handle all bookkeeping and traffic responsibilities crucial to smooth business performance.

Figure 4.2 shows the organizational structure of an agency with forty clients and $8 million annual billings.

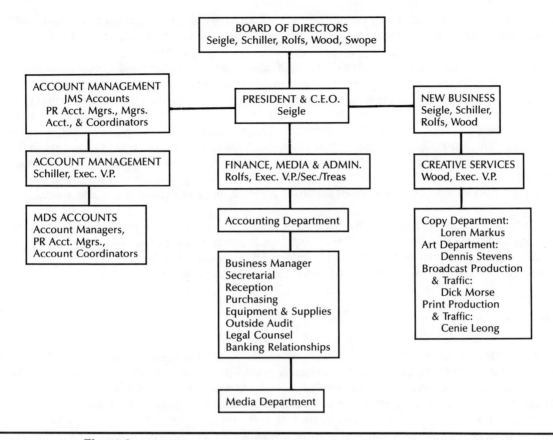

Fig. 4.2. SSR&W, Inc., organization chart. (Courtesy of Seigle, Schiller, Rolfs, and Wood, Inc., Honolulu)

Choosing an Agency

How does an advertiser choose the right agency—one that will do the best job in all of the above departments? It is rarely an easy decision, so a prospective client often asks a number of different agencies, usually within reasonable proximity, to bid for its account by delivering proposed ad campaign ideas in a formal presentation. Involved can be everything from rough scripts to actual recordings and media plans on slides, along with research proposals, suggested merchandising appeals, and related budgetary breakdowns.

Of course, an advertiser whose media concerns are mainly broadcast oriented also will want to check out an agency's track record (and professional contacts) in radio and TV, such as past successes and failures for a variety of clients whose advertising efforts were concentrated in these media. Similarly, a degree of broadcast research expertise may be of importance to certain advertisers.

A few other key advertiser questions might be:

1. Is a prospective agency team familiar with my specific type of product? And if they already handle a competing account, do I want them to work for me?
2. How long does this agency generally keep its clients, and what is the size and overall nature of the existing client roster?
3. What kind of people (and how many) would service my account, especially if I have a product

requiring creative input from young people, women, minority groups, or other specific individuals?

4. What methods of payment does this agency follow, and are they satisfactory to me?

Some of the nation's largest advertisers, such as Procter & Gamble and General Motors, use nearly a dozen different advertising agencies to handle their many products. While there is no law prohibiting one agency from working on competing accounts (even for the same manufacturer), many agencies refuse to do so on ethical grounds and/or for fear of losing an existing client. There are notable exceptions, however. Foote, Cone & Belding, in Chicago, created TV advertising that was highly successful in positioning Klear and Bravo floor waxes (both made by Johnson Wax) as two very different products in the minds of consumers. One was presented as a "floor-beauty" product, and the other as an "easy-to-care-for" item. Both Klear and Bravo succeeded in taking sales away from competitors, but not from each other, since each carved out its own separate, distinct market niche and share.

On the other hand, a given advertiser might use a full-service ad agency for only part of its advertising campaign. The rest is then farmed out to one or more suppliers, who, it is felt, can do a particular job more effectively, more efficiently, and/or less expensively (without sacrificing quality). We will consider the specific responsibilities of these outside service organizations shortly.

Agency Payment

As pointed out in Chapter 1, the broadcast media as we know them today could not survive without advertising. Similarly, if it were not for media outlets to carry commercial messages to consumer prospects, advertising agencies could not function. Binding this dependency relationship is what is called the recognition system. As long as an agency is reputable—that is, it pays its bills when they are due, is free from outside manipulation or financial control, and generally conducts business in a professional manner—it is recognized by the major media. It then qualifies for a media commission, one of two major methods of payment for advertising agencies.

THE COMMISSION SYSTEM

The commission system, or *straight commission*, dates from the very earliest ad agencies, which served merely as sales agents for newspapers. Under this plan, a recognized agency is compensated through (1) the media commission, a 15 percent discount on the prevailing nationally quoted time cost for the exact hours, minutes, and/or seconds involved; (2) a markup on the costs incurred outside of the agency—mainly advertising production and research materials and services; and (3) standard agency rates for any internal charges that may arise, again usually in connection with production and research, although merchandising efforts may also be involved. In most cases, the major portion of a national agency's income is derived from media commissions.

THE FEE SYSTEM

The fee arrangement, on the other hand, involves payment by advertiser/clients to agencies on (1) an hourly basis, for specific tasks performed; (2) a cost-plus-profit basis, taking into account broadcast advertising materials and activities, plus an agency markup; (3) a fixed or flat fee basis, usually covering a year-long time span and based on anticipated work loads during the period; or (4) any numerous offshoots of these methods or combinations thereof.[8]

A report from the Association of National Advertisers notes that the percentage of advertisers paying under the commission system is about 68 percent; 17 percent claim to operate strictly fee, and the other 15 percent of those surveyed indicated use of both systems (or adaptations thereof).[9] Whatever the plan, however, there are almost always supplemental fees involved for extra client services such as new product development, research, and sales promotion.

THE MATHEMATICS INVOLVED

Regardless of the exact payment system used, it is important to understand two basic, but different, mathematical procedures involved in determining costs. First, in the case of discounts on the cost of media time (the commission system), the process is simply one of multiplication and subtraction. If total time costs from one station amount to $2,500, 15 percent of the figure is $375–the amount the ad agency "pockets" on the deal. For bookkeeping purposes, the procedure looks like this:

Station bills agency	$2,500
Agency pays station	$2,125
Agency bills advertiser/client	$2,500

Finally, there is an added incentive for agencies to pay media bills promptly (usually within ten days), as is true in the case of some water and electric bills sent to consumers in many parts of the country. It is a 2 percent on-time (or cash) discount, granted to the agency, and based on the agency's total cost (which, in the given example, is $2,125). So, since 2 percent of $2,125 is $42.50, the agency may pay as little as $2,082.50 of the original $2,500 bill.

Often, in the spirit of goodwill, agencies pass along this 2 percent dollar savings to their clients. If such were true in this example, the advertiser would wind up paying $42.50 less, or a total of $2,457.50.

Second, we come to the situation in which a markup on a face cost is desired (as may be true under both commission and fee systems). Unfortunately for the nonmathematically inclined individual, the add-on procedure is not quite as simple as the subtraction process. Still, it is just a matter of remembering a two-step rule: (a) the markup percentage is subtracted from 100 percent; and (b) the *remainder* becomes the *divisor,* while the face cost of the item or job in question becomes the *dividend* in a simple division problem. The final quotient is the amount the agency charges the client–enough to clear the face cost and make the intended markup profit. For instance, an "on the books" procedure for a $1,700 face cost and a desired 15 percent markup is:

Outside supplier bills agency	$1,700
Agency pays supplier	$1,700
Agency bills advertiser/client	$2,000
(because 100% − 15% = .85; and $1,700 ÷ .85 = $2,000)	

If no outside supplier is involved and the agency merely sets a $1,700 fee on a particular job, the middle agency payment step disappears and the markup is figured directly. There is no set markup percentage across agencies and specific jobs, but because the 15 percent figure is so firmly established under the media commission system, it is frequently applied to markups as well. On-time and cash discounts, however, apply only under the media commission system.

WHICH SYSTEM TO USE

The commission system, critics complain, may result in agency selection of the most expensive media available (since related commissions are thereby the highest possible). Further, a straight media commission may not reflect the amount of effort required to produce a campaign. Small accounts may consume more agency time than the relatively low-cost media buys would indicate; large accounts, however, resulting in very expensive national media commitments, may demand only moderate amounts of agency input (especially in the case of sustaining creative campaigns utilizing already-proven audio/video treatments).

On the other hand, the fee system has been said to penalize the agency's fast genius and to reward the slow thinker; obviously, if payments are made according to hours worked, it is to the agency's advantage not to hurry. A system proposed to help resolve this controversy is one in which clients would pay their agencies (beyond media and production costs) only if specific advertiser goals were achieved. That is, agency compensation would (somehow) be tied to sales and profits, which would (somehow) be related directly to the creation and placement of ads.[10] As Chapter 12 will discuss, however, defining specific advertising goals and measuring specific advertising achievements are very complex operations.

JOB TERMINOLOGY

Before leaving this section, two terms that are closely associated with the foregoing discussion should be mentioned—nonbillable services and billable services. *Nonbillable* services are the day-to-day, routine operations of an advertising agency. The media commission is said to cover all of these activities, because under this plan the agency receives no other payment for such services.

Billable services are those that occur outside of the agency and that are performed by professional interviewers, cinematographers, acting talent, and the like. Why should the agency receive a markup profit on the work done by nonagency personnel? It is because agency representatives must (1) handle all of the planning activities before making contact with any outside suppliers and write commercials, questionnaires, and other materials; (2) negotiate with several bidders before selecting the right company for the job; and (3) either supervise the commercial production process or handle interpretation and presentation procedures after the research legwork has been completed. Obviously, a great deal of agency time and talent may be involved even in the case of billable services.

The Station Representative

We now need to consider the input of an outside, but closely associated, business partner to the advertising agency—the station representative. Not even the largest radio and television stations have large enough sales staffs and travel budgets to permit calling personally on advertisers throughout the country. Hence, just as an advertising agency serves its advertiser/clients in the creation and placement of ads and commercials, so a station representative (often called simply a *rep*) serves media clients in the sale of time to national spot advertisers.

Local stations do maintain their own salespeople who cover limited geographical areas (and network O&O stations have sales staffs separate from those of their network "parents"); reps thus sell time only in areas other than a station's home market. Since a large number of advertisers today, however, are interested in nonnetwork media schedules, the role of the station rep is a vitally important one.

There are probably two dozen major radio sales reps in this country today, with about half that number in TV. Most are independently owned organizations. In-house rep firms, however, handle national ad sales for network O&O stations, and some firms operate as subsidiaries of station licensees, such as the Westinghouse Group. A possible trend in self-representation also may be emerging as a result of the acquisition of broadcast stations during the 1980s by John Blair & Co., a prominent station representative.

Another trend in sales representation has been specialization of effort by some firms toward types of stations represented in the advertising marketplace. For example, Katz Television and Blair have established divisions that specialize in handling independent outlets. Blair also has specialized lists of stations arranged by network affiliation.

A distinction should be made between the *short-list* and *long-list* rep firms. The first type usually handles national sales for a select list of perhaps 12 to 15 stations, while the latter may represent dozens, even 100 or more outlets. Although the most attractive stations usually receive the greatest amount of sales attention from a rep, it does not necessarily follow that a station is neglected if its rep firm handles a large number of other stations. For example, two of the largest and most successful TV rep firms, Blair Television and Katz Television, each representing more than 125 stations, are structured into numerous divisions. Each of these units handles the national sales effort for a relatively small number of TV stations, thus assuring each outlet strong sales representation.

In 1988, the ABC, CBS, and NBC Spot Sales units represented only their respective network's O&O stations for national spot sales. Group W Television Sales handled only the five TV stations licensed to Westinghouse Broadcasting, its parent firm. In contrast, larger numbers of stations were represented by some firms: Seltel, Inc. (100), Petry Television, Inc. (88), MMT Sales, Inc. (65); and Telerep (50). Several radio reps have numbers in the 200 and higher range. For obvious competitive reasons, though, any one rep firm handles only one radio or TV station per market. (*Television Factbook* provides complete rep/client rosters.)

JOB SPECIFICS

The rep's function is to sell as much time as possible for each station represented, while providing money-saving, time-saving services for advertisers and their agencies. Reps advise station management personnel on programming, cooperative advertising plans (to be discussed in Chapter 16), and overall operating policies. Sometimes they design (or help design) station promotional pieces and conduct or commission research studies for use as selling tools. They study all available market and competitive data and, based on analyses of competitive rate packages, program offerings, and services, may assist in the development of rate cards and special package deals covering selected time periods.

Once they have become thoroughly familiar with their station-clients' facilities, programs and formats, ratings, rates, advertiser services, and accumulated track records, reps call on advertiser and agency media directors. Often, the presentation is for a rep's entire line-up of stations (covering multiple markets).

The Television Bureau of Advertising (TVB) and Radio Advertising Bureau (RAB), trade associations that promote TV and radio as advertising vehicles, can provide valuable assistance to reps as well as to individual station salespeople; it is important to note, however, that the best sales ammunition in the world can backfire if the carrier falls apart at the point of contact. The actual sales delivery, often a full-scale audiovisual presentation before advertising agency personnel, frequently makes or breaks the sale; successful reps are well versed in professional sales tactics and are highly talented presenters in their own rights.

METHOD OF PAYMENT

Most reps are paid on a commission basis, though it is often a negotiated figure rather than the standard 15 percent used between media and agencies. The normal range is about 5 to 20 percent, with lower averages in TV than in radio because of the higher actual dollar involvement in TV.

When a national time-sale transaction has been completed, stations normally deduct 15 percent of the total cost (the agency commission) first, and then base the rep's commission on the rest. In some instances, however, both commissions may be figured on the gross sale.

Alternatives to the Full-Service Agency

A number of companies today, among them major national advertisers such as Lever Brothers, have begun experimenting with in-house (self-contained) advertising agencies. The Singer Company recently moved a $10 million account from an internationally known advertising agency back under its own roof.[11] In such cases, of course, the company's own staff becomes responsible for the advertising campaign, although these people rarely work without a considerable amount of outside assistance.

By dealing directly with media, in-house agencies can obtain media commissions (much to the chagrin of full-service agencies, who maintain that ethically this special discount belongs only to them). On the other hand, although this 15 percent commission stays within the company, it is often spent (many times over) for top-notch writers, film producers, research designers, media buyers, and other specialists whose jobs would otherwise be part of a full-service agency package.

Three so-called a la carte services (the ones most commonly sought) are specifically organized and referred to as creative boutiques, research specialists, and media buying services. All generally work on a negotiated fee basis. The first two jobs are fairly obvious; creative boutiques prepare everything from rough scripts to fully packaged commercials, and research specialists design questionnaires or follow through with actual interviewing, tabulate results, and prepare and present final reports.

Media buying services, however, which purchase radio and TV time schedules, deserve some added attention here. These organizations have been increasing in strength since the mid-1960s, and nearly all major services do the largest percentage of their business in television. The *Standard Directory of Advertising Agencies* provides up-to-date lists of companies in this field. Table 4.1 shows how young some of these companies are.

Table 4.1. Media buying services

Media Buying Service	Founded	Business in TV (%)
Bohbot & Cohn	1985	71
Media Placement Services, Inc.	1985	70
Media Headquarters, Inc.	1984	70
Active Media Services	1983	80
KSL Media, Inc.	1981	60

Source: *Standard Directory of Advertising Agencies,* February-May, 1988.

When media buying services engage in spot buying, negotiation is the name of the game. In fact, when buyers go directly to stations (bypassing the station rep), an example of a transaction that might occur is:

1. Buying service negotiates with station and gets $12 million worth of time for $8 million.
2. Buying service peddles the time to an advertiser for $10 million (saving the advertiser $2 million over the published cost).
3. Buying service pockets a $2 million profit.

In this instance, the station winds up with $8 million, and its rep with nothing. If this same $12-million schedule had been sold through normal rep and ad agency channels, the station would have paid the agency 15 percent (or $1.8 million) of the total, leaving itself with $10.2 million. Then, even if the station paid its rep as much as 15 percent of the rest (or $1.53 million), it would be left holding $8.67 million—a figure solidly above the $8 million it got from the media buying service.

Although buying services can purchase fairly worthwhile blocks of time during periods of light demand, the situation changes when demand is heavy. At that point, stations are reluctant to deal with low-paying media buying firms and generally let them have only leftover time availabilities. Then, too, weaker stations tend to work more freely with these services than do their first-line competitors.

It is important to note that money is not the only form of payment for media time. A number of stations also engage in various bartering activities.

The Barter Alternative

Regardless of its official name, the system of barter (or simply trade) dates back to the early days of commercial radio. When a station owner needed a new car but could not afford one and a local car dealer needed commercial air time but could not afford it, a trade seemed the logical solution. Then, when it came time to buy gasoline for that car, the owner found that relatively low-cost items could be bartered just as easily, and local service station operators were pleased to oblige. Undoubtedly, such necessities as clothing, grocery items, and even furniture for a station and/or its staff were bartered, too.

THE BARTER HOUSE

Some items that a station needs, such as studio equipment and even programs, cannot be traded for air time, because these manufacturers and producers are not in need of broadcast advertising to mass audiences. Thus, another intermediary, called a barter house, has joined the ranks.

Its philosophy is simple: if a station makes major equipment purchases by itself, it either depletes its cash reserves or borrows the money and winds up paying interest. If a barter house buys the equipment, however, and trades it to the station for air time, both problems disappear.

Barter houses get the money needed to purchase equipment from advertisers or agencies who buy time from them instead of going to stations themselves (or to their reps). In examining the situation in detail we find that first, the blocks of time a barter house buys from stations are generally at unpopular hours, available only on a preemptible basis (see Chapter 14), or otherwise not easy to sell. Payment is normally in the form of merchandise—items the station needs for day-to-day operations, those that can be used for prizes in connection with contests and other promotional activities, or, perhaps, things the station can sell later to banks and other nonretail establishments for use as premiums. It should be noted that payment, or partial payment, may also be made in cash.

Second, armed with its supply of time, the barter house turns around and sells the time to advertisers (or to their agencies, since bartered time today can be fully commissionable to advertising agencies). The cost is less than these companies would pay if they dealt with stations directly but still assures a profit to the barter house over the value of the merchandise traded. It should be mentioned, though, that even when a barter house intervenes, each station remains in charge of its commercial line-up; each must clear all product messages scheduled for air time.

The Local Scene

The term barter is used usually with reference to national transactions, while exchanges made locally between stations and businesses are known as *tradeouts* or *tradeoffs*. Time that would otherwise go unsold might be given (as it was decades ago) to a local car dealer, who, in turn, would provide the station with a news car for use in covering local events. In addition, local restaurant tabs (incurred when salespeople entertain clients), as well as airline tickets, are frequently tradeouts, and new stations often find it convenient to trade time for office equipment and furnishings. Unless such transactions are short-lived, however, or at least conducted on a very small scale, stations may foster less than reputable images.

BARTER AND PROGRAM SYNDICATION

Sometimes, advertisers and agencies develop actual TV and radio program series to appeal to audiences in selected markets. Barter syndication involves the exchange of such programs for a certain amount of air time (within these shows) on stations in the chosen areas. It grew out of the demand for lower priced national programming (lower than network fare), as more advertising dollars spent resulted in fewer commercial exposures (because of continuing increases in the cost of time).

Here's an example of how it works. Suppose an advertiser offers a half-hour TV series free (or at a greatly reduced cost) to a station in exchange for two commercial minutes within each program, during which the advertiser can air its own messages. Both sides benefit: the station makes money by selling the remaining commercial minutes within the program (while saving the effort otherwise needed to sell the first two minutes and also saving program production costs); and the advertiser gets into its desired market area at less than the cost of full program sponsorship.

A *pure barter* show in a major market usually gives the national advertiser between two and three minutes for commercials and leaves three or four minutes for the station to sell itself, either to a local advertiser or through its national rep. In a *barter-plus-cash* arrangement, the syndicator requires the station to pay a license fee in addition to giving up one or two 30-second spots.[12]

Examples of well-known advertiser-supported syndicated programs are "Wheel of Fortune," "PM Magazine," and "Entertainment Tonight."

THE SCOPE AND SHORTCOMINGS OF BARTER

Barter is known to be a budget-stretcher, and a reasonable estimate today is that at least 75 percent of all radio and TV stations and more than 1,000 different advertisers are involved in some manner. Approximately 50 program syndicators are active in the industry, but as few as 10 of them probably handle 90 percent of the business. Three of the largest are LBS Communications, Television Program Enterprises, and King World.[13]

Whereas the percentage of national TV revenues claimed by barter in 1980 was only 1 percent (with 1 percent going to cable television and 98 percent to networks), the Television Bureau of Advertising estimates 7 percent for barter in 1990 (and 9 percent for cable, 84 percent for networks). In 1985, independent stations carried an average of 28.5 hours of barter syndication weekly, and for network affiliates the average was 7.7 hours. Both figures represented substantial increases from the previous year, and since independent stations cover 85 percent of the United States, barter is lucrative at present.[14] Although the overall business represents well under 10 percent of all broadcast revenues, the annual outlay is now approximately three quarters of a billion dollars.[15]

Some disadvantages of barter, from the station's point of view, are that it may reduce advertisers' budgets (through the savings it offers); result in a "cheap" image for the station (if too many tradeouts are requested); and cause numerous accounting and other bookkeeping headaches (if excessive tradeouts occur, especially in the areas of food, accommodations, and travel).

There are split feelings as to whether barter funds are drawn from network or from spot budgets, but some ad agencies believe barter is often used to pressure the networks into lowering their advertising rates. In 1990, however, when the financial interest and syndication rule lapses, the big three networks are expected to reenter the syndication market themselves.[16]

From the buyer's viewpoint (advertiser, agency, or barter house), the less-than-ideal time segments available may be seen as a disadvantage, and in some areas the dominant (or, at least, very popular) stations do not make any time available for barter.

As these first four chapters have shown, there is a large number of different people and organizations involved in the broadcast advertising business. And, as is true in the case of all American businesses today, some form of regulation is needed to help ensure smooth operations among them and between them and those they serve. Chapter 5 will discuss the legal front as the next area of concern.

Study Questions

1. Explain how a background in (a) marketing and sales, (b) the behavioral sciences, and (c) English and the humanities would benefit employees in the advertising agency positions described in Chapter 4.

2. For an agency operating under the fee system, which activities do you think would be most difficult to document in terms of time spent working on them?

3. Find some in-store examples of merchandising activities tied in with broadcast advertising. Discuss their strengths and weaknesses.

4. Select a current national radio or TV commercial (or a series of commercials) and identify all of the background steps you believe led to the ultimate airing of the message(s). Then indicate which of those steps would fall under nonbillable services and which would fall under billable services.

5. What exactly is the job of a station representative?

6. Discuss both the advantages and the disadvantages of the system of barter.

ASSIGNMENT 4-A

You have been given an assigned client, media schedule (with costs), and production schedule (with costs). Compute the answers called for.

CLIENT:

SCHEDULE:

MEDIA COSTS:

PRODUCTION SCHEDULE:

PRODUCTION COSTS:

NONBILLABLE SERVICES

1. The stations bill the agency: $_____

2. With no "on-time-payment" consideration, the agency pays: $_____

3. Then, the agency bills the advertiser/client: $_____

4. Now, if the agency had paid its original bill "on time," the total amount paid would be: $_____

5. And then the agency bill to the advertiser/client would be: $_____

6. Finally, the stations (assuming an even division of billings) each pay their representatives: $_____

BILLABLE SERVICES

1. The production house bills the agency: $_____

2. The agency pays: $_____

3. Wishing to make a ___ percent profit on the deal, the agency then bills the advertiser/client: $_____

ASSIGNMENT 4-B

Assume you are the station rep for an assigned station. Prepare a presentation (suitable for delivery before the media department of an agency) on behalf of your client, keeping assigned time limits in mind. Remember the competitive nature of your task, and plan to "sell" accordingly.

ASSIGNMENT 4-C

Given an assigned commercial or campaign, recommend research studies in each of these categories: market/consumer research, message research, and media research. List questions that you feel should be asked to (1) assist the advertiser's current competitive status and (2) indicate how it might be improved.

Notes

1. *Advertising Age* (September 4, 1986):168.
2. *Broadcasting* (August 31, 1981):8.
3. *TV Guide* (June 6-12, 1987):A-69.
4. *Advertising Age* (March 26, 1987):8.
5. *Ibid.*, 18.
6. *Ibid.* (December 21, 1981):35.
7. *Ibid.* (May 11, 1987):86.
8. Burton Vaupen, Robert F. Lyman, and Thomas R. Vohs, "Agency Compensation and Fee Arrangements" (Paper from the 1976 Annual Meeting of the AAAA, May 12-15, 1976, White Sulphur Springs, WV).
9. *Advertising Age* (May 10, 1976):1.
10. *Ibid.* (May 18, 1981):63-64.
11. *Ibid.* (March 15, 1976):2.
12. *Broadcasting* (February 13, 1984):102.
13. *Ibid.* (July 22, 1985):97.
14. *Advertising Age* (September 22, 1986):S-2; and *Advertising Age* (November 3, 1986):108.
15. *Ibid.* (April 27, 1987):2.
16. *Ibid.*

Suggested Readings

American Association of Advertising Agencies. *A Handbook for the Advertising Agency Account Executive.* Reading, Mass.: Addison-Wesley, 1969.

Association of National Advertisers. *A.N.A. Member Practices and Views on Advertising Agency Compensation.* New York: Association of National Advertisers, 1972.

_____. *Selecting an Advertising Agency: Factors to Consider . . . Steps to Take.* New York: Association of National Advertisers, 1977.

Cowan, D. S., and R. W. Jones. *Advertising in the 21st Century: A Model of Advertising Agency Development during the Next Fifty Years.* London: Hutchinson, 1968.

ALSO: Check recent issues of *Advertising Age, Journal of Advertising,* and the *Journal of Advertising Research.*

5

Regulation of Broadcast Advertising

No matter how many companies are involved in their creation and production, commercials must comply with several types of laws. In fact, advertising over the air is regulated at two distinct governmental levels—federal and state—and through enlightened self-regulation by both broadcasting and advertising industries. Federal jurisdiction is divided between the Federal Communications Commission (the broadcasting side) and the Federal Trade Commission (advertising side). The two work closely with each other, particularly when Federal Trade Commission rules have been violated.

Self-regulation of broadcast advertising once operated primarily through the "Codes of Good Practice" adopted by code-subscripting members (stations and networks) of the National Association of Broadcasters. The two codes—one for radio and another for TV—are no longer recognized by the industry, but the principles they set forth still serve as operational guidelines.

Federal Regulation

The federal government keeps a watchful eye on all aspects of broadcast advertising. Sometimes it takes action on behalf of or against an industry member or organization, and sometimes it merely recommends a behavioral course or specific procedure.

THE FEDERAL TRADE COMMISSION (FTC)

The FTC is responsible for protecting the public against unfair and deceptive business practices, including false and misleading advertising. Established by Congress in 1914, the FTC's original purpose was to protect businesses from unfair methods of competition. Under subsequent amendments, it has been granted not only broad antitrust authority, but also the broadest consumer protection powers of any federal agency. The FTC is composed of five members who are appointed to seven-year terms by the president (subject to Senate confirmation). No more than three commissioners may belong to the same political party, and the president designates one commissioner to serve as chairperson. Approximately 1,500 employees work for the FTC in its various bureaus.

Responsibilities of the FTC

The FTC has two principal responsibilities, which have been assigned to its major bureaus:

Working with the antitrust division of the Justice Department, the FTC seeks to maintain free and fair competition in the nation's economy. Its *Bureau of Competition* enforces antitrust and price discrimination laws and conducts broad studies to determine how well antitrust laws are being obeyed and whether new legislation is needed.

Working through its *Bureau of Consumer Protection,* the FTC protects the public from unfair or misleading practices in commerce. Under broad powers granted by Congress, the FTC has authority to bring action against false and deceptive advertising, mislabeling, and misrepresentation of products and their terms of sale (truth in lending and fair credit reporting).

To the FTC, deceptive advertising is any statement or demonstration that could possibly deceive consumers. No proof of deception is required—just proof that a commercial has the capacity to deceive. Recently, the FTC has ruled that celebrities must sign written testimonials for the products they plug, recognizing that occasional exceptions will be made. (Joe Namath, for example, never had to wear the pantyhose his TV commercials promoted.)

Hidden-camera testimonials are bound by the same requirements as all other commercials: everything said must be true, and all demonstrations must be genuine. In addition, however, the people being interviewed must not know their testimonials will be used on the air until after they have spoken, without prompting, of their own free will. Further, affidavits attesting to this situation must be signed. Finally, no interview material may be used out of context in commercials, and there may be no editing of remarks so they appear in an unnatural order.

One last note here concerns messages for detergent products. The law now requires that "dirty clothes" must be stained with the exact type of soil mentioned in the commercial. And these same clothes must be washed in the advertised detergent before they are shown to the viewing audience as "clean."

In addition, the FTC enforces the antiprice-discrimination legislation contained in the Robinson-Patman Act of 1936. One of the major provisions of this law deals with advertising *allowances,* requiring that national or regional firms that make advertising monies available to local retailers do so on a proportional basis without discrimination. When issued, such advertising allowances must be used for bona fide advertising and not as trade discounts. Business organizations that grant financial support to local retail dealers for cooperative advertising (to be discussed in Chapter 16) normally require affidavits from broadcast stations as proof that funds have been used properly.

The FTC and Consumer Protection Legislation

Under the original Federal Trade Commission Act of 1914, protection was provided for the competitor who was conducting business fairly; consumer protection was only incidental until the act was broadened and strengthened by the Wheeler-Lea Amendment. The impetus for this 1938 amendment came in a Supreme Court decision in which the Court held that the FTC was powerless to ban false advertising. Subsequently, Congress enacted the Wheeler-Lea Amendment, which provided the consuming public with the same protection against unfair and deceptive practices as that previously given to business competitors. It also specifically prohibited the dissemination of false advertising about food, drugs, cosmetics, and therapeutic devices and gave the FTC power to obtain temporary restraining orders to prevent allegedly false ads from running until a case could be heard and appropriate action taken.

In 1975, FTC powers were strengthened further with enactment of the Magnuson-Moss Warranty Federal Trade Commission Improvement Act. This measure (1) gave the FTC authority to spell out standards for written warranties given by manufacturers or sellers of consumer products priced at more than five dollars; (2) broadened the FTC's jurisdiction to cover activities affecting commerce as well as those in commerce; (3) permitted the agency to file civil suits seeking consumer redress from unfair or deceptive practices; and (4) established detailed legal procedures to be followed by the FTC in setting rules and policy statements on unfair or deceptive advertising practices.

Activities of the FTC

In carrying out its responsibilities to the nation's business community and its consumers, the FTC does the following:

1. Issues *rule-making orders,* which inform marketers and buyers of legal requirements in particular industries or trades
2. Issues *guidelines* suggesting acceptable advertising practices
3. Issues *advisory opinions* providing advice from the commission on request from individual marketers contemplating specific courses of action
4. Monitors *advertising copy and claims* in all media
5. Enforces an *advertising substantiation program,* which requires that all advertisers be able to support all claims made about products or services
6. Investigates *complaints* made against producers, marketers, and advertisers

Complaint Procedures

Any citizen, group, or company may file a complaint with the FTC concerning advertising (or other practices) regarded as false or deceptive. Complaints must be in written form and must set forth the facts that seem to violate laws administered by the FTC or the Commission's rules. The FTC acknowledges all complaints (involving interstate commerce) and, after evaluation, investigates to determine whether or not a violation has occurred. In addition, the FTC itself may initiate investigations and take corrective action in the public interest.

Complaints involving advertising practices by a business organization may be investigated in person by FTC attorneys or through correspondence. The severity of the alleged violation determines the method of investigation. In any event, a case against an advertiser must show that a substantial number of people have been affected to warrant FTC action and its spending of taxpayers' money.

It should be noted that direct, literally false statements rarely appear in ads or commercials; companies have learned that today's consumer simply will not accept them. False or misleading impressions, however, given through implication (even though an ad contains no tangible falsehoods), are more common. And it is as much an FTC role to match wits with those advertisers who attempt to mislead through implication, as it is a responsibility to take action against those whose advertising is blatantly false.

Once an investigation of deceptive advertising gets under way, the FTC may, if it chooses, obtain a *temporary restraining order* (a court injunction) to prevent the advertiser from continued use of the claim until the case is resolved. The advertiser may then take one of three courses of action:

Voluntary compliance. To speed up action on a case, the FTC permits an alleged violator to sign a voluntary agreement to refrain from the unfair or deceptive practice. No guilt is admitted in such a statement. Although voluntary compliance cannot be enforced legally, the FTC may reopen the case if terms of the pledge are subsequently violated.

Consent order. When an advertiser is charged with a more serious violation, the FTC issues a formal legal complaint. The accused party then has a 30-day notification period before a hearing is scheduled, during which time it may elect to fight the case to conclusion or agree to an out-of-court settlement through a consent order. If the latter approach is chosen (within ten days of the complaint), the consent order is drafted by FTC staff attorneys in conference with the defendant's counsel. Unlike voluntary compliance, the consent order legally binds the respondent; its subsequent violation may result in a severe penalty.

A recent example here was a Firestone Tire & Rubber Company case involving commercials that misled audiences to believe that certain tires were safe under all conditions. The consent agreement called for $550,000 to be spent on a TV commercial shown in primetime news and sports programs; the message made it clear that tire safety depends to a large extent on proper maintenance and careful driving.

Legal opposition. When an advertiser chooses to oppose an FTC complaint (and only a minority of defendants do), it is up to the FTC to prove a violation of the law or the FTC's rules. The case is heard before an FTC Administrative Law Judge, who may ultimately dismiss the complaint or issue a cease-and-desist order, which is a permanent injunction to prevent recurrence of the illegal practice.

The decision of the Administrative Law Judge is subject to appeal to the full five-member commission. And, a respondent may appeal a lost decision (within 60 days) to a Federal Court of Appeals. If an appeal is not filed, the cease-and-desist order becomes final, and its subsequent violation may subject an offender to substantial monetary penalties through civil suits brought by the FTC.

In summary, the FTC attempts to promote competition between business organizations while prohibiting unfair advertising practices. In this regard, the FTC sometimes requires advertisers found guilty of misleading claims to devote a portion of future commercials toward correcting the false impressions. Such corrective advertising has been ordered by the FTC in only a few instances, but it represents another tool for deterring unfair competition and protecting the public.

A Few Cases

A precedent-setting U.S. Supreme Court decision in 1965 made mandatory the disclosure of substitutions, mock-ups, and special props used in TV commercial demonstrations. (A TV spot for Rapid Shave shaving cream had claimed that sandpaper could be shaved successfully if softened with Rapid Shave. In commercial production, however, the "sandpaper" used was a piece of Plexiglas covered with sand.) Then, in 1970, the Campbell Soup Company was called on the carpet for putting marbles in the bottom of a bowl of vegetable soup used in a commercial, because the marbles forced the (lighter) vegetables to the top of the bowl. It seemed, therefore, that the soup contained more vegetables than were actually present.

Granted, a kind of trick was employed by Campbell, but before we join forces with those denouncing the "overstatement of product contents," let us look at the other side. The television camera is not equivalent to the human eye in terms of perceptibility—especially at close range. Hence, when a bowl of vegetable soup is placed under studio lights, no camera can pick up the vegetables that sink to the bottom of the bowl. Left untouched, therefore, the sales message is understated, because commercial viewers cannot see what is "really there" (and what is visible to the naked eye when the product is on the home table). Unfortunately, there are no easy solutions to this dilemma—or to dozens like it.

In the fall of 1975, the Vermont Attorney General's office, on behalf of the State Agricultural Department and the Vermont Maple Industry Council, asked the FTC to investigate television commercials for Golden Griddle syrup. The spots used local people saying they preferred the taste of Golden Griddle to that of real maple syrup. The charge was that spots gave a false impression that residents unanimously preferred this product, though only 223 of 1,000 residents of the town concerned were sampled. Furthermore, that sampling showed that only between 51 and 64 percent preferred Golden Griddle and that only one of numerous varieties of maple syrup was used in the test. In this case, the advertiser voluntarily withdrew the commercials.

In another important case, the FTC ruled that the Warner-Lambert Company be required to spend more than $10 million to tell the public it had been making false claims about its Listerine mouthwash since 1921. Warner-Lambert refused to agree to a voluntary consent order, however, denying that it had advertised Listerine as a cold preventive or cure. The company appealed the FTC ruling, but the U.S. Court of Appeals for the District of Columbia upheld the FTC's action. Upon further appeal, the Supreme Court declined to review the case.

In a recent decision, the FTC found fault with Anacin's commercials, which led consumers to believe the product's claim was based on research evidence when, in fact, no clinical tests had been conducted to support Anacin's assertion that it was superior to other analgesic medications. However, the advertisement contained no specific claim that such superiority had been proven. As a result, the FTC ruled that comparative advertising claims for over-the-counter pain relievers that do not refer to specific medical proof must be supported by test evidence or be qualified by a disclosure that the claim has not been proved or that there are "substantial questions" about its validity.[1]

These are but a few of many cases questioning commercial claims and practices. It is important for readers about to enter this field not only to determine their own personal standards of integrity, but also to remember that they may, at times, wear several different hats, for instance, that of an advertiser, a commercial producer, a legal representative, and a consumerist.

THE FEDERAL COMMUNICATIONS COMMISSION (FCC)

The FCC is another independent government agency directly responsible to Congress. Established under the Communications Act of 1934, the FCC has broad discretionary power to regulate both foreign and interstate electronic communications "in the public interest, convenience, and necessity." Both wire and wireless communication systems come under its jurisdiction.

The FCC is composed of five commissioners, appointed to five-year terms by the president. No more than three of the five commissioners may belong to the same political party, all must be confirmed by the U.S. Senate, and one is designated by the president to serve as chairperson. Some 1,900 people are employed by the FCC in its various bureaus and branches.

Legal Foundations of Broadcast Regulation

During the earliest years of commercial broadcasting, from 1920 to 1927, the radio industry was governed by the Department of Commerce under the Radio Act of 1912. Regulation was minimal, however, and resulted in severe problems of technical interference between stations. In 1927, Congress sought to bring order to the new industry with passage of the Federal Radio Act and the creation of a Federal Radio Commission (FRC). Subsequently, in a move to consolidate the regulation of all electronic communication, Congress passed the Communications Act of 1934. The FRC was replaced with the new and expanded Federal Communications Commission (FCC), a permanent agency empowered to issue rules and regulations as needed to assure that the public's interest was served. Now, as then, the FCC licenses stations, assigns power and frequencies, and requires operating information from licensees on a regular basis.

In addition, it determines whether radio stations operate full-time or part-time, and whether their antenna systems are directional or nondirectional. Finally, it designates the call letters each radio and TV station will use, although licensees are usually granted those they request. For example, WGN radio-TV in Chicago refers to the "World's Greatest Newspaper"—the *Chicago Tribune*—owner of the stations. Other stations in Chicago were named for that area's famous "Windy City" nickname (WIND radio) and for the Chicago Federation of Labor (WCFL).

In other cities, WSB (Atlanta) stands for "Welcome South, Brother," and WIOD (Miami) for "Wonderful Isle of Dreams." WACO was named for its home (Waco, Texas), and KGBS (Los Angeles) for its owner, George B. Storer. San Francisco identifies its famous cable cars through station KABL.

We should note here that while the FCC does license all traditional TV stations, cable systems are answerable only to the local government bodies that franchise them. The argument is that a cable operation is not really broadcasting. Rather, it is *narrowcasting;* the TV signals go through privately owned cables to subscribers who choose to buy each particular service. This issue is a highly controversial one, however.

Under the philosophy adopted in the acts of 1927 and 1934, Congress specifically denied the FCC the power to censor programs or to dictate program policies to stations. Thus, the FCC has no direct control over program content or advertising; such control is exerted mainly through self-regulation by the broadcasting industry and by public opinion. Nevertheless, the FCC indirectly influences stations' programming efforts, as well as the amount of advertising they carry.

FCC Functions and Organization

The FCC is expected to fulfill three major functions: to direct the orderly development of the nation's broadcast and cable communications services; to promote economical and efficient telephone and telegraph services; and to facilitate use of the nation's communications systems in the interests of safety and defense. Like the FTC, the FCC administers laws of Congress and issues its own rules and regulations. It levies penalties against licensees that violate these laws (including fines up to $20,000 per violation, short-term licenses, and license revocation), and issues cease-and-desist orders to halt the violation of its rules.

The FCC staff is divided into five major bureaus:

The Mass Media Bureau is responsible for allocating spectrum space, granting licenses, and reviewing station service.

The Cable Television Bureau handles cable and related matters.

The Common Carrier Bureau deals with telephone, telegraph, and domestic satellite activities.

The Safety and Special Services Bureau handles aviation, industrial, and amateur radio services.

The Field Engineering Bureau monitors and inspects station equipment.

An FCC organization chart is shown in Figure 5.1

The FCC and Broadcast Advertising

Although the Communications Act forbids direct FCC involvement in programming matters, it also requires the FCC to regulate radio and TV broadcasting "in the public interest." Practically speaking, the FCC must make decisions based on its evaluation of the service (programming and advertising) proposed by applicants and that provided by licensed stations; all licensees assume full responsibility for providing programming that does, in fact, "serve the public."

While accepting commercials as a necessity for economic support of the broadcast media, the FCC historically has opposed "excessive commercialism." Therefore, until the deregulation era of the 1980s, the FCC required all applicants for stations to specify the maximum amount of time per hour they would devote to advertising. Then, at license-renewal time, broadcasters were required to do content analysis of past program logs, making comparisons between original promises (maximum number of commercials to be allowed) and actual performance (number of commercials broadcast).

Under "deregulation," however, the commission follows the marketplace theory that competition will resolve public interest issues. In this instance, it believes the public, with its wide choices among stations, will respond favorably to those broadcasters who reasonably limit their advertising loads and negatively to those who accept too many (undefined number) commercials. Thus, the FCC relies on competition among stations to regulate the amount of advertising material broadcast. Indeed, in today's competitive radio and TV environment, stations often limit the number of advertising messages and commercial interruptions to avoid audience loss.

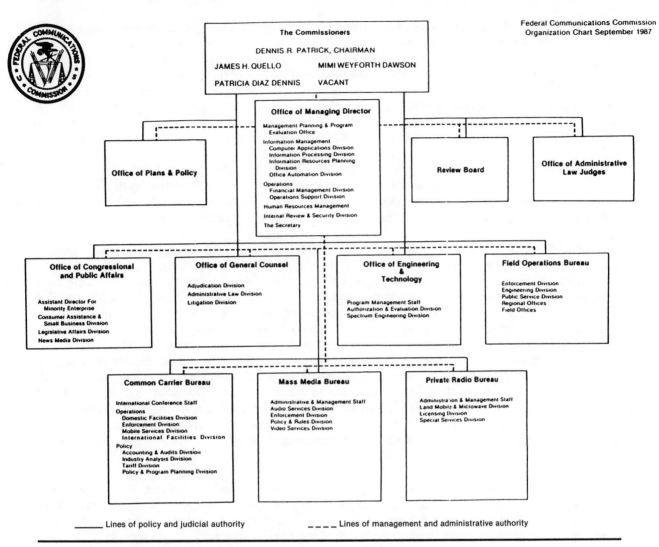

Fig. 5.1. Organization of the Federal Communications Commission. (Courtesy of Federal Communications Commission)

The FCC also enforces laws concerning:

Sponsorship identification. Section 317 of the Communications Act requires that commercial announcements and sponsored programs carry sponsor identification. This rule is intended to safeguard the public from the presentation of anonymous ideas; but since advertisers are primarily interested in registering their names with the audience anyway, problems here have seldom arisen. However, in certain circumstances, special statements must be made to indicate the names of sponsors whose payment—regardless of the form—is used to purchase time or to defray the cost of programming:

1. Sponsorship of political broadcasts must be stated clearly.
2. Advertiser identification must be revealed for any "teaser" announcement (promoting, for example, an upcoming sale, product introduction, or new sponsored program, the details of which are not given until later).
3. Disclosure must be made of payola/plugola types of payment that may be used in support of program production (for instance, payment for air-play of phonograph records or incidental mention of usage of a firm's products in a show).

4. Names of donor firms or organizations must be given when prizes or other promotional materials or services are contributed to a program.

Political advertising. Section 315, the well-known *equal-time* section of the Communications Act, requires stations that broadcast political material to provide time on an equal basis to all candidates for political office. Time charges for such political ads also must be at the lowest (discounted) rate available to any advertiser. In addition, each station must maintain a public file (at its principal office) containing, among other things, all requests for political advertising and the disposition of those requests.

Fairness Doctrine. Adopted by the FCC in 1949 and rescinded in 1987, the Fairness Doctrine required that stations present a reasonable balance of viewpoints on controversial public issues. Since Congress has indicated an interest in codifying the doctrine as part of the nation's statutory laws and because many stations continue to follow its rules, the provisions of the Fairness Doctrine will be set forth.

The Fairness Doctrine was particularly applicable in news broadcasting, for example, when a station took editorial positions on debatable issues. The doctrine was applied to advertising in 1967 when the FCC upheld the complaint of a New York attorney, John Banzhaf III, who wanted cigarette commercials balanced with antismoking messages on a New York TV station. The Commission agreed with Banzhaf and applied the doctrine to cigarette advertising; but the FCC also promised that this application of the doctrine would be the only extension of the rule. A number of other complaints were brought to the commission, however, and were followed by a series of decisions. The FCC upheld stations that denied reply time to (1) environmentalists who sought to refute certain oil company commercials, and (2) anti-Vietnam War groups wishing to express their editorial viewpoints. In both instances, the Commission's decision was reversed by the U.S. Court of Appeals for the District of Columbia. Ultimately, though, the U.S. Supreme Court reversed the lower court, holding that station licensees have the right to exercise editorial judgment and may not be required to sell time for editorial advertising merely because they sell time for commercial advertising.

Fraudulent billing. The FCC attempts to police the stations it licenses regarding the integrity of their client billing procedures. Historically, through various devices, some broadcasters, along with other media, have engaged in fraudulent billing practices. The activity typically involves cooperative advertising in which a national manufacturer reimburses a local retail outlet for a portion of incurred advertising expenses. For example, a retail establishment being reimbursed 50 percent of its time charges could report twice the number of messages actually run, thus recouping 100 percent of the media charges. Hence, *double billing* occurs, since the original bill (from the station to the retailer) is not the same as the one passed on from the retailer to the national manufacturer.

Fraudulent billing is strictly illegal under FCC rules. Penalties against guilty stations may range from $20,000 fines to revocation of licenses. In a few instances manufacturers have brought lawsuits against deceitful dealers.

Rigged promotions. Another area in which the FCC has been especially vigilant is that of rigged promotions conducted by stations and/or their advertisers. Illegal contests, for example, may involve "hidden treasures" that actually have not been hidden or reportedly "randomized" winning in contests that are controlled by either stations or advertisers. Again, a station engaging in this form of deceit may be subjected to severe penalties, such as a $20,000 fine or loss of license.

U.S. Criminal Code violations. The FCC also enforces two sections of the U.S. Criminal Code that have application to broadcast material. First, the code prohibits the airing of lottery information (with the exception of legalized state lotteries). Persons responsible for contests and other promotions at stations, therefore, should be alert to the three elements that together constitute a lottery: (1) a prize, (2) the element of chance, and (3) some form of *consideration,* usually defined as a monetary exchange. Violation of the lottery statute by a station may result in a $20,000 fine.

To avoid legal entanglements, many contests and promotional announcements include a "no purchase necessary" statement. Or, if a purchase is required before a free gift is given, everyone who buys is, in effect, a winner (so there is no element of chance).

Despite this tough regulatory stance taken with respect to lotteries, recent changes in the law do permit lotteries operated by state governments to advertise over the air. Such commercial messages, however, must not unduly "encourage" the public to engage in betting.

The second section of the U.S. Criminal Code that is enforced by the FCC forbids the broadcast of material that contains "obscenity, profanity, or vulgarity." Of course, with changing attitudes and mores in society, the definition of what is obscene, profane, or vulgar is subject to change. Thus, while licenses have been revoked for gross violations of this statute, media regulators have become more tolerant toward once-taboo material.

OTHER FEDERAL LAWS

A number of other federal laws that apply, in part, to broadcast advertising deserve mention here:

The Consumer Protection Act of 1969. Under this law, the Federal Reserve Board requires full disclosure of the credit cost paid by consumers when they purchase items on credit. Specifically, creditors must put in writing all finance charges including interest, plus the annual percentage rate of such carrying charges. This legislation, popularly known as the *truth-in-lending law,* also requires that commercials mentioning the availability of credit terms include all pertinent facts, among them the number of payments and size of the down payment.

The Federal Food, Drug and Cosmetic Act of 1938. Administered by the Food and Drug Administration, this act primarily affects the labeling of food, drug, and cosmetic products. However, its advertising implications require full disclosure of information for items that pose potential dangers to health. For example, analgesic products must not suggest that they provide cures; rather, commercials must state that they provide "fast, *temporary* relief," or that if pain persists, one should consult a physician.

Post Office regulations. The U.S. Post Office becomes involved in broadcast advertising whenever offers are made that involve shipment of items through the mails. Any such mailing must conform to postal regulations with respect to the acceptability of products for mailing, weight limits, and package sizes. Promotion and merchandising items mailed to retail outlets in support of broadcast campaigns are likewise affected. The growth of direct marketing has included an increased use of the broadcast media; wise advertisers, therefore, check postal regulations thoroughly before such campaigns are launched.

State Regulation

Although the principal watchdogs over broadcast advertising are federal agencies, all of the fifty state governments provide some forms of regulation. Consumer protection laws exist in practically all states to discourage false or misleading advertising; many of these statutes are more rigorous than federal laws.

In addition, many states have passed laws controlling or banning the on-air advertising of lotteries and alcoholic beverages, as well as such merchandising devices as premiums, coupons, and trading stamps. Since such restrictions vary widely from state to state, advertisers must investigate them carefully.

Recently, a few states have applied their state sales taxes to various forms of advertising; some enforce a tax on materials used in the production of commercials. Even some municipalities, including New York City, impose taxes on all forms of advertising appearing in their cities.

Self-Regulation

Perhaps the most effective force in regulating television and radio advertising is administered by advertisers, agencies, and the media themselves. Admittedly, some of the impetus for this self-regulation lies in the fact that it reduces the likelihood of increased government control (which both broadcasters and advertisers abhor); but enlightened self-regulation by responsible practitioners also results in higher standards and better service to the consuming public.

THE NATIONAL ASSOCIATION OF BROADCASTERS

The National Association of Broadcasters, established in 1923, is the principal trade association of U.S. commercial broadcasting. Headquartered in Washington, D.C., the NAB represents the industry before congressional committees, the FCC, and other governmental agencies. Beyond its lobbying function, the association provides member stations with information useful to station managers, including economic studies, interpretations of governmental rules and regulations, and industry guidelines.

For more than fifty years (1928-1982), an additional NAB activity of considerable importance was the sponsorship and administration of self-regulatory codes of good practice. Early in its history, members of the NAB formulated their first radio code in 1928. The original code for television, based on both the Radio Code and the Motion Picture Code, was established in 1952. Each code dealt specifically with programming and advertising standards and included prohibitions and recommendations that subscribing stations were expected to follow.

However, in 1982, the NAB radio and television codes were suspended after the Antitrust Division of the Justice Department brought suit, charging that the codes violated certain restraint-of-trade statutes.[2] A year earlier, there were 4,162 subscribing radio stations and 512 subscribing television stations, representing approximately 52 percent of all U.S. commercial radio stations and 67 percent of all commercial TV outlets. Although a substantial number of stations never subscribed, code standards were widely followed throughout the industry.

Even though withdrawn by the NAB, the radio and television codes still exist as documents and, in fact, are frequently consulted by network and station executives even today. A brief summary of the contents and administration of the NAB codes is included here because of their continuing influence.

Administration of the NAB Codes

While they were in effect, both the radio and the television codes were administered and enforced by the NAB's Code Authority under the general direction of the Radio Code Board and the Television Code Review Board. Daily administration was delegated to the NAB Code Authority, which derived its support from fees paid by code-subscribing stations. With offices in New York, Hollywood, and Washington, the Code Authority reviewed advertising materials to determine broadcast acceptability; recommendations were made to subscriber stations through a monthly publication, *Code News*.

Other responsibilities of the Code Authority included investigating advertising complaints and informing subscriber stations, monitoring program logs to verify whether a station was in compliance with the code's advertising and time standards, and making recommendations to the code boards concerning violations. In addition, the Code Authority maintained liaison with governmental agencies.

The code boards initiated formal charges against stations accused of violating the codes, considered appeals stemming from any decision made by the Code Authority, and consulted with the Code Authority's director on matters affecting code administration.

Contents of the Codes

The NAB radio and television codes bear a strong resemblance to each other. Both consisted of a prefacing statement that presented the philosophy and purpose of self-regulation, program standards, and advertising standards. Philosophically, the codes recognized the need for thoughtful attention to the content of material broadcast and suggested that advertisers and viewers also share in the responsibility for upholding high standards:

> Advertising messages should be presented in an honest, responsible and tasteful manner. Advertisers should also support the endeavors of broadcasters to offer a diversity of programs that meet the needs and expectations of the total viewing audience. . . .
>
> The viewer also has a responsibility to . . . make criticisms and positive suggestions about programming and advertising known to the broadcast licensee. Parents particularly should oversee the viewing habits of their children, encouraging them to watch programs that will enrich their experience and broaden their intellectual horizons.[3]

With respect to programming, the codes acknowledged that broadcasters have a special obligation to present episodes of violence only "in responsibly handled contexts." When depictions of conflict are present during hours when children normally view television, it is the broadcaster's responsibility to see to it that they are handled with sensitivity. Other responsibilities affect news broadcasts, discussion programs for the expression of views on public issues, political forums, and religious presentations.

The Advertising Standards sections of the radio and TV codes were almost identical except for differences in time allowances for advertising and other nonprogram material segments. Major topics in the codes were:

Product acceptability: including proscriptions against the advertising of certain products and limitations on the advertising of others (especially personal products, alcoholic beverages, fortune-telling, astrology, and tip sheets).

Good taste: in both production and presentation of commercials (especially in the case of personal products and the naming of competitors).

Special considerations: in the advertising of medical products, contests, premiums, and offers and in the delivery of testimonials.

Commercial time standards: wherein radio stations were merely advised that the amount of time used for advertising should not exceed eighteen minutes within any clock hour. Exceptions were permitted in special circumstances, such as those that might arise with the heavy demand for political advertising during an election campaign.

The Television Code was much more complex. It included different standards for network affiliates and independent stations and for primetime hours (any three consecutive hours between 6:00 P.M. and midnight) and other hours. The following were among major code provisions in these areas:

1. For network affiliates, nonprogram elements, all of which were counted against commercial time, included billboards (announcements of sponsorship at the beginning and end of programs);

promotional announcements for sister (commonly owned) stations; promotional announcements for programs (network and local) carried by an affiliate; and excessive program credits, as well as actual commercials.

2. In primetime, nonprogram material may not exceed 9½ minutes per clock hour, and in other time periods it may not exceed 16 minutes.

3. Program interruptions (during which time the nonprogram material is aired) may not exceed two per half hour in primetime, and four per half hour at other times.

4. The number of consecutive nonprogram announcements aired may not exceed four when the interruption comes during a program *stopdown* and three when it comes at the station break.

Independent TV stations, because of their different economic circumstances, were permitted more nonprogram material time per hour; they also had a slightly different definition of nonprogram material. News, special events, and variety programs, as well as feature films, were exempt from some of the previously given conditions. Also, certain weekend hours were set aside as children's programming time, during which separate standards—often as strict as those for primetime—applied.[4]

Finally, code policies generally paralleled FTC guidelines in the area of false and misleading claims, lottery information, and bait-and-switch advertising (the promotion of goods or services used merely to lure customers into purchasing higher-priced substitutes). The outright federal ban on cigarette advertising by the broadcast media in 1971 was seen by many broadcasters and advertisers as a serious threat to the freedoms guaranteed by the U.S. Constitution, as well as a dangerous precedent. It is interesting to note, however, that broadcasters themselves had proposed such a ban—and even had it written into their codes—to be effective in 1973.

OTHER SELF-REGULATION

In addition to the former NAB Code Authority, several other entities have been actively engaged in the self-regulation of broadcast advertising. These include network Standards and Practices (S&P) departments, individual stations, and the National Advertising Review Board (NARB). The latter is a relatively young organization created by advertisers to promote high standards of truth and accuracy in national and regional advertising.

Network Standards

Each of the radio and television networks maintains a continuity acceptance department that must approve all programs and commercial materials before they are aired. Commercial messages, as many as 50,000 per year, are scrutinized for product acceptability, method of presentation, and substantiation of claims. Following examination, the network standards office takes one of three actions: (1) it accepts a proposed message without revision; (2) it accepts a commercial message, subject to specified revisions; or (3) it rejects a message outright. Many network advertisers submit plans for commercial messages in script and storyboard form before production actually begins, so required revisions may be made at minimum cost.

As many as one-third of the commercials submitted to the networks each year are either rejected completely or sent back to advertisers and agencies for revisions. Problems cited range from disparagement of competitors to unsupported claims and material presented in poor taste. Even material that passes muster often does so only after repeated screenings, detailed discussion, and numerous headaches.

In a 1987 article on decision making related to advertising and programming standards,[5] Dr. Bruce A. Linton of the University of Kansas reported that, after the demise of the NAB codes, the broadcast networks beefed up their S&P staffs and activities. Linton observed that the game, as it has been called by those involved, continues to be played under the same basic rules. "These require the editors to attempt to balance the (often excessive) desires of the agencies and producers with the standards of the network while not upsetting the public."[6] The main difference seems to be that the networks now must deal with the agencies at an earlier time.

The former vice president of broadcast standards for NBC, Herminio Treviesas, noted that network censors now heed three voices in their gatekeeping functions—the press, the affiliates, and the public. During recent years, organized and vocal pressure groups have emerged "to make life (for the network censors) more complicated."[7]

According to Linton, most of the major problems in advertising 20 years ago continue to exist today. These include suspicious claims and questionable taste of proprietary drugs and personal products ads. Comparative advertising is now quite common. Changes in advertising time standards and program interruptions have resulted in clutter-related criticism, and commercials directed to children continue to raise questions from citizen pressure groups. Two new areas of concern have emerged; these relate to alcohol and issue advertising.

Local Station Standards

During the years of the NAB Code, self-regulation at the local station level was fairly simple. Managers had easy access to expert opinions on commercial acceptance matters from the code staff and from their network S&P editors. Now, with the code gone and many stations operating as independents, local stations must make acceptance decisions largely on their own. In his 1986 survey of 125 television stations, Dr. Linton found that almost all (98 percent) now have commercial acceptance guidelines in some form.

Nearly twice as many managers reported that their standards were in written rather than oral form. But relatively few stations have organized (codified) manuals, and the majority depend on the memorandum. More than a third of the stations reported using the old NAB Code as a policy source.[8] Dr. Linton added:

> It was especially evident in the interviews that many managers miss the Code. While not perfect, it was accepted, telling all parties where the lines would be drawn. Managers could call a Code editor and get expert opinion, or they could read the monthly advisories in the "Code News."[9]

Certain problem areas were cited by local station managers in 1986. These included political advertising, issue advertising, and movie trailers. Station personnel also expressed concern that growing competition for ad dollars could force management to relax its stance on some long-held guidelines.[10] Nevertheless, as Dr. Linton concluded, "The Code is gone, but the *process* of self regulation has continued."[11]

National Advertising Review Board

The NARB was established in 1971 (during a period of consumer activism) by four advertiser organizations: the American Advertising Federation, the American Association of Advertising Agencies, the Association of National Advertisers, and the Council of Better Business Bureaus. Fifty volunteer members make up this self-regulatory agency, forty of whom are advertising professionals, and ten of whom represent the public.

Unlike the network standards departments and the NAB Code Authority, the NARB does not prescreen broadcast advertising materials. Its main activity is to review decisions made by the National Advertising Division of the Council of Better Business Bureaus that have been disputed. Whenever an NARB panel concurs with complainants, the advertiser involved is notified and urged to remove the ad or commercial in question from the media.

No formal cease-and-desist orders are issued because the NARB has no official legal powers, but if its recommendations are not carried out, cases may be taken directly to the FTC. Thus, the NARB gives those advertisers found to be "at fault" the chance to redeem themselves without any legal involvements.

Well over 2,500 complaints have been funneled through NARB channels. Approximately one-third of them were dismissed because the respective advertisers substantiated the claims, and another one-third involved ads and commercials that were subsequently modified or discontinued. The advertisers affected by the final one-third chose to appeal the NARB decisions. It is interesting to note, too, that although each case is considered on its own merits (as is true in FTC proceedings), seven different "complaint categories" in broadcast advertising have emerged over the years:

1. *Dangling comparatives* such as "more" (of what?), "better" (than what?), and "longer" (than what?).
2. *Semantics* such as "a lot" (how much?), "lasts" (how long?), and "easy" (for whom?).
3. *Omission of relevant information* when, for example, only one important feature of a warranty is given, or only one similar ingredient is pointed out between an expensive product and an inexpensive substitute.
4. *Testimonials* and the different effects on audiences when celebrities merely endorse a product and claim personal use.
5. *Puffery* and the different effects of exaggeration in qualitative areas where measurement is impossible versus obvious fantasies, satires, and parodies.
6. *Misuse of research data and surveys,* especially material lifted out of context, findings that cannot be projected because of inadequate samples, and assumptions of the overall superiority of products based on studies of single characteristics.
7. *Comparative commercials* and fairness to both named and unnamed competitors.

Regardless of the nature of the complaint, however, and in keeping with court precedents set in FTC cases, NARB panels have consistently affirmed that a commercial's objective (that is, the advertiser's intent) is irrelevant in determining whether or not deception has occurred. Rather, the criterion is the impression left on listeners and viewers. What has not been established, and may never be, is the proportion of an intended (target) audience that must feel "deceived" before a commercial is ruled misleading. In a number of instances, the cut-off point has been more than 50 percent; however, it has also been a low as 15 percent.[12]

The overall effect of self-regulation in broadcasting and advertising is difficult to assess. However, it is encouraging to note the far-sighted steps taken by leaders in both industries to eliminate the abuses that can only work against media and commercial acceptance and credibility.

On the other hand, it should be obvious to the reader by now that not all of the areas of concern in broadcast advertising can be regulated. Some simply call for good judgment and responsible behavior on the part of industry personnel. It is to this kind of decision-making activity that we turn our attention in the next chapter.

Study Questions

1. Find and discuss a recent case involving bait-and-switch advertising on TV or radio, the illegal broadcast of lottery information, fraudulent billing, or the violation of some other state or federal statute. Do you agree with the action(s) taken or proposed? Why?

2. Do you feel the federal government should have banned the advertising of cigarettes on TV and

radio as they did in 1971? Should other products be banned in the future? If you *agree,* explain why you think the federal government should take the initiative here; if you *disagree,* indicate what other organization(s) should be responsible, and why.

3. Take and support a stand on the issue of the Fairness Doctrine and its application to broadcast advertising.

4. Suppose the former NAB code was being reinstated. Suggest one addition to the code with respect to advertising that you feel would strengthen it. Explain your suggestion and indicate its value.

5. Find and discuss a case currently before the National Advertising Review Board affecting broadcast advertisers. Then, predict the outcome and give reasons for your prediction.

6. In your opinion, does the FCC have too much, too little, or the right amount of control over broadcasting? And does the FTC have too much, too little, or the right amount of control over advertising? Explain your feelings.

(Helpful sources for these questions include *Advertising Age, TV/Radio Age,* and *Broadcasting.*)

ASSIGNMENT 5-A
Monitor an assigned hour of radio or TV programming. Set up a chart showing the amount of nonprogram material included (and its nature), the number of program interruptions, and the number of consecutive announcements during each interruption. Check your findings against the standards set forth in the NAB codes.

ASSIGNMENT 5-B
List the steps you think should be taken to enforce advertising standards on radio and television. That is, how might a nongovernmental body both police and prosecute effectively?

ASSIGNMENT 5-C
Find examples of current commercials that might possibly come before the NARB in each of the following categories discussed in Chapter 5: dangling comparatives, semantics, omission of relevant information, testimonials, puffery, misuse of research data and surveys, and comparative commercials. In each instance indicate the problem claim.

Notes

1. See Debra L. Scammon and Richard J. Semenik, "The FTC's 'Reasonable Basis' for Substantiation of Advertising: Expanded Standards and Implications," *Journal of Advertising* 12 (1983): 4-11.
2. U.S. v. N.A.B., 8 Media L. Rep. 2572 (Dist. Ct. Washington, D.C., 1982).
3. *The Television Code* (Washington, D.C.: NAB, 1980), 1.
4. *The Television Code* (Washington, D.C.: NAB, 1980); *The Radio Code* (Washington, D.C.: NAB, 1980).
5. Bruce A. Linton, "Self-Regulation in Broadcasting Revisited," *Journalism Quarterly*, 64 (Summer-Fall 1987):483-90.
6. Ibid., 484.
7. Ibid.
8. Ibid., 487.
9. Ibid.
10. Ibid.

11. Ibid., 489.

12. See Eric J. Zanot and Lynda Maddox, "An Analysis and Evaluation of the Performance of the National Advertising Review Board" (Paper presented at the American Academy of Advertising Conference, Minneapolis, March 28, 1977).

Suggested Readings

Cole, Barry, and Oettinger, Mel. *Reluctant Regulators: The FCC and the Broadcast Audience.* Reading, Mass.: Addison-Wesley, 1978.

Diamond, Edwin et al. *Telecommunications in Crisis: The First Amendment, Technology, and Deregulation.* Washington, D.C.: Cato Institute, 1983.

Krasnow, Erwin G., and others. *The Politics of Broadcast Regulation.* 3d ed. New York: St. Martin's, 1982.

Legal and Business Aspects of the Advertising Industry 1984. New York: Practising Law Institute, 1984.

Neelankavil, James P. *Advertising Self-Regulation: A Global Perspective.* New York: Hastings House, 1980.

Nelson, Harold L., and Dwight L. Teeter, Jr. *Law of Mass Communications: Freedom and Control of Print and Broadcast Media.* 5th ed. Mineola, N.Y.: Foundation, 1986.

Noam, Eli M., ed. *Telecommunications Regulation Today and Tomorrow.* New York: Law and Business/Harcourt-Brace-Jovanovich, 1983.

Posner, Richard A. *Regulation of Advertising by the FCC.* Washington, D.C.: American Enterprise Institute for Public Policy Research, 1973.

Rohrer, Daniel M. *Mass Media, Freedom of Speech, and Advertising: A Study in Communications Law.* Dubuque, Iowa: Kendall-Hunt, 1979.

Strong, William S. *The Copyright Book: A Practical Guide.* 2d ed. Cambridge, Mass.: MIT Press, 1984.

ALSO: Check recent issues of *Advertising Age* and *Broadcasting*, and publications from the National Association of Broadcasters.

6

Commercials and Social Responsibility

In chapter 5, we noted that the long-standing NAB Radio and Television Codes have been laid to rest in favor of more informal self-regulatory policies and procedures. Still, because broadcasters in this country most certainly wish to remain free from government control, they must establish and adhere to some kind of advertising standards; commercials that are presented honestly, tastefully, and in a manner that meets the wants and needs of audiences help enhance a station's favorable image in the community.

Practicing Advertising Ethics

Many stations today maintain a crusade against the advertising of questionable products—messages they feel would be objectionable to a substantial number of listeners and viewers. All such commercials may be refused by station management, regardless of whether or not the respective advertisers' businesses are advertised through other media.

Studies show that young people who have been exposed to television commercials for beer and wine generally drink more than those who have not.[1] Additionally, they tend to be more favorably inclined toward alcoholic beverages that feature young people in their advertising.[2] Recognizing this issue, the Reagan administration required beer and wine advertisers to drop athletic spokespeople (peer emulators) from their commercials.[3]

Many years earlier, however, broadcasters themselves became concerned with the mere mention of alcoholic beverages in connection with restaurant commercials. *Code News,* a former NAB Code Authority publication, printed questions and answers dealing with advertising guidelines. One example was:

> *Question:* Would copy language such as "All the beer or wine you can drink with your meal" be acceptable in a commercial?
>
> *Answer:* No. Such language is believed to encourage over-consumption and should not be permitted.

More and more advertisers agree that consumer research holds the key to effective communication of ethical concerns. For example, studies have been conducted to determine the kinds of messages that do the best job of conveying the dangers of taking drugs, and advertising research has assessed the effects of specific messages on changing attitudes toward drugs.

One study of high school students tested two versions of each of three different commercials: (1)

the threat of serious versus minimal harm (death versus parental disapproval); (2) the drawing of an explicit conclusion versus no summary statement at the end; and (3) a monologue versus a dialogue format. No differences were found in the first and third instances, but explicit conclusions were proven necessary if commercials were to have any influence.[4]

Along with concerns about alcohol and drugs is the concern about sexually transmitted diseases. At this writing, a number of stations are currently running condom commercials and public service announcements (PSAs) dealing with AIDS. It may be a while before this kind of televised communication is accepted by all broadcasters (and viewers), but note that it was only recently that commercials for any kind of feminine hygiene products were seen in this country; even today, not all consumer response to the airing of such messages is positive.

On the programming side, the NAB wrote *Family Viewing Time* into television codes from 1975 through 1981; stations were asked to keep the hours from 7 to 9 P.M. (or 6 to 8 P.M., depending on specific time zones) free from the sex and violence deemed inappropriate for young viewers. Nationwide polls taken in 1975 and 1976 showed that more than 80 percent of the American public favored this programming idea.[5] In addition, a number of practitioners regarded the concept of Family Viewing Time as an example of industry self-regulation at its best.

The Advertiser/Agency Side

From the earliest days of wireless communication, broadcasters have been asked to operate in the public interest, convenience, and necessity in as responsible a manner as possible. On the advertiser/agency side, however, steps also have been taken to help assure that obligations to society will be met through commercials. For example, recent years have all but seen the demise of the so-called BRAND X—the unnamed competitor/villain against whom the advertised product/hero always emerged victorious in comparative commercial showdowns. When the advertising industry decided (with the approval of legal watchdogs) that competitors could be named in commercials, questions immediately arose—not only in terms of message effectiveness, but also with regard to responsible comparisons.

In 1974, therefore, the American Association of Advertising Agencies (AAAA) drew up a set of guidelines for comparative advertising that commercial writers now adhere to as closely as possible (see Figure 6.1). Two problems experienced by broadcast advertisers attempting to follow this plan are basically the same ones faced in trying to apply NAB Code guidelines: (1) how to interpret the very general statements in specific contexts and (2) how to follow through completely in as little as ten seconds. Still, the social concern this policy represents is noteworthy.

On the other hand, the Ogilvy & Mather advertising agency might ask just what responsibility it is that copywriters are fulfilling for clients when comparative commercials are prepared. A 1975 study conducted by that agency found that comparative commercials (as opposed to noncomparative ones) made consumers more aware of the competition; lessened the credibility of claims and the persuasiveness of the overall message; and decreased brand identification and increased confusion.[6]

Looking at ethics in another way, a 1988 survey examined advertiser, agency, and media responses to questionable business practices. One situation involved a group of restaurants that offered "good tasting" food at low prices. They asked their agency to develop a "better price story," because they were about to cut their prices even further. Before creating any commercials carrying this message, however, the agency learned that the restaurants had found a supplier of "still edible but nearly spoiled" food that could be "doctored" with additional seasonings and preservatives. That's how they were going to be able to sell at rock-bottom prices.

1. The intent and connotation of the ad should be to inform and never to discredit or unfairly attack competitors, competing products, or services.

2. When a competitive product is named, it should be one that exists in the marketplace as significant competition.

3. The competition should be fairly and properly identified but never in a manner or tone of voice that degrades the competitive product or service.

4. The advertising should compare related or similar properties or ingredients of the product, dimension to dimension, feature to feature.

5. The identification should be for honest comparison purposes and not simply to upgrade by association.

6. If a competitive test is conducted, it should be done by an objective testing source, preferably an independent one, so that there will be no doubt as to the veracity of the test.

7. In all cases, the test should be supportive of all claims made in the advertising that are based on the test.

8. The advertising should never use partial results or stress insignificant differences to`cause the consumer to draw an improper conclusion.

9. The property being compared should be significant in terms of value or usefulness of the product to the consumer.

10. Comparatives delivered through the use of testimonials should not imply that the testimonial is more than one individual's thought unless that individual represents a sample of the majority viewpoint.

Fig. 6.1. Policy statement and guidelines for comparative advertising, The American Association of Advertising Agencies, April, 1974.

Hundreds of replies were received from across the country, nearly 90 percent of which (85 percent of agencies, 87 percent of media, and 88 percent of advertisers) said that this kind of advertising would be unethical.[7]

The Question of Truth

No matter what organizations or individuals are shouldering the responsibility for commercials, one of the most difficult questions faced concerns the communication of truth. Literal truth or falsity is regulated by federal, state, and local governments. Today, for example, it is illegal for an advertiser to claim in a commercial that a cereal has vitamins and minerals in it if, in fact, it does not. Furthermore, advertisers who make such claims are responsible to the FTC for proving in actual laboratory tests that these elements exist. Or, if commercials state that a detergent will remove a specific stain, or an automobile tire will withstand a particular kind of torture test, or one brand of battery will outlast another, the respective advertisers must always be ready to demonstrate proof.

Granted, these examples are not usually categorized in terms of social responsibility—except insofar as responsible broadcast advertisers do uphold the law. At least one major television network required proof of competitive claims (before commercial airing) long before the FTC began demanding it. Indeed, seeing to it that viewers received only truthful information in commercials was deemed a broadcaster responsibility before consumer advocates ever gained recognition.

When it comes to perceived truth, however—truth as interpreted by commercial recipients—there is no regulation per se; broadcasters and advertisers alone must assume responsibility for this kind of truth-communication. *Credibility* is a term often used for perceived truth, and it is vitally important to commercial effectiveness. Unfortunately, it is also a quality whose presence cannot really be proved because its total existence is in the minds of individual listeners and viewers.

Consider, for example, the commercial that promises: "When you use this product, you'll be more confident," or the one that advises: "Try this service and you'll feel a new sense of pride and accomplishment." Testing the accuracy of such claims is next to impossible because people interpret such messages (as well as the results of product usage) in their own, often different, ways. What obligation, therefore, does this situation place on those who write and air commercials? Should all such emotional claims be banned? Hardly. In fact, the psychological value that advertising has been shown to add to goods and services is often welcomed by consumers. The satisfaction gained from usage of personally selected products is in keeping with many an American's pursuit of happiness.

THE POWER OF PERSUASION
Consider a brand-name product that you buy and use because you believe it is better for you than its competitors. Now, assume that a new company has just manufactured a product that is identical in physical composition to your favorite brand but costs less; further, assume that you are generally interested in saving money. The question is, would you switch brands? And if you would, do you know someone in a similar situation who would not, even if the price continued to decline? Your authors, for example, are loyal Crest toothpaste customers concerned with saving money. They are aware that many competing brands are identical in terms of ingredients, but no cents-off promotions by other brands are acceptable. Both authors fully admit to a belief that Crest is better—thanks to its image-creating and -sustaining advertising program. Intellectually speaking, several brands do match Crest in value, but emotionally speaking, not one of them can.

In most cases, consumers are not eager to admit being, as they see it, taken in by commercials. But our contention is that no one is ever coerced by advertising to do anything. True, most commercials are designed to persuade, but listeners and viewers are always free to accept or reject messages, products, and ideas. If they choose to buy a particular brand, and then find it unsatisfactory (for whatever reason), the most persuasive, creative, ingenious commercials ever produced cannot force a repeat sale. On the other hand, if the selected product lives up to its claims (however they have been interpreted), advertising has helped its audience fulfill particular wants or needs. For those who insist that it is morally wrong for people to have those wants and needs or that truth is an absolute with which broadcast advertising dare not tamper, we suggest tête-à-têtes with philosophers or spiritual advisers; such concerns lie beyond our spheres of marketing and communication.

THE IMPORTANCE OF CONFIDENCE
Advertisers are generally the first to admit that commercials that do not maintain a high level of consumer confidence stand little chance of succeeding in their various communicative tasks. No blatantly false, misleading, or deceptive commercial is going to do a snow job on today's sophisticated consumers. Because the vast majority of broadcast advertisers attribute a high degree of effectiveness to their commercials, however, it is obvious that listeners and viewers do regard many of them not only as acceptable, but also as helpful.

In a national attitude survey, the most frequently volunteered reason for positive opinions about advertising was its ability to provide information and stimulate overall awareness of products and services. On the other hand, in this same study, a low level of credibility was cited most often as the reason for negative opinions of advertising.[8] Other surveys have examined public reactions to the whole idea of having commercials on television. For more than 20 years, the Roper Organization has asked viewers whether commercials are a fair price to pay for so-called free TV. The most positive response,

84 percent favorable, was recorded in 1974. Even today, though, figures hover around 70 percent—despite the increasing availability of cable and satellite-distributed programs without commercials.

When asked to think specifically of children's programming, well over 60 percent of respondents over a 10-year period have continued to approve of having commercials instead of paying direct program fees.[9]

THE ETERNAL TIME QUANDARY

Some critics maintain that commercials tell only half-truths, never spelling out the bottom line. The response from broadcasters and copywriters, however, is often: "Well, what do you expect in 30 seconds (or 15)?" Inherent in our two media that run on time is the inability to tell whole sales stories. There are never enough seconds to provide all the details that may appear in printed ads. Still, although few people today seriously advocate limiting advertising to printed media, many do call for more information (such as negative disclosures or comparative data and competitive rebuttals) in commercial messages. Obviously, copywriters must pay as much attention to how commercials are presented as they do to what is said and shown.

Looking at time in another way, for many years, the NAB Code restricted radio advertising time to 18 minutes per hour. Yet, many stations voluntarily reduced their daily commercial loads to 16, 14, and, in some cases, even 12 minutes per hour. Listeners benefit (they hear less commercial clutter), advertisers benefit (their messages face less competition), and the stations benefit (in terms of public image and FCC approval). Ultimately, if such policies lead to larger audiences, the stations involved may even raise their advertising rates and thereby make up for the money otherwise lost.

On the other hand, in the fall of 1987, CBS-TV added a full 3½ minutes of network commercials to its weekly primetime schedule, a move designed in part to help hold the line on network pricing.[10]

The Advertising Council

Next to the Advertising Council logotype superimposed at the end of its televised messages appear the words: "Advertising contributed for the public good." This socially concerned organization is dedicated to achieving two major goals: (1) improvement of human welfare through creation and dissemination of public service messages and (2) demonstration of the fact that advertising can be a powerful force for the public good.

Formed in 1942 as the War Advertising Council, this group was and is a voluntary, nonpartisan, and nonpolitical operation, made up of representatives from all branches of advertising, communication, business, and the media. In the early 1940s, the Council's main objective was to marshal the forces of advertising to aid the war effort; promotions centered around war bonds, recruitment, conservation, and rationing. In 1945, the term *War* was dropped, and the organization became simply the Advertising Council; offices today are located in New York, Washington, D.C., and Los Angeles.

Some two dozen major Ad Council campaigns reach millions of listeners and viewers annually, with literally billions of radio and TV audience impressions. Broadcast research organizations have also climbed aboard the social responsibility bandwagon; A. C. Nielsen provides TV circulation estimates at no cost to the Council (while the networks spend millions of dollars per year for ratings).

Examples of familiar campaigns receiving heavy broadcast support over the years are: U.S. Savings Bonds, since 1942; the National Safety Council (seat belts) and the American Red Cross, since

1945; the United Way, since 1947; and the Help Fight Pollution (Keep America Beautiful) campaign, since 1953. More recently, listeners and viewers have been exposed to Ad Council announcements promoting drug abuse information, the National Alliance of Businessmen's JOBS program, and rehabilitation of the handicapped.

Overall results have been staggering: more than a million lives saved on America's highways, a tripling of annual contributions to private colleges and universities since the middle 1950s, and billions of dollars raised for the Red Cross, United Way, and Community Chest.

All major TV and radio networks, together with some of their national advertisers, cooperate in the Radio-TV Public Service Plans administered by the Ad Council. Under these plans, networks carry a minimum of one Ad Council message every five weeks in weekly half-hour programs, one message every four weeks in hour-long shows, and one message every three weeks in programs broadcast more than once a week. In practice, however, both networks and individual stations schedule public service announcements daily and many are sponsored by the Ad Council.

THE LOCAL SCENE

On the local level, stations give the Ad Council a tremendous amount of support through use of announcement kits provided monthly by the Ad Council, in cooperation with the NAB. In addition, the *Public Service Advertising Bulletin* is issued every two months through the American Advertising Federation to local ad clubs. Typical examples of locally supported broadcast campaigns are: Boys' and Girls' Clubs and Scouts, Cancer Control, Multiple Sclerosis, Christmas and Easter Seals, the Heart Fund, Mental Health, Physical Fitness, the United Negro College Fund, and the YMCA and YWCA. Figure 6.2 is a public service spot personalized by a local radio station.

```
MUSIC:          BACKGROUND (UP & UNDER)

ANNCR:          This is National Boys' Club Week -- celebrating the
                activities of more than a million youngsters at eleven-
                hundred Boys' Clubs across the country.  Boys' Clubs are
                more than just places to hang out.  They offer
                understanding, guidance, skills, and self-respect.  The
                Boys' Club of Westville is on the campus of Washington
                Intermediate School, and people there are ready now to
                tell you all you need to know.  Visit the Boys' Club
                today -- and introduce your kids to a lifetime friend.

MUSIC:          UP AND OUT
```

Fig. 6.2. Boys' Club public-service spot for radio.

THE SPIRIT OF GIVING

It is often interesting to advertising critics to learn that Ad Council membership consists of many of the same people who write, produce, and air the commercials that draw complaints from opponents of product advertising. In fact, advertising agencies do much of the Ad Council's creative work—the planning, writing, and designing of commercials—free of charge, while the national broadcast media contribute vast amounts of air time (close to a billion dollars a year in terms of regular commercial rates).[11] And it's encouraging to find that even though the FCC has relaxed its regulation of TV stations, the time these stations allot to PSAs has not declined.[12]

Why all the effort on the part of both broadcasters and advertisers? According to one Ad Council spokesperson, "Because of the American people. They need an Advertising Council to remind them of the things that need to be done. And to help them recognize that there is much unfinished business in America, and to urge them to work together for the common good."[13]

Combined Campaigns: Public Service and Commercial Advertising

Goodwill efforts are often supplemented by commercial advertiser involvements. The annual Aloha Week Festival in Hawaii, for example, pays tribute to the diversity of cultures and traditions that make up our 50th state. (Part of the Aloha Week Parade is retelecast nationally by CBS-TV during its Thanksgiving Day special.) The festival's major fund-raising project is the sale of Aloha Week ribbons, which serve as admission tickets to shows and events.

The promotional staff always plans a dramatic campaign kickoff, as demonstrated in Figure 6.3. In 1980, Hawaii's governor, George Ariyoshi, bought the first Aloha Week ribbon from Danny Kaleikini, celebrity entertainer and the festival's Ambassador of Aloha. (Fortunate, indeed, is the public service campaign team that gains the wholehearted support of state officials and show business stars.) The scene shown in Figure 6.3 appeared in citywide publicity releases, and the camera crew in Figure 6.4 made sure the event was seen by viewers of local TV newscasts.

Fig. 6.3. Public service campaign kick-off. In 1980, Hawaii's Governor Ariyoshi accepts an Aloha Week ribbon from popular entertainer Danny Kaleikini. The ribbon symbolizes the official start of Hawaii's annual Aloha Festival.

Fig. 6.4. Television news/publicity crew in action.

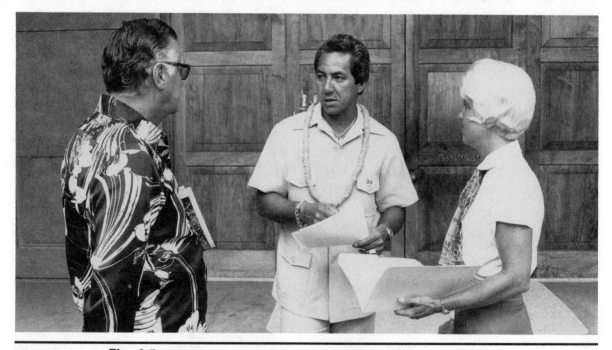

Fig. 6.5. Informal prerecording session. Danny Kaleikini also agrees to record radio announcements to publicize the campaign.

Mr. Kaleikini agreed to record some radio spots promoting ribbon sales (Figure 6.5). The festival's executive director suggested several different approaches, and his staff writer prepared a variety of scripts. Briefly, these were the tasks of the promotional team, paralleling the jobs of an advertising account group:

1. To determine creative and broadcast media objectives for the campaign in terms of communication effects; to make people aware of the festival and to stimulate their desire to participate in it.

2. To decide on execution in terms of audio and video appeals, celebrity input, and broadcast reach and frequency.

3. To measure results of the campaign so that the next year's efforts might benefit therefrom.

Informal research studies, conducted by telephone and through personal interviews, determined TV and radio stations' receptivity to the creative materials presented and to their treatment on the air, and consumer reactions to the messages in terms of content and repeated exposure.

Finally, shortly before the Aloha Week Parade, the advertising director of one of Honolulu's major department stores put together a Parade Pack—a Styrofoam cooler filled with six cans of soda pop, some suntan lotion, and an Aloha Week ribbon and sun visor (the latter with the store's name on it as well)—all tied up with an Aloha Week banner (see Figure 6.6). Related TV spots featured a well-known radio disc jockey with his own Parade Pack. And, of course, the store not only promoted its products, but scored a public-relations plus by supporting the Aloha Festival.

Fig. 6.6. Retail store promotion tied to public service.

A second example, familiar to Christmas shoppers across the nation each year, is the annual Salvation Army Kettle Drive. In Hawaii, bell-ringers include celebrities such as Danny Kaleikini, mentioned above, and U.S. Senator Daniel Inouye. Photos like the one in Figure 6.7 serve as effective print ads and poster illustrations and tie in with the radio and television spots (Figures 6.8 and 6.9) as well. The message is the same: join in the spirit of giving and feel good about helping others.

From a marketing point of view, the success of this campaign (it's now an annual event) was

Fig. 6.7. Local version of a national public service campaign. U.S. Senator Daniel Inouye and Hawaiian entertainer Danny Kaleikini appear on behalf of the Salvation Army Christmas Kettle Drive campaign.

```
SALVATION ARMY CHRISTMAS KETTLE DRIVE CAMPAIGN

30-Second Radio Spot/Celebrity Participation

FOR AIR:  Thanksgiving through Christmas, Hawaiian Islands


CELEBRITY
(DANNY KALEIKINI):      ALOHA - THIS IS DANNY KALEIKINI, CHAIRMAN

                        OF THE SALVATION ARMY CHRISTMAS KETTLE DRIVE.

                        WE NEED YOUR SUPPORT IN SPREADING THE

                        CHRISTMAS SPIRIT TO NEEDY FRIENDS AND

                        NEIGHBORS THROUGHOUT HAWAII. AND IT'S SO

                        EASY TO HELP. JUST JOIN ME IN GIVING GENEROUSLY

                        WHENEVER YOU HEAR THE FAMILIAR BELLS AND SEE

                        THE RED KETTLES. IF WE CARE ENOUGH, WE CAN

                        MAKE CHRISTMAS MERRY FOR EVERYONE.

                        (BRING IN "CHRISTMAS MEANS ALOHA" THEME SONG)
```

Fig. 6.8. The tie-in with radio.

SALVATION ARMY CHRISTMAS KETTLE DRIVE CAMPAIGN

30-Second TV spot/Celebrity Participation

FOR AIR: Thanksgiving through Christmas, Hawaiian Islands

VIDEO	AUDIO (DANNY): ALOHA - DANNY KALEIKINI,
OPEN ON CLOSE-UP OF DANNY AND SALVATION ARMY SIGN	CHAIRMAN OF THE SALVATION ARMY CHRISTMAS KETTLE DRIVE. YOU KNOW, CHRISTMAS IS A TIME FOR GIVING -- AND THOUSANDS OF
ZOOM BACK TO REVEAL RED KETTLE	OUR ISLAND FAMILIES NEED YOUR HELP. SHARING IS CARING -- AND WITH YOUR
DISSOLVE TO PICTURES OF PEOPLE HELPED BY FUNDS	SUPPORT, THE SALVATION ARMY CAN BRING COMFORT TO THOSE LESS FORTUNATE THAN
BACK TO DANNY - IN SALVATION ARMY CAP WITH BELL IN HAND	YOU AND ME. SO, COME ON -- HELP ME SPREAD CHRISTMAS ALOHA THIS YEAR. GIVE GENEROUSLY WHEN YOU HEAR THE
DANNY RINGS THE BELL AND DROPS COINS IN KETTLE	FAMILIAR BELLS AND SEE THE BRIGHT RED KETTLES. MERRY CHRISTMAS, EVERYONE!
	(BACKGROUND MUSIC: "CHRISTMAS ALOHA")

Fig. 6.9. The tie-in with television.

partly the result of strategic placement of celebrity bell-ringers—on the mall level of the largest shopping center in the state. Passersby not only recognized the celebrities but also recalled the radio and TV spots; further, being in a holiday spending mood, they were even more favorably encouraged to make contributions.

The Issue of Violence

Turning now to a very sensitive issue in broadcasting (and to a lesser extent, in advertising as well), we find that some advertisers, including such giants as General Motors, Kodak, and Kraft, actually have withdrawn their commercials from various TV programs deemed violent by research and consumer-interest groups. As mentioned earlier, such programs themselves do not generally appear during the early evening period known as *Family Viewing Time*. Amidst all the national clamor over excessive violence portrayed by a medium viewed more than 7 hours per day in the average American home, broadcasters and advertisers alike are taking steps to alleviate the problem. The number of situation comedies on the air has increased markedly in the last few seasons, while crime series have declined.

As we have shown repeatedly, however, the question of responsibility is a multifaceted one. Consider that shows like "Magnum P. I." and "Cagney and Lacey" both contain a fair amount of violence. Yet they attracted loyal audiences throughout their tenure as first-run features and continue to do so now in syndication. We might well ask, therefore, whether responsible advertising agencies should withdraw commercials from such programs when it may clearly be in a client's best interest to leave them there.

In other words, if commercials are designed as sales tools intended to reach those viewers who happen to like watching violent programs, does the agency have a responsibility to follow through here? (Some viewers have even volunteered the suggestion that part of the crime-show audience may, in fact, deplore violence, but take pleasure in seeing "the law" capture and prosecute those responsible for violent crimes!)

The same question applies also to commercial messages, which some people regard as exploitative and, hence, irresponsible. If such commercials persuade their intended audiences to act in a specified manner, and if the ultimate purchases result in the desired consumer satisfaction, to whom is the advertiser and/or the station responsible?

Unfortunately, these are not questions that can be answered easily or objectively. Students striving to make valuable contributions to broadcasting and advertising will do well to ponder these issues seriously.

Commercial Portrayals

When compared with their counterparts of a few years ago, commercials today are portraying women in increasingly responsible and authoritative roles, children's products in increasingly unadorned, depressurized situations, elderly persons in occasional roles, and minority groups in increasingly greater numbers and degrees of prominence. It is true that recent pressures from a variety of governmental and consumer groups helped instigate such changes; still, many advertisers, and the broadcasters who approve their commercials for airing, now regard the furthering of these efforts as a personal responsibility.

WOMEN IN COMMERCIALS

An advisory panel for the NARB undertook a major study to determine whether the women portrayed in commercials reflected current statistics in terms of education, occupation, and current attitudes held by women toward home and family. A number of stereotypes deemed inaccurate by proponents of women's liberation were detected, although gradual improvements have been noted over time.[14]

Advertisers and broadcasters are recognizing women's changing social roles and have incorporated a number of them into commercials and programs. Social responsibility, however, must extend to more than just selected segments of the broadcast advertising audience. For example, pollster Daniel Yankelovich has found that there are still many women in America who feel threatened by women's lib and who are comforted by the reassertion of traditional values in commercials.

CHILDREN'S COMMERCIALS

The National Advertising Division of the Council of Better Business Bureaus has formulated "Children's Advertising Guidelines," which are used as aids both in writing and in evaluating commercials. Still, concerns are voiced about commercial effects on young minds.

Continuing studies are sponsored by the National Institute of Mental Health, the Marketing Science Institute, and the Office of Child Development of the Department of Health and Human Services; as a result, broadcasters and advertisers must keep an ever-watchful eye on their commercial output. On the positive side, however, findings from the national attitude survey discussed previously did include consumer endorsement of the notion that commercials actually help children mature, because "they learn from what they see."[15] The difficulty here, of course, lies in determining just what kinds of material children should be learning.

The "TV watchdog" group known as Action for Children's Television (ACT) has long believed that children's programs are "30-minute commercials." In fact, there has been a significant increase in licensed toys based on TV cartoon characters. (Sometimes the licensed toy is introduced simultaneously with the TV character so that each bolsters the promotion of the other.) Parents and consumer advocates claim that children don't distinguish between the commercials for the toys and the programs.[16]

Interestingly enough, however, a significant decline in ratings has made the industry skeptical about the ability of TV shows to sell toys. Ratings of animated shows built around specific toys dropped an average of 39 percent in the mid-1980s.[17]

As we go to press, the FCC is still considering new time limits on commercial advertising in children's programming.

THE ELDERLY IN COMMERCIALS

Among the elderly (now considered to make up more than 12 percent of the U.S. population), television viewing accounts for the single most time-consuming leisure activity.[18] Further, research suggests that these people rely heavily on TV to provide them with purchase-related information.[19] Yet, based on an analysis of 36 hours of network television programming (more than 800 commercials) in the mid-1980s, only 7 percent of commercials with people in them portray any elderly characters.[20] Progress is being made, but slowly.

MINORITIES IN COMMERCIALS

Finally, although many concerned citizens will maintain that changes were far too long in coming, today's commercials do feature an increasing number of minorities in increasingly important roles (beyond mere token appearances). Numerous research studies have documented this progress, and more are undoubtedly on the horizon.[21] Unfortunately, there are still complaints about alleged national-advertiser discrimination against minority- and female-owned broadcast stations.[22]

Political Concerns

Advocates and critics of political advertising on television and radio have become progressively more vocal in recent years. One side holds that competing candidates for public office have just as much right to the airwaves as competing products do; after all, both kinds of messages are designed to inform and persuade, lend themselves to communication through aural and moving visual channels, and reach a majority of American consumers and voters easily, efficiently, and repeatedly day after day.

The other side, however, maintains that politicians are not at all like bars of soap. Although the latter can be purchased and (if so desired) discarded in a matter of minutes, the former, once elected, may hold powerful offices for four years or longer. Clearly, these people feel, consumers' decisions here are so much more important, the commercials they see should conform to special standards. For example, some individuals and organizations have advocated a ban on the sale of political time in less than 5-minute segments. Yet, a 1971 amendment to the Communications Act requires that broadcasters give candidates "reasonable access" to the time-controlled airwaves—a term which a number of stations have taken to mean 30- and 60-second spots.

No matter which side you personally feel is right in this case, consider the intended recipients of these commercial messages. Would they benefit more from longer messages on behalf of fewer candidates (and would they really watch and listen carefully) or from shorter messages on behalf of more candidates (and would they really remember what was said and shown)? Research has found that political commercial recall is highly related to candidate preference. People remember more information from a preferred candidate's commercials than they do from opponents' commercials.[23]

Looking Behind the Scenes

Occasionally, broadcasters are criticized for what seem to be irresponsible acts but which, in fact, are far from deliberate. Let us consider just one example—the complaint that a station has aired competitive commercials too close together, especially when their respective claims seem to cancel each other out. What advertisers and/or audiences may fail to realize is that extenuating circumstances sometimes force even the most responsible stations into scheduling quandaries.

For example, a Dial soap commercial aired close to one for Dove may be a *make-good* called for because a technical difficulty prohibited clear transmission of the spot at its earlier, scheduled time (and the slot next to the Dove commercial was the only one readily available). Or, American Air Lines and Continental spots might appear together because both had been postponed from previously separated slots, following a widely publicized plane crash. (In such cases, concerned advertisers frequently do pull their commercials in an attempt to minimize negative listener and viewer reactions stemming from the unfortunate occurrence and its related news coverage.) Finally, a local fire or flood may necessitate a damaged goods sale, calling for the immediate airing of commercials by the store involved. Sometimes, these squeezed in spots wind up very close to those for competing establishments.

The Challenge

One last finding from the AAAA consumer attitude study is worthy of note in concluding this chapter. The study was a follow-up to one conducted 10 years earlier and showed a general increase in public skepticism regarding advertising's value as a socioeconomic force.[24]

Is there any hope that broadcast advertisers can reverse this trend in the future? Fortunately, yes. The AAAA report, based on survey results, contains a strong implication that the key to improving the public's attitude toward advertising lies to a large extent in creating commercials that are more useful, more credible, and more enjoyable than those on the air today.[25]

That does not mean, as some members of society would have us believe, avoidance of so-called persuasive tactics in favor of purely informational ones. Many messages both inform and persuade consumers simultaneously; then again, a given commercial may inform those shoppers not previously familiar with a product and persuade those who are trying to decide between brands. The challenge is to inform without inveigling, to convince without conning, and to help without harassing. One of the most important keys to unlocking this challenge is knowing and understanding those audiences who watch and listen with varying degrees of interest and expectation.

Study Questions

1. How do you feel about the advertising of beer and wine on TV? Does your feeling change depending on the time the commercial is shown and the way in which it is presented?

2. Argue for and against the naming of competitors in radio and TV commercials.

3. Are there any products or services you believe should never be advertised on TV? Why?

4. How would you propose dealing with the problem of TV commercial clutter? Suggest alternatives to establishing time standards and rules for the number of program interruptions and consecutive announcements therein. Remember to be fair to advertisers who depend on the broadcast media for a large part of their survival.

5. Examine an existing local public-service campaign in your area (on either radio or TV). How could it be improved?

6. How do you feel about the issue of TV violence? Do you think advertisers are wise to withdraw commercials from certain programs? What else could and should be done? Why?

7. Discuss your opinion of the current status of women and/or minority groups in TV and radio commercials. What could and should be done in this area?

8. In your opinion, what should be done in the area of children's commercials? Consider both message content and commercial placement.

9. On the issue of political advertising on radio and TV (5-minute segments versus 30- and 60-second spots), how would you decide if you were: (a) a station manager, (b) a political candidate, (c) a product-advertiser competing for air time, (d) an FCC commissioner, or (e) a representative of a consumer-interest group?

ASSIGNMENT 6-A

Examine commercials for one of your favorite products and list the reasons why you believe they do a good job of persuading. Compare your reactions with those of other students and where there are differences, try to identify reasons why.

ASSIGNMENT 6-B

Select a local public-service concern that has not yet received attention in the broadcast media. Prepare a radio or TV announcement for your chosen cause; follow the spirit of work done by the Advertising Council. Exchange messages with another student and provide critiques.

ASSIGNMENT 6-C

Indicate the steps you think should be taken to improve the image of broadcast advertising in society. List the group or groups you believe should take the initiative in each instance and the type of activity that should be initiated.

ASSIGNMENT 6-D

Analyze a selected comparative commercial to determine whether it would meet AAAA standards. Explain why certain parts would and would not be acceptable (even if you think the entire commercial passes the test, see if you can detect areas with which some societal group might take issue).

Intent and Connotation

Significant Competition

Competitor Identification

Related Properties Compared

Honest Comparison

Objective Testing Source

Claims Supported

Proper Conclusions

Significant Value

Testimonial Implications

Notes

1. Charles Atkin, John Hocking, and Martin Block, "Teenage Drinking: Does Advertising Make a Difference?" *Journal of Communication* (Spring 1984):157-67.

2. Charles Atkin and Martin Block, "The Effects of Alcohol Advertising," in Thomas C. Kinnear, ed., *Advances in Consumer Research* (Chicago, Association for Consumer Research) XI(1983):688-93.

3. *Advertising Age* (March 25, 1985):10.

4. Paul C. Feingold and Mark L. Knapp, "Anti-Drug Abuse Commercials," *Journal of Communication* (Winter 1977):20-28.

5. *Advertising Age* (June 7, 1976):14.

6. *Advertising Age* (October 13, 1975).

7. *Advertising Age* (April 18, 1988):88.

8. Rena Bartos and Theodore F. Dunn, *Advertising and Consumers, New Perspectives* (New York: American Association of Advertising Agencies), 44-45.

9. "Evolving Public Attitudes Toward Television and Other Mass Media 1959-1980" (New York: The Roper Organization, Television Information Office, April, 1981), 19-20.

10. *Advertising Age* (March 16, 1987):2.

11. "Your Advertising Council" (New York: Media Department, The Advertising Council).

12. "Free TV Time Abounds for Public Service Messages," *Marketing News* (August 16, 1985):7.

13. *Annual Report* (New York: The Advertising Council, 1972-1973), 4.

14. *Advertising Age* (April 21, 1975):72-76.

15. Bartos and Dunn, *Advertising and Consumers,* 56.

16. John Wilke, Lois Therrien, Amy Dunkin, and Mark N. Vamos, "Are the Programs Your Kids Watch Simply Commercials?" *Business Week* (March 25, 1985):53-54.

17. *Advertising Age* (July 6, 1987):27.

18. Robert W. Kubey, "Television and Aging: Past, Present, and Future," *The Gerontologist* (February 1980):16-35.

19. Elliot S. Schreiber and Douglas A. Boyd, "How the Elderly Perceive Television Commercials," *Journal of Communication* (Winter 1980):61-70.

20. "The Portrayal of Older Americans in Television Commercials, *Journal of Advertising* 16, no. 1(1987):47-54.

21. James D. Culley and Rex O. Bennett, "The Use of Stereotypes in Mass Media Advertising: Blacks in Magazine, Newspaper, and Television Ads," in Leonard W. Lanfranco, ed., *Making Advertising Relevant* (American Academy of Advertising) (1975):132-33; and Bradley Greenberg and Sherrie Mazingo, "Racial Issues in Mass Media Institutions" (Report No. 16, Project CUP: Communication Among the Urban Poor. Department of Communication, Michigan State University), 42-44.

22. *Broadcasting* (September 29, 1986):38.

23. Ronald J. Faber and M. Claire Storey, "Recall of Information from Political Advertising," *Journal of Advertising* 13 (1984):39-44.

24. Bartos and Dunn, *Advertising and Consumers,* 51.

25. *Ibid.,* 84.

Suggested Readings

Cater, Douglass, and Richard Adler. *Television as a Social Force: New Approaches to TV Criticism.* New York: Praeger Publishers, 1975.

Divita, S. F., ed. *Social Responsibility Advertising and the Public Interest.* Chicago: American Marketing Association, 1974.

Liebert, Robert M., John M. Neale, and Emily Davidson. *The Early Window: Effects of Television on Children and Youth.* Elmsford, N.Y.: Pergamon, 1973.

Preston, Ivan L. *The Great American Blow-Up.* Madison: The University of Wisconsin Press, 1975.

ALSO: Check recent issues of *Advertising Age, Broadcasting, Television/Radio Age,* the *Journal of Advertising,* the *Journal of Advertising Research,* the *Journal of Broadcasting,* the *Journal of Marketing,* and *Journalism Quarterly.*

7

Broadcast Media Audiences

As noted in Chapter 1, the purpose of advertising is, essentially, to communicate a persuasive message to prospective users of a product or service. Not all such prospects, however, can be reached with any one message (or even a series of messages) because not all are tuned in to the specific medium carrying the message at a given time, and even if they are listening or watching, all may not be in a receptive mood when the commercial (in its particular delivery form) appears. Although we refer to potential purchasers as people in the *market* for a product or service, those subsets of each market that meet the two criteria expressed above are known as (media) *audiences*.

Both of the electronic media, of course, reached the level of near-universal saturation and acceptance by the American public years ago; however, the overall broadcast audience is both a heterogeneous mass audience and a mosaic of audience subsets. Understanding personal characteristics, therefore, is essential to successful use of these media.

Audience behavior is quite predictable today on an aggregate basis. Overall listening and viewing levels generally follow regular daily and seasonal patterns. But the popularity of specific TV and radio programs constantly fluctuates, thanks in large part to vigorous efforts of competing stations and networks to win large audience shares. A vast amount of expensive research is conducted annually to assist advertisers, agencies, and stations in developing specific schedules appropriate for target-audience needs. (Chapter 13 explores the subject of audience research in detail.)

Growth of Television Households

Although TV broadcasting was officially introduced to the United States just before the start of World War II, because of wartime restrictions, receiving sets could not be manufactured in large quantities until after the war. By 1948, television stations were authorized on a hodge-podge geographical pattern in some 50 scattered U.S. cities. Nevertheless, the growth in TV households began immediately, reaching 9 percent penetration by 1950. TV ownership grew so rapidly that it approached 65 percent in five years and exceeded 90 percent by 1965. Today, as shown in Table 7.1, more than 98 percent of all households in the United States have at least one television set.

The impact of color television, as manifested in the sale of receivers, developed slowly after the FCC adopted color telecasting standards in 1953. However, color TV truly caught the public's fancy in 1965 when all three commercial networks began presenting most of their primetime programming in color. Substantial gains followed in successive years until color-set penetration reached almost universal proportions. Similarly, there has been steady growth in multiset households during recent decades. The latter development enlarged the total amount of viewership by permitting individual selection of programs by family members. In 1989, the A. C. Nielsen Company estimated that 97 percent

Table 7.1. Growth of television households

Year	Total U.S. Households (thousands)	TV Households (thousands)	Percentage with TV	Color TV Homes (thousands)	Percentage of TV Homes	Multiset Homes (thousands)	Percentage of TV Homes
1950	43,000	3,880	9.0	...	...	40	1.0
1955	47,620	30,700	64.5	5	0.0	875	2.9
1960	52,500	45,750	87.1	340	0.7	5,500	12.0
1965	56,900	52,700	92.6	2,810	4.9	10,225	19.4
1970	62,700	59,700	95.2	20,910	35.7	18,840	32.2
1975	70,520	68,500	97.1	46,850	68.4	28,360	41.4
1980	77,900	76,300	97.9	63,350	83.0	38,260	50.1
1985	86,530	84,900	98.1	77,660	91.5	48,220	56.8
1990	93,900	92,100	98.1	89,300	97.0	58,000	63.0

Sources: NBC, 1950-74; A. C. Nielsen Co., 1975-89 (used with permission from Nielsen Media Research).

of all U.S. households had at least one color TV set and that 63 percent had two or more television sets.[1] In addition, by the end of 1989, approximately 57 percent of all U.S. households subscribed to cable television, and about 65 percent had home videotape (VCR) equipment.

Characteristics of U.S. Television Households

During the first decade of American television broadcasting, set ownership exhibited an uneven distribution through society. Early TV receivers were expensive, resulting in a higher level of set ownership among upper-income than among lower-income families. In addition, set ownership was especially heavy among urban households, young homes, and homes with large families. Set ownership also was most concentrated in the Northeast, where most pioneer TV stations were located, and least concentrated in the South.

Television set ownership, which stood at more than 92 million households at the beginning of 1990, approaches the universal level in all sections of the United States and among all levels of society. Of the more than 227 million persons over two years of age who live in TV households, the vast majority live in an urban or suburban environment. With adults now making up about 75 percent of our population, the ratio of adults (18 and older) to nonadults in television homes has risen from 2:1 to 3:1 within the past 15 years.

Growth of Radio Households

Radio broadcasting, which officially began in 1920 with only a few thousand receiving sets, quickly became a popular medium of communication. The number of radio-equipped households grew to an estimated 5.5 million, or roughly 20 percent of all U.S. homes, by September 1925.

The public's eagerness for radio was so intense that Secretary of Commerce Herbert Hoover, addressing the first national radio conference in 1922, described it as "one of the most astounding things that has come under my observation of American life."[2] The percentage of radio-equipped homes continued to increase, reaching 30 percent by 1929, 66 percent by 1935, and about 87 percent by 1941. The 97-percent level was attained in 1952, according to the Radio Advertising Bureau, which estimated in 1987 that 99 percent of all U.S. homes had at least one radio.[3]

Despite many changes in radio broadcasting since the advent of television, radio set ownership has continued to expand. At the beginning of 1988, Americans owned an estimated 505 million radio receivers, an average of 5.4 sets per household. That total includes about 366 million home or personal receivers and 129 million radios in automobiles.[4]

Recently, the sale of radio receivers has averaged more than 45 million sets per year, compared with about 21 million TV sets sold annually. Approximately 84 percent of all radio sets sold each year are now equipped as AM-FM receivers. Table 7.2 provides data on the ownership of radio receivers from 1950 to 1985.

Table 7.2. Estimated radio sets in use, 1950-1985

Year	Radio Sets (Except Auto) (thousands)	Automobile Sets (thousands)	Total Sets (thousand)	Number of Sets per Household
1950	67,200	18,000	85,200	2.0
1955	92,000	29,000	121,000	2.5
1960	116,007	40,387	156,394	3.0
1965	171,408	56,871	228,279	4.0
1970	240,200	80,500	320,700	5.1
1975	301,200	100,400	401,600	5.7
1980	341,000	112,000	453,000	5.5
1985	380,000	127,000	507,000	5.4

Source: Radio Advertising Bureau, from *Television Factbook*, 1986-87 ed., No. 55, A-18 (used with permission from Warren Publishing, Inc.).

Location of Radio Sets

While radio set count has increased consistently during the past four decades, listening patterns have changed dramatically. Once the principal home entertainment parlor medium, radio has been transformed into a personal companion medium, used primarily by individuals in single as opposed to group listening situations. An estimated 41 percent of all rooms have radios (Table 7.3). The estimated share of listening in various locations is shown in Table 7.4.

Table 7.3. Location of radio sets in the home

Room	Percentage
Living room	67.0
Bedroom	58.4
Kitchen	49.8
Den/family room	21.9
Dining room	9.3
Bathroom	7.2
Other	38.4

Source: Radio Advertising Bureau.

Table 7.4. Radio listening by location

	At Home	In Cars	Other Places
	(percentage)		
Teens 12-17	69.2	15.5	15.3
Men 18+	40.7	28.5	30.8
Women 18+	60.0	17.2	22.8
All persons 12+	52.5	21.9	25.6

Source: Radio Advertising Bureau.

Today's radio has moved into offices and business establishments, farmlands and beaches, lakes and mountains, and most important of all, into 95 percent of the nation's automobiles.[5] The slogan, "Wherever you go, there's radio," continues to be very appropriate; and, certainly, radio's mobility has provided additional opportunities for successful advertising through careful media selection.

Radio and Television Set Usage

In practical time-buying situations, the media specialist must understand the complexities of radio and TV set usage in detail. To what extent is broadcasting's vast potential audience converted into actual listeners and viewers? What are the characteristics of different audience groups? And how can these specific target audiences be reached most effectively through the broadcast media?

The total amount of all television or radio set usage at any given time is usually expressed as a percentage of the total potential audience. For this purpose, the terms *homes-using-television* (HUT) and *persons-using-radio* have been adopted by audience measurement firms to indicate the estimated audience levels for TV and radio, respectively. For example, a HUT figure of 60 indicates that 60 of every 100 homes equipped with television had a set turned on at a particular time. How the audience was divided between competing stations, networks, and cable services, of course, is a different matter, related to the quality of reception and program popularity. The subject of audience *shares* will be covered in Chapter 13.

Americans spend an impressive amount of time each day with television and radio. Research by the A. C. Nielsen Company reveals that today's typical family watches TV an average of more than seven hours a day on an annual basis. This amount of viewing, of course, is subject to seasonal variations. The amount of viewing time, as Table 7.5 illustrates, increased steadily from 1950 through 1985.

Table 7.5. Average time spent viewing television per household per day

Year	Average Hours per Day
1950	4 hr. 35 min.
1955	4 hr. 51 min.
1960	5 hr. 6 min.
1965	5 hr. 29 min.
1970	5 hr. 56 min.
1975	6 hr. 7 min.
1980	6 hr. 36 min.
1985	7 hr. 10 min.
1986	7 hr. 8 min.
1988	7 hr. 2 min.

Source: Nielsen annual averages (used with permission from Nielsen Media Research).

Broadcasters and advertising executives pay close attention to viewing levels, particularly since new technological developments have fostered increased competition for viewers. Traditional broadcasters are particularly concerned with any slippage in the audience of broadcast channels due to cable and VCR competition.

Although total viewing has remained at a very high level, some notable changes have occurred within the total viewing framework. Substantial viewership shares have been carved out of total viewing hours by cable networks, pay television, and hundreds of new independent stations. Where the three networks once controlled about 95 percent of primetime viewing, their dominance has been reduced to 70 to 75 percent. A later section of this chapter will examine viewing patterns by broadcast and nonbroadcast television.

As television viewing grew during the early 1950s, the American public devoted less of its leisure time to radio. By the end of that decade, however, in-home radio listening had stabilized at slightly less than two hours per day per family. That level persisted throughout the 1960s and 1970s, although out-of-home listening increased dramatically. In 1989, according to the Radio Advertising Bureau, adults 18 and older listened to radio an average of three hours per day (both at home and away). The heaviest listening levels were recorded by men and women in the 18-24 age groups, and the lightest levels were registered by men and women over the age of 50. Hours of daily listening by various demographic groups are shown in Table 7.6.

Table 7.6. Daily time spent listening to radio (Monday - Sunday)

				Ages			
	12+	Teens	18+	18-24	25-34	35-49	50+
				(*hours: minutes*)			
Men	...	...	3:01	3:35	3:17	3:01	2:29
Women	...	...	2:59	3:28	2:54	3:01	2:46
Men and women	2:57	2:32	...	...	...	...	...

Source: Radio Advertising Bureau.

Daily radio listening among two important ethnic groups—African-Americans and Hispanic-Americans—significantly exceeds the general population averages shown in Table 7.6. Hours of daily listening for these ethnic groups are shown in Table 7.7.

Table 7.7. Daily time spent listening to radio (Monday - Sunday)

	Blacks	Hispanic Americans	General U.S. Population
		(*hours: minutes*)	
Men and women 12+	3:51	3:48	2:57
Men 18+	3:49	3:41	3:01
Women 18+	4:02	4:04	2:59

Source: Radio Advertising Bureau.

A 1979 Simmons study found that professional/managerial men used radio 42 percent more each day than they did TV. Single working adults spent 34 percent more time with radio, and upper-income men used radio 33 percent more. For adults in upper-income households, radio claimed a 14 percent greater audience, and for adults in the 18-24 age bracket, the figure was 40 percent higher.[6]

DAILY AUDIENCE PATTERNS

Listening and viewing patterns strongly suggest a complementary rather than a competitive relationship between the two electronic media, though both have high and low periods of usage. Radio achieves its highest audience levels from 6 to 10 A.M. as stations provide light entertainment and valuable information to assist listeners in starting the day. Millions are awakened by clock radios, hear the news while they eat, check their watches against radio time, and dress according to weather reports supplied by radio. In most major cities, radio stations also provide commuters with useful traffic information.

By midmorning, in-home radio listening begins to drop, and the decline progresses through the day. But overall radio listening (including out-of-home) exceeds that of television until mid-to-late afternoon. During late afternoon drive time, which varies somewhat with local business schedules and commuting hours, listening picks up again as stations escort listeners home with more traffic information, music, news, market reports, sports, and weather. Finally, radio's audience declines to its lowest level of the day during evening (prime television) hours.

Although TV's in-home audience trails that of radio until midmorning, the number of households using TV increases throughout the day as more and more people have time to watch. Viewership increases sharply toward the late afternoon when students come home from school and working adults return from their jobs. A high level of viewing is normally maintained during the early evening when most stations offer network and local newscasts. Television attracts its greatest audience, often exceeding 60 percent of all households, during evening primetime viewing hours (generally from 8 to 11 P.M.) when elaborate network entertainment is presented.[7] TV's audience then gradually declines as viewers retire for the evening, and drops off sharply by 11:30 P.M. after late news broadcasts.

Clearly, radio's greatest potential for most advertisers lies in its ability to reach large audiences during the morning and substantial but somewhat smaller audiences during midday and afternoon drive time. Hence, the two drive-time periods are usually regarded as radio's primetime. Television's audience level becomes significantly large by afternoon, exceeding that of radio from late afternoon hours through the rest of the evening. Thus, it is during these hours that TV advertising is most in demand. Figure 7.1 charts overall audience patterns for radio and television for a typical broadcast day.

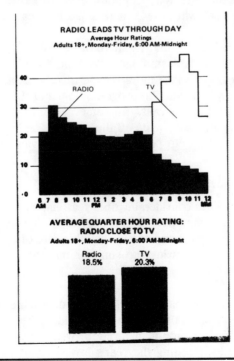

Fig. 7.1. Average radio and TV usage per day. (Courtesy of Radio Advertising Bureau)

Increased attention also is being given to the crossover audience between television and radio. Recent studies suggest, for example, that heavy primetime TV viewers tend to be heavy radio listeners, too, between 6 and 10 A.M. And many advertisers have used both radio and TV successfully during so-called off-hour periods. Television and radio rates are scaled to correspond closely with audience levels at various times of the day.

For the first 60 years of broadcasting, AM was the dominant radio service. Although the superiority of frequency modulation was well known, FM broadcasting languished for more than three decades after its beginnings around 1940. The public's enthusiasm for FM radio developed slowly, much as it did for color television; however, a significant shift toward FM occurred during the late 1970s. By 1980, FM's share of audience surpassed that of AM in the nation's combined metropolitan (MSA) communities. According to Arbitron data published in Duncan's *American Radio,* FM accounted for 71 percent of all radio listening in measured MSA markets during Spring 1988.[8]

The impact of FM varies somewhat on a market-by-market basis. FM listening in such markets as Evansville, Lancaster, and Lansing exceeded 90 percent in 1987. However, FM levels in many of the largest cities, including New York, Los Angeles, Chicago, Boston, St. Louis, and San Francisco were substantially lower, ranging from 60 to 68 percent. In these same markets, some AM stations even now consistently register among the top five stations in their areas. Markets ranking even lower in FM listenership, usually in the 50 to 60 percent range, include Asheville, Amarillo, Honolulu, and Stockton.[9]

The dominance of FM radio represents a fundamental change in the listening patterns of Americans. The once-laggard medium has benefitted greatly from increased set sales, especially those in automobiles; superior sound quality; and stereophonic sound transmission. The FCC's encouragement of separate programming on commonly owned AM and FM outlets resulted in the introduction of attractive programming, further stimulating FM listenership. As it grew into the choice radio medium, the FM service blossomed into a full spectrum of music-based formats, allowing effective targeting of audiences through demographically oriented programs. FM's greatest acceptance has been among teenagers and younger adult listeners, while AM has retained its greatest loyalty among older listeners.

Today, AM broadcasters, with their minority share of the listening audience, must seek innovative ways to remain viable. Indeed, some AM stations have gone silent because they lost the ability to compete effectively. Attempts at making AM more competitive have included the introduction of AM stereo, greater emphasis on talk and information programming, and the development of nostalgic music and other niche formats. Although there is cause for some pessimism, especially for low-power, urban AM stations, few industry leaders completely write off the AM service. High-powered outlets, particularly those on clear channels, should continue to provide a valuable service to listeners and advertisers well into the future.

SEASONAL VARIATIONS IN VIEWING AND LISTENING

Time devoted to television varies considerably on a seasonal basis and slightly on a regional basis. Inasmuch as one of TV's biggest competitors is the outdoors, viewing is heaviest during the winter months when daylight hours are shortened and outside activities are often limited by weather conditions. On the other hand, viewing is lightest during the summer months when long daylight hours permit outdoor enjoyment until 9 or 10 P.M.

A. C. Nielsen data show that January historically produces the season's highest daily viewing levels—now approaching seven and one-half hours per household. This peak occurs, of course, during what is usually the most severe winter month in terms of weather and early darkness. Then viewing declines through the spring months, reaching the year's lowest levels in the vacation months of June and July (about five and one-half hours in the early 1980s). Normally, the summer TV audience is about three-fourths as large as the winter one. Viewing levels reverse again in September, with the start of the new TV season, rising toward the fall-winter peak.

The influence of seasons also is noticeable in the level of viewing during different hours of the day. As Table 7.8 illustrates, although seasonal variations are minimal during the morning and early afternoon hours, they are distinct during late afternoon and evening hours. Note that the peak viewing hour occurs progressively later in the evening as summer approaches.

Table 7.8. Average percentage of TV households using television, 1988

	7AM	9AM	11AM	1PM	3PM	5PM	7PM	9PM	11PM
Sept/Aug. average	10	20	22	28	30	37	52	60	54
February	12	24	25	31	34	43	60	68	61
July	8	18	22	26	28	29	40	57	48

(Used with permission from Nielsen Media Research.)

Finally, television usage levels, to a limited degree, reflect local and regional weather conditions. During the winter, viewing tends to be heaviest in the North and lightest in the deep South. All such variations are reflected in advertising time costs charged by stations and networks.

In-home radio listening remains relatively constant throughout the year. In contrast to TV, however, radio does gain additional audiences during the summer season when millions of car and portable radios are used more extensively by an out-of-home public.

Audience Composition

The term *audience composition* generally refers to the demographic makeup of a television or radio audience at any given time or for any particular program. Audience composition data tell us the proportions of men, women, and children within the audience, as well as their age groups and other characteristics. Because each program is somewhat unique in its audience attraction, a general understanding of audience composition is helpful to those involved both in buying and in selling broadcast time.

The characteristics of broadcast audiences are determined to a large extent by the nature of listeners and viewers available at any given time, and are limited by work and school schedules and competing leisure pursuits. TV viewers generally watch at home, or in public places where TV sets are located. Radio's available audience is greater because it includes individuals in radio-equipped automobiles and those with portable receivers, as well as persons who are at home; in addition, many individuals use radios while they are at work. Potentially, therefore, the broadcast media can reach a large heterogeneous audience during evening hours, but the available daytime audience, especially in the case of TV, is weighted toward homemakers and retired persons.

THE TELEVISION AUDIENCE
Viewing levels in television households vary according to the characteristics of those households. For example, in November 1987, those that viewed the most were households having three or more people, pay cable households, and households with nonadults. Even the lowest viewing group, single-person households, had their sets on more than 37 hours a week, almost as much as most people spend at their jobs.[10]

As a general rule, women view television more than men, and older men and women tend to watch more than younger adults. Younger children view more than older children and teenagers. The Nielsen Television Index (NTI) also reveals that women over 55 are the heaviest TV users and teenage girls are the lightest. Women also outnumber men as viewers of primetime evening programs of all types other than sports. Despite this viewing pattern, evening viewership represents television's closest approximation to a universal mass audience. According to NTI estimates, about 96 million people watched TV between 8 and 11 P.M., local time, on an average day in November 1987.[11]

Sunday evening is the most popular night for TV viewing. Monday is the runner-up, followed by Thursday, Tuesday, Wednesday, Friday, and, finally, Saturday. Nielsen estimates that 105.8 million people watched Sunday primetime television during November 1987 and, even on Saturdays, viewership exceeded 87 million persons in an average primetime minute.[12]

Television also reaches selective target audiences during certain time periods. As suggested above, daytime hours are particularly useful for reaching homemakers. Late weekday afternoons and Saturday mornings attract large audiences of children. Many employed persons may be reached during early evening. However, television's most elusive audience—adult males—may be reached only as part of the large primetime audience, or, in more concentrated numbers, during news and sports broadcasts.

One of the newest innovations in television viewing has been the widespread ownership of home videocassette recorders (VCRs). TV households tend to use their VCRs mainly to play rented tapes such as movies and other nonbroadcast material and to record broadcast programs for later viewing. Such *timeshifting* involves taping one program while watching another, thus avoiding a forced choice, or taping shows automatically at times when the viewer cannot watch television. Recent Nielsen studies have shown that most recording is done during primetime (41 percent) and weekday daytime (29 percent). Most recordings are made when the television set is off, and 67 percent of all recordings are of programs telecast by network stations.[13] Playback activity, which includes use of rented tapes in addition to home recordings, is strongest on the weekend with Saturday evening the highest.[14]

THE RADIO AUDIENCE

Although the radio audience is much more evenly balanced between men and women than is the television audience, listening patterns often differ markedly among individual stations. In yet another comparison, radio is used extensively by teenagers, a light TV-viewing group, who represent a significant segment of the total radio audience. During the school year, of course, teens listen most during after-school hours and on weekends.

During the day, when radio's audience is at its highest level, adult women outnumber men by approximately a 6:4 ratio; but the ratio approaches 1:1 during afternoon drive time when commuting men and working women have greater access to radio. Males generally outnumber females during the evening hours, partly because of sportscasts.

AUDIENCE CONCENTRATION AND FRAGMENTATION

In a final note of comparison, fewer television stations normally compete for the viewing audience than radio stations for the listening audience. Television households, however, must be regarded as two separate universes—cable homes and noncable homes. In 1988 each accounted for about 50 percent of all households. Cable subscribers may have 30 or more programmed channels, including broadcast and nonbroadcast sources, from which to choose. Fewer choices are available to the noncable households that receive only network, independent, and public TV stations; however, Nielsen reports that, as of 1987, 71 percent of U.S. TV households received nine or more television stations.[15] (See Figure 7.2.)

In both universes, traditional network-affiliated stations garner the largest share of the audience. In noncable homes, three network stations usually attract an aggregate of about 80 percent of all

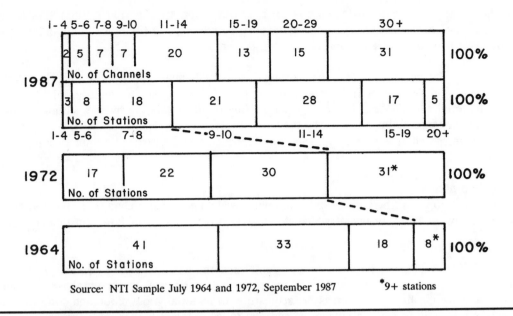

Fig. 7.2. Stations and channels receivable per TV household, percentage share of TV households. (Courtesy of Nielsen Media Research)

viewing, with the rest shared by a few independent and public stations. In the wired universe, the networks usually attract about 65 percent of primetime viewers, while an abundance of cable networks, pay services, and independent stations fragment the remaining viewership into numerous narrow target audiences. In this anomalous situation, the dominance of national network-affiliated TV stations gives advertisers access to mass audiences, while the narrowcasting cable networks fragment a lesser portion of the audience into easily targeted demographic and special interest audiences.

Despite the situation just described, cautious observers note a steady decline in aggregate viewing of network stations due to improved programming on both independent and public TV outlets and the attractiveness of an ever-increasing number of cable networks. The increasing number of cable subscriptions also accentuates the trend toward more nonnetwork viewing. Nielsen's 1988 report on television stated that cable subscribers tend to view more TV than noncable households and pay-TV households watch even more. On an aggregate basis, cable network and pay-cable programming reach audiences of significant size during primetime hours.

The number of radio stations in a given market almost always exceeds the number of available TV signals, often by a 5:1 ratio. With rare exceptions, radio listenership is highly fragmented in most U.S. markets. Because of the proliferation of radio outlets, few stations attract average quarter-hour shares greater than 20 percent; leading stations in large cities, which may have 40 or more radio stations, rarely attract more than 10 to 12 percent shares. The result of the fragmentation of the radio audience with segmented programming is twofold. First, an advertiser can reach a large mass audience via radio, but only by including four, five, or perhaps even more individual stations in a media plan in any given market. Second, an advertiser can reach audience subsets of specific demographic or ethnic character by placing schedules on individual stations that have developed audience loyalties among selected target groups.

Unfortunately, many media planners must be content with limited demographic data in making daily decisions. In some cases, additional quantitative information is available on (1) audience shopping and buying behavior (for example, where, when, and how often people shop, and how much they buy and spend in terms of product classes and specific brands); (2) ownership and activity patterns (for example, how many cars people own and how far they travel in a given period of time, how many clubs they belong to, and how often they participate in sports activities); and (3) educational and occupational status, along with family size and total purchasing power.

Obviously, the more data the better, though much of it may be expensive and time consuming to gather. Even more important and harder to come by is *psychographic* information: highly qualitative, attitudinal material that sheds light on why people buy or do not buy, why they choose to watch or listen or to refrain from doing so, and why they are attracted to or repelled by particular products and services, companies and stores, programs and commercials, and even specific appeals and production techniques.

Emerging Life-styles

In the past 20 years, the United States has witnessed some massive changes in basic values, goals, and outlooks toward living, many of which are having direct effects on how consumers spend their money.

Focus on self. The traditional emphasis on self-denial and the downplaying of personal drives in favor of family needs, company norms, and peer pressures has given way to an emphasis on individual pleasures and accomplishments. Whereas the acquisition of material goods stood and continues to stand for advancement on life's various ladders of success, today there also is much concern given to self-esteem and the satisfaction derived from increased leisure time.

Pluralism. Men and women of the 1980s have found they can lead alternate life-styles, depending on circumstances and time of day or year. People hold more than one type of job, live different places during different seasons, and belong to clubs and organizations that cater to vastly different interests. Young and old alike are seen on jogging trails, behind administrative desks, and in college classrooms, while both men and women do the weekly grocery shopping and care for the house and children.

Focus on time. The value of time is approaching that of money in many respects. Americans cry out against inflation, but they are learning to live with it as an inevitable occurrence (like death and taxes). The loss of time, however, to tasks deemed meaningless or unproductive, is much harder to take.

Morality. Private morals do not claim as much attention as they once did. What was morally wrong for individuals and families of past generations now is tolerated and even acceptable within limits. Ethical eyes have turned toward institutions, business, government, education, the military, and the medical and legal communities. Many a skeptical glance is directed toward their modus operandi, keeping spokespersons for these groups often on the defensive.[16]

Now, what does all of this mean to the broadcast advertiser? For one thing, greater care must be given to media strategy. As people seek the "rich, full life," they demand an increasing amount of information, faster than ever before and available to them at ever more convenient times. And as more commercials beg for air time, they will have to be shorter and more hard hitting just to get through the clutter.

Turning to creative concerns, we find a need for multiple-role models in commercials. A woman may be a full-fledged career woman, a homemaker, and a participant in social and civic activities. A man too may wear several different hats—businessman and babysitter, athlete and investor, volunteer and cook. The personal benefits derived from products and services will be emphasized as never before, as the "me orientation" runs its course. Hence, the effects of traditional creative approaches will have to be monitored carefully; classic status symbols, humorous appeals, and price/value stories may require some major renovations.

Inputs from Behavioral Science

Sometimes broadcast advertising can borrow knowledge gained from behavioral science research. The following examples illustrate how such findings can aid media sales personnel in promotional endeavors and media buyers in crucial station-selection processes:

Repetition. Research shows that people learn most effectively when they are exposed to information over a period of time (across day parts, stations, or even media).[17] Also, people's rate of forgetting tends to be very rapid immediately after learning; an initial recall figure of around 60 percent drops quickly and levels off at about 30 percent after two to four weeks.[18] The frequency of broadcast commercial exposure, therefore, is an important advertiser concern.

Involvement. When mechanical skills are involved, psychologists have found that learning is enhanced when people can place themselves (mentally if not physically) in the roles of performers.[19] In other words, if a person can see a task completed as it would appear if he or she were doing the job personally, the gain, from a learning point of view, should be maximal. Advertisers whose products fall into such categories would probably do well to include television in their broadcast buys.

Source credibility. Although respect for authority is learned at an early age and more or less accepted throughout a lifetime, the value of including an authoritative source in a commercial is debatable. Some studies suggest that the positive effects derived are temporary and tend to wear off before any actual purchasing behavior occurs.[20] Yet advertisers often flock to secure the talents of respected film stars, recording artists, and athletes. It would behoove them, however, to check the credibility of, say, a local radio or TV newscaster before using him or her as a commercial spokesperson. One may be more popular in terms of program ratings but would actually lose prestige if associated with certain types of commercial presentations.

On the other hand, companies suffering from negative images may benefit greatly from the positive association of strong radio and TV personalities, especially if target audiences hold highly favorable attitudes toward the broadcast media themselves. (A 1975 R. H. Bruskin study found that 82 percent of U.S. adults considered television the most influential advertising medium.)

Attention levels. Advertisers are justifiably concerned about the amount of attention viewers and listeners give to their commercials. The power of television to attract audiences is obvious, given its capabilities; however, additional research is needed to understand more fully the degree to which various types of programs and commercials command attention and hold interest. It is widely accepted that viewers pay greater attention to evening TV programs and commercials than to those aired during the day because of differing viewing circumstances and distractions. Homemakers who watch daytime TV are often simultaneously engaged in work activities; hence, some daytime viewing consists of listening to the TV audio, while glancing periodically toward the set. Evening viewing, in contrast, tends to involve individuals more fully because they are less likely to be preoccupied.

One of the advantages claimed for radio is the fact that it can be used while listeners perform other activities. Thus, radio's attention level is naturally lower than that of television. But because radio programming varies from background music to foreground information broadcasts, it is reasonable to assume that attention levels vary, perhaps significantly.

Although further study of attention levels in both radio and television is needed, it is obvious that successful commercials must be distinctive. Chapters 9 and 10 will discuss some proven techniques of creating effective commercial messages, after we take a look at the program environment within and around which commercials are housed.

Study Questions

1. Amidst all of the clamor over televised sex and violence, the sameness of programming, and the rapid demise of a number of series each year (indicating public disfavor), how do you account for the ever increasing number of hours spent by Americans with TV?

2. Do you think that radical changes in radio or TV programming would result in significantly altered listening or viewing patterns by the American public? Explain your answer.

3. Chapter 7 noted some social-psychological studies of value in planning effective broadcast advertising campaigns (for example, those dealing with repetition, involvement, source credibility, and attention levels). What other behavioral science concerns do you perceive as helpful in this regard?

4. Thinking of your own program preferences, or those of friends and relatives, explain the appeal of specific programs and personalities on both radio and television.

ASSIGNMENT 7-A

For a period of one week, keep a diary of your personal radio listening and TV viewing. Then make a chart indicating (a) the total amount of listening and viewing, (b) the average daily amount, and (c) the percentage of listening to AM and FM stations, VHF and UHF stations, and network and independent stations.

ASSIGNMENT 7-B

Consulting your data obtained for assignment 7-A, make a list of programs you heard or watched, dividing them into the following categories: (a) high level of attention, (b) medium level of attention, and (c) low level of attention. List a few reasons why the respective programs received these attention levels.

Notes

1. *1989 Report on Television* (Northbrook, Ill.: A. C. Nielsen, 1989).
2. Department of Commerce, "Minutes of Open Meeting of Department of Commerce Conference on Radio Telephony," (1922, mimeographed), 2.
3. *Radio Facts 1987-1988* (New York: Radio Advertising Bureau, 1987), 3.
4. *Ibid.*, 5-6.
5. *Ibid.*, 6.
6. See *Broadcasting* (February 23, 1981).
7. The evening network schedule is presented from 7 to 10 P.M. in the central standard time zone.
8. James H. Duncan, Jr., *American Radio: Spring 1988* (Kalamazoo, Mich.: Duncan's American Radio, August 1988). 13(1):A3.
9. *Ibid.*, A18.
10. *1988 Report on Television*, 7.
11. *Ibid.*, 9-10.
12. *Ibid.* 10.
13. *Ibid.* 12.
14. *1987 Nielsen Report on Television* (Northbrook, Ill.: A. C. Nielsen, 1987), 2.
15. *1988 Report on Television*, 2.
16. See Florence R. Skelly. "Emerging Attitudes and Life Styles" (Paper from the annual meeting, American Association of Advertising Agencies, White Sulphur Springs, W.Va., May 16-19, 1979).
17. Steuart Henderson Britt, "How Advertising Can Use Psychology's Rules of Learning," *Printer's Ink* 252 (September 23, 1955):74-80.

18. Carl I. Hovland, Irving L. Janis, and Harold H. Kelly, *Communications and Persuasion* (New Haven, Conn.: Yale University Press, 1953), 245.

19. Britt, "Rules of Learning."

20. Arthur R. Cohen, *Attitude Change and Social Influence* (New York: Basic Books, 1964).

Suggested Readings

Beyond the Ratings. New York: Arbitron, 1978-present.

Bower, Robert T. *The Changing Television Audience in America*. New York: Columbia University Press, 1985.

Comstock, George et al. *Television and Human Behavior*. Santa Monica, Calif.: Rand, 1975.

Division, W. Phillips, James Boylan, and Frederick T. C. Yu. *Mass Media Systems and Effects*. New York: Praeger 1977.

Duncan, James H., Jr. *American Radio*. Indianapolis, Ind.: Duncan's American Radio.

Frank, Ronald E., and Marshall G. Greenberg. *Audiences for Public Television*. Beverly Hills, Calif.: Sage, 1982.

Frank, Ronald E., and Marshall G. Greenberg. *The Public's Use of Television: Who Watches and Why*. Beverly Hills, Calif.: Sage, 1980.

Nielsen Report on Television. Northbrook, Ill.: A. C. Nielsen.

Radio Facts. New York: Radio Advertising Bureau.

8

Television and Radio Programming

Programming is at the very heart of successful broadcast advertising; it is the essential element that attracts viewers and listeners. Alert media buyers need a working knowledge of the fundamentals of TV and radio programming, as do all those within the broadcasting industry who try to attract audiences. This chapter provides an understanding of programming fundamentals through emphasis on program schedules, sources of programs, programming strategies, and the relationship between commercials and program fare.

Television Programming

Six types of telecommunications organizations provide TV programming to the U.S. public—television networks, network affiliated stations, independent TV stations, public TV networks and stations, cable networks, and cable television systems.

The primary source of broadcast programming in the United States is the commercial networks, which originate programs and secure television productions from outside sources. ABC, CBS, and NBC each provide approximately 90 hours of programs each week to some 200 individual stations, both network-owned and network-affiliated local outlets. A fourth organization, the Fox Broadcasting Company, provides a limited-time network service that is carried by more than 100 affiliated stations.

Local television stations regard their networks as major sources of programming and fill as much as 70 percent of their weekly schedules with network material. Unlike affiliates, however, independent stations must program all of their airtime from other sources. Those independents that have affiliated with the Fox Network receive roughly 10 percent of a typical weekly schedule from that source. Independent stations must rely heavily on syndicated programming, such as movies, network reruns, and original syndicated shows, as well as local-live productions. The amount and the quality of syndicated programming products have improved immensely during recent years, due in part to barter arrangements, enabling independent TV stations to compete more effectively with network outlets.

Although we are concerned mainly with commercial broadcasting, it is important to note that public television now commands a significant audience in many markets. The Public Broadcasting Service (PBS) provides an extensive schedule of daytime and evening programming, including instructional, cultural, and public affairs broadcasts. Local stations supplement the national feed with their own material, much as commercial network affiliates do. Many of the programs on both the PBS national service and local public TV stations are underwritten by commercial businesses as part of their public relations activities.

For half or more of today's audience, the viewing options also include cable networks and local cable-originated programming. Although originally a provider of better reception of over-the-air television stations, cable TV now originates a great amount of its own programming. As with broadcast television, cable networks are the primary source. Many advertising-supported cable networks exist, as well as pay-cable networks, all of which feed their material to local cable systems by satellite. In addition, as noted earlier, a few large-market independent TV stations, commonly called superstations, are widely carried by cable systems. Superstations, along with the more specialized cable networks, attract national advertising for their widespread audiences.

Locally, cable systems sometimes provide community news and public affairs programming, especially in small cities that do not have local broadcast TV stations. Local cable advertising may be sold on local origination channels and as inserts on cable network programming. Local cable programming considerations will be discussed later in this chapter.

NETWORK PROGRAMMING

Network programming efforts are directed toward two principal goals: (1) reaching as large an audience as possible at any given time, particularly among those viewers who exhibit the demographic characteristics sought by advertisers, and (2) reaching all of the desirable, specialized audience subsets at some time during the week. Each network tries to develop a diversified program schedule with sufficient appeal to compete effectively for viewership and advertisers.

During TV's formative years, networks produced most of the programs they broadcast. Today they obtain practically all of their primetime programming and much of their daytime material from outside production sources. Such familiar names as Universal Television, Quinn-Martin, Columbia Pictures TV, Paramount Television, Norman Lear's TAT Productions, and MTM Productions dominate the schedules. In addition, TV agents, who book jobs for actors and actresses (usually through major production studios), also package programs — complete with producers, directors, writers, and stars — and sell them to the networks. The "big three" program and performer agents in the TV business today are the William Morris Agency, International Creative Management (ICM), and the Creative Artists Agency. ICM, for example, has supplied to the networks such packaged primetime series as "Taxi," "Archie Bunker's Place," "Charlie's Angels," and "The Waltons." The networks themselves produce their own news, public affairs, and sports programs as well as numerous daytime serial dramas.

All programs purchased are carefully scrutinized by network administrators and by advertisers and their agencies before they are accepted; production companies submit *pilot* shows for examination and review. Such representative programs are often pretested through theater screenings before live audiences, or they are actually broadcast as special telecasts, so the networks can analyze at-home audience reaction. Specific network schedules are normally announced each spring for the fall season beginning in September.

Network program budgets relate closely to the potential audience that may be attracted during various *day-parts*, or times of the day and week. During the 1987-88 season, primetime network programming expenditures averaged approximately $1 million per hour, while elaborate entertainment specials, blockbuster movies, and major sports telecasts cost even more. Networks have paid such staggering prices as $10 million to show *The Godfather*, $5 million for *Gone With The Wind*, and $4 million for *Dr. Zhivago*. In contrast, daytime TV programs are budgeted by the networks at a fraction of nighttime cost figures. In fact, an entire week of daytime soap operas—five hours of programming—may be produced for the cost of one primetime hour.

Weekly network schedules may be subdivided into six program blocks: evening primetime, daytime, evening news, early morning, late night, and weekend daytime. The programming scheduled during each period fundamentally reflects the interests of the available audience.

As noted earlier, television's largest audience assembles at night. Under the FCC's primetime access rule, the networks may program three evening hours (except Sunday, when the rule permits four), which they generally fill with programs for adult and family viewing. Daytime network programs, between 10 A.M. and 4 P.M., consist mostly of serial dramas, game shows, and reruns of former primetime shows, intended primarily for homemakers.

Each of the three major TV networks programs a half-hour of news during the early evening, and local affiliates may select from two or more time periods when the newscast is fed through the network system.

Early morning network programming, which consists mainly of news and feature material, serves much the same purpose as early morning radio. NBC pioneered this time period with its long-running "Today" show. ABC's "Good Morning, America" also has been successful. CBS also offers a morning news magazine program. Viewership of these broadcasts consists largely of adults.

The late-night network block, again pioneered by NBC with its "Tonight" show, attracts an audience composed mainly of young adults, including college students, and late-shift factory workers. ABC nightly news talk program, "Nightline," has been very successful in this time period. CBS historically has offered reruns and movies, and the Fox Network has experimented with late-night variety shows. Programming after midnight also may be found on the networks in varying degrees.

Finally, the networks use weekend daytime periods to reach specialized audiences. Saturday mornings are programmed with cartoon shows and other children's fare, and early Saturday afternoon shows often are targeted toward older children and teenagers. Two networks now provide relaxed Sunday morning news magazine programs ("Sunday Today" on NBC and "Sunday Morning" on CBS). However, from an advertising perspective, the most important weekend audience subset is the hard-to-reach adult male, who may be attracted to network sports programs and play-by-play telecasts. Figure 8.1 presents a typical weekly network program schedule.

		7:00	8:00	8:30	9:00	9:30	10:00	10:30
S	ABC	Life Goes On	Free Spirit	Homeroom	ABC Sunday Night Movie		----------------------	
U	CBS	60 Minutes	Murder, She Wrote ----		CBS Sunday Movie ------		----------------------	
N	NBC	World Disney	Sister Kate	My 2 Dads	Sunday Night at Movies		----------------------	
	FOX	Booker	Most Wanted	Hid'n Video	Married/Chl.	Open House	----------------------	
M	ABC		MacGyver ---------------		Monday Night Football		----------------------	
O	CBS		Major Dad	Next Door	M. Brown	Teddy Z	Design Women	Newhart
N	NBC		ALF	Hogan Family	NBC Monday Night Movies		----------------------	
	FOX		21 Jump Street ---------		Alien Nation ----------		----------------------	
T	ABC		Who's Boss	Wonder Yrs.	Roseanne	Moment On	thirty something ----	
U	CBS		Rescue 911 -------------		Wolf -------------------		The Hawaiian --------	
E	NBC		Matlock ---------------		Heat of the Night -----		Midnight Caller -----	
W	ABC		Grow'g Pains	Head/Class	Anything	D. Howser	China Beach ----------	
E	CBS		A Peaceable Kingdom ----		Jake and the Fatman ---		Wiseguy --------------	
D	NBC		Unsolved Mysteries -----		Night Court	Nutt House	Quantum Leap ---------	
T	ABC		Mission Impossible -----		The Kid ---------------		Prime Time ----------	
H	CBS		48 Hours ---------------		Top of the Hill -------		Knots Landing -------	
U	NBC		Cosby Show	Diff. World	Cheers	Dear John	L. A. Law -----------	
F	ABC		Full House	Family Mttrs	Strangers	10 of Us	20/20 ---------------	
R	CBS		Snoops -----------------		Dallas -----------------		Falcon Crest --------	
I	NBC		Bay Watch --------------		Hardball --------------		Mancuso, FBI --------	
S	ABC		Belvedere	Living Dolls	ABC Sat. Mystery Movie		----------------------	
A	CBS		Paradise ---------------		Tour of Duty ----------		West 57th -----------	
T	NBC		227	Amen	Golden Girls	Empty Nest	Hunter --------------	
	FOX		Cops --------—Reporters	-------------		Beyond	Tomorrow	

Fig. 8.1. 1989-90 weekly primetime network TV schedule. (Compiled from various trade publications)

PROGRAMMING BY AFFILIATES

The relationship between networks and their local outlets, as discussed previously, is a contractual one, subject to FCC rules on chain broadcasting. Program managers of affiliated stations usually rely heavily on their networks for the bulk of their program material; in exchange for carrying network commercial broadcasts, each local affiliate receives agreed-upon compensation. Under FCC rules, each individual station licensee is totally responsible for its programming and retains the right to turn down a network program for any reason whatsoever. As a matter of practice, however, affiliates clear most of the network time requested; to do otherwise would increase program costs and risk loss of affiliation. Exceptions sometimes include preemptions of low-rated network shows in favor of better-rated syndicated product and one-time preemptions for broadcasts of high local interest.

Local programming time for network outlets usually consists of a few scattered hours during weekdays (such as before 7 A.M., 9 to 10 A.M., and noon to 1 P.M.); the period from 4 to 8 P.M., except for a half-hour network newscast; and the 11 to 11:30 P.M. slot. (For stations in the central time zone, network feeds are generally one hour earlier than these local times.) Nonnetwork time on weekends includes Saturday morning hours before 8 A.M., some of Sunday morning, and various blocks of time on Saturday and Sunday afternoons, depending upon the amount of sports provided by the networks.

The most important of these blocks is unquestionably the time between 4 and 8 P.M., a transitional period between homemaker-oriented daytime hours and evening primetime programming. It is also a major revenue-producing time for local stations because all advertising availabilities, with the exception of those in the network news, are fully controlled by the stations, and the audience level increases rapidly throughout the period.

The usual highlight of the segment from 4 to 8 P.M. is a news block, consisting of both network input and the local station's news effort. The total amount of time devoted to news varies among stations from one hour to two and one-half hours but is almost always vitally important as an advertising vehicle and image builder. Stations usually program the preceding hours very carefully to develop a large carry-over audience—one it is hoped will stay tuned for the news.

Local TV stations have two principal means for filling their nonnetwork time: local live production and syndicated programs. In most cases, two nightly newscasts, one during the early evening and another immediately after the network primetime schedule ends, constitute the major local production effort. The amount and quality of additional local live production varies widely among stations throughout the country.

Three distinct types of syndicated TV shows are available, including first-run or original programs made for syndication, reruns of off-network shows, and feature movie films. The chief advantage in using syndicated programs is that, by spreading the cost among many users, stations may obtain quality program material at a fraction of the production cost. Syndicated shows are sold on an exclusive basis to one station in any given broadcast market.

First-run syndicated programs have become increasingly available during the 1980s, mainly because demand expanded with the growth of independent stations. Network affiliates also must rely heavily upon syndicated shows to program much of their nonnetwork time. Prominent first-run syndicated programs at the time of publication include "Donahue," "The Oprah Winfrey Show," "People's Court," "Entertainment Tonight," "Wheel of Fortune," and "Jeopardy."

As noted in Chapter 4, many syndicated shows and sports broadcasts (minor bowl games, for example) are offered to stations on a *barter* basis. Under this arrangement, production and distribution costs are underwritten by one or more advertisers who provide programs free of cost to a number of stations in exchange for free broadcast of their commercials within the shows. Stations benefit two ways from this arrangement. They obtain competitive programming at no direct cost, and they can generate advertising income by selling additional commercial messages within the barter programs. Participating advertisers benefit by achieving an overall lower cost for their advertising time. Also, the presence of barter syndication as a viable option for national advertisers tends to hold down rates charged by the networks.

Upon completion of successful runs on network television, most primetime series, other than variety shows, go into syndication. Sometimes local stations obtain syndication rights for popular programs one or more years before the shows end their network schedules. Reruns of well-established shows can be used quite effectively to meet programming needs and to serve as advertising vehicles on local stations. Frequently, they are *stripped*—scheduled across-the-board at the same time, Monday through Friday, during local station time. A few of the numerous successfully syndicated shows include vintage favorites such as "I Love Lucy," "Gilligan's Island," "Star Trek," and the "Andy Griffith Show," as well as more recent successes including "M*A*S*H," "Three's Company," "Taxi," "WKRP in Cincinnati," "The Cosby Show," and "Benson." Literally dozens of others could be added to the list. Table 8.1 lists some of the major program syndicators and shows offered.

Table 8.1. Typical syndicated programming of eight major distributors

Distributor	Selected Programs Offered
Columbia Pictures TV	Barney Miller, Benson, Diff'rent Strokes, Good Times, The Jeffersons, One Day at a Time, Sanford & Son
King World	Wheel of Fortune, Jeopardy!, The Oprah Winfrey Show
Lorimar Telepictures Corp.	Mama's Family, It's a Living, The People's Court, Superior Court
Multimedia Entertainment	Donahue, Sally Jesse Raphael
Paramount Pictures Corp.	Bosom Buddies, Cheers, Family Ties, Happy Days, The Lucy Show, The Odd Couple, Star Trek
Twentieth Century Fox TV	A Current Affair, Fall Guy, M*A*S*H, Room 222, Trapper John
Viacom International	Hawaii Five-O, The Cosby Show, All in the Family, The Andy Griffith Show, Gunsmoke, The Mary Tyler Moore Show
Worldvision Enterprises	The Jetsons, The Love Boat, Little House on the Prairie, Barnaby Jones

Rental fees charged for each episode of a syndicated program, whether off-network or first run, vary according to market size, competition, desirability of the specific show, intended time slot, and the number of previous showings in the market. The reputation of the syndicator and the negotiating skills of the buyer and seller also are factors in determining the final price for a show in a given market. Each episode may be used several (usually seven) times by the stations that contract for a series.

Some top-rated off-network programs (for example, "Three's Company," "Family Ties," "Mary Tyler Moore Show," and "M*A*S*H,") have commanded prices in excess of $50,000 per episode and currently cost stations in the three largest markets more than $100,000 per episode. By comparison, some small-market TV stations obtain half-hour programs for less than $100. In 1986-87, the successful

"Cosby Show" was initially offered to local stations on a "cash plus barter" basis for fall 1988 airing, even though the program likely would continue indefinitely on NBC's primetime schedule. Indeed, "The Cosby Show" set the all-time record for highest price in program syndication, earning a projected $600 million for the initial three-and-a-half years of its syndicated run.[1] Obviously, from a station's standpoint, prices for programs must make economic sense with respect to audience and advertising potentials.

Network license fees usually cover the original basic production costs for most primetime shows, but studios rarely see real program profits until after shows have entered the syndication market. Many producers aim to complete approximately 175 shows, or about seven years of original production, to facilitate Monday-through-Friday across-the-board programming for one full season.

Syndicated shows normally are transmitted to local stations via satellite feed for recording and playback at desired times.

Feature films, movies originally produced for theatrical showing, also are available to local TV stations through syndication. A variety of types of movie packages, ranging from vintage films to recent productions, may be acquired to meet programming needs. Sometimes these features run within locally produced shows. For example, one of the most original approaches to Sunday afternoon movie programming ran for nearly ten years on the airwaves of KHON-TV, the NBC affiliate in Honolulu. From 2 until 4:30 P.M., viewers were treated not only to a feature film, but also to musical performances, engaging dialogue, informative services, and lively promotions—all hosted by a popular local entertainer.

Packaged as "The Danny Kaleikini Theater," the program featured the star of Hawaii's longest running nightclub show in program segments preceding and following the movie and in minisegments during station breaks. Each was presented in the Hawaiian spirit of *ohana* (translation: family style). As Danny Kaleikini himself explained it, the show's objective was threefold: to introduce talented local performers and to help establish their careers in entertainment; to promote youth activities, benefits for the underprivileged, and charity drives for a variety of organizations; and to advise audiences of community needs and public services in areas such as health and safety.

Each show was taped just five days before air date to insure its current information and fresh appeal and to stimulate a sense of audience involvement as well as enjoyment. The producer/director called the format "personable and relaxed" (it was a totally nonscripted show) but was quick to point out a never-ending quest for excellence. That is why 30 minutes of "Theater" program time took three hours to set and shoot, despite the use of the most advanced production and electronic editing equipment.

And audiences willingly responded. In fact, "The Danny Kaleikini Theater" consistently attracted major advertisers—perhaps because they, too, felt part of the *ohana*.

PROGRAMMING BY INDEPENDENT STATIONS

With a few notable exceptions, independent TV stations always have operated in the shadows of their network-affiliated neighbors. Their unenviable task has been to compete against network programming almost entirely with local and syndicated productions. However, the fortune of many independent stations improved dramatically during the 1980s. The reasons include the public's appetite for greater choices of programming and a substantial increase in the amount and quality of available nonnetwork program material. A marked growth in the number of independent stations also has occurred, further stimulating the production of first-run and barter syndication programming.

Two different types of independent stations compete in major television markets: *general service independents*, which compete directly with network affiliates for the mass audience; and *specialty independents*, which program to specific target audiences. The latter type includes stations targeted to Spanish-speaking and black viewers and stations that emphasize religious programming and financial information. Table 8.2 gives a profile of independent and affiliated TV stations in three major markets.

Table 8.2. On-air TV programming in three major markets

Network or Programming Specialty	Boston		Chicago		San Francisco	
	Call	Channel	Call	Channel	Call	Channel
ABC	WCVB	5	WLS	7	KGO	7
CBS	WNEV	7	WBBM	2	KPIX	5
NBC	WBZ	4	WMAQ	5	KRON	4
FOX	WFXT	25	WFLD	32	KTVU	2
Telemundo	...	...	WCIU	26	...	...
Univision	...	...	WSNS	44	KDTV	14
PBS	WGBH	2	WTTW	11	KQED	9
PBS	WGBX	44	WCME	20	KQEC	32
Independent (General)	WSBK	38	WGN	9	KBHK	44
Independent (General)	WLVI	56	WPWR	50	KTSF	26
Independent (General)	...	...	...	...	KOFY	20
Independent (General)	...	...	...	...	KWBB	38
Independent (Religious)	WQTV	68	WCFC	38	...	...
Independent (Shopping)	WHSH	66	WEHS	60	...	...

Independent stations need an enormous amount of nonnetwork program material, estimated at 200 hours per month by management consultant Ward L. Quaal.[2] To fill this requirement, which is far greater than that of network affiliates, independent TV stations rely on syndication as their most important source of programming. These stations have discovered that viewers like reruns of familiar shows that have left network schedules, as well as feature films and first-run syndicated productions.

Other programming sources include local live productions such as news and sportscasts, feeds from limited or special networks (Fox, INN, Mislou and Raycom Sports), and, occasionally, a regular network program that has been refused by an affiliate station in the market. Finally, programs sometimes are exchanged among independent stations.

General appeal independent stations usually build their schedules on feature movies, children's shows, strong blocks of situation comedies, and sports. Major-market independent stations generally enjoy a significant advantage in the latter area because they have the flexibility to clear large amounts of time for major league baseball and other professional sporting events.

Although there are decided disadvantages to operating as an independent station, certain benefits also accrue. Nonnetwork outlets retain greater control over their programming than affiliates do, resulting in total flexibility of scheduling. Hence, independents may obtain certain types of broadcasts, especially local sports, for which affiliates have difficulty clearing time. Major-league baseball, basketball, and hockey games are, therefore, usually carried by independent, rather than affiliated, stations. Also, unlike affiliates, independent stations can sell most commercial positions within shows, as well as break spots.

Independent stations usually compete against affiliates through the strategy of *counter programming*. Many have been successful in programming entertainment fare against newscasts, and some independents have garnered significant audiences for their own news programs by scheduling them earlier than the competition does. Specifically, many independent stations successfully program their main newscasts from 10 to 10:30 or 11 P.M., one hour earlier than network stations do in most time zones. Independent stations also attract viewers with niche programming such as sports, kiddie cartoons, and an abundance of movies.

Nonnetwork stations usually offer their strongest competition from 4 to 8 P.M. when affiliates have no network service; whereas independent stations normally reach an average of 10 to 15 percent of the audience, their shares frequently exceed those of network stations during this important time block. Thus, primetime for many independent television broadcasters becomes the late afternoon and early evening period.

Specialty-programmed independent stations usually serve ethnic minorities, such as Hispanic Americans, urban blacks, or religious viewers. Spanish-programmed stations are located mainly in New York City, Chicago, Southern Florida, Texas, California, Arizona, and New Mexico. Two television groups are the primary competitors for the Spanish-American viewership: Blair Television's Telemundo service and the Hallmark Company's Univision, formerly the Spanish International Network. In contrast, black-programmed TV stations exist in only a few of the large metropolitan centers. Television stations that emphasize paid religious programming, however, have proliferated in many cities across the country. Specialty stations do not claim broad audience reach, but they do provide a means for advertisers to reach important specialized audiences.

Another recent development in specialty programming has been the rise of "shop-at-home" services via television. This movement's main thrust has been on dedicated cable channels, but some shopping services, notably Home Shopping Network, have acquired numbers of UHF stations to assure significant market coverage.

PROGRAMMING BY CABLE SYSTEMS

As noted in Chapter 1, cable systems mainly provide subscribers with a variety of programming services, including local TV stations, distant independent stations, advertising-supported cable networks, and pay-TV services. A few enterprising cable systems also engage in aggressive local program origination, typically using one of their channels much like a local TV station. This arrangement is most suitable for small cities that have no broadcast TV outlets.

Until the 1980s, cable television was supported almost exclusively by subscription fees. A typical cable system still charges a basic monthly fee for wired reception of over-the-air stations and basic cable networks. Additional monthly fees are charged for each of a number of pay-TV (usually movie and sports) channels offered. Although income from subscriber fees still constitutes the bulk of the cable industry's revenues, advertising has become an important additional source of income. National advertising is handled by the cable networks, while local advertising may be scheduled on individual cable systems or, in many locations, on "interconnects" of all systems in a given metropolitan area. The commercials usually are placed during local availabilities on cable network channels, as well as on local-origination channels.

As advertising has become increasingly important to local cable systems, many cable operators have strategically realigned their channel offerings to place their commercial-carrying services on the most advantageous channels. For example, such major cable networks as ESPN, USA Network, and Cable News Network (CNN) might be interspersed among the ABC, CBS, and NBC affiliates and major independent stations, thus assuring a greater opportunity for viewer sampling of the channels on which the cable operator sells advertising. Systems participating in areawide interconnects usually standardize their channel offerings to facilitate program promotion and advertising sales.

Greater emphasis undoubtedly will be given to the sale of advertising by the cable industry, not only through placement of commercial messages on cable networks, both nationally and locally, but also via leased channels. In some cases, newspapers and radio stations have leased cable channels to expand their communication services and advertising bases. Other users of leased channels include shopping services, either independent or affiliated with established retail store organizations, which display merchandise and encourage viewers to order products seen on TV without visiting a retail outlet. Thus far, the Home Shopping Network has been the most visible of the shop-at-home services. Another unique advertising opportunity available in some cabled markets is the *split-feeding* of different messages to various sectors of a city in order to reach various target audiences with appropriate product appeals.

Probably, the 1980s were to cable television what the 1920s were to radio and the 1950s were to broadcast TV—a developmental period in which the industry expanded greatly in public acceptance and economic viability. All indications suggest that advertising via cable will continue to grow and become an increasingly important function for cable television in the United States.

PROGRAMMING STRATEGIES

In the competitive U.S. system of broadcasting, television networks and stations utilize a variety of methods to attract and hold viewers. Some prove more effective than others, but three warrant special consideration: station image, competitive scheduling techniques, and specials versus regular program series.

Station Image

Basically, station image refers to the personality projected by a station through its choice of programs, its on-air talent, and the manner in which it produces shows. Station image is what the public thinks of a particular station. TV affiliates, as suggested earlier, reflect to a great degree the personalities of their networks; because they devote much of their local time to syndicated shows, they have fewer opportunities than do radio stations to exhibit individual characteristics. However, alert and creative managements can develop distinctive station images during local program segments and even during station-break periods.

As noted previously, news is the most prominent form of local television programming; recently, much attention has been given to upgrading news presentations, because of the widely held belief that vital, aggressive news reporting produces a favorable image that enhances a station's entire schedule. News consultant firms, which proliferated during the 1970s, may be hired by station managements to assist in analyzing strengths and weaknesses of newscasts and in recommending ways to improve public acceptance.

A number of stations have used their brief station-break periods for image enhancement. Station WMC-TV, Memphis, for example, has incorporated a sketch of a Mississippi riverboat, complete with audio foghorn, into its breaks in an effort to tie the station to the region it serves. Others have turned their studio buildings into community landmarks through station-break exposure. One of the earliest to do so was WSB-TV, Atlanta, whose modern antebellum style home on Peachtree Street is promoted as White Columns. Two station ID slides, reproduced in Figure 8.2, contain elements designed to bolster station image.

Viewer impressions of stations may range from trustworthy to unreliable, from warm and sincere to cold and indifferent, from enthusiastic and ethical to boring and even unprofessional. Nuances of station images, as held by the viewing public, can sometimes be discovered only through in-depth qualitative research; as collective perceptions of a station's personality, however, these images must be of concern to station managements. Similarly, both national and local advertisers would do well to consider station images when placing schedules.

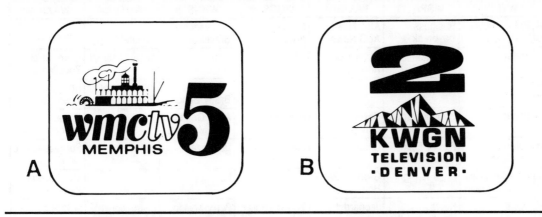

Fig. 8.2. ID's reflecting areas served by TV stations. A. WMC-TV, Memphis, displays a Mississippi riverboat in its station ID, complete with audio riverboat whistle. (Courtesy of WMC-TV, Memphis) B. KWGN Television, Denver, incorporates a Rocky Mountain background into its signature. (Courtesy of KWGN Television, Denver)

Competitive Scheduling Techniques

The primary concern in building a television program schedule involves placing each program at the most opportune time for reaching a maximum number of target viewers. Since the viewing audience exhibits varying characteristics in composition throughout the day, the *audience flow* (reflecting collective tuning-in and tuning-out) is a vital factor in schedule building.

Program decisions focus on both individual shows and total schedules; hence, a second consideration requires the placement of programs in sequences that maximize audience carryover from one show to another. The most common strategy for achieving favorable carryover is block programming, which involves scheduling a series of shows with similar audience appeal consecutively over a period of time, usually two hours or more. The idea is that viewers, once attracted to a strong lead-off show, will remain tuned for subsequent programs that satisfy the same needs. Several examples of block programming may be found in the typical large city program log shown in Figure 8.3. Note the three-hour soap opera blocks on all three networks and the two-hour block of situation comedies carried by the ABC affiliate from 8 to 10 P.M. The three hour-long drama programs scheduled on the CBS outlet from 8 to 11 P.M. represent still another program block.

A variation of block programming is the *blockbuster,* a segment usually 90 to 120 minutes in length, which is scheduled directly opposite a competitor's block of shorter programs. In some cases, a blockbuster may start prior to the beginning of the opposition's block of programs. In either case, the intent is to weaken effectiveness of the competition's programming by capturing viewers early and holding their attention through a long period of time with a strong, single program. A blockbuster may be a regular weekly series, a movie slot in which the content varies from week to week, or a special one-time broadcast. Note the blockbuster movie scheduled from 8 to 10 P.M. on an independent station in Figure 8.5.

How to compete against an opposing station's high-rated programs is a challenge faced by every station or network at some time. Essentially, two strategies are available for such situations—*power programming* and *counter programming*—and, they are diametrically opposed.

Power programming involves pitting a strong show against one already entrenched by a competitor. Usually the aggressor appeals to the same type of audience in an effort to increase an existing audience share. Thus, in power programming viewers are forced to choose between desirable

	WYFF ④	WSPA ⑦	WLOS ⑬	WGGS ⑯	WHNS ㉑	WNTV ㉙	WAXA ㊵
6 AM / 30	Before Hours / NBC News	Business Daybreak	ABC News / ABC News	Exercise / Ag-Day	J. Swaggart / BraveStarr	To Life! Yoga	
7 AM / 30	Today / "	This Morning / "	Good Morning America	PTL Club / "	Jem / G.I. Joe	Sesame Street / "	Morn. Stretch / Zoobilee Zoo
8 AM / 30	" / "	" / "	" / "	Nite Line / "	Woody / Brady Bunch	Instructional Programming	Heathcliff / Teddy Ruxpin
9 AM / 30	Donahue / "	Superior Court / Love Connec.	Newlywed / Dating Game	Nite Line	Andy Griffith / Real McCoys	" / "	Crook / Record Guide
10 AM / 30	Sale / Cl. Conc.	Family Feud / Card Sharks	Geraldo / "	700 Club / "	Bonanza / "	" / "	Success-N-Life / "
11 AM / 30	Wheel-Fortune / Lose or Draw	Price Is Right / "	Growing Pains / Home	PTL Club / "	Fall Guy / "	" / "	Matchmaker / Password
12 PM / 30	News / Scrabble	News / Young and the	Jeopardy! / Loving	Ernest Angley / "	Perry Mason / "	Instructional Programming	MOVIE "Boot-leggers"
1 PM / 30	Days of Our / Lives	Restless / Bold/Beautiful	All My Child-ren	Peggy Denny / Exercise	Incredible Hulk / "	" / "	" / "
2 PM / 30	Another World / "	As the World / Turns	One Life to / Live	Alive / Closer Look	BJ/Lobo / "	" / "	Tarzan
3 PM / 30	Santa Barbara / "	Guiding Light / "	General Hospi-tal	Secret Place / Gospel Bill	Ghostbusters / Smurfs	" / "	Dinosaucers / Superfriends
4 PM / 30	Silver Spoons / 3's Company	Hour Maga-zine	The Judge / Gimme Break	Zoo Revue / Sing Out	DuckTales / Double Dare	Sesame Street / "	Saber Riders / Defend'r/Earth
5 PM / 30	Oprah Winfrey / "	Divorce Court / People's Court	A-Team / "	Richard Rob-erts	Happy Days / Facts of Life	Mister Rogers / Learn to Read	B. Hills Teens / Jetsons
6 PM / 30	News / "	News / CBS News	News / ABC News	J. Swaggart / J. Robison	Family Ties / WKRP	MacNeil/ Lehrer	Pyramid / Rawhide
7 PM / 30	NBC News / PM Magazine	Lose or Draw / Hollywood Sq.	Wheel-Fortune / Jeopardy!	Frederick K. / Price	Family Ties / Cheers	Business Rpt. / World/Animals	" / Superman
8 PM / 30	ALF / "	Newhart / Cavanaughs	MOVIE "Holly-wood Wives"	Nite Line / "	MOVIE ★★½ "Kissin' Cous-	Evening at Pops	Fight for Free-dom
9 PM / 30	MOVIE ★★½ "Blood Vows:	Memories / Then & Now	" / "	" / "	ins"	Crosstalk / "	MOVIE ★★ "Seizure: The
10 PM / 30	The Story of a / Mafia Wife"	Magnum, P.I. / "	" / "	INN News / 700 Club	Star Trek / "	America's Tes-tament	Story of Kathy / Morris"
11 PM / 30	News / Tonight Show	News / Sanford & Son	News / M*A*S*H	" / Isaiah Vision	Andy Griffith / Barney Miller	MacNeil/ Lehrer	Hit Squad / Late Show
12 AM / 30	" / David Letter-	Hunter / "	Nightline / Ent. Tonight	" / Prophecy	Gunsmoke / "	Sign-Off	" / Sign-Off
1 AM / 30	man / S.J. Raphael	Copacabana / "	Saint / "	Sign-Off	Hug Tight / "		

Fig. 8.3. Typical newspaper log. This log shows the diversity of TV programming even in medium-size markets. (Courtesy of the *Greenville* [S.C.] *News*)

programs. Although this strategy has worked well in many instances, stations do risk wasting a strong program by engaging in such a struggle; a frequent result is withdrawal of one of the two shows after audience ratings reveal the winner of the confrontation.

In counter programming, it is conceded that an entrenched program will do well. Instead of engaging in power strategy, a competing station now offers viewers a sharply different kind of show. Counter programming not only saves strong shows from destructive competition, but also tends to enlarge the total viewership by attracting additional viewers through alternative programs. A classic example of counter programming, shown in Figure 8.5, was WTTG's placement of the comedy "M*A*S*H" opposite the 11 P.M. news on the three network affiliated stations.

A final strategy used extensively in television is *across-the-board programming*. Also known as *strip* or *horizontal programming,* this approach involves airing a given program at the same time every day, usually Monday through Friday. Across-the-board scheduling takes advantage of the tendency of individuals to form regular viewing habits. Most daytime programs, as well as evening newscasts, adhere to this plan and independent stations use it heavily along with the counter programming technique.

As television has become fiercely competitive, a number of secondary programming techniques have been devised. Perhaps the oldest of these is the *spectacular,* or one-time special broadcast. Others include:

1. *Miniseries*—a short series of full-length programs is devoted to a single subject of great importance or wide interest. The miniseries often is an adaptation of a literary work.
2. *Hammock programming*—the program slot between two successful shows is used to provide exposure to a new program or one that needs additional positive exposure.
3. *Serialization of regular programs*—a single plot is spread across two or more weeks instead of the normal procedure of presenting a single complete episode within one program.
4. *Long-form programs*—the length of a popular program is extended to boost network ratings. Typically, half-hour shows are expanded to a full hour, or hour-long programs are extended to two hours.
5. *Stunting*—highly irregular tactics are used to draw the audience to a program. An unusual degree of suspense is one form. Probably the best example was the summer-long (1981) curiosity as to "Who shot J.R.?" on the CBS show, "Dallas." Another type of stunting involves *front-loading,* in which early programs of a series are loaded with unusually strong personalities or appeals. The use of prizes as rewards for viewing also represents a form of stunting.

TV Specials and Regular Series

TV's voracious appetite for programs results in a certain amount of repetitiveness in content. Successful new shows usually beget imitators, and programming tends to follow cyclical patterns. At various times in the history of the medium, primetime has been dominated by westerns, by big prize game shows, by crime dramas, and by situation comedies. Each year's network schedules include both carry-over programs from the previous year and new shows that are expected to compete effectively for viewers. In practice, only a few of each season's new programs become hits; by the same token, some of the old standbys wear out their welcome and are dropped. Rapid obsolescence is, indeed, one of the basic characteristics of TV programs.

The majority of network shows are regular, weekly program series. In addition, the three networks schedule numerous one-time *spectacular* broadcasts each year. Such specials can outdraw even the most popular regular programs when they are well conceived and attractively promoted. Keys to successful specials generally include elaborate budgets, prominent talent, ample time for careful production, and a high degree of creative imagination. Whereas the production costs for an average hour of primetime programming now exceed half a million dollars, an elaborate special may be budgeted at twice as much or more.

Most TV advertisers prefer to place commercials within various regular programs to achieve a desired level of audience reach and frequency of exposure. However, specials appeal to those who need high impact at particular times of the year or who seek the prestige associated with sponsoring high-quality programs. For instance, specials may be particularly appropriate advertising vehicles for automobile manufacturers who need high visibility for the introduction of new cars or during peak selling periods. Another good example is the Hallmark Greeting Card Company, which sponsors several

"Hallmark Hall of Fame" specials annually. These one-time programs are scheduled prior to such occasions as Christmas, Valentine's Day, Easter, and Mother's Day—all appropriate times for sending cards.

Overall, the most popular season for television specials is the 4-week period between Thanksgiving and Christmas when many manufacturers wish to bring their products to the attention of the country's Christmas shoppers.

PROGRAMMING COMMERCIAL CONTENT

Recall from Chapter 5 that the NAB codes limited the proportion of broadcast time that can be allocated to advertising (both within and around programs), the number of permissible TV program interruptions for commercial and other "nonprogram" material, and the number of consecutive announcements that may be aired during any one interruption.

Audiences obviously have gained from these restrictions, but advertisers also benefitted because of the limited number of commercials competing for viewer attention. Commercial availabilities are still normally spaced 10 to 14 minutes apart on primetime TV shows, as illustrated in Figure 8.4, to facilitate the development of program plots.

	Time	Length	Element
1.	9:58:00	:30	Network promo
2.	9:58:30	1:30	Local promo/commercial/commercial
3.	10:00:00	3:30	Program time/teaser/main credits
4.	10:03:30	:10	Opening billboard
5.	10:03:40	1:00	Commercials 1 & 2 (30/30)
6.	10:04:40	11:20	Program segment
7.	10:16:00	1:00	Commercials 3 & 4 (30/30)
8.	10:17:00	12:38	Program segment
9.	10:29:38	1:00	Commercials 5 & 6 (30/30)
10.	10:30:38	:42	Local break promo/commercial/ID
11.	10:31:20	10:00	Program segment
12.	10:41:20	1:00	Commercials 7 & 8 (30/30)
13.	10:42:20	12:00	Program segment
14.	10:54:20	1:00	Commercials 9 & 10 (30/30)
15.	10:55:20	1:00	Trailer
16.	10:56:20	1:00	Commercials 11 & 12 (30/30)
17.	10:57:20	:40	Credits (voiceover promo)
18.	10:58:00	:30	Public service promo
19.	10:58:30	:30	Network promo
20.	10:59:00	1:02	Local promo/commercial/commercial/ID
21.	11:00:02	--	Local news program

Recap

Total time	62:02 Minutes		100%
Program segment time	45:58	"	74%
Commercial time	8:30	"	14%
All other	7:34	"	12%

Fig. 8.4. Typical prime network format/one-hour program (six network commercial minutes in six positions).

Radio Programming

As noted in Chapter 2, radio broadcasting is also composed of networks and local stations; however, unlike television, radio is primarily a local medium. Programming is the responsibility of each station, and networks serve essentially as sources of national and international news coverage, plus other short feature material.

Because radio stations are numerous in every major city, the basic programming strategy is to devise a format that will differentiate one station from all others and attract a loyal audience. Again, station image is vitally important as a reflection of station personality and is closely entwined with program format. It also includes such items as on-air talent, quality of production, and the attitude exhibited toward listeners.

Because radio programming focuses so intently on choice of format, we need to examine the major ones currently in use.

GENERAL SERVICE PROGRAMMING

Although most radio stations program in a very specialized manner to attract a well-defined target audience, many small-town outlets and a few large-market stations provide a broad range of program fare. A typical general service station provides extensive news and sports coverage, emphasizes service features that are directly beneficial to listeners, and often provides a broad mix of music. Service features usually include helicopter traffic reports and detailed weathercasts.

Some prominent general service radio stations include WCCO, Minneapolis; WGN, Chicago; WTIC, Hartford; WRVA, Richmond; WJR, Detroit; KDKA, Pittsburgh; and WIVK AM-FM, Knoxville. Most large market general service outlets are 50,000 watt clear channel or 100,000 watt class C FM stations.

MUSIC-BASED FORMATS

Stations having music-based formats emphasize music of a given type as their main attraction. News varies in importance from one station to another, and other program material usually is secondary. Musical formats presently attracting large audiences include adult contemporary (AC) and current hit radio (CHR), based on currently popular music; album-oriented rock (AOR), soft rock, and other rock categories; country formats; and beautiful music or easy listening, emphasizing both instrumental and vocal arrangements. Other music-based formats include jazz, classical, ethnic, nostalgic, and religious music.

These categories, however descriptive they may seem, do not begin to show potential advertisers how customized radio can be. For instance, there are more than 20 country music formats alone, with names like "Country Fresh," "Countrypolitan," "Country Sunshine," "Progressive Country," and "All American Country." Similarly, nostalgic formats range from the big band music of the 1940s to rock hits of the 1970s. We should also note that there is a tremendous amount of syndicated radio programming—everything from "drop-in" features to complete program formats.

TALK-BASED FORMATS

Numerous large-market radio stations have achieved significant shares of audience with talk programming. The most expensive of all formats is the all-news approach, which depends heavily on rapid audience turnover resulting in a large *cume* audience. Variations include the news-talk format, which consists largely of newscasts, telephone-talk programs, and interview shows.

Figure 8.5 shows the weekly schedule of a typical block-programmed news-talk radio station, 50,000 watt WPTF, Raleigh, N.C.

 WPTF
the Air of Success

 Program Schedule.

	Monday	Tuesday	Wednesday	Thursday	Friday	Saturday	Sunday
12 MID.	Nightsong With Tom Avery						
1 AM	ABC Talk Radio with Ira Fistell						
2 AM							
3 AM	ABC Talk Radio with Ray Briem						
4 AM							
5 AM	The Early Bird Hour — With Johnnie Hood					Ray Briem	
6 AM	The Great Morning Wake-Up With Maury O'Dell and Garry Dornburg					Mike Raley Music	Religious & Public Affairs
7 AM							
8 AM						Weekend Gardener	
9 AM	Ask Your Neighbor — With Maury O'Dell					Ask Your Neighbor	
10 AM						Tom Russell Music With Paul Harvey (12:10-12:25)	
11 AM	In Touch — With Lowell Shumaker						Live Worship Service
12 Noon	The Noon Report — With Johnnie Hood						*
1 PM	Open Line — With Bart Ritner						Michael Harris Music
2 PM							
3 PM						Kathy Reid Music	
4 PM	Focus Hosted By Lowell Shumaker						
5 PM							
6 PM	Focus Hosted By Mike Raley					Tom Smither Music	The N.C. Collection With J.C. Knowles
7 PM	Sportsline — With Garry Dornburg						
8 PM	Monday Only Jim Valvano	The Allan Handelman Show				Solid Gold Saturday Night	Our Best To You — With Tom Kearney
9 PM							
10 PM							
11 PM	Nightsong — With Tom Avery						

*Reporter's Notebook (WPTF News)

680 AM STEREO

3012 Highwoods Blvd., P.O. Box 29521, Raleigh, NC 27626, 919-876-0674

Fig. 8.5. Block-programmed radio station. (Courtesy of WPTF Radio, Raleigh)

ETHNIC FORMATS

Programming to ethnic minorities is a significant type of broadcasting in many parts of the United States. Black-oriented stations are commonly found in large cities with a substantial black population and in smaller communities throughout the South. A few stations program to American Indians in such states as New Mexico, Oklahoma, and North and South Dakota, while Eskimo broadcasts are common in Alaska.

In addition, Spanish-programmed radio stations are located in Florida, Texas, Arizona, California, and major cities such as New York and Chicago. Broadcasts in Polish, Russian, Greek, Chinese, Ukrainian, and Slovak also may be heard in cosmopolitan centers.

OTHER SPECIALTY PROGRAMMING

A rapidly emerging program concept is all-religious broadcasting. Stations involved here may be either institutional or commercial by nature and have been established in most large cities. Also, sports and agricultural programs often occupy large blocks of radio time. Frequently, one or two radio outlets in major cities devote much of their time to play-by-play broadcasts of professional baseball, football, and other local games. Similarly, collegiate athletics often forms a nucleus for extensive sports programming in university centers. Agricultural programming receives a great amount of attention from stations in the Midwest and the central part of the United States, although farm broadcasts rarely, if ever, constitute a station's total format.

Thus, advertisers may design their radio campaigns very precisely. Either broad audience reach or saturation of special or unique target audiences can be attained through judicious choice of stations. Table 8.3 illustrates the variety of programming available among radio outlets of a major market.

Table 8.3. Diversified radio formats in a large U.S. city (Denver)

Station	Frequency	Network	Format
AM Stations (1988)			
KLZ	560 kHz	ABC-I	Country
KHOW	630 kHz	US-2	Middle-of-the road
KNUS	710 kHz	NBC	Talk
KOA	850 kHz	CBS	News/talk
KPOF	910 kHz		Religion
KYBG	1090 kHz		Oldies
KRZN	1150 kHz		Oldies
KBNO	1220 kHz		Spanish
KXKL	1280 kHz	MBS	Oldies
KDEN	1340 kHz	MBS, ABC-E	News/talk
KPPL	1390 kHz		
KEZW	1430 kHz	MBS	Nostalgia
KDKO	1510 kHz		Black
KMVP	1600 kHz	MBS, ABC-E	Adult contemporary/talk
FM Stations (1988)			
KADX	92.1 mHz	APR	Jazz
KHIH	94.7 mHz	US-1	Classical hits
KSYY	95.7 mHz	MBS	Soft album rock
KBCO	97.3 mHz		Album rock
KYGO	98.5 mHz		Country
KVOD	99.5 mHz		Classical
KMJI	100.3 mHz		Adult contemporary
KOSI	101.1 mHz		Easy listening
KOAQ	103.5 mHz	CBS/R.R	Adult contemporary
KXKL	105.1 mHz	MBS	Oldies
KBPI	105.9 mHz	NBC/Source	Album rock
KAZY	106.7 mHz	ABC-Rock	Album rock
KRXY	107.5 mHz		Current hits

Source: *Duncan's American Radio.*

A FINAL NOTE

From Table 8.3, we see that both the AM and FM bands now include a considerable variety of formats. In a sense, each radio station "narrowcasts" its programming to a distinctive target audience.

With this background in programming, we are ready to move into the creation of broadcast commercials—first radio and then television—after which we will discuss their actual production.

Study Questions

1. From what sources do TV networks get their programs? How about independent stations? Cable TV systems?

2. Explain the difference between power programming and counter programming, and give examples of each.

3. Rarely, if ever, does a competitive TV station schedule its daily news block in the middle of its primetime hours. Can you think of any instance in which such a move (as a counter-programming tactic) would prove effective? Why or why not?

4. What are syndicated programs? Explain how they differ from other types.

5. Discuss the various images your local stations have. What specific items or activities work to support these images?

6. Define the following terms: Hammock Programming, Stunting, Blockbuster.

7. Consider a typical music/news/commercials format on one of your local radio stations. What suggestions can you make for improvements in this pattern, considering its values to both advertiser and listener?

ASSIGNMENT 8-A

Using *TV Guide* or listings from a local newspaper, prepare a composite schedule for one assigned day of the week for the TV stations serving your community. Compare your chart with those of other students and indicate where weekly stripping of programs occurs.

ASSIGNMENT 8-B

Analyze the schedule you prepared for assignment 8-A with respect to target audience considerations, paying special attention to the major program periods: (a) evening primetime, (b) daytime, (c) early morning, (d) late night, and (e) weekend daytime.

ASSIGNMENT 8-C

Analyze the schedule you prepared for assignment 8-A in terms of competitive strategies, looking particularly for examples of (a) block programming, (b) blockbusters, (c) power programming, and (d) counter programming.

ASSIGNMENT 8-D

For a given community, obtain a schedule of local-origination programming for a CATV system. List the target audiences served by these programs, as well as the competitive strategies employed. Then indicate what types of advertisers use the facility and how extensively they use it.

ASSIGNMENT 8-E

List the radio stations serving your community, indicating the type of program format used by each. Select two of these stations for closer examination, and analyze their formats in terms of (a) program elements (music, news, other items), and (b) sequencing patterns within a typical hour.

Notes

1. " 'Cosby' barter minute goes to P&G, GF, Group W," *Broadcasting* (May 9, 1988):29.
2. Ward L. Quaal, and James A. Brown, *Broadcast Management* (New York: Hastings House, 1976), 197.

Suggested Readings

Baldwin, Thomas F. *Cable Communication*. Englewood Cliffs, N.J.: Prentice Hall, 1983.

Clift, Charles, III, and Archie Greer. *Broadcast Programming: The Current Perspective*. Washington: University Press of America, 1974-present.

Eastman, Susan Tyler, Sydney W. Head, and Lewis Klein. *Broadcast Programming*. 2d ed. Belmont, Calif.: Wadsworth, 1985.

Howard, Herbert H., and Michael S. Kievman. *Radio and Television Programming*. 1st ed. New York: Macmillan Publishing, 1983. (Second edition forthcoming. Ames: Iowa State Univ. Press.)

Morganstern, Steve, ed. *Inside the TV Business*. New York: Sterling Publishers, 1979.

Routt, Ed, James B. McGrath, and Fredric A. Weiss. *The Radio Format Conundrum*. New York: Hastings House, 1978.

9

Writing Radio Commercials

Even with a solid background in broadcast advertising organizations and audiences, regulation, and programming, the job of writing effective radio commercials is a tremendous challenge. Because an aural stimulus requires relatively little in the way of conscious effort from its audience, people tend to get careless in their listening habits; they hear with only half an ear because they are either doing or thinking of something else while receiving the message. In fact, no other medium has quite as distracted an audience as radio. (Of course, herein lies a strength as well as a weakness. Thanks to transistors, tiny radios fit handily into pocket and purse, and they accompany their owners almost everywhere; hence, radio's audience is very large and very consistent.)

The Nature of the Task

Radio has no visual channel, so words and sounds must create pictures in the listener's mind and still not overpower the product or sales message with their literary value, humor, or irrelevant chatter (no matter how entertaining these approaches might be). A clever approach may be tempting, because radio is, at least in part, an entertainment medium. Yet, the best commercials are not necessarily those that elicit the most praise or laughter from an audience. The ultimate strategy must be one of sales communication, not the all-too-frequently appearing substitute we will call *commercialitis.*

This unfortunate "disease" manifests itself in situations where audiences remember the commercial (a melody, a pun, a celebrity presenter, a fancy sound effect) but forget the sales message (the brand name and sometimes even the type of merchandise). The product must get top billing in the listener's mind, or advertising has not done its job.

Radio commercials are also interrupters—intruders in the midst of musical programming, sports coverage, or a newscast. Messages must be pleasant but businesslike, interesting but sales-oriented, commanding but never pushy. Granted, there are times when a funny line or light-hearted approach does prove the best means for establishing a brand name or making a sales claim especially memorable or clear. Writers must avoid the kind of humor that tries to be funny but isn't and the kind that is funny but doesn't do anything for the product (commercialitis). Comedy is not for amateurs, and good comedians are the first to admit it. However it is used in radio commercials, humor is delicate and risky; it can make or break a sales message but rarely does much in between.

The Elements of Radio Communication

Radio copywriters have three main ingredients with which to work: words (the human voice), music (including lyrics), and sound effects. All have promising potential (and some perilous pitfalls) in terms of sales communication.

WORDS AND VOICES

Each word in a commercial must be weighed for its contribution to the selling power of the message and for its goodness of sound. A spray disinfectant may be odoriferous, but the vast majority of prospective customers would rather hear about its fresh, clean smell. Globule is a short, simple term referring to a small drop of something, usually a liquid. It is a perfectly harmless word, as is assuage (to lessen pain), but if your favorite radio announcer advised you to "assuage your eyes with a few globules of Brite-Eyes," would you be eager to act accordingly? Or would you prefer a message that promised "soothing relief with just a few drops of Brite-Eyes"? The sound of words can spell the difference between a pleasing claim and one that is actually repulsive.

Words that produce a sibilant, hissing effect over the microphone (such as surreptitious, supercilious, or so sensitive it's simply sensational) should be avoided. It is also wise to be wary of excessive use of the first person (the advertiser-we). Too much "believe me, I know you'll love it . . ." or, "we're so proud of our name . . ." or "take our word for it—we're sure it's right for you . . . ," and the listener is apt to react in one of two ways. He either feels the advertiser is shoving the product at him, or figures the copywriter is basking in the glory of an ego trip. Neither sensation does much to help sell.

What about the voice behind the words? Sometimes the difference between a male and a female spokesperson can be crucial; occasionally, a child makes a good presenter. Character voices can aid communication of a humorous or offbeat message and help build a memorable image. The major criterion for selection must be relevance—appropriateness to the advertising objective.

The human voice adds realism to messages, something not available in printed media. There is a warmth and companionship quality inherent in radio that wise copywriters use to full advantage. Interpretation of selling points in terms of genuine consumer interests is often facilitated by use of a friendly (sometimes well-known) voice.

Finally, all radio copy should be read aloud before the copywriter is through with it. Sometimes a seemingly innocent line on paper can come out sounding cold or pompous when actually spoken. Few things repel a listening audience faster than detection of a belittling quality or boastful, snobbish sound in copy.

MUSIC AND JINGLES

Music for radio commercials may either be originally composed or be transcribed, instrumental library music that often is used simply for background. In some instances, melodies in the public domain are used (and for jingles, the copywriter develops new lyrics).

The major criterion, again, is suitability to the occasion: music that is current for a fashion boutique, quiet for a gentle medication, nostalgic for a bakery product's homemade taste, uplifting for an airline or a refreshing cosmetic, romantic for an engagement ring, or adventurous for a sports car or a dashing cologne. In short, music can help establish a mood that carries listeners into a desired state of mind, involving them in the sales message. It can also punctuate a point through use of what is called a musical *stinger*. For example, the twang of an out-of-tune guitar might accentuate a sudden feeling of heartburn or indigestion, while a single chime can indicate A-OK again.

Music can carry an audience through time and space by means of a *segue* (pronounced seg-way), an immediate transition from one type of music (say, a 1920s Charleston number) to another (a progressive rock song from the 1980s) without pause. Or we can gradually mix one source of music with another, in such a way that the one originally dominant slowly gives way until the other takes over completely. Such a technique is called a *crossfade*, and may be utilized, for instance, to take listeners from a dancing studio's "beginner's waltz" to a church's Wedding March.

A recent survey of advertising creative personnel found that music is assigned several different, critical tasks in commercials: (1) creating an emotional atmosphere for a selling message that stands out from the competition; (2) emphasizing specific copy points and building a distinctive brand personality; (3) lending a feeling of continuity throughout the sales presentation; (4) providing a friendly incentive for audiences to stay with the commercial from beginning to end; and (5) serving as free advertising (through, for example, spontaneous humming or whistling on the part of consumers) long after a commercial has been aired.

Experts at the Ogilvy & Mather advertising agency, who advocate using music as a powerful selling tool for consumer products, suggest that music is best suited to simple selling promises (ones that are easy to repeat and, if possible, contain both product names and sales promises in the lyrics); messages with emotional benefits; and commercials for products that are leaders in their fields. But the tone of the music, they advise, must match the advertised product's personality—relaxed, upbeat, or whatever.[1]

One trouble spot in the case of music is the choice of such a popular, or otherwise appealing, theme that listeners would rather follow the music than the message. On the other hand, getting listeners to sing along can be a fine example of audience involvement. (Research in the area of consumer behavior shows that participation is a valuable learning device.) Now, of course, we are talking about the jingle—a catchy tune whose words, we hope, tie in directly with an advertiser's sales message.

Some jingles come directly from popular songs, but others are more original (and may be adapted to fit a particular selling emphasis or season). The one in Figure 9.1 does an excellent job of reinforcing the sales message.

```
CLIENT:      Rainbow Shoppes, Southeast      DESCRIPTION:   30-sec w/jingle
STORES:      Kentucky & East Tennessee       FOR AIRING:    June, afternoons
MEDIUM:      MOR, Kentucky & East Tenn.      TITLE:         Take a Break
```

```
JINGLE:     (SUNG TO THE TUNE OF "ON TOP OF OLD SMOKY")
            It's ice cream and candy,
            A colorful treat ...
            A Rainbow ice cream cone
            Is frosty and sweet!

MUSIC:      CONTINUES UNDER ANNCR

ANNCR:      How would a delicious candy ice cream cone taste right now?
            At Rainbow Ice Cream Shoppes you always get a special two-in-
            one treat.  Your frosty-cold ice cream cone comes with a
            candied topping you have to taste to believe.  There's a
            whole rainbow of flavors -- so come on in and choose your
            favorite!

JINGLE:     (MUSIC UP FOR LAST TWO LINES)
            Your Rainbow ice cream cone's
            Refreshment complete!
```

Fig. 9.1. Radio jingle commercial.

Figure 9.2 shows a commercial in which the jingle plays a smaller, but nonetheless specific and appropriate, selling function. Notice how it is set off by a single (memorable) sound effect.

CLIENT:	Robin & Roy Restaurants, Midwest	DESCRIPTION:	60-sec w/jingle and sound
STORES:	Chicago and Suburbs	FOR AIRING:	Fall, weekends
MEDIUM:	AOR, Chicago	TITLE:	Family Fun

SOUND: BONG

MUSIC &
CHORUS: Courtesy and service, at Robin-and-Roy,
          You'll get a meal your whole family will enjoy.

SOUND: BONG

MUSIC &
CHORUS: Courtesy and service -- that's Robin-and-Roy! (MUSIC UNDER)

ANNCR: That's right -- along with every delicious Robin-and-Roy
          meal, you'll discover Robin-and-Roy courtesy and service.
          It's what makes the difference between just another meal away
          from home, and a refreshing, relaxing experience. What does
          Robin-and-Roy service mean? It means taking your order
          accurately and bringing it to your table piping hot -- or
          frosty cool. It means free comic books for your kids, and an
          alert waitress who makes a point of being around when you
          need her. And Robin-and-Roy courtesy? That's a cheerful
          response to a last-minute change in your order. It's per-
          sonal attention -- even during the busiest part of the day or
          evening. It's a greeting when you enter and a thank-you when
          you leave. Stop in at Robin-and-Roy today and enjoy the
          courtesy and service that come with every meal.

SOUND: BONG

MUSIC &
CHORUS: Courtesy and service -- (DRAW THIS OUT): Rob-in...and...Roy!

SOUND: BONG

Fig. 9.2. Jingle-and-sound combination commercial.

SOUND EFFECTS

Strange as it may seem, radio has been called the most visual of all media. Sound effects can create characters, situations, and worlds of fantasy that cannot be duplicated in television or print; then, through imagination, audiences project themselves into the "pictures." For instance, the clinking of glasses over low background voices and soft music can put listeners at a candlelit table in a fine restaurant; boat whistles and the lapping of waves against wooden boards can take them dockside; and electronic synthesizers can transport them across a bridge in gale force winds, pelting rain, and heavy traffic.

Other effects can signify an entrance or exit (to or from a party or parade), indicate a specific season, or describe a geographical spot. A word of caution in the area of sound effects, however, involves the use of identifiable sounds. Most everyone recognizes a siren, but how many would correctly visualize the "wrapping of Christmas presents," or the "dining-room chair pulled out from the neatly set table"?

Also important is the use of effects that supplement, rather than overpower, the sales key. Sometimes, copywriters get so caught up in their own audio shows, they forget to keep the product in proper perspective and commercialitis gains the upper hand. Along this same line, if several different effects are employed (with or without music or dialogue), they must work together, not fight each other for the listener's attention. (See Figure 9.6 for an example of a commercial that handles the dialogue/sound/music combination effectively.)

The Copy Platform

Before a copywriter begins writing, he or she should have a copy platform—a kind of map that points the way toward successful completion of the advertiser's sales story. There are many forms for such platforms (also called copy strategies, or policies), and sometimes, under severe pressures of time, the writer must work from only a partial strategy.

Assuming ideal circumstances, however, the copy platform we will use for both radio and TV commercials will contain the following ten points; it will serve to keep us on course as we develop and analyze broadcast sales messages.

1. *Client and product, service, or store.* The first marker on our map is merely a signpost: the name and supporting identification of our client and the specific product, service, or store we are being asked to advertise. For example: The Nestle Company, White Plains, New York, and Taster's Choice Freeze-Dried Coffee; or J. C. Penney, the stores in Miami, Florida.

2. *Medium and commercial description.* The second marker also serves mainly as an identifier: the intended medium (or media) and relevant dates and times, plus a brief general description of the commercial itself. For example: progressive rock stations in the top 10 U.S. markets, morning drive time, January to March; 30-second production spot with jingle.

3. *Objective.* Next comes the all important purpose—the objective we hope to achieve with our commercial. Recall from earlier discussions that advertising is a communication force and a marketing tool. Its function is to communicate a specific message in a specific way to a specific media audience, thereby (in most cases) helping the other marketing elements in a given campaign to sell a product, service, or retail establishment.

Forms of radio and TV communication are probably infinite in number, but some common ones, stated in commercial-objective format, include:

To inform through factual commentary.
To prove through documentation.
To enhance believability through testimonial.
To remind through musical or animated repetition.

To convince through demonstration.
To call attention to by dramatizing.
To clarify through explanation.
To reassure with scientific support.
To interest through slice-of-life presentation.
To emphasize through aural or visual associations.
To suggest through symbolism.

(The serious student of broadcast advertising, however, will want to make a personal list.)

4. *Target audience.* In Chapter 7 we differentiated between markets (people in the market for a product or service), and audiences (those subsets of markets attending to specific media at specific times). Further, we noted that both demographics and (especially) psychographics are needed in audience definition. Now we need to add one other element. Ideally, the target-audience portion of a copy platform should also spell out those audience characteristics that make people receptive to our message as it is presented. (In a sense, these qualities are psychographics, but in a very specific form, required only when we deal with one particular commercial message instead of an overall campaign.)

Suppose our intended audience members are (demographically) brides-to-be, aged twenty-five and under, students who work part-time, residing in Lansing, Michigan, and (psychographically) animal lovers, interested in foreign affairs, and afraid of airplanes. Granting that both categories of information would be helpful to the radio copywriter on a bridal consultant's account, consider the added value of knowing that these women enjoy classical music, prefer saleswomen to salesmen, are extremely money conscious, and watch soap operas.

In short, broad psychographic characteristics may aid creative teams in developing long-range campaign themes and ideas—fabric soft as a kitten's fur, for animal lovers; designs that communicate in any language, for those interested in foreign affairs; and dreams brought down to earth, for those afraid of flying. The more specific, the better, when it comes to selecting words and music for an individual commercial. In this instance, classical music behind a spot that stressed savings, delivered by women in a dialogue format, would seem ideal regardless of the choice of theme.

5. *Style.* Commercial style (mood, tone, color, or flavor) must be developed to suit the overall objective and target audience. A light, bouncy, or humorous style would be inappropriate for delivery of a mortuary commercial. On the other hand a somber, melodramatic tone would do little to communicate the youthful exuberance of customers enjoying a new pizza parlor or amusement park. Copywriters must match mood to message and remember the psychographics involved.

6. *Technique.* The technique portion of the platform performs another matching job, by explaining how the selected style will be implemented, using available media facilities. For example, a dashing, high-spirited, masculine style (for men's cologne) might demand a crisp, even rhythmic copy technique, supplemented by adventuresome music, the sound of a roaring surf, and the bold, rugged voice of a sea captain.

7. *Competition and competitive claims.* Although we are building a copy platform for our intended commercial, it is valuable to list a few major competitors and the claims they are currently making (against which we will attempt to position our product). Suppose that we are going to advertise a new dishwashing detergent and that commercials for existing detergents stress the following claims:

Brand A: strong enough to cut through stubborn stains.
Brand B: a little goes a long way so you save money.
Brand C: perfumed scents make dishwashing a pleasure.

The value of this information becomes apparent in the next part of the platform.

8. *Positioning.* Our commercial must now carve out a private little niche for our detergent in the consumer's pattern of thought; our product must be seen as an individual entity, rather than merely one of the crowd. Hence, we might choose a "new container is easier to handle" position or a "powerful formula cleans without a lot of scrubbing" position. Granted, our product—and the other A, B, and C brands—might be able to claim several of these positions. The point is to take one position at a time (for the sake of comprehension and credibility), and a different one from current competition (for the sake of brand image and memorability).

Looking at the matter another way, positioning explains the mind's-eye picture (of product, service, or store) that, it is hoped, audience members will have after exposure to the commercial. This desired image will affect the style and technique selected for the message. If a cereal manufacturer wants his product positioned as a nutritious hot cereal that needs no cooking, the resulting commercial must establish this informational mood, and then develop it in a framework free from distracting elements.

9. *Sales key.* It seems appropriate to hold the heart of the copy platform until the end. The creative sales key, which ultimately determines whether a message succeeds in its role as a marketing tool, is a three-pronged device powerful enough to unlock doors to successful message communication. Carrying this analogy one step further, we might note that the doors referred to are often rusted shut thanks to the indifference paid them by members of the listening audience who, consciously and unconsciously, tune out many radio commercials. It takes a strong key to do the job, and the thrust behind it (the message that carries and turns the key) also has to be substantial.

In essence, the sales key is a valuable selling point, linked to a valuable benefit, and expressed in an original way. Without question, this is the most complex and crucial side of effective commercial writing. Let us consider each part separately. A valuable selling point refers to a special feature of a product, service, or store, important enough to the target audience to command attention and stimulate interest. A valuable benefit link is a result of the selling point—a believable effect that meets and strengthens audience desires for the advertised brand. And an original expression is the copywriter's brainstorm—a memorable and creatively unique manner of summarizing the selling point/benefit package that helps convince consumers to act.

As an example, assume that the selling point is delicious food you don't have to prepare, and that the benefit is a satisfying meal in a relaxed atmosphere. In the hands of one copywriter the unique expression became "You deserve a break today" (McDonald's). Another copywriter, however, came up with "You're a Wendy's kind of people," and still another with "Aren't you hungry for Burger King now?"

The crucial point is that usually (except in the rare case of a genuine physical difference between brands) the same selling points and benefits can be claimed by two or more competing advertisers. Although the copywriter naturally must spend some time deciding which selling point and which benefit to feature in a given commercial, much of his or her effort goes toward creating that original expression. Another case in point found two leading toothpaste manufacturers claiming "I love the fight!" (Crest), and "Take aim against cavities" (Aim). In each case, the selling point (a proven cavity-fighting ingredient) and the benefit (healthier teeth) were the same, but the sales keys (and the commercial styles) were different because of the way in which the selling-point/benefit match-up was expressed.

10. *Bonuses, if any.* Last, and optionally, we may wish to include a limited number of minor selling points or benefits in a given commercial above and beyond our major sales key. Unless these bonuses are few in number and of relatively little importance, however, they will overpower the sales key.

Examples of generally acceptable bonuses might be three different sizes, a new yellow box, open 24 hours, free parking available, and ten cents off this week. (Of course, in select circumstances, any one of these points could be developed into a complete sales key.) Copywriters should never feel obligated to include bonuses in commercials. A solid sales key may be all that is needed (in which case additional points would bog down the communication process).

Finally, always remember that a copy platform is designed for a specific commercial, and not for an entire campaign. (See Figures 9.3 and 9.4.) The audience that is not reached, the sales key that is not developed, the objective that is not met by one message may be picked up by a second, third, or thirtieth. Each individual commercial is part of an overall campaign, of course, and should lend unity to it; often, however, the connecting factor is simply a theme line or slogan.

1. Client and Product

   Sun-Glo Products, N.Y.,
   Sun-Glo Car Wax

2. Medium and Commercial Description

   Top-40 stations in New York & New Jersey; 60-second straight sell.

3. Objective

   To convince car buffs that Sun-Glo does the job beautifully without extra effort, and to associate the product name with the look of sunshine.

4. Target Audience

   College-age students who wash their own cars often, and enjoy keeping them shiny. Married or single, they don't have a lot of extra time, so work-savers are welcomed. Still, they're sophisticated enough to demand quality and don't appreciate commercial gimmicks or extravagant claims. They're at least partially self-supporting, and depend on their cars for job and school transportation as well as pleasure. Money is tight, so value is important.

5. Style

   Friendly, but convincing; a rational appeal combined with emotional satisfaction.

6. Technique

   Straightforward, authoritative male presenter

7. Competition and Competitive Claims

   ECONO-SHINE: "Professional results without the cost"

   CAR-SO-NEW: "Give your old car a face lift -- hide those extra years"

8. Positioning

   Positioned as a reliable, double-duty product; a carefully blended compound that cleans and polishes simultaneously.

9. Sales Key

   Sunshine quality in work-saver form: does two jobs at once, thanks to a combination of ingredients. Memorable "sun" name and association.

10. Bonuses

    Convenient availability.

Fig. 9.3. Example of a copy platform for a straight announcement commercial.

1. Client and Product

   Sterling Sound, N.Y.,
   stereo kits

2. Medium and Commercial
   Description

   MOR stations in the
   Midwest; 60-second production spot

3. Objective

   To inform not-so-
   technically-inclined
   music enthusiasts, through
   credible dialogue, that
   Sterling Kits are economical and easy to assemble;
   and to convince them to
   examine the product
   firsthand.

4. Target Audience

   Primarily males, 25-34,
   single or recently
   married, with a serious
   interest in music and at
   least a passing acquain-
   tance with light mechanical work. Apartment or
   small-home dwellers, they
   have at least two years of
   college or trade school
   education, and combined
   family income is $10,000-
   $15,000. Occupations
   vary; the "workshop" may
   be purely an avocation.
   These men prize personal
   accomplishments and appreciate recognition.
   They're not apt to spend
   money foolishly.

5. Style
   Light and personal; fast-
   paced, triumphant at end.

6. Technique

   Snappy dialogue; bright
   and conversational.
   Workshop sounds help set
   locale, and two musical
   crescendos reinforce copy
   claims directly.
   Crossfade builds image for
   Sterling and credibility
   for the announcer.

7. Competition and
   Competitive Claims

   TRU-SOUND: "Lowest prices
   in town, and guaranteed
   satisfaction"

   MASTER KITS: "The thrill
   of building it all
   yourself; become an expert
   in your spare time"

8. Positioning

   The Sterling Sound Stereo
   Kit will be positioned as
   a partner in musical
   adventure; a companion
   that's fun to work with,
   and a delightful investment in lasting entertainment.

9. Sales Key

   Easily obtained, high
   quality results; economical because you do your own
   assembling. Sterling is
   your partner in musical
   adventure and a sound
   investment for the future.

10. Bonuses

   Convenient availability.

Fig. 9.4. Example of a copy platform for a radio production commercial.

The Commercial Message

Unfortunately for the aspiring get-rich-quick copywriter, but fortunately for the sake of creativity, there are no copy formulas for instant success. If there were, radio spots would probably be ground out by computers—each with prescribed words, sound effects, and music in a set fashion. If such were the case, the art of persuasion would be lost; the personal voice of commercials—speaking directly to the wants and needs of listeners—would be missing.

On the fortunate side, however, a number of guidelines for beginning radio copywriters have been compiled and handed down from one successful copywriter to another. Textbooks present such tips in a variety of ways, but it is important to realize that no one prescription is more effective than any other; it is up to each writer to know the product (or service or store) involved, the medium (its characteristics and available resources), the competition (products and ads), and the target audience thoroughly.

It is then that copywriters are free to pick and choose from existing guidelines, occasionally (with good reason) ignoring some, and creating others to fit the circumstances. They view copywriting rules as thought prodders or directional signals, not as mandates that must be interpreted literally and obeyed meticulously. Ultimately, the job does get easier, though not necessarily less challenging.

HOW EASY it all is—once you know how. In fact, if you will forgive a touch of advertisingese, we call our own copywriting formula "HOW-E-ZE," and present it as six guidelines that can help bring a sales key to life. Each deserves special emphasis:

Hit home with your audience. If there were a first law of copywriting, it would probably be to start where your audience is (not where you would like it to be) in terms of predispositions. Behavioral scientists have found that the stronger an attitude is, the more it will resist change; hence, copywriters must recognize and relate to existing attitudes (opinions, beliefs, values) before trying to alter them in some way. In other words, the copy in a commercial should move with the audience from point to point along the sales communication path. Commercials cannot yank listeners across attitudinal lines.

Offer a reward—a promise. We already have discussed the importance of this endeavor, but its value cannot be overemphasized. Even ancient philosophers recognized that human beings strive to maximize pleasure and minimize pain; this is the best promise a commercial can make.

Win loyalty with brand image. Remember that in selective advertising we are working with brands, not general classes of products. A commercial that merely emphasizes the advantages of flying over traveling by bus does nothing to differentiate American from Delta, or United, or whichever airline is paying for the message. The brand name must be clearly, unmistakably related to the sales claim, or the promises we have worked so hard to establish may go to work for a competitor in the minds of listeners.

Earn trust through proof of claims. Psychologists tell us that a real understanding of principles does more than rote memorization to stimulate genuine learning. By substantiating claims (even briefly), the copywriter helps build understanding. The more logical and precise the sales argument, the greater chance there is for solid audience conviction to occur. Even emotional presentations shouldn't be flimsy.

Zoom in on personal value. Advertising succeeds only when it shows consumers how and why it is in their own best interests to try a given product. Whether or not you accept the cynical view that man is basically a selfish animal, it is hard to quarrel with the pursuit of happiness that almost all of us seem dedicated to in one way or another. The value of the sales promise must be stressed again and again—not just what the product will do or why, but what it all means to the individual message recipient in terms of his or her own life-style, goals and ambitions, present and future.

End with a clincher to make action easy. A brief closing summary of a commercial's main point can help pave the way for action, especially a memorable summary ("Clout knocks dirt out!"). Then the actual call for action may be either hard sell (direct, immediate action: "Buy today"), or soft sell (indirect, delayed action: "Keep us in mind"). In radio it is more often the former, but in either case, listeners must be given whatever particulars are necessary and appropriate, such as where and when they can buy. In addition, the more motivated a response is, the easier it will be to make; hence, price reductions and other incentives are offered frequently.

Armed with this formula, we can now examine three specific categories of message-content concern: the field of information from which we draw selling points and benefits; the structures or formats around which we build sales stories; and particulars on word choice, sentence construction, and sequencing.

WHAT TO SAY

In selecting and constructing a sales key, the copywriter has at least four areas of information from which to choose: background material (history of the company, store, or brand name, management philosophy, past success stories, continuing research studies, improvements and expansions); in-use information (descriptions of physical make-up, such as size, shape, weight, texture, color, sound, smell, and taste; or location, hours of operation, prices, available services and guarantees; or usage details, including when, where, why, and how); results-of-use information (physical and emotional reactions, results of studies conducted on consumer attitudes, evidence obtained to support claims); and incidentals (current specials, holiday or seasonal tie-ins, contests, premiums, coupons, and even packaging details).

Granted, these are only partial lists, but it is easy to see the field is wide open; copywriters must be aware of the tendency, however, to crowd too much information into a single message. One sales key per commercial is a very important rule.

HOW TO PRESENT IT

Radio commercial formats are many and varied, and sometimes two or more may be combined. Especially popular ones follow.

Straight Announcement

The straight announcement commercial often focuses on product advancements and competitive benefits. There are no dramatic frills, musical accompaniments, sound effects, or dialogue and no attempt at storytelling. Figure 9.5 is an example of the straight format. Notice that the sales key is repeated, in different words, no fewer than four times.

A variation of this approach accelerates the pace of delivery, as a barker does at a carnival, and a salesman does in a used car lot. It is the hurry-hurry-hurry, step-right-up format that is obviously only suitable in select instances (not in the case of fine jewelry or intimate cologne).

Personality/Testimonial

Sometimes, a well-known individual talks about a product without actually endorsing it and thereby lends an accepted personality to a message urging listeners to try a particular brand. An actual testimonial, on the other hand, features a celebrity (or simply a Mr. or Ms. American who endorses a product from personal experience). The implication is clear; if a professional model or movie star uses a specific type of skin cream, it must be good.

CLIENT:	Sun-Glo Products, N.Y.	DESCRIPTION:	60-sec. Straight Sell
PRODUCT:	Sun-Glo Car Wax	FOR AIRING:	Fri.-Sun., ROS
MEDIUM:	Top 40, N.Y. & N.J.	TITLE:	Duststorm/Mudbath

ANNCR: Does your car look like it's just come through a duststorm? Or a mudbath? Well, now picture a Sun-Glo sparkle instead. Almost everyone likes to drive a clean, shiny car, but no one likes extra work. That's why you need Sun-Glo -- the golden, rich-textured wax that cleans and polishes your car at the same time. Results you'll be proud to show off! And, when you use Sun-Glo, there's no hard rubbing at all. Sun-Glo's special formula actually does two jobs at once. You simply apply it, pressing just hard enough to loosen old dirt. Then, let Sun-Glo dry to a white powder. When you wipe it off, all that old road grime goes with it, and your car's bright enough to dazzle in the sun -- really beautiful! You'll love driving your Sun-Glo car . . . so why wait? Get this easy-to-use cleaner and polisher now at your favorite hardware store. Wipe out that duststorm -- or mudbath -- with Sun-Glo . . . today!

Fig. 9.5. Straight radio commercial.

Dialogue

Dialogue takes place between real or imaginary characters, or between one or more of them and an announcer who serves as official spokesperson. The conversation usually involves some sort of product endorsement (whether or not it takes the form of a full testimonial) and may tell a story or simply discuss product features and benefits. A word to the wise, however—idle chitchat, by itself, can seriously hinder genuine sales communication.

A frequent problem with dialogue is believability; the feeling created is often artificial or rehearsed. Phrasing may be stilted, almost as if the various speakers were reading off a package. Sales messages need to flow with dialogue instead of being sandwiched in between conversational lines.

One other problem concerns the clear-only-if-known fallacy. Here the meaning of an exchange is clear only to conversational participants (and the copywriter); it never comes across to listeners. For example, a man and woman might talk for 30 seconds about a "great, really different" cracker without ever explaining meanings: Cheese crackers or wheat? Salty, sweet, crispy, large, small, round, square, or something else entirely?

Figure 9.6 is an example of a dialogue commercial in which both music and sound effects contribute to the sales message; the conversation is relevant, and the announcer lends credibility.

CLIENT: Sterling Sound, N.Y.   DESCRIPTION: 60-sec. Production
PRODUCT: Stereo Kits   FOR AIRING: M-F, Drive Time
MEDIUM: MOR Stations, Midwest   TITLE: Hubby's Hobby

SOUND: HAMMERING & GENERAL WORKSHOP NOISES UP AND UNDER

LINDA: Honestly, my husband came home with a Sterling Sound Kit, and

         said he was going to build a stereo, if you can imagine . . .

FRED: Linda, it's finished! Listen!

MUSIC: SYMPHONIC CRESCENDO UP FULL, THEN MUSIC UNDER FOR:

LINDA: Fred! That's not coming from something you built!?

FRED: Sure! Sterling gave me the parts, and I was the partner --

         just put 'em together.

LINDA: (REFLECTING) Hmmm . . . must've had easy instructions . . .

FRED: Step-by-step -- just like a map. My own little adventure!

         And what was a Sterling Sound Kit a little while ago is

         now . . .

MUSIC: UP FULL AGAIN, THEN UNDER AS SHE SPEAKS

LINDA: . . . beautiful! A little bit of work and a whole lot of

         music. You and Sterling make a super team.

FRED: And a money-saving team, too. Great investment.

MUSIC: CROSSFADE CHANGE OF PACE AS ANNCR SPEAKS

ANNCR: Team up with Sterling. Ask to see the whole line of Sterling

         Sound Kits at your favorite appliance store. Find out how

         easy it is to save money -- beautifully.

MUSIC: UP AND OUT

Fig. 9.6. Radio production commercial.

Interview

If the dialogue takes more of a question-and-answer form, it may be classified as an interview (the familiar man-on-the-street approach). Unfortunately, this particular format is used so often it may tend to sound canned and, thus, lose whatever sales punch it hoped to achieve.

Drama

In this case, the structure assumes a narrative approach. A dramatic situation (often a little playlet) presents the product as a problem-solver and may even wind up sounding like a soap opera. Still, this format occasionally offers some verbal proof of claims in a more realistic framework than is true of other approaches.

CONTENT SPECIFICS

As noted, the heart of any commercial is its promise to the consumer—an advantage, a problem-solver, a reward, a benefit available through purchase of product or service (or through store patronage). It is the copywriter's job to present this promise as the reason why consumers should buy one brand instead of another.

In most cases the presentation is:

1. *Rational.* Ingredient Q is a cavity-fighter; brand X has ingredient Q in it; therefore, brand X is a cavity-fighter; or

2. *Emotional.* Product A is made to give you that wonderfully refreshed feeling you've been missing; wear it tonight and know you're irresistible; or

3. *Both.* You know a good, nutritious breakfast is important to your family's health; you've come to trust company Y; you can rest assured that Y's new cereal, with eight essential vitamins and minerals, is just what your family needs for a great start each day.

In any case, the argument must be both truthful and believable. The following tips should be considered in this light.

Immediate Attention

Breaking through the wall of indifference radio listeners often set up toward commercials—in a manner appropriate to the sales message—is not an easy job for copywriters. Unexpected words often prove successful as stoppers, or any unusual beginning that jars the listener can do the job, as can a familiar piece of music, a thought-provoking question, or a sing-along.

Well-written jingles can pack a strong selling message in four opening commercial lines:

> Are hot feet your worry?
> Get cool in a hurry!
> Here's speedy relief news
> From Comfort-Style Shoes!

On the other hand, rhyming lines set to music may simply waste a client's money by neither describing the advertiser nor suggesting any part of the sales key:

> At last you've decided
> You're due for a rest;
> So come out to Swenson's
> It's really the best.

Can humor serve as an effective attention-getter? It can . . . although it is often accused of getting in the way of real brand-sell. The commercial in Figure 9.7 was cited by *Advertising Age* as one

WAITER: I got an order for you, chef.

CHEF: What is it?

WAITER: Table six wants the blimp cocktail.

CHEF: You mean shrimp cocktail.

WAITER: And the beer soup.

CHEF: Bean soup.

WAITER: And a bowl of the beef glue.

CHEF: What? Let me see that menu.

WAITER: Okay.

CHEF: Who made this copy. It's all smeared and wrinkled.
           I can hardly read it.

WAITER: Booth four wants chicken frisbee.

CHEF: Fricassee.

WAITER: What the heck is corn on the cat?

CHEF: Oh, these copies are terrible.

WAITER: What do you want from me -- our copier jams up all the time.

CHEF: Get me a Minolta.

WAITER: I don't see a Minolta on the menu. Oh, you mean the
           minestrone.

CHEF: I mean the Minolta EP 310 copier.

WAITER: Ahhh.

CHEF: The Minolta EP 310 has this incredibly short paper path that
           virtually eliminates paper jam.

WAITER: No kidding.

CHEF: And the Minolta EP 310 even has a self-diagnostic system.

WAITER: How about the bowling banquet in the back room.

CHEF: Yeah?

WAITER: They want the nude cake.

CHEF: You mean nut cake.

WAITER: No, nude cake -- where the girl jumps out at the . . .

CHEF: Oh, that.

WAITER: Yeah.

CHEF: That.

ANNCR: The Minolta EP 310 copier. A business partner you can
           depend on.

Fig. 9.7. "Humorous" radio spot. (*Advertising Age* [August 24, 1981]: 54)

of the best-of-the-year spots in 1981. Its message is brief and clear, and it probably would appeal to non-users of the product (who might someday pass along its story to a user) as well as to those in the market for the product.

Extensive research by McCollum/Spielman & Company does indicate that it is inadvisable to use humor to launch new products.[2]

Early Selling

Some experts argue that a product name need not jump out at listeners in the first couple of words, thereby cueing them immediately that it is a commercial they are about to hear. Still, in highly competitive fields, or when there is something different to report about the product, it rarely pays to keep listeners in suspense and risk losing them entirely before the advertiser's name is ever mentioned. For beginning writers especially, a good rule of thumb is product name and at least a hint at the sales key in the first ten seconds of a message. Figure 9.8 is a local commercial in which selling begins immediately, yet the message is light, interesting, and easy to follow.

AMERICAN:	Oh, yes . . . here at King Street Carwash we wash every model, and we do it right.
BRITON:	Really?
AMERICAN:	And we wash any model for just a dollar-ninety-nine.
BRITON:	I say!
AMERICAN:	'Course, with 5 to 7 gallons of gas, we wash 'em for only 99 cents.
BRITON:	Good heavens!
AMERICAN:	And with a full tank, we'll wash any model free of charge.
BRITON:	Extraordinary!
AMERICAN:	We're open every day, too, 'cept Sunday -- at 829 South King.
BRITON:	And you say you wash every model?
AMERICAN:	Just open that door there and see for yourself.
SOUND:	DOOR OPENS TO SOUND OF SPLASHING WATER
GIRL:	Oooo . . . could . . . you . . . pass me that towel?
BRITON:	Oh . . . my!

Fig. 9.8. "Early-sell" radio spot. (Courtesy of K59 Radio, Honolulu)

Importance of News

In their pursuit of achievement and success, Americans are ever anxious to learn what's new—to keep up with the very latest fads and fashions, hair styles, photographic equipment, and automobiles. Hence, new products (and new features, uses, and designs of existing products) are appealing in part just because they are new.

Unfortunately, some commercials exploit this interest in novelty by emphasizing new or improved features of little or no value. Still, legitimate news is never out of place in advertising, and should not be buried in copy, especially in a perishable message on radio.

"You" Attitude

You is often regarded as the most important word in advertising. Consumer-oriented copywriters fulfill *your* wants and needs, speak to the problems *you're* confronting, and appeal to the goals *you've* set, or to the dreams *you'd* like to see materialize. The personal approach is mandatory in the personal-companion medium of radio. Also, it helps copywriters remember to zero in on personal audience psychographics.

Short Words and Sentences with Smooth Tracking

Radio is a conversational medium, and consumers simply do not talk in polished prose (five-syllable words, for instance). Even sentence fragments are perfectly acceptable, because most of us converse without regard for dangling participles and the like. Similarly, radio copywriters cannot afford to waste time with the long lists of items often seen in newspaper ads. "Family" or "loved ones" can replace "Mom and Dad, the kids, teenagers, grandparents, and toddlers," and "dozens of styles and colors" would probably be used in a radio commercial for a shoe store, rather than an enumeration of items.

Tracking is another term for sequencing. Commercials must move smoothly, clearly, logically from point to point; choppy, disjointed thoughts muddle messages and lose audiences.

Contractions

Formal papers are usually prepared without contractions, but in everyday conversation we use them constantly. Hence, they are expected by radio listeners. Can we ever leave out a contraction to emphasize a point? Of course: *It is* your responsibility to recognize exceptions to these rules!

Action Verbs and Visual Nouns

Long sets of descriptive adjectives may do well in an exercise on word imagery or an assignment designed to paint flowery scenes with flowery words. When every second is measured, however, as a carrier of hard-working dollars meant to differentiate one highly competitive brand from another, there is no time for excess verbiage. A long string of adjectives frequently does little more for a commercial than point to its writers as boastful. Verbs can be action-getters and action-setters (mixing, swirling, digging, racing), and visual nouns (wedding, ballgame, circus, volcano) create mental pictures much faster than do adjectives. Figure 9.9 is a graphic radio commercial for a local home supply store.

Active Voice

Active voice is less wordy (shorter), and usually gets a point across with more punch than passive voice. "Stores carry" is much better than "stores can be found to be stocked with." Usually, the livelier the pace of commercial copy, the more interesting it is to follow.

Positive Claims

In most cases, copy with sales power spells out its claims positively rather than negatively. (One exception might be "Don't miss your chance.") Then, too, a long series of negative terms and

```
ANNCR:          Among our early pioneers was a woodsman, name of

                "Slammin' Sammy" Sunida!  He swung a mean ax, that Sammy

                . . . felling those big-ones till you couldn't see the

                forest for the trees.  But think of the work he'd have

                saved if only he'd gone to Pioneer Home Supply instead.

                All kinds of lumber, building supplies, hardware,

                roofing, plumbing -- listen:  if you want to "ax" the

                high cost of home-improvement, hurry (CHOP-CHOP) to

                Pioneer Home Supply, 930 Kilani Avenue.
```

Fig. 9.9. "Graphic" radio spot. (Courtesy of K59 Radio, Honolulu)

associations, used repeatedly to support a product can have a negative effect. A cleaning agent consistently presented as an end to housekeeping drudgery, the woes of a homemaker's day, the burden of never-ending grime, and the everlasting chore of getting things really clean just may wind up with a woeful image in the minds of potential customers. Also, consumers are generally more impressed by what a product will do than by what it won't do, so why call attention to a product's weaknesses?

Simple and Specific

Simple expressions communicate much more quickly and easily than complex ones. For example, "grime-busting ammonia power" makes sound sense, but "composed of sufficient chemicals and other ingredients to enable removal of undesirable residue in a vigorous manner" is an auditory nightmare.

Likewise, only specific claims will really differentiate one product, service, or store from another. Better and greater have become watered-down claims (when applied to "taste," "appearance," or "performance"); isn't it *better* to say richer flavor, brighter shine, or stronger grip?

Repetition

Obviously, broadcast audiences cannot refer back to messages once they have been aired. Hence, unless the product name is extremely well known (unmistakably associated with the commercial message), it must be repeated two, three, or more times. So should the sales key, though not necessarily in exactly the same terms; repetition with variation adds interest. (Check again the example in Figure 9.5.)

Memorability

Catching the listener's ear is only the first step of a radio copywriter's job. Communicating the sales message memorably—linking the product name and sales key together in a memorable way—is a monumental challenge. Sometimes, a little rhythm helps, such as alliteration or words that rhyme ("Everything's better with Blue Bonnet on it"). On other occasions, sound effects and music help or, perhaps, a jingle.

We don't mean to construe the idea that claims must be dressed up in media garb to communicate effectively. It is important to avoid mere trite expressions, which writers seem to fall back on when there is not enough time (or effort) available to search for something more suitable. Of course almost everyone uses cliches in conversation; it's often difficult to keep from using them. "Green as grass," "white as snow," "free as a breeze," "happy as a lark"—copywriters may have dozens of them at their fingertips. Unfortunately, they often fall flat when it comes to selling consumers on a new product design or idea, or on a special brand characteristic or high-quality ingredient. Here, then, is another creative challenge: to find a new way to say the thing that already has been said so well it's become a cliche. Figure 9.10 plays on the word "cut" very effectively; Cutter Ford comes out ahead as a result.

ANNCR: Let's see . . . there's the "cost-cutter," the "red-tape-cutter," the "nonsense-cutter" -- as a matter of fact, <u>all</u> the cutters are at your service all the time: at Cutter Ford! On beautiful, new, affordable Ford cars . . . and practical, rugged, affordable Ford trucks . . . <u>they</u> cut-the-clowning, 'cause they want to deal. And <u>you</u> cut-the-corners, 'cause you do the dealing! Cutter Ford is <u>always</u> a-cut-above. Come see us today!

Fig. 9.10. "Play-on-words" radio spot. (Courtesy of K59 Radio, Honolulu)

No Tongue Twisters or Figure Flings

As already pointed out, alliteration can aid message retention. The wise copywriter, however, avoids such lines as "Get Bressler's best in bread," or "Come to all five free Friday Fresh-Fish-Fries," for obvious reasons.

Sets of figures are best omitted also—the weights and prices of numerous package sizes, complete with the number of servings each provides, lengthy addresses, and even telephone numbers. The ear cannot receive signals as quickly as the eye and cannot assimilate as much information. There are exceptions; a memorable address such as 1776 Liberty Way might be included for a shop known as American Spirit. Or, The Up & Down Boutique might plug its 123-4321 telephone number. Otherwise, listeners may be advised to "check the yellow pages" for needed information, or locations can be generally specified as "downtown on Main Street," or "next door to Macy's."

Call for Action

Summarizing the sales key at the close of a commercial is often a good way to ease listeners into a sale, but it is also important to tell the audience exactly what the advertiser wishes them to do: come in, buy, or simply remember.

If commercial copy is to convince consumers to do business with one particular company or store, it must respect and support that organization's existing or desired image. The line "So cheap you'll want to pick up several today" might fit well with a discount store sale on sweaters or scarves. The same line used to promote a sale at an exclusive fashion boutique, however, would obviously be in very poor taste.

Beginning copywriters would do well to heed as many of these suggestions as possible, but should not feel restricted by them; creativity is still an art. Figures 9.11 and 9.12 are examples of a special kind of challenge: creating separate radio commercials for separate audiences without changing the product or sales key.

A challenge to the reader will be to keep all of these radio guidelines in mind as we turn to the more complicated world of TV commercials.

SOUND:	TRUMPET FANFARE
ANNCR:	It's Darcy's Home Store sale of the year! All major appliances are reduced up to forty percent through Saturday! That means great savings for you on that new Darcy dishwasher you've been dreaming about . . .
SOUND:	SPLASHING WATER AND GENTLE WHIR OF DISHWASHER (UP & OUT)
ANNCR:	. . . Such a time-saver! Or, how about a Darcy vacuum cleaner . . .
SOUND:	HUM OF VACUUM CLEANER (UP & OUT)
ANNCR:	. . . It's lightweight, but does a heavy-duty job every time. There's lots more -- and a full year's warranty on every appliance! (SNEAK TRUMPET FANFARE IN BACKGROUND) So come in today while there's still a big selection!
SOUND:	FANFARE UP FULL
ANNCR:	(LOUDLY) Hurry to Darcy's Home Store Sale of the year!

Fig. 9.11. Radio spot for top-40 station.

MUSIC:	THE PARTY'S OVER (UP & UNDER)
ANNCR:	When the party's over, your clean-up jobs begin . . . (SEGUE LIGHT CELEBRATION MUSIC AND HOLD UNDER) . . . but <u>this</u> time Darcy's Home Store comes to your rescue. It's Darcy's annual appliance sale -- up to forty percent savings through Saturday on dishwashers, vacuum cleaners, and much more! Now's your chance to buy some of that famous Darcy quality -- fully guaranteed for a year -- at low prices you simply must check out. (MUSIC OUT)
SOUND:	DOORBELL RINGING
ANNCR:	Let your holiday entertaining be a pleasure even after your guests have gone. Come to Darcy's Home Store sale of the year -- today!

Fig. 9.12. Radio spot for middle-of-the-road (MOR) station.

Study Questions

1. Name three products or services that you think could benefit from a humorous approach in radio commercials and three that should avoid it.

2. Think of some celebrities who are not currently endorsing products. Match them with particular brands or stores (based on their characters or personalities), and explain why you think their images would enhance those of the advertised items on radio.

3. List some instantly identifiable sound effects and suggest a variety of radio commercial moods they might represent.

4. Select a local store or service currently running radio commercials, and explain how the organization is positioned in listeners' minds through this form of advertising.

5. Use the HOW-E-ZE formula to analyze selected radio commercials. Where violations occur, discuss possible reasons and overall effects.

6. Which specific radio commercial do you find the most believable? The most unbelievable? Why?

ASSIGNMENT 9-A

Listen to a half-hour of programming on a commercial radio music station and log the following information for the commercials you hear. Write in each advertised item, the length of each spot, and the number of product name repetitions. Then, check all other relevant columns. Summarize what you have learned from the exercise and include appropriate comments regarding general content.

Advertised Item	Length of Spot	Product Name Repetition	Straight Annct.	Dialogue	Music	Sound Effects	Jingle/Song	Celebrity Presenter	Hard Sell	Soft Sell	Male Voice	Female Voice

Summary and Comments

ASSIGNMENT 9-B

Read the following 60-second radio commercial carefully. Find and mark at least 15 serious shortcomings in content (disregarding the straight announcement format, which might well be improved with the addition of music).

ANNCR: After a lengthy and tedious day of work, there are times, especially during snow-filled, sleet-filled, shivery, slippery winter months, when a sweet, flavorful, yet light, not-too-filling dessert is better tasting than anything one would be able to think of. It is not possible to imagine a person who would not be satisfied by the delightful, delicate, and truly delicious aroma of Brookenhines new cherry dessert. None of the ingredients in this dessert can fail to please—whether it be grandparents, Dad, the kids, teenagers, or even toddlers. The housewife who fills those dessert plates with this wonderful treat keeps everyone pleased, and finds that the days are left free of time-consuming dessert preparations. Food stores everywhere can be found to be stocked with the regular, and the economy-sized packages—enough for four, or for eight, servings. It is the product to be kept on top of Mother's shopping list . . . for a treat that is tops with the whole family.

ASSIGNMENT 9-C

Given an assigned objective, audience, commercial length, station, and air time, rewrite the message you analyzed in assignment 9-B.

ASSIGNMENT 9-D

Given an assigned product, service, or store, prepare a 10-point copy platform for a prospective straight announcement commercial, following guidelines presented in Chapter 9.

ASSIGNMENT 9-E

Prepare a straight announcement commercial following the platform you completed in assignment 9-D.

ASSIGNMENT 9-F

Given an assigned product, service, or store, prepare a 10-point copy platform for a prospective radio production commercial, again following guidelines presented in Chapter 9.

ASSIGNMENT 9-G

Prepare the production commercial for your platform completed in assignment 9-F.

ASSIGNMENT 9-H

Given one product (service or store) and one basic sales key, prepare two different 30-second commercials—one for each of the two audiences described. Both groups share the same demographics (presented below), but the psychographics are quite different.

Demographics for Audience 1 and Audience 2

Married women, 25 to 30, who live in suburbs of major cities. They have 1 to 2 children, work part-time, have a combined family income of $20-25,000. They have at least two years of higher education, listen to radio an average of three hours per day, and belong to at least one social club or service organization. They visit a supermarket twice a week, department stores twice a week, and other stores and service establishments four times a week. They drive approximately 100 miles per week and have an average of five radios per household (including car radios).

Psychographics for Audience 1

These women are basically liberal in their thinking—innovators in most areas. They are highly emotional, often restless, and would almost always prefer going out than staying at home; they have no qualms about hiring babysitters. They love the beach scene and thrill to big city entertainment. They are sports enthusiasts, and prefer movies and TV to books and cards. Political activities rank high, and they are extremely interested in personal grooming and physical fitness.

Psychographics for Audience 2

These women are basically conservative in their thinking—followers rather than leaders. They are practical, enjoy entertaining at home, and like to spend free time with their families. They enjoy rural and mountain trips and vacations, like to cook and sew, and prefer books and cards to movies and TV. Religious activities rank high, and they are extremely interested in culture and the arts.

Notes

1. See *Advertising Age* (January 23, 1978):54; and *Broadcasting* (March 24, 1980):16.
2. *Topline* 3, no. 3 (July, 1982):6 (McCollum/Spielman & Company, New York).

Suggested Readings

Field, Stanley. *Professional Broadcast Writer's Handbook.* Blue Ridge Summit, Pa.: Tab Books, 1974.
Peck, William A. *Anatomy of Local Radio-TV Copy,* 4th ed. Blue Ridge Summit, Pa.: Tab Books, 1976.
Zeigler, Sherilyn K., and J. Douglas Johnson. *Creative Strategy and Tactics in Advertising.* Columbus, Ohio: Grid Publishing, 1981.

ALSO: Check recent issues of *Advertising Age, Broadcasting,* the *Journal of Advertising,* the *Journal of Advertising Research,* and the *Journal of Broadcasting.*

10

Writing Television Commercials

Like radio, television is an exciting medium for delivering powerful sales impact; its combination of sight, sound, motion, and emotion brings it closer to personal, face-to-face communication than does any other medium. Product and sales messages can literally come to life before viewers' eyes, involving them in a very personal way. With careful planning, even low-cost production methods can achieve many of the dramatic effects associated with high-budget Hollywood creations.

The Nature of the Task

As noted earlier, television today is omnipresent. Sets are found in living rooms, family rooms, and bedrooms and accompany owners to outdoor events, college dormitories, and weekend retreats. As a companion and friend, therefore, television is expected to be compatible and interesting, helpful and credible, stimulating and inoffensive.

Because TV is an entertainment medium, though, its commercials, like those on radio, appear as intruders—unwelcome guests who arrive to disrupt audience enjoyment and concentration. Still, if they provide needed product information in a refreshing yet relevant manner, they may be welcome after all. Indeed, if they can offer pleasant solutions to annoying tasks, they may even leave audiences with a feeling of genuine satisfaction.

PROBLEMS

TV commercials that are sheer entertainment may win prizes for creativity but fail miserably when it comes to influencing product purchase. The copywriter must always remember that the purpose of any advertising message is first to convey a sales story—usually a brand-differentiating story—and only secondarily to tie in appropriate conversation, narrative details, humor, or other elements.

Difficult but important questions to face are (1) how can the sales key best be set in visual motion; (2) how can the selling-point/benefit match-up be dramatized so the viewer sees clearly the relationship between it and the specific brand in question; (3) how can the overall sales message be related directly to the viewer's own life-style; (4) how can effective sales communication be accomplished in as little as 15 seconds; and (5) how can it all be done with a minimum of commercialitis? Then, too, competition is fierce. According to the Television Bureau of Advertising, well over 10,000 brands of products are now featured in TV commercials.

OPPORTUNITIES

On the positive side, television can expose every word of advertising copy—every element of a sales story—within the context of a moving, talking world. This challenges copywriters to create product personalities (such as the Jolly Green Giant, the Pillsbury Doughboy, and the Dow Chemical Scrubbing

Bubbles) and to delve into unexplored worlds inside packages and products through slow-motion and time-lapse photography.

Looking at the matter a little differently, television can also serve as both an initiator and a reinforcer when it comes to campaign themes. Often, a product spokesperson, trade character, jingle/slogan, or promise of service is introduced on TV (amidst, perhaps, much celebration and fanfare), and then picked up by other media as consumers follow through and cash registers start ringing. Product news may be dramatized on television when a campaign is first launched, or a cautious advertiser might choose to try out a new approach on radio before moving into costly TV ventures.

The Elements of Television Communication

Television copywriters, of course, have both aural and visual ingredients with which to work—and action. The communication potential is almost limitless, and the need to guard against wasted entertainment effort greatly enhanced. Reason-why appeals must be keyed to brand names and need-fulfillment, not to the cuteness of a message. Likewise, perceived truth is of concern in TV commercials; the line between scoring a hit and missing the mark is just as fine as it is in radio spots. First we will examine the video channel and then compare the audio track with that of radio.

VISUAL ELEMENTS
Television employs both still and moving pictures, though the more the latter are emphasized the better the copywriter justifies use of the TV medium. Granted, scenes that constantly bounce and jerk an audience along for the sheer sake of perpetual motion can tire and irritate viewers to the point that they tune out completely. But an increasing percentage of today's audience grew up with television, so it is a rare commercial that moves too fast for them.

Talent
TV commercial *presenters* (as they are often called when they deliver sales messages) or *players* (as they are referred to in performers' union contracts) may serve a variety of commercial purposes. They may be victims of nonproduct use, recipients of product benefits or rewards, heroic bearers of good tidings (such as news of a store-wide clearance sale), information seekers, or demonstrator-salespeople.

Because these persons can be objects of viewer dissatisfaction (if they appear as gullible housewives, dimwitted servicemen, or unusually precocious children), the copywriter must portray them carefully and make sure that they serve a function appropriate to genuine brand positioning. Not every commercial requires on-camera talent to be effective.

Props
Products (unless they are large, durable items better classified as part of a commercial's set) and all other objects used in presentation and display are generally termed *props*. Again, the question of relevancy arises; obviously, certain kitchen utensils are required to demonstrate a cake mix, but an eye-and-ear-catching cuckoo clock on the kitchen wall or a whistling teakettle on the stove could easily be considered distracting.

Sets
Sets, whether interior or exterior, have the power to support a commercial message or to provide extraneous visual material that steals viewer attention away from the product or service at hand. A winding mountain road might be ideal for demonstrating the maneuverability of a small car, but if the product were a Schwinn bicycle, the copywriter would have to be careful not to focus entirely on neighborhood riding scenes, because they alone wouldn't differentiate Schwinn from other brands.

Graphics

Cards or other visual materials containing pictures of a product or its component parts (or just lettering—a store name and address, a price, or a line of copy) are known as *TV graphics*. Some provide a limited amount of action as they are flipped or spun before the camera or moved in some other way; others merely appear as stills, often on photographic slides, either alone or as part of a set or prop display.

Graphics may increase commercial impact by reinforcing the sales message already being demonstrated by on-camera talent or described by an off-camera announcer. Used alone or too frequently, they tend to bog down an otherwise lively message. Next to the real thing, a picture of the circus that's coming to town appears disappointingly tame.

Animation

Finally, any of the above commercial ingredients may appear in animated form. Talent and props may be cartoon characters, sets may be fairytale locations, and graphics may sing and dance merrily away. Because animation by itself is entertaining, copywriters must appraise the nature of each product, sales key, and competitor with an extracritical eye. Never-never land might help sell chewing gum, but it could be a very poor choice for medicinal products. Only about 5 percent of today's commercials are animated.[1]

AURAL ELEMENTS

TV audio is delivered by people on the set (addressing the audience directly or each other through dialogue), or presented *VO* (off-camera, voiceover the action performed). Saying and showing the same thing at the same time is valuable in helping to achieve commercial impact, but let us turn now to some additional roles TV's aural channel may play, as we review elements of the audio track.

Words and Voices

Our earlier discussion of the importance of each word in a radio commercial and of characteristics of the human voice applies directly to TV as well. In television, however, audio is usually secondary in importance to video; graphically oriented people sometimes maintain that one way to test a good TV commercial is to turn off the sound and see if the product and sales message are still perfectly clear. Yet a commercial capitalizing on celebrity image may use audio as a vital partner to visual presentation. In addition, the audio track may explain what a visual scene change doesn't show (for example, an overnight facial skin treatment); describe an intangible that cannot be visualized (for example, a "feel the fun of driving" claim for a new automobile); or verbalize the thoughts of presenters or personified objects (for example, a girl's hopes as she goes to meet a new date, or an animated bug's challenge to a can of insect spray).

The actual word count in TV commercials is often less than that of radio commercials of similar length, depending in many instances on how self-explanatory the video is. Sometimes the music and sound effects, which serve only as background in a radio commercial, might sustain much of a TV spot's track while the visual message unfolds by itself.

Music and Jingles

More than half of today's commercials contain some form of music, though not necessarily throughout the message.[2] Sometimes, as in radio, it is an original score, created specifically for a given TV spot; on other occasions it is established music, lifted from a musical library.

Often, commercial creative teams choose the latter form because costs are considerably less and the role of the music is minor anyway—often simply to provide transitions between scenes or to serve as a pleasant background over which copy is delivered. Still, music may serve the important function of accenting copy points or visual actions and, hence, enhancing a sales key. Music used this way is usually composed from scratch. For example, an energy-producing food might promise to deliver a "spring to your step, a bounce to your walk, a lift to your spirits" and benefit in large measure from music that springs, bounces, and lifts in time to performers' movements. Then, again, music that overpowers demonstration of a sales message—that drowns out the commercial presenter, diverts attention away from the product, or annoys through tone, pitch, beat, or volume—can easily ruin an otherwise effective spot.

Turning again to the commercial jingle, few will dispute the audience-involvement power of the "Weekends were made for Michelob" theme, or the sing-along/clap-along value of Vaseline Intensive Care Lotion's "Let the healing begin." Experts in this field will differentiate between a commercial song and a jingle, but for our purposes a single classification will suffice. When lyrics and music combine to form a toe-tapping, finger-snapping, hand-clapping phenomenon, we are talking about potent communication. The creative team's job, as always, is to make sure that communication is sales oriented.

Jingles can help build and maintain distinct product personalities, and their messages may live on long after commercial copy has been forgotten. Special values accrue, therefore, to jingles that contain product names and (at least partial) sales keys. Finally, TV jingles usually transfer easily to radio for added reinforcement.

Sound Effects

Although sound effects in TV do not face the same identity problem as radio sounds because the visual channel is there for support, they can both enhance and hinder development of a commercial's sales key. For instance, consider where a commercial for winning basketball shoes would be without the roar of a crowd behind it, or how one for an electric saw would feel without appropriate precision instrument sounds.

In addition, sound effects (with or without music) may aid the creation of suspense in the opening scene of a commercial. Examples might be a creaking door opening slowly to reveal a new product or a mystery egg thumping and cracking as it prepares to hatch. On the other hand, you should be able to hear the commercialitis behind the scene that features a girl brushing her long hair while birds sing, a chorus hums, a man whistles, and the off-camera announcer notes that "these are the sounds of happy hair."

The Commercial Message

Now let us see HOW-E-ZE it is to write TV commercials (again, of course, with that all-important know-how firmly in hand). We return to our six-point formula here, but it is recommended that the reader review the presentation in Chapter 9.

Hit home with your audience. As before, we must know our prospective customer viewers well, both demographically and psychographically, if we expect to influence them in any way. If the target market for new Brand Y spot remover is currently sold on Brand X, we would be in big trouble if we began our commercial with a shot of Mrs. Homemaker throwing Brand X in the wastebasket over the line: "Ladies! Get rid of your favorite Brand X forever!" With that approach, we would probably wind up much like a rude salesman who finds the door shut in his face; viewers would either change channels or mentally tune out.

A much better attempt to hit home with this audience would be a statement of "great news for Brand X users," followed by a message showing how Brand Y fulfills their needs even more efficiently and effectively. Or, if we are aiming for an undecided cereal market, we might open with an attention-getting display of boxes and query: "Having a tough time deciding which cereal's best for your family?" In short, we must respect viewers' current positions if we want them to respect ours. The challenge is to discover and present what TV commercial consultant Harry McMahon has called a "visual plus," or "memory picture" for the advertised product—one that can be played to the hilt on the TV screen.[3]

Offer a reward--a promise. Here we can add a word of caution to our previous maximize-pleasure/minimize-pain example. Beginning TV copywriters have a tendency to maximize the story of the pain (problem) and to minimize the selling of the pleasure (solution). Most of the problems presented (dirty dishes, chapped skin, stalled engines) are almost instantly communicated, and we need not belabor them. It takes a relatively long period of time, however, to present a believable product-solution, differentiate one brand of that product clearly and specifically, and convince viewers to act accordingly.

Win loyalty with brand image. TV is an ideal medium for stressing the quality behind the name. Demonstration scenes can show employees serving customers' needs, scientists working to improve product offerings, and satisfied users over long periods of time. Short case histories can help instill confidence in a brand or store and pave the way for action.

Earn trust through proof of claims. TV's potential as a demonstration medium can now be utilized fully. Close-ups can focus attention exactly where the copywriter wants it and lead viewers step-by-step through the reason-why sales story. Further, instant replays and time-lapse photography can dramatize the evidence that proves claims are true.

Zoom in on personal value. The benefit of audience participation becomes clear as we relate our sales key directly to viewer life-styles. Can Grandma ride a motorcycle to show she's one of the think-young generation? Sure she can, and she can bring a whole young-at-heart segment of the market with her. Or a rugged male athlete might drum up new uses and new users for a product such as baby oil.

End with a clincher to make action easy. Sometimes a TV commercial ends with an aural reminder of the sales key while the visual segment adds terms of a sale, special prices and store hours, or, perhaps, an address. Such a procedure is often followed for local commercials, or for cooperative spots—national commercials that are jointly sponsored by retail outlets, which then receive individual tag lines at the end of each message. A commercial that reinforces audio with video in the action clincher, however, has its own kind of impact. (Recall the "Clout knocks dirt out!" example from Chapter 9, and picture an active visual reinforcement of this claim as a commercial send-off.) Close-ups of logos and graphically dynamic packages also make effective closing shots.

Now let us turn to the category of message content presented in Chapter 9 and relate it to television.

WHAT TO PRESENT

The areas of information from which we can choose in developing a TV commercial message remain the same, but a specific example may prove helpful here. Suppose our sales key for a rug cleaner spot is "Soil-cutting power to get rugs clean, with a protective ingredient to keep them clean longer than ever before." Housed in a *background* setting, the bulk of such a message might feature development of the product's cleansing properties (in a test laboratory, for example), and addition of the protector (perhaps right through the packaging process, so viewers could see elements combined in can or bottle).

In an *in-use* situation, carpet stains would be no match for the grime-cutting suds. Here would be a good chance to take viewers into carpet fibers to examine the reason-why firsthand, and they might observe soil-resistant material soaking into the rug during the cleaning process.

Third, plans might call for a *result-of-use* story, putting the same sales key in still a different framework. Now the majority of scenes would focus on aftereffects—beautiful carpets for an evening's entertainment. Or time-lapse might compare two rugs over a period of days or weeks, one easily soiled again and the other remaining clean thanks to the advertised brand.

Finally, the tough-on-grime-with-protection-too message could be told with reference to *incidentals:* the easy-to-handle container, the variety of applicators available, or the selection of sizes and prices.

A careful study of target-audience psychographics and competitive strategies will help determine the best creative plan; but regardless of which setting seems most appropriate, copywriters need not avoid others entirely. To show a complete sales key, it often is necessary to borrow from several different creative approaches. For instance, the background situation above should probably include at least a scene or two of in-use or after-use benefits of the cleaner, to underscore relevance to the viewing audience.

The in-use and after-use situations also might tie in a here's-why scene (from the background approach) to enhance credibility. Finally, in the case of incidentals, an abbreviated version of the in-use setting may be needed; people are unlikely to buy even the most convenient cleaner if it does not do the basic job for which it was designed.

HOW TO PRESENT IT

TV commercials may be laid out in two different ways (although neither is ever referred to as a layout). One is a *script* and the other a *storyboard*. Depending on circumstances, one or both may be prepared for any given spot.

Two-Column Script

TV commercial scripts take varying forms, but all include two kinds of material: visual instructions and the audio (actual spoken copy, plus instructions for music and sound effects). Normally, a sheet of typing paper is divided into two columns (either half-and-half, or one-third for video and two-thirds for audio) to accommodate these two types of information. Figure 10.1 is an example of a two-column script. (Notice the reference to *talent*—a term TV copywriters often use to stand for any and all on-camera presenters and performers; it is both singular and plural. Because space is often a problem in scripts and storyboards, abbreviations are used liberally in instructions.)

Audio terms are used in television the same way they are in radio, and a popular format involves capitalizing everything not spoken over the air and capitalizing and underlining sound effects and music. The major concern in script preparation usually is how much description is necessary (because individual scenes, called *frames*, represent only a small part of the moving picture). Unfortunately, there is no all-encompassing answer. Space prohibits lengthy explanations, but key props and vital action must be specified.

Storyboard

When a visual rendering of every frame in a TV commercial accompanies video instructions and the audio, the resulting structure is called a storyboard. Actually, it is a sort of comic strip—a series of pictures (illustrated panels representing scenes) that together reveal the commercial message in step-by-step fashion. The video instructions in a TV script are included here in condensed form. As a rule, each

---

<pre>
              30 SECONDS: 50TH STATE FRESHEST

FADE IN TALENT ON BICYCLE.   (SUNG THROUGHOUT): Coming home
SHE'S RETURNING HOME, HAPPY.
ZOOM IN ON HER.   to eat...

CUT TO MLS TALENT IN KITCHEN.   My mom's cooking a treat...
SHE WATCHES AS DINNER IS
PREPARED. SHE KNOWS HOW GOOD
IT IS.

CUT TO CU CHICKEN COOKING ON   The freshest chicken she can find...
STOVE. HOT AND SIZZLING.

CUT TO CU TALENT'S FACE. KEY   I've got 50th State chicken on my
IN '50TH STATE BRAND'
THOUGHT-CLOUD. A DELIGHTFUL   mind.
IDEA.

CUT TO PACKAGED CHICKEN. IT'S   Fresh 'cause it's home grown...
SURROUNDED BY A FRESH HAWAIIAN
LEI. ZOOM IN TIGHT.

CUT TO CU TALENT EATING A   Best taste a kid has ever known...
DRUMSTICK. OBVIOUS ENJOYMENT.

CUT TO MS TALENT IN GROCERY   Freshest chicken mom can find...
STORE. ONE PUTS PACKAGED
CHICKEN IN CART AND THE OTHER
LOOKS ON WITH APPROVAL (MOTHER
AND CHILD).

CUT TO MS TALENT WITH   I've got 50th State chicken on my
DRUMSTICK AND KEY IN
THOUGHT-CLOUD AS BEFORE.   mind.

FADE TO BLACK.
</pre>

Fig. 10.1. Script for local TV spot. (Courtesy of Clancy Fuchigami Advertising, Inc.)

frame presents a completely new scene, a continuation of previous action (sequential action), or a combination of both.

Storyboards are prepared in varying degrees of artistic finish; locations, sets, and props may be clearly detailed or merely suggested. When photocopies are taken from actual films, however, the result is called a *photoboard*. It usually appears on heavy paper stock with the audio track indicated; visual instructions are omitted because the action has already been produced.

Whatever its form, a storyboard is a plan—a blueprint of the desired message structure and the first graphic illustration of a TV commercial idea. Designs may be crude, but, as is true in the case of architectural blueprints, positions and proportions are quite exact. Commercial producers and clients must be able to see clearly the proposed actions, settings, talent functions, and special effects. Figure 10.2 is an example of a TV storyboard.

The more detailed the storyboard, the more clearly it approximates the finished commercial. Beginning TV writers, however, often work under a four-to-five second plan, creating one frame for every four or five seconds of commercial time. Hence, a 30-second spot contains between six and eight frames. Of course, the actual number of visual scene changes will have considerable influence on the number of frames needed, and commercials that are especially active may feature a staccato pace with new scenes every second or two.

Video Terminology

The TV writer, as we have noted, must provide visual instructions along with audio copy so that artists, commercial producers, and management personnel can understand clearly the scenes suggested. Three kinds of information are called for in each instance. After we examine them, we will see how they apply to specific messages.

Composition Terms. Actual shot-by-shot make-up in a TV commercial requires a composition term, a video instruction that indicates how much of each scene the viewer will see. For example, a *long shot* (LS), or *wide shot* (WS), shows a person from head to toe, a room from floor to ceiling, or an outdoor scene from a distant perspective.

Granted, this type of picture does include some extraneous information—elements that are not essential to the sales message. Still, it is helpful in establishing location, in orienting viewers to a new setting, and in acquainting them fully with the surroundings of a presentation. Long shots can accentuate a feeling of depth, speed, and distance, but they may also call attention more to the entertainment value of a message than to any real brand differentiation. A word to the beginning TV copywriter: use long shots sparingly.

A *medium shot* (MS) shows talent from approximately the waist up. Scenes are not as wide or expansive as they are in long shots, but show more detail of setting and background. Frequently, a medium shot does an excellent job of establishing locale with fewer distracting elements to divert attention.

An unfortunate but very common shot in TV commercials today is the *headless* medium shot of talent standing behind a table-top product demonstration (a shot your authors like to call a *belly shot*). Aside from being generally unappealing, its major problem is one of boredom or sameness and of failure to further the sales message in any dramatic or exciting way.

The *close-up* (CU) or *tight shot* (TS) is generally the copywriter's best bet. It zeroes in on the talent's face, eyes, or teeth; on a given product feature or part of one; or on a specific detail that clearly sets one brand apart from another. This focusing of attention gives added emphasis to a sales key and to the reasons behind it (proof that makes it both credible and memorable). Close-ups can climb into mixing bowls, washing machines, or balloons. They can put us in the driver's seat as we whiz around a race track, or drop us front-row-center for a product spectacular.

The long shot, medium shot, and close-up are basic composition terms; others are variations and combinations thereof, such as a *medium-long shot* (MLS), a *medium-close-up* (MCU), or an *extreme-close-up* (ECU or XCU). There is no magical cutoff point for determining when one has moved from one type of composition to the next; the above descriptions, however, provide convenient guides.

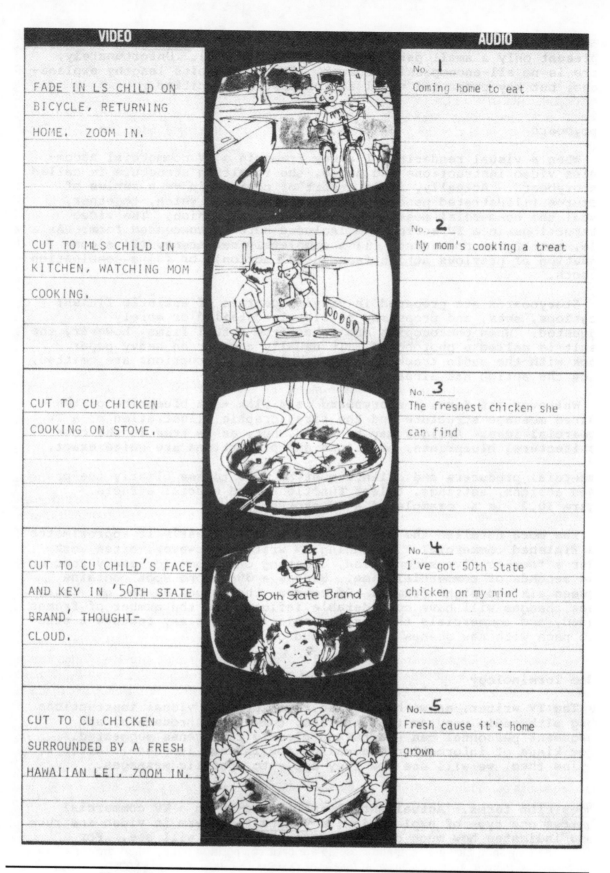

VIDEO		AUDIO
FADE IN LS CHILD ON BICYCLE, RETURNING HOME. ZOOM IN.		No. 1 Coming home to eat
CUT TO MLS CHILD IN KITCHEN, WATCHING MOM COOKING.		No. 2 My mom's cooking a treat
CUT TO CU CHICKEN COOKING ON STOVE.		No. 3 The freshest chicken she can find
CUT TO CU CHILD'S FACE, AND KEY IN '50TH STATE BRAND' THOUGHT-CLOUD.	50th State Brand	No. 4 I've got 50th State chicken on my mind
CUT TO CU CHICKEN SURROUNDED BY A FRESH HAWAIIAN LEI. ZOOM IN.		No. 5 Fresh cause it's home grown

Fig. 10.2. Storyboard for local TV spot. (Courtesy of Clancy Fuchigami Advertising, Inc.)

VIDEO		AUDIO
CUT TO CU CHILD EATING DRUMSTICK.		No. **6** Best taste a kid has ever known
CUT TO MS CHILD WITH MOM IN GROCERY STORE PUTTING CHICKEN IN CART.		No. **7** Freshest chicken mom can find
CUT TO MS CHILD WITH DRUMSTICK AND KEY IN THOUGHT-CLOUD AS BEFORE		No. **8** I've got 50th State chicken on my mind.
FADE TO BLACK.		No.
		No.

171

Finally, a few more literal composition terms are sometimes used for the sake of clarity. *One-shot, two-shot,* and *three-shot* refer to a single-talent scene, a two-talent shot, and a scene with three different performers. A *top shot* photographs a scene from above (putting talent, products, and other objects in a little different perspective); a *waist shot, chest shot,* and a *head-and-shoulders shot* have obvious references.

Transition Terms. All TV messages must travel somehow from one scene to another; a new scene simply does not pop up mysteriously, even though it may seem that way to viewers. Transition terms tell the television director just how the commercial's creative team wants the progression of scenes to flow: rapidly, in staccato fashion; lazily, in a sort of dream sequence; or somewhere in between, perhaps a combination of the two in an alternating pattern.

Transition terms, which usually are placed before composition terms in actual shot-by-shot instructions, may refer to two different types of movement: physical camera movement and optical motion (electronic effects that indicate a change of time and/or place). The following glossary encompasses the most common forms of both.

1.   Physical Camera Movement
A *dolly* (in or out) is movement of the entire camera base either toward or away from its subject matter; the subject usually remains stationary or engages in only minimal action. As the dolly progresses, the visual elements naturally grow larger or smaller. Because the camera operator must actually push or pull the camera (or be pushed or pulled on a platform), copywriters must realize that some time is required for the dolly movement to occur (and to occur smoothly and in proper focus). Because commercials are short, if dollies are used at all, it is recommended that they cover only very small distances—especially since a special camera lens (a zoomar) is readily available today.

A *zoom* is movement of a camera lever that shoots this zoomar lens forward or back, achieving basically the same effect as that of a dolly (in or out). In this case, however, the movement is perfectly smooth, regardless of how fast it occurs, and the lens is designed to maintain constant focus. The focal length of the lens is the only thing that changes, creating the illusion of approaching or moving away from a scene. A zoom can thus create the effects of close-ups, medium shots, and long shots, all from the same camera position.

A *truck* (right or left) involves movement of the camera base with moving talent and objects on the set: right to left, or left to right. Valuable seconds are needed to complete this action properly.

An *arc* (right or left) is almost a combination of the truck and dolly. It is actually a semicircular movement often requiring more time than any other.

Although not a technical word, the term *follow* is often used because of its instant communicability. As talent moves across a set, the camera operator may simply be asked to follow them or move with them.

A *pan* (up or down, right or left) is movement of the camera only, while its base remains stationary, in a vertical or horizontal plane. Often, the pan follows a moving object, or reveals a series of objects one by one in much the same way spectators follow a horse race through binoculars. Sometimes an up-and-down pan is called a *tilt*.

A *boom* or *pedestal* (up or down) is movement of the camera and its attached cylinder while the base stays put. The effect is almost a vertical zoom; over musical crescendos, drum rolls, or other appropriate sounds, scenes may thus take on very dramatic perspectives.

2. Optical Motion

A *cut* or *take* is an abrupt change from one frame to the next. It is the fastest scene change because it indicates no real time lapse. In fact, this instant switch is all but unnoticed by viewers; it is so common, they merely take it for granted. Cuts are often used to reveal new people or objects on the screen as they are being introduced verbally.

A *dissolve* (DISS, DIS, or DS) is a melting or blending of one scene into another until the first is completely replaced by the second (similar to the crossfade in radio). Sometimes the process is called a *lap dissolve* because the scenes actually overlap briefly. Dissolves are slower than cuts, although the speed of the dissolve can be controlled to fit a desired mood. Dissolves are usually used to indicate a short lapse of time in a sales story or to move from one place to another, where the action is either simultaneous with the first or occurring shortly after the first. For example, one frame might show a cake being placed in the oven. Obviously, there is not enough commercial time to wait for the baking process to occur so the picture simply dissolves to the finished cake (and viewers willingly acknowledge and accept the transformation). Or a dissolve between night-before and morning-after scenes will show viewers the overnight effects of a particular medication. Finally, dissolves provide a smooth transition between different visual media—from a slide to live action or from a live-in-studio demonstration to a filmed insert (and back again.)

When a new scene ripples across the screen the term is *ripple dissolve*. A *match dissolve* is used when the object ending one scene or sequence matches (at least approximately) the object beginning the next. For instance, if one frame in an airline commercial showed a family seated side-by-side in their living room, the next (matched dissolve shot) might show the same people in the same positions—this time seated on board a 747 jet.

A *wipe* is the pushing or sweeping of one picture off the screen as a new one moves in. The visual change is often faster than a dissolve but not as fast as a cut and is especially effective when a rapid succession of short or quick scenes is desired. Types of wipes include *horizontal, vertical, diagonal, closing doors (barn doors)* coming in from either side, and *iris* (or *circular),* sweeping around like the hands of a clock.

A *montage* is a series of quick wipes or cuts, beginning and ending with a dissolve. Sometimes several images appear simultaneously in the same scene to produce a special optical effect, much the same as a poster board montage appears in printed media; this time, though, there is the addition of movement.

A *fade* involves the appearance of a scene *from nothing* (total black) or its disappearance *into black* (blank scene). Fades usually indicate the passage of days, weeks, even years between action sequences. They require more time to achieve than any of the above optical effects, and although they are popular in soap operas, in commercials they are reserved mainly for the opening (fade in) and closing (fade out) shots.

Obviously, communication of time changes is no problem in the world of TV commercials and neither is presentation of changes in locale. Just as viewers can watch seasons pass, crops and flowers develop and bloom, and people grow old (or young!) right before their eyes, so they can be transported from city to country, from east to west, even from earth to the moon. Dissolves, wipes, and fades cue the TV audience that such changes are imminent.

Descriptive Terms. The last part of each set of video instructions is description—a few words that explain the setting, action, and other scene content not described by transition and composition terms. This additional information is needed because each scene laid out on paper is only a brief representation of the moving picture that will appear before viewers. Descriptive terms follow no set pattern; rather, the copywriter chooses whatever words seem appropriate to explain a selected scene's content. A few pieces of jargon here may be helpful.

A *background* refers to elements in the rear of a scene or behind talent.

A *flashback* is past action introduced into current action to show the "how" or "why" behind it (or behind reaction).

Foreground elements are located in that part of a scene nearest the viewer.

Freeze frame is a scene held stationary on screen, temporarily frozen in place.

An object or talent in *limbo* is photographed without a set or scenery of any kind (excellent for product shots at the end of a commercial).

A *matte shot* blanks out part of a picture during exposure—as in a view seen through a keyhole or telescope.

Reverse motion is usually a comic effect in which performers do everything backwards (often used to dramatize or overdramatize a problem, such as housecleaning chores).

Slow motion is action slowed down (often to emphasize the need for a product).

Picture content in *soft focus* is shot slightly out of focus to achieve a hazy effect, as in dream sequences and highly emotional scenes.

Speeded-up action is the reverse of slow motion used to punctuate both problems and solutions.

A *split screen* occurs when two different scenes appear simultaneously, side-by-side (excellent for demonstration sequences showing the advertiser's brand and a competitor—often followed by a wipe, which removes the competing side).

A *super* is short for the *superimposition* of one scene or object, character, or lettering over another; the impact power of television is really at its peak when a sales key is stated verbally, demonstrated visually, and supered over the action all at the same time. Two words of caution are in order here. First, supers can easily be overdone; they are tempting because they can zero in so well on a selling point or benefit. They should be short, easy to read, and used as only one way of emphasizing a claim. Second, if supered words correspond to spoken words, they should correspond exactly. An awkward feeling arises if the audio says "easy to clean" while the super reads "easily cleaned."

Titles are letters or other printed materials that appear on the screen by themselves and are not supered over something else. They emphasize a product or store name, sales key, price, terms of a guarantee, or test results. Titles—and supers—can "wipe on," "zoom up," "pop on one letter at a time," "slide in," or "hold" while a scene changes.

Working with Visual Content

Although the possibilities for descriptive content are virtually endless, a few words of wisdom may be helpful to beginning TV writers. Beware of over-emphasizing talent. As a rule, people like to look at other people—it's human nature. So when the talent's face (especially in the case of attractive talent) vies with a can of peas for attention, the former usually wins and steals viewer attention.

Stay away from intricate features; the television camera simply cannot pick them up. Add the brief exposure time television affords, and the often preoccupied audience, and it should be clear that "the simpler, the safer."

Strive for presentation of crucial action, not just action. Sheer story details waste valuable brand-differentiation time. For example, an instant dessert commercial could either show the product being purchased, driven home, carried into the kitchen, and finally opened, or show it opened, served, eaten, enjoyed, and finally supported with reason-why demonstration.

Make sure the commercial has active, visual variety. If successive scenes are identical in composition, viewers tend to get bored. Television is a moving medium; if the sales message is mainly in the audio channel (over dull, repetitive shots), it might as well be done on radio a lot more cheaply. Something (camera, product, talent, special effects) should move in a relevant way in every scene.

Do not play tricks on your audience. A fancy shot may be OK (for example, a genie appearing from a magic lamp) if it is honestly presented and relevant to the sales message. Copywriters must let viewers know, however, that action is intended to be fantasy. In this example, "Genie" furniture polish might be "shedding light" on a major cleaning problem or "lightening" a workday load. Granted, there is a fine line between entertainment that's really conducive to communication of a sales message and mood, and story details that don't contribute to either; usually it takes an educated judgment based on experience to perceive it.

The Copy Platform

The same kind of copy platform we designed for radio commercials can guide TV copywriters to successful completion of their tasks. In fact, the differences are so limited that we can dispense with them by simply filling in a few details where needed.

1. *Client and product, service, or store:* No change.
2. *Medium and commercial description:* TV stations are not generally referred to in terms of format. Rather, they are classified as affiliates of major networks (ABC, CBS, or NBC) or as independent stations. If the commercial is slated to air within a specific program, the title is indicated; otherwise, common listings are primetime, daytime soap operas or game shows, and news or weekend sports programming.
3. *Objective:* No change.
4. *Target audience:* No change.
5. *Style:* TV's visual element might come directly into play here as in a face-to-face confrontation style or a picturesque travelogue. Because moods are intangible, however, the same terms used in radio are often just as relevant for TV.
6. *Technique:* This is the only portion of the TV platform that is necessarily quite different from radio. Reference should be made to specific shot composition and scene transition, as well as to descriptive video information and audio devices. We need not supply a complete synopsis of commercial scenes or frames, but we should highlight the camera, studio, and electronic procedures that will be utilized to implement the selected style. For example, quick cuts and zooms, combined with an emphasis on close-ups, will set a fast-paced commercial mood, with attention focused on details. On the other hand, slow ripple dissolves over harp music, coupled with use of soft focus and slow-motion photography, produce an imaginary quality or nostalgic air.
7. *Competition and competitive claims:* No change.
8. *Positioning:* No change.
9. *Sales key:* No change.
10. *Bonuses, if any:* No change.

Television Commercial Formats

Although the number of individual formats is practically unlimited, five overall structures serve as basic vehicles in carrying sales messages to TV viewers.

STORYTELLING/SLICE-OF-LIFE

Within this popular framework are miniature soap operas—little skits usually featuring one or more players with a problem (lifeless hair, meals that are too expensive, or a car that won't start) and a solution carrier (a friend or relative with a new shampoo, an inexpensive way to satisfy hearty appetites, or an effective antifreeze). The Leo Burnett agency calls these vignettes "heartsell."

Of course, the problem-solution format need not be presented as a drama. A single character (celebrity or unknown) might simply advise the audience, much as Ann Landers advises her newspaper readers. A third variation involves an off-camera announcer who speaks with on-camera talent or with the audience while the visual sequences progress. These may involve a problem and solution or merely a story about the product and its role in the life of consumers. Such formats provide an excellent opportunity to capitalize on the credibility of a commercial presenter and on his or her trustworthy image, which develops over time due to repeated commercial showings.

Storytelling has traditionally been a favorite human pastime; thus, it is often an excellent method of obtaining viewer involvement (see Figure 10.3). It can identify important consumer concerns and provide strong support for product benefits, but storytelling copywriters must be careful that their characters don't steal the show. Sometimes a beautiful girl or handsome escort, an appealing child, adorable pet, emotional grandparent, or comic can pull viewer attention completely away from the product and sales key.

If the problems presented are too trivial or their solutions too corny, viewer reaction may range from fatigue to insult or from disgust to actual offense. Finally, there is the credibility gap—the too-quick conversion or remedy that is too close to a miracle cure. A popular pitfall here is what we call the "I-Am-A-Camera" phenomenon—a scene in which talent is struggling with some chore when a voice from off-camera queries, "Having a tough day?" Talent responds, talking with the camera as if it were a person. More often than not, a mysterious hand then appears with a remedy for housekeeping blues.

In real life there is no magic sorcerer a homemaker can consult—no genie to pop up with an instant pacifier. It may be fun to fantasize, but the I-Am-A-Camera approach has become such a cliche in TV commercials, we may well question whether it's now any more than a cheap way around the demands of advertising creativity.

In other words, the success of the "real-life situation" format hinges on consumers' ability to accept and relate to the characters and events depicted. In a 1984 study that used a sample of 1,000 viewers, 35 percent of respondents said they found this commercial format "very persuasive."[4]

Looking specifically at the "dramatic" side of storytelling, we can identify at least five different approaches. First, a writer may dramatize a benefit and then show that the advertised brand of product offers it. Second, a product feature or attribute may be dramatized, followed by a presentation of how personal benefits are derived.

Third, dramatization of a problem may precede the solving of that problem with a specific product (its selling point and related benefit). Fourth, if a consumer life-style is being dramatized, the product is depicted as a natural and necessary part of it. Finally a commercial writer may dramatize some part of the advertiser's method of operation, but only if it is personally related to consumers' own lives and it shows consumers how and why it is to their own advantage to use the brand in question.

DOCUMENTARY

Although stories are usually associated with fiction, a nonfictional approach to commercial delivery is the *documentary*—a short case history. Here, the sales message usually unfolds in a chronological fashion, with emphasis on the mood or atmosphere created by an institutional or otherwise dignified theme. Studies of product development, reasons behind guarantees, or company reputation and backing of merchandise are popular examples.

Absolute integrity, factual proof of benefit claims, and strong visual identity move to the front in this type of presentation. Copywriters are also faced with the challenge of maintaining both brand-name awareness and interest in a message that is usually presented in a more serious vein than those delivered under other formats.

1. SINGERS: McDONALD'S AND YOU. . .

2. McDONALD'S AND YOU. SHARING GOOD TIMES TOGETHER,...

3. WHEREVER, WITH YOU. TO-GETHER, McDONALD'S AND YOU... AND YOU. . .

4. AND YOU, AND YOU, A BIG MAC AND A COKE ON A MISSISSIPPI RIVERBOAT. McDONALD'S AND YOU. KIDS: CHEESEBURGERS AND FRIES!

5. SINGERS: IN AN AIRPLANE RIGHT OUT OF THE SKIES TOGETHER, ...

6. McDONALD'S AND YOU, AND YOU, ...   RONALD: YOU, TOO. KID: ME, TOO!

7. SINGERS: AND YOU COME AROUND AND HAVE A BALL... KID: WHEEEEEEEEEEE!

8. SINGERS: AN EGG McMUFFIN UNDER A WATERFALL...

9. AROUND THE CORNER, AROUND THE BEND, YOU KNOW WHEN YOU SEE AN OLD FRIEND...

10. THAT IT'S GREAT TO GET TOGETHER AND NO MATTER WHERE WE DO...

11. REMEMBER, THERE'S ONLY ONE McDONALD'S.

12. AND THERE'S ONLY ONE YOU. . .

13. TOGETHER. . .

14. McDONALD'S. . .

15. AND YOU!

Fig. 10.3. Storytelling commercial. (Courtesy of McDonald's Corporation)

PERSONAL ENDORSEMENT

Most people are familiar with celebrity endorsement of products and services. Well-known sports figures, popular TV and movie stars, and leading corporation executives may speak on behalf of anything from insurance to ice cream, cosmetics to cameras, appliances to airlines. In addition, a teacher, sales clerk, or homemaker unknown to viewers, yet with whom they can easily identify because of obvious demographic and psychographic make-up, may support a particular brand of deodorant, drain cleaner, or dog food.

In either case, one of two different patterns may appear: (1) the actual testimonial in which the commercial presenter cites personal experience with the product, supports its performance and claims, and recommends purchase; or (2) the personality spot in which the celebrity (either alone or with family, other celebrities, or unknowns similar to those mentioned above) lends his or her image (personality) to a commercial message; no claim of personal use is required.

Sometimes endorsements are run in printed media and carried over into broadcast or vice versa. The ad in Figure 10.4 ran in regional editions of *Time, Newsweek, U.S. News,* and *Sports Illustrated,* as part of a campaign in the Hawaiian Islands for the local outlet of GTE (Hawaiian Telephone). Popular entertainer Danny Kaleikini (see Figure 6.3) appealed to residents who made calls to a variety of foreign countries, and each ad featured a different language in the headline.

Then television was added to the media lineup, and the storyboard in Figure 10.5 shows how the endorsement carried over. This commercial ran on all three network affiliates, plus independent stations, throughout Hawaii at the rate of 40 times per week during the first couple of months of the campaign. For the rest of the year, the schedule was constant but less frequent.

The visual element of the spot was such a dramatic part of the message that when radio came on the scene, new copy had to be written; it wouldn't have been effective to have lifted the audio track from TV. In fact, this final example, in Figure 10.6, is even more personal than the other two.

It's worth noting that the television commercial business is currently witnessing a boom in the endorsement field, and celebrity brokers have the job of matching stars and product images. In recent years, Bill Cosby has appeared both for Jello and for Kodak, Karl Malden for American Express, and Tom Watson for *Golf Digest.*

Featured characters may provide a valuable form of continuity throughout a campaign (often extending over a period of years) in both broadcast and other media. Familiar examples are Mr. Goodwin (Crest toothpaste), Rosie (Bounty paper towels), Mikey (Life cereal), and certainly the lonely Maytag repairman. In animated form, we have Charlie the tuna, the Keebler cookie elves, and Dow Chemical's scrubbing bubbles.

Because celebrities command much higher fees than noncelebrities, research is often conducted to determine their specific values in terms of sales communication. McCollum/Spielman & Company recently examined hundreds of television commercials featuring celebrity and anonymous presenters representing a wide range of product categories. Their first finding was that celebrities consistently drew higher audience awareness and attitude change scores than noncelebrities. They also found that female presenters outscored males in both celebrity and noncelebrity situations.[5]

The 1984 study cited previously also looked at commercial spokespersons and found that "experts in the field" had more persuasive power than celebrities and sports figures who, in turn, were slightly more persuasive than company presidents (although it's hard to dispute the image boost that Chrysler's Lee Iacocca has received following his TV commercial exposure). Hidden-camera testimonials were found to be the least persuasive of all commercial formats tested.[6]

"Cantando y jugando golf– ¿qué es más importante que eso?"

0 1 4 ¹ 0 POINTS

Even if you don't know what Danny's saying, you should know that his international calls are now more rewarding than ever.

That's because Hawaiian Tel's new Frequent Caller Program awards him 10 points for every minute of every international call he makes.

Use Hawaiian Tel for your international calls and you, too, can start racking up points. And use them for credit on your Hawaiian Tel phone bill or for special catalog merchandise. (You're eligible for awards with just 3,000 points and you get 1,200 bonus points just to get you started.)

Plus, every three months we'll be having drawings with a unique feature: lots of winners! We'll be giving away mainland and international trips, VCRs and portable TVs. And since every 10 minutes of calling time equal one entry in these drawings, your chances of winning are quite good.

To enroll automatically, just use Hawaiian Tel for international calling. Then, every international call you make will be translated into points.

(If you're wondering how we translate what Danny's saying on the phone... well, it's something along the lines of, "Singing and golf—what else is there?")

For more information, call 643-1000. On Molokai and Lanai call toll-free 1-643-1000.

INTRODUCING HAWAIIAN TEL'S FREQUENT CALLER PROGRAM

HAWAIIAN TEL GTE
Beyond the call

Fig. 10.4. Celebrity endorsement advertisement featuring Hawaiian entertainer Danny Kaleikini. (Courtesy of Hawaiian Tel GTE)

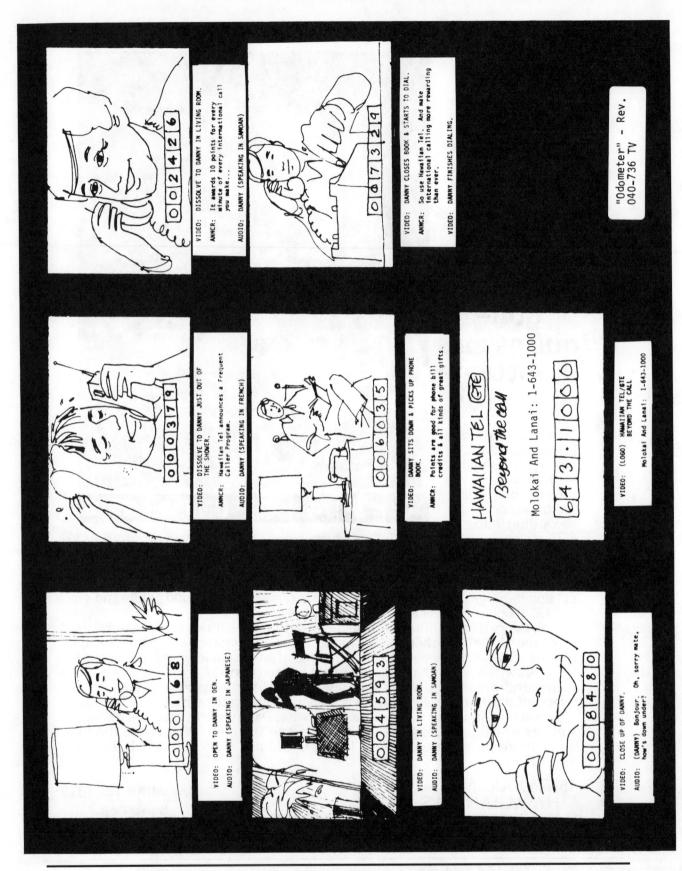

Fig. 10.5. Endorsement commercial. (Courtesy of Hawaiian Tel GTE)

Milici Valenti Smith Park Advertising

Client   Hawaiian Tel

Spot Title   "Frequent Caller"

Spot Length   :30   ☒ Produced   ☐ Live

Job No.   040-737 R

Rev. #1

---

1.   (DANNY FINISHING CONVERSATION IN JAPANESE)

       SFX: (PHONE RECEIVER DOWN)

2.   DANNY: ALOHA I'M DANNY KALEIKINI. YA KNOW,

3.   THESE DAYS MAKING AN INTERNATIONAL CALL

4.   IS MORE REWARDING THAN EVER. SEE, HAWAIIAN TEL

5.   HAS A FREQUENT CALLER PROGRAM, THAT AWARDS

6.   10 POINTS FOR EVERY MINUTE OF EVERY

7.   INTERNATIONAL CALL YOU MAKE. YOU CAN GET

8.   CREDIT ON YOUR PHONE BILL, AND ALL KINDS OF

9.   GREAT MERCHANDISE. SO IF YOU MAKE CALLS

10.   TO FOREIGN COUNTRIES, MAKE SURE TO USE HAWAIIAN TEL,

11.   AND TAKE ADVANTAGE OF THEIR FREQUENT CALLER PROGRAM.

12.   DOMO ARIGATO GOZAI MASU.

A DOYLE DANE BERNBACH GROUP COMPANY 700 BISHOP STREET 12TH FLOOR HONOLULU, HAWAII 96813 (808) 536-0881 TELEX: RCA (723) 8304 MEMBER: AAAA

Fig. 10.6. Radio endorsement spot. (Courtesy of Hawaiian Tel GTE)

THE DEMONSTRATION

Any of the above structures may incorporate product demonstration. This television phenomenon is so important in driving home a commercial message that we'd be remiss if we did not consider it as a separate commercial framework. Though some may claim that demonstration is used ad nauseam, as a TV exclusive it can never outlive its value. Often, it represents a superb means of proving how and why claims are true; it is TV's trump card for involving and convincing the viewer. More than a third of today's spots use demonstration. See Figure 10.7.

Some words of caution are in order here. If the desired demonstration is too technical, the result is more likely to be confusion than real involvement. Television simply cannot handle examination of minutiae (standard camera lenses aren't capable of clear, detailed magnification in extreme close-up), and severe time limitations prohibit any prolonged explanation of schematic diagrams or working parts.

Although camera dissolves can handle the passage of time (viewers go along with anything reasonable), TV copywriters must take care not to exploit an audience's willing suspension of belief. The rise of consumerism has led to laws demanding, among other things, that dirty dishes shown on camera actually be washed with the advertised detergent while shooting stops and then be shown officially clean. However, today's TV viewers are wary of camera tricks perceived merely as gimmicks.

Also, the persuasive power of commercials comparing competing brands (usually in side-by-side demonstration) is low, although proponents of this technique still claim that it helps consumers make informed decisions.[7]

For those who maintain that the informative kind of advertising doesn't persuade as well as its more entertaining counterparts, it might be noted that a substantial percentage of women, who make most shopping decisions regarding products featured in demonstrative commercials, still claim they are attracted to demonstrations.[8]

FANTASY LAND

Now we enter the wonderful world of imagination—of beautiful maidens, knights in shining armor, and animated characters who are absolutely invulnerable to any of life's realities. Fantasy commercials look like they are easy to write, but they are actually among the most difficult. The danger of commercialitis is tremendous, and the task of creating credible, memorable brand differentiation is monumental. But fairy tales and dream-world techniques may create genuine product enjoyment by association.

Regardless of the commercial structure selected, today's TV sales messages must communicate instantly (clearly and specifically). People are busier than ever before, and the competition for their attention is overwhelming. Relevant action in a TV commercial helps speed development and comprehension of the advertiser's message; irrelevant illusions lose audiences fast.

Research conducted by McCollum/Spielman & Company has revealed some valuable guidelines on the use of "real people" in commercials, as opposed to celebrities, regardless of the format. Real people are just as effective as celebrities in gaining initial attention and in persuading audiences to take a suggested action. Single real-people presenters, however, fare much better than groups of them.

Within a demonstration framework, real people are most effective when they are employed to test products (serving, so to speak, as guinea pigs). They are least effective in a man- or woman-on-the-street situation. In between these two extremes is the format that involves a semi-staged testimonial from a satisfied customer or qualified expert.

1. ...

2. DAD: So, she think it was worth a two thousand mile trip to visit her first grandchild?
MOM: Are you kidding?

3. (SFX: WAAA!)
MOM: Uh-oh.
GRANDMA: I'll check on him...

4. MOM: No Mother, I'll get it.
GRANDMA: Oh, Karen, he's wet... his sleeper...his sheets...

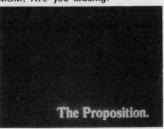

5. (Anncr VO): If you could buy a thin diaper that dramatically cut leakage...

6. even overnight -- wouldn't you try it? This is it. New Luvs Deluxe.

7. No diaper has ever worked like this.

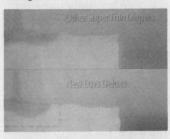

8. If baby only wet once during the night, almost any thin diaper would do.

9. But only Luvs' new Night-Guard system quickly distributes wetness throughout the padding.

10. So as baby wets throughout the night, other diapers can leak, but Luvs can still absorb without leaking.

11. GRANDMA: Sssh...

12. everything's dry as a bone. That new diaper you found really works.

13. MOM: Yeah. You know, Mom...

14. I just want him to have the best of everything...

15. all the time.
GRANDMA: I know.

Fig. 10.7. Demonstration commercial. (Courtesy of The Procter & Gamble Company)

Though viewers show much higher levels of identification and empathy with celebrities (or at least professional actors) than they do with real people, a personable, reasonably attractive, confident real person can shine in several ways: in realistic comparative product demonstrations, in confirming expectations about well-established products, and where the product itself is clearly the star of the commercial.[9]

Content Specifics

All of the specific tips given for radio commercials hold for TV audio as well, with the possible exception of the reference to figures. Television is as fleeting as radio, but the addition of video makes presentation of a few well-chosen numbers acceptable. The guidelines we present here deal with visual content.

GAINING ATTENTION

If the opening shot of a TV commercial fails in its attention-getting function, following shots stand little, if any, chance of registering with the viewer. If the opening frame sends its audience out to the kitchen for a snack, many thousands of dollars and months of creative effort play to empty rooms. Unfortunately, it seems to be getting increasingly difficult to get TV viewers' attention. A recent Audits & Surveys study found that only two-thirds of primetime viewing audience members remain in the room during a TV commercial break. Further, only one-third of those who do stay actually watch the commercial.[10] Among those who tape-record programs for later viewing, it's a common practice to "zap" (fast-forward) through all commercials so none are seen. And VCR penetration is predicted to be 85 percent of U.S. TV homes shortly after we go to press.[11]

Some TV copywriters will argue for an establishing shot at the beginning—a scene-setter that orients viewers to the environment of the forthcoming message. Indeed, if viewer attention can be snagged in the first few seconds with material that clearly sets the stage for sales key development, there is no need to jump immediately into the sales pitch. If a lively beach party, for instance, successfully prepares the eyes, ears, and minds of its audience for a commercial dealing with the "best refreshment under the sun," more power to it.

Another school of thought maintains that the sales key may begin effectively in the opening shot—in a suspenseful atmosphere, for example, that motivates viewers to stay with it. No one rule always applies. Careful analysis of the product and sales message, audience characteristics, the competition, and available resources must precede creative decisions.

When presenting introductory or especially noteworthy information about products, we can cite the experience of commercial testing experts at Communicus, Inc., in Los Angeles. They maintain that the best way to attract viewer attention to new and important material is to feature it in the opening few seconds of the message.[12]

HOLDING INTEREST THROUGH SEQUENCING

Television has a built-in curiosity factor in terms of what scene is coming next, and the wise copywriter uses it to full potential. Years ago, the American Dairy Association opened a commercial with a camera pan across the bare legs of what appeared to be a stage full of beauty contestants; slowly the camera moved up to reveal the trim female figures in bathing suits and then came the shocker: the faces belonged to senior citizens, radiant with health and drinking milk.

The three-step sequence was crucial here to achieve the desired effect. If the opening shot had been one of the women from head to toe, the dramatic impact would have been lost completely.

REINFORCING VIDEO WITH AUDIO

As a commercial unfolds, the audio track must keep pace with the visual sequence, and vice versa. Each new scene must match up with copy; viewers find it extremely difficult to assimilate material from two different channels simultaneously. Research has found that maximum TV recall can be obtained when audio and video elements complement each other.[13] Advice to beginning copywriters here is simply say what you show and show what you say—at the same time. A superb example is the long-running Dentyne gum commercial that showed an actual product package doing a back-and-forth toothbrush swish to the jingle beat: "Brush your breath, brush your breath, brush your breath with Dentyne."

It is also important to watch out for irrelevant visual material. If the audio for a paper towel spot says "Drinks up the whole spill," the center of attention on screen should not be a supermarket check-out line, a child opening a soft drink, or a freshly waxed floor. A demonstration of the product in action (with or without the presence of the paper towel) is both more appropriate and more beneficial to the advertiser.

MAXIMIZING THE VALUE OF TRANSITIONS

The proper sequencing of scenes is vital to effective message communication, but it is the transitions between them that determine whether or not the sequence flows naturally, logically, and believably throughout. If the transition is too abrupt, confusion often results; if it is drawn out too long, viewers may tune out because of boredom.

What we call a *tracking problem* arises when the TV audience is asked to bridge a communication gap by filling in missing elements mentally (a task the viewer won't bother to do if the effort is anything more than minimal.)

Timing is important, too. Consider two scenes: a baseball batter making a winning hit, and the same player eating the advertised nutritional snack in his locker room. A transitional cut between the two shots might well cause a tracking problem; a (slower) dissolve or wipe would transport viewers more comfortably.

A related area of concern involves not just comprehension of the visual message but proper emphasis on it. Since TV communication can occur in both verbal and nonverbal spheres, gestures and facial expressions may convey as much, and often more, of an advertiser's message than can mere words. A copywriter faced with such an opportunity does well to include such reactions as part of the transition between action shots.

For example, study the four two-frame couplets in Figure 10.8. No apparent tracking problems exist, but consider the audience involvement value of the suggested addition in each case. Keep in mind that such viewer participation (both intellectual and emotional) can enhance believability, aid recall, and stimulate action.

CHECKING COMMERCIALITIS AND VAMPIRE VIDEO

We already have noted that humor is a fragile creative form best left in the hands of experts but, also, that effective humor does entertain. A good joke, an amusing scene, and clever dialogue can provide a powerful sales vehicle. Take-offs, parodies, and satires are common in TV spots today because selling doesn't preclude humor—if consumers come away from the commercials genuinely interested in the advertised products. When the impression is simply one of having seen a funny commercial, however, commercialitis has scored again.

Even the best-written comedy, of course, may poke fun at something someone believes is serious

VIDEO	AUDIO

1. CUT FROM SON AND DAD BEARING   Jean's family knows how to
   FLOWERS ...   make Mother's Day special ...

   TO WHOLE FAMILY (BG) WITH   ... because they know about
   FLOWERS AND "DEL'S" SUPER (FG)   Del's Florist.

       (<u>Suggested Addition</u>: A scene showing the happiness
       Jean knows when her family gives her the flowers.)

2. CUT FROM LS BOB AND COLLEAGUES   A hot day and a hot interview,
   IN HARRIED MEETING ...   and Bob's really feeling the
                                                  heat.

   TO COOL POWER PRODUCT BEING   If only he'd used new Cool
   SPRAYED INTO THE AIR   Power ...

       (<u>Suggested Addition</u>: A scene showing the discomfort
       Bob feels in his tight collar and tie.)

3. CUT FROM MLS BILLY EATING AT   Touchdown! And somehow the
   FOOTBALL GAME, AND CHEERING   game's even more fun ...
   A TOUCHDOWN ...

   TO BEEF-O SUPER HOT DOG   ... with a Beef-O Super Hot
                                                  Dog.

       (<u>Suggested Addition</u>: A scene showing the enjoyment
       Billy gets from the hot dog.)

4. CUT FROM ACCIDENT SCENE AND   A tragic accident ... and a
   "COVERED" STRETCHER, WITH   tragic loss. But she knows ...
   GRANDMA AND OTHERS IN BG ...

   TO REGAL INSURANCE LOGO   ... Regal Insurance can help.

       (<u>Suggested Addition</u>: A scene showing the heartache
       Grandma experiences over the loss of her daughter.)

Fig. 10.8. Two-frame couplets from TV commercials.

or otherwise important. Sensitive individuals frequently embarrassed by perspiration stains might object to deodorant gags making light of the situation. The more diverse any audience is, the harder it is to make them all laugh.

Then again, a careless use of humor may lead to *vampire video*—scenes totally unrelated to the product or sales key. These are shots that literally feed on the commercial vehicle to serve the ends of pure creativity. Unfortunately, these same scenes are often brilliantly witty, highly memorable, and thoroughly enjoyed by audiences; further, they sometimes help commercials win artistic awards. But with no audience recall of product name and no application of the content to any real selling message, advertising creativity has gone out the window. Then, as we noted previously, the campaigns often prove disastrous at the cash register.

Television commercials appeal directly to two of the five human senses and indirectly to the other three. Good copywriters can use TV's impact power to involve viewers in tasting, smelling, and touching. But how much real creative potential is there in the increasingly shorter spots advertisers are now using (not just 30, but 20, 15, and even 10 seconds)?

In any communication process, time is only relative; it is not a question of how long, but rather, of how good. A speaker may talk for an hour and convey nothing but boredom. Or an idea expressed in three seconds may arouse a nation: "Give me liberty or give me death"; "Peace on earth, good will toward men"; "One small step for man, one giant leap for mankind."

In a TV commercial, the important thing about an idea is its communication effect, not the number of words and pictures crammed into a given period. Will the idea be remembered? Will it influence consumers? Will it stir them to act? We know TV has the disadvantage of perishability, but somehow it must help each message keep on working long after the communication process is completed. Words and pictures must join in pinpointing the crux of a message clearly, simply, believably.

If someone says "Do your own thing," it relates a general picture and mood to the audience, though not the same picture to everyone. Some may visualize physical activity, and others a specific form of mental or emotional release, but an idea has been formed. If you hear "Soup is good food," the picture becomes more specific (a piping hot meal with the special goodness and quality that only comes from Campbell).

"Own a piece of the rock" is even more directed. This means not just an insurance company, but Prudential's solid, secure, trustworthy kind of image. When we hear, "You're not fully clean until you're 'Zestfully' clean," we see Zest soap, because the shower models who serve as spokespersons for this product have helped position it as a refreshing kind of skin cleanser. An idea with appropriate repetition and added impact can communicate quickly. The creative team's job is to make certain that an idea is the right one to set a particular brand of product apart from its competition and to stimulate purchasing behavior among consumers.

Few 60-second TV spots are produced today because of the increased cost of running them, but for the record, this commercial length allows for the product name, a sales claim, demonstration, supporting claims, plus mood or atmosphere and dramatization if desired. These latter elements are not requisites but can be effective communication aids. Supporting claims often help prove, explain, and develop a sales key; then, too, they may just muddle up a message.

In 30 or 40 seconds, we're restricted to the name, a claim, demonstration, and supporting claims, but in 20 seconds, the supporting claims must be eliminated.

Until recently, the only other commercial length in regular use was 10 seconds (allowing only for the product name and claim). Today, however, the 15-second commercial has become a cornerstone of television advertising, representing more than 20 percent of network spots on the air.[14] Experts believe that 15 seconds is an ideal time frame for a strong, to-the-point message that doesn't need embellishment. It saves clients money and helps keep up the message weight level when 30-second units become too expensive to buy.

Each message, however, no matter what its length, is best when designed from the ground up and not as a "lift" cut down from a longer spot.

Use of Children

Children have a way of making commercials seem honest and very human. Kids have a universal appeal (for example, the Oscar Mayer kids) that's hard to dispute. Considering only saleskids commercials aimed at adults, a recent study found such presentations were as effective as those using adult presenters in their ability to generate brand awareness but less effective when it came to persuasion and attitude change. But results were tied very strongly to product category. Children scored exceptionally well in areas such as candy and gum, ice cream, cereal, pancakes and waffles, and high-energy drinks. On the other hand, they did very poorly with pet products, electronic games, and most major food categories, and only came out average in areas like milk, snack foods, household products, and fast-food restaurants.

Special consideration must be given to kids used to appeal to kids (commercials within children's programming). Experts recommend the following:

- Choose child characters slightly older than the target age group (because children strive to be older than they actually are);
- Keep visualized activities within range of viewer capabilities (for easy identification);
- Remember that girls for the most part accept boys in commercials, but boys are much less likely to accept girls (if a casting decision must be made between the two, the boy is the safer bet); and
- Because children often feel weak and insecure, it's a good idea to play up to their desire to control and master the situations with which they are faced (but beware featuring child characters who brag or show off).[15]

Developing a Recognizable Style

In selecting commercial formats and content specifics, wise copywriters strive to develop recognizable styles for their clients. Similar camera techniques, settings, and commercial pacing, as well as the consistent appearance of specific talent and musical accompaniments, can do as much as a familiar slogan or package design to maintain levels of audience awareness and response.

Veteran consultant Harry McMahon recently examined more than 100 highly successful commercials and found the following common key factors in decreasing order of magnitude:

1. An emotional story;
2. A demonstration of product relevancy to consumers' lives;
3. The appearance of celebrities;
4. A continuing central character (such as the Campbell Soup kids or the smiling face on pitchers of Kool-Aid);
5. A consistent "visual look" (such as the contest between Kraft Parkay margarine and a tub of butter, or the releasing of Contac's tiny time pills);

6. Catchy, product-relevant phrases (such as Wisk's "ring around the collar" and Visine's "gets the red out");

7. Jingles that position a brand name with an appropriate image (such as "If you've got the time, we've got the beer—Miller beer.").[16]

We focus next on the hardware side of broadcast advertising, the physical implementation of copywriters' ideas that results in the radio and TV commercials we hear and see every day.

Study Questions

1. Which do you think makes the best commercial TV spokesperson: the glamorous star, trim athlete, respected authority, or the man- or woman-on-the-street (the actual consumer)? Give reasons for your answer.

2. Use the HOW-E-ZE formula to analyze selected TV commercials. Where violations occur, discuss possible reasons and overall effects.

3. Which specific TV commercials do you find the most believable? The most unbelievable? Why?

4. Explain clearly the difference between transition terms and composition terms and give examples of each.

5. Find current on-air examples of vampire video in commercials and discuss its effect.

6. Select a national product currently running TV commercials and explain how the advertiser is positioning the brand name in viewers' minds.

7. What guidelines would you give to a creative team that was discussing the possibility of using celebrities instead of "real people" in a TV commercial? How about children?

8. List at least five ways in which copywriters can build a recognizable style into their commercials.

ASSIGNMENT 10-A

Consider the following sales key. Then, thinking in an active, visual, television framework, without regard to any specific product, come up with two different lists, one for possible ways to visualize the selling point, and the other for ways to visualize the benefit. Use your imagination but watch out for commercialitis!

SALES KEY: Locks in freshness and flavor (selling point) and locks out mildew and odor (benefit).

Ways to Visualize Selling Point   Ways to Visualize Benefit

ASSIGNMENT 10-B

For an assigned product, service or store, prepare the video portion of a 30-second TV commercial below (storyboard frames and video instructions only). Make sure that your brand name and sales key are perfectly clear, but no form of audio is permitted. When you have completed the assignment, exchange papers with a classmate and ask him or her to identify your sales key.

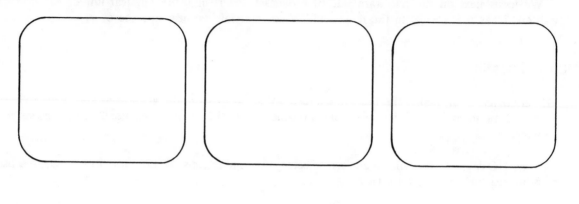

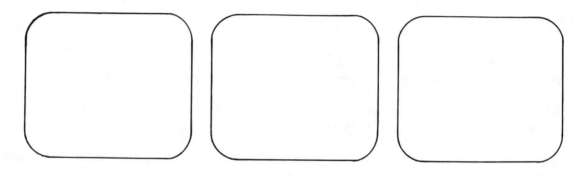

ASSIGNMENT 10-C

Select one of the ways you listed in assignment 10-A for visualizing the selling point, and one of the ways you listed for visualizing the benefit, and choose an appropriate product. Prepare a script for a 30-second TV commercial.

ASSIGNMENT 10-D

Study carefully the storyboard presented in Figure 10.2. Prepare what you believe is an appropriate copy platform for it (one you think might have preceded actual creation of this commercial).

ASSIGNMENT 10-E

Select any of the commercial exhibits in Chapter 10 and redo the audio track (improving on it as you go). Write a justification for your changes.

ASSIGNMENT 10-F

Prepare a complete storyboard for an assigned product (30 seconds). Emphasize the demonstration format, and use it to the "best of TV's ability." Prepare television frames similar to those used in assignment 10-B.

ASSIGNMENT 10-G

Given one product, service, or store, prepare four storyboards: one for 60 seconds, one for 30 seconds, one for 20 seconds, and one for 10 seconds. Use the same basic sales key but vary your choice of format. Use as many different frames as you need; start each new commercial on a separate page and indicate length. Prepare frames similar to those used in assignment 10-B.

Notes

1. See *Advertising Age* (January 2, 1978):17.
2. *Ibid.*
3. *Advertising Age* (April 27, 1981):50.
4. See "Pitches That Persuade Viewers," *Adweek* (February 20, 1985).
5. *Topline* 4, no. 4 (February 1986) (McCollum/Spielman & Company, New York).
6. "Pitches That Persuade Viewers," *Adweek* (February 20, 1985).
7. *Ibid.*
8. *Ibid.*
9. *Topline* 2, no. 3 (May 1981).
10. *Topline* 2, no. 6 (December 1981).
11. "TV Week," *Honolulu Star-Bulletin & Advertiser,* May 4, 1986.
12. "Pretesting Television Commercials: The Sequence Method" (Mimeographed Pamphlet, Communicus, Inc., Los Angeles), 2.
13. Thomas Frederick Baldwin, "Redundancy in Simultaneously Presented Audio-Visual Message Elements as a Determinant of Recall." (Ph.D. diss., Michigan State University, 1966).
14. *TV Basics 1987-88,* Television Bureau of Advertising, New York.
15. *Topline* (December 1986).
16. *Advertising Age* (December 17, 1979):41–42.

Suggested Readings

Baldwin, Huntley. *Creating Effective TV Commercials.* Lincolnwood, Ill.: Crain Books, 1982.
Brook, Albert C., Norman D. Cary, and Stanley J. Tannenbaum. *The Radio and Television Commercial,* 2nd ed. Lincolnwood, Ill.: Crain Books.
Moriarty, Sandra E. *Creative Advertising: Theory and Practice.* Englewood Cliffs, N.J.: Prentice-Hall, 1986.
Peck, William A. *Anatomy of Local Radio-TV Copy,* 4th ed. Blue Ridge Summit, Pa.: Tab Books, 1976.
Price, Jonathan. *The Best Thing on TV, Commercials.* New York: Viking Press, 1978.
Zeigler, Sherilyn K., and J. Douglas Johnson. *Creative Strategy and Tactics in Advertising.* Columbus, Ohio: Grid Publishing, 1981.

11

Broadcast Commercial Production

As we begin our discussion of commercial production, we admit that some listeners and viewers object rather strenuously to noisy, gimmicky announcements, high-pressured sales tactics, and unreal situations and characters. Others, however, firmly maintain that certain radio commercials are more listenable than much of the between-record patter that stations provide. And they can cite TV commercials that they believe are more logical and better produced than a lot of the program fare those commercials accompany.

Although there are exceptions, six weeks is generally the minimum time required for production of a 30- or 60-second TV spot from storyboard approval to finished tape or film, unless the commercial is animated (and then the time needed usually doubles). Interestingly enough, an hour-long program in a TV dramatic series often takes that same 6-week period to produce. Although the actual filming for one episode may be accomplished in five to ten days, post-production activities (processing and editing) go on for several weeks thereafter.

Who's in Charge

Numerous organizations and job personnel are involved in commercial production, and it will be helpful to review their roles before examining some of the materials with which they work. It is important to stress, however, the interrelated aspects of these jobs; teamwork is the name of the game, even though not all commercials involve the same number or type of players. The commercial writing process is so closely related to production that we will include brief mention of people thus engaged as well.

THE RADIO STATION TEAM
Radio stations may supply writers for local commercials at the request of advertisers. Sometimes a company representative works with the actual writer (although it may be only by telephone), and sometimes the contact is merely a mailed fact sheet for the product, service, or store. Frequently, however, station copywriters must dig for all of their own information.

Radio engineers obviously handle the bulk of the production process and sometimes the announcing portion as well. Or program personalities take on the talent part of the advertising function and their engineers are responsible for any music and sound effects called for in the script.

THE TELEVISION STATION TEAM
TV stations may be asked to provide not only writers and audio and video engineers, but also artists and photographers, set designers, film editors and projectionists, and the entire studio crew (camera operators, lighting specialists, floor directors, and special service personnel, as required to

192

handle props and microphones), plus the director, and sometimes talent (especially if it's only an off-camera announcer).

THE ADVERTISING AGENCY TEAM

The commercial production department in a large advertising agency may have its own studio and a limited amount of both film and videotape equipment. Even if agency personnel shoot their own commercial footage, however, they nearly always send it to a local TV station for post-production operations (editing). In many instances, though, agencies contract with film production companies and then send their own representatives along to supervise.

There are literally hundreds of such firms throughout the country, but relatively few do most of the business and are located in major production centers such as Los Angeles, New York, and Chicago. Some smaller companies, however, specialize in certain types of commercials (such as animated productions, tabletop presentations, and food demonstrations) and turn out highly professional work.

The agency team accompanying a film crew may include copywriters, creative supervisors, production specialists, and/or account executives and supervisors, often depending on the size and nature of the account being serviced. A major client investing $200,000 in a commercial venture might be much more anxious to see a number of qualified representatives riding herd on the filming than would a relatively small advertiser for whom TV was only a minor medium. Figure 11.1 shows some of the additional expense categories involved in TV production.

```
AUDIO (TV/RADIO)
   Talent (    ) @ $ ...........................  $_____
          (    ) @ $ ...........................  $_____
   Recording Studio ...........................  $_____
   Tape Editing/Dubbing .......................  $_____
   Tape Dubs ..................................  $_____
   Cleared Music/Jingle/SFX ...................  $_____
   Musicians ..................................  $_____
   Other (                         ) .........  $_____
   Contingency ................................  $_____

            Sub Total .........................  $_____

            A/C @ 17.65% ......................  $_____       $_____

VIDEO (VTR/FILM)
   Talent (    ) @ $ ...........................  $_____
          (    ) @ $ ...........................  $_____
          (    ) Extras @ $ ..................  $_____
   Film Production (Motion/Stills) (        )  $_____
   Additional Film Prints .....................  $_____
   VTR Production (                 ) .........  $_____
   VTR Orig. Tape/Dubs ........................  $_____
   Graphic Supplies ...........................  $_____
   Other (                         ) .........  $_____
   Contingency ................................  $_____

            Sub Total .........................  $_____

            A/C @ 17.65% ......................  $_____       $_____

   Props/Supplies .............................  $_____
   Special Charges/Creative Fees ..............  $_____
   Art Director (    ) hours ..................  $_____
   Artist (    ) hours ........................  $_____
   Broadcast Prod./Dir. (    ) hours ..........  $_____
   Broadcast Assistant (    ) hours ...........  $_____

            Total Net Charges..................  $_____

            TOTAL ESTIMATE.....................  $_____
```

Fig. 11.1. Broadcast production estimate request. (Courtesy of Seigle, Schiller, Rolfs, and Wood, Inc., Honolulu)

Forms established by the Association of Independent Commercial Producers list well over 200 cost considerations that may be involved in commercial film production. Some of the categories covered are preproduction fees (including casting); the shooting crew (including all audiovisual equipment operators); location and travel expenses (including interior and exterior permits, crowd control, food, lodging, security, and insurance); props and wardrobe costs, plus animal care; studio rental and set construction costs; equipment rental charges; film stock, developing, and printing costs; special director and creative fees; talent costs and expenses; and post-production fees (everything from musical scoring and voiceovers to editing, titling, and duplicating).[1]

TALENT AGENCIES

Before filming can begin, of course, all necessary talent must be cast and rehearsed. Talent agencies can supply almost every imaginable type of performer—singers, dancers, acrobats, clowns, mimics, and models, to name but a few. Finding the right presenters for a specific brand of product and type of sales message, however, is not an easy job. Frequently, advertisers and agencies handle auditions, but there are also free-lance casting directors whose job it is to match people with parts, speakers with copy lines, and characters with roles.

Casting

Research studies dealing with source credibility indicate definite values in careful commercial casting. Celebrity presenters have been discussed in previous chapters; now we need to emphasize a few priorities in the selection of commercial talent.

For the Ear. In choosing those all-important voices for radio commercials, casting directors look for projection of character (the roving reporter, the sophisticated shopper, the tired traveler) and an ability to present the sales message effectively through straightforward delivery, dialogue, humor, or whatever. Inflection, vocal emphasis, and pacing are often just as vital as actual words in communicating a sales key; such qualities as pitch, tone, resonance, and contrast (if there are two or more voices involved) are also important.

For the Ear and Eye. TV talent agencies produce long rosters of attractive commercial spokesmen and spokeswomen, lovable children, and sprightly senior citizens who stand ready to sell anything from health foods to home furnishings. They represent a wide range of ethnic backgrounds and, hence, can appeal to a variety of target audiences. But again the questions must be asked: How convincing are they in terms of a specific brand name? And do they enhance a sales key or overpower it? Obviously, both looks and speaking abilities are involved here, but so is the intangible substance known as empathy or charisma.

If celebrities are involved in any way, their agents must be consulted, and personal managers often accompany the stars to film sites and remain with them for the duration of the shooting. Also, no matter what the size or composition of the on-location team, if travel arrangements and overnight accommodations are needed, the people involved in setting them up must be added to the growing list of personnel engaged in all aspects of the commercial production business.

MUSICIANS, COMPOSERS, AND CHOREOGRAPHERS

Elaborate TV commercials may call for original choreography, but even simple ones on both radio and TV often feature specially composed (and/or arranged) jingles, themes, or background music. Copywriters may play large or small roles in the actual creation of lyrics; sometimes talented composers doctor agency-suggested song lines considerably. Still, a basic idea is just as valuable as its execution, if not more so. No one part of the creative job can stand alone.

Actual musicians need not appear on camera for their performances to be in evidence. Occasionally, however, a well-known group may be called on specifically to sing and/or play on behalf of a product, and thereby lend its own prestige. In such instances, sets and costumes can add special emphasis, too.

When copyrighted music is involved, the American Society of Composers, Authors, and Publishers (ASCAP), and Broadcast Music Incorporated (BMI) come into play. These are performing-rights organizations for music; they obtain license fees from radio and TV stations for the right to play copyrighted music. Each has devised formulas for computation of payment for music in commercials, whether the owner of such music is the advertiser, ad agency, jingle writer, production company, or music publisher. Changes in payment plans occur frequently and vary between commercials on radio and television and between local stations and networks.[2]

TALENT UNIONS

Traditionally, talent appearing in filmed commercials belonged to the Screen Actors Guild (SAG), and those appearing live on both radio and TV belonged to the American Federation of Television and Radio Artists (AFTRA). With the advent and widespread use of audio and videotape recordings of commercials, however, AFTRA contracts were broadened to include them. Today, SAG and AFTRA commercial contracts are very similar, and many performers belong to both unions (though only AFTRA covers radio talent).

What's more, the similarity of working conditions and requirements in film and videotape situations, plus the fact that an advertiser using a filmed TV commercial sometimes runs the audio portion separately as a radio commercial (thereby cutting across both SAG and AFTRA lines) leads to much discussion over the possible merging of the two groups. Currently, SAG has some 50,000 members; AFTRA has somewhat fewer.

SAG and AFTRA *players* (the union term used for talent, or performers) are paid under a variety of circumstances: when they act in commercials or simply speak or announce (with different pay scales for on- and off-camera roles); when they sing or dance (here, individual pay will vary depending on how many singers and dancers there are in the performing group); when they are required to perform so-called dangerous or unusual feats such as underwater stunts or staged auto accidents; when they participate in commercials presented on location (sometimes great distances from the studio—requiring air travel and lodging accommodations); and when rehearsals, filming, or recording schedules go beyond those specified in union contracts. Examples might include overtime work (beyond a normal, 8-hour work day or on weekends), missed guaranteed rest periods, or prolonged activity without meals, which are also guaranteed on a time basis (for instance, a certain number of hours after the morning call time).

The term *scale* refers to the minimum pay given to commercial players for their efforts (currently, well over $300 for an on-camera session and more than $100 for a very minor role as an *extra*); stars, however, may receive many times the base fee.

Residuals

In most cases, especially at the national level, the outlay of money for commercials does not end when the spots are "in the can" (safely packaged on film or tape). Since commercials are very rarely aired just once, an important part of the production costs may occur in the form of *residuals* paid to talent. Under union contracts, basic talent fees cover only performance during production, plus a limited number of commercial airings. Additional fees must be paid for successive airings, usually based on 13-time cycles, and depending in part on the number and size of markets in which the commercials are run. Widely used spots can cost an advertiser, in residual payments, many times what was paid for production in the first place.

Nonunionized Talent

If nonunion talent is desired for a particular commercial (an honest-to-goodness marine biologist and mother of three, for example) an advertiser may make what is known as a *talent buy* or *buy-out* of talent; the actor or actress involved receives a single, negotiated, outright payment for services. This figure is a one-shot sum, which normally includes an unlimited-use clause with no residuals. Persons appearing in these commercials are usually given 30 days after the production in which to join a union if they decide they would like to continue in this branch of the acting business.

The above discussion applies mainly to commercials aired nationally (produced in major production centers). In other situations, especially at the local level, union talent is often unavailable. Payment is usually worked out solely by negotiation and tends to be at much lower rates than those encountered with union personnel. Principal sources of talent in small markets are modeling agencies and local TV and radio stations (though certain station personnel sometimes are members of AFTRA).

Other Performers' Unions

A third union we need to mention is the 10,000-member Screen Extras Guild (SEG), for players who appear only incidentally in crowds or group scenes or whose contributions to a commercial otherwise do not include speaking or the direct appearance of faces. A hand model would fit this description if his or her task consisted merely of product assembly or display, and many SEG contracts are set up under the buy-out arrangement mentioned above. SEG does allow waivers for photographing shots of normal crowd activities. Some crowd waivers, however, stipulate that a certain number of SEG members must be included in the shooting.

Finally, if symphony musicians appear in commercials, pay scales are determined by the American Federation of Musicians (AFM). Residuals here come mainly from TV performances (on either videotape or film) because contracts with recording companies absolve radio stations from paying residuals to members of AFM whose music might appear behind a commercial.

Unions for Crews

Other unions involved in commercial production include the International Alliance of Theatrical Stage Employees (IATSE), the personnel who assemble and move sets and handle props; the International Brotherhood of Electrical Workers (IBEW) for, among others, electricians and those responsible for some of the special effects seen in commercials such as a cloudburst or explosion; and the Directors Guild. Contracts spell out requirements for working conditions, overtime pay, and special services performed and are the same ones involved in the production of TV programs.

EQUIPMENT, STUDIO, AND SET PROCUREMENT

Locally produced commercials requiring special equipment (not available at local TV stations) necessitate negotiation procedures between advertisers and suppliers (although broadcast personnel are glad to act as go-betweens for nontechnically oriented clients). On the other hand, an advertising agency looking for a nearby studio in which to shoot some test or finished commercials may contact a local TV outlet. Stations are usually willing to rent their studios when vacant.

On occasion, part of a public street, park, building, utility, or vehicle may be needed for on-location filming or taping. An *advance person* generally secures permission with appropriate officials and may arrange for crowd control and other police assistance and protection during the shooting. Certain fees may be involved, depending on the specific sites selected, the duration of the shooting, and any inconveniences caused in normal routine. Private homes also may be rented to serve as sets. Terms are established with individual owner/residents.

TRAFFIC AND ACCOUNT SERVICE DEPARTMENTS
AND LEGAL ASSISTANCE

Some less visible, but highly active and vitally important, team members handle the paperwork behind commercial production. Ordering and processing, scheduling and tabulation, paying bills and checking deliveries, these people become involved at almost every stage of the production process. As departments of traffic (at stations) and account service (at agencies), they keep watchful eyes on commercial budgets and expenditures, make sure union fees are paid on time so there are no late penalties, and place and follow through on orders for all materials and supplies needed between the time scripts and storyboards are approved and finished commercials are delivered. Staff size varies from less than one (in the case of a small station where one person performs several different functions) to several dozen at a large advertising agency.

Legal advice may be sought when commercials contain claims or demonstrations that might in any way be construed as misleading, defamatory, or plagiaristic; sometimes a simple production change can save a lengthy court battle. Many TV and radio stations, ad agencies, and client firms have their own legal departments; if they don't, they almost always are within easy reach of outside legal assistance.

Commercial Production Equipment

Dividing commercial broadcast equipment into hardware and software categories, we'll consider both in-studio and on-location production, first for radio and then for TV. Even though commercial scripts and storyboards have already been completed before people in this area of the business begin working, effective production techniques still demand creative discipline. Transferring a sales message from paper to tape or film is no easy task, and there are always limitations in time, money, and talent, as well as facilities and other resources. It is noteworthy, too, that developments in computer and other technologies are very rapid. Some of the innovations predicted and discussed in forthcoming pages might be well established by the time you read about them.

RADIO HARDWARE

Standard radio equipment includes microphones, turntables, cartridge machines, reel-to-reel tape recorders, and some kind of audio control board permitting the mixing of output from various sources, as well as volume control. Portable gear for on-location recording usually takes the form of easy-to-operate, hand-held cassette tape machines with built-in mikes.

The majority of radio stations today use condenser mikes for in-studio operations (either table-top models or those suspended from movable, mechanical arms). They provide excellent frequency response and are often used as lavaliere mikes for news crews and "on the spot" commercial interviews. Mikes may pick up sounds from one side only (unidirectional), from two sides (bidirectional), or from all sides, in a circular pattern (nondirectional). Turntables are of various types, and most can handle all speeds of play. Figure 11.2 shows an audio console set up at a radio station. Notice the presence of a microphone and copy displayed for the announcer/engineer.

Cartridges, simply called carts, are compact, case-enclosed, self-threading tapes, recorded and played back over a cartridge machine (successor to the reel-to-reel recorder). The tapes are reusable and are divided into two tracks. One holds the actual audio material and the other carries a cue tone positioned right before the first word or note of sound. (Or, if several different spots are recorded on a single cart, a cue tone precedes each one. An engineer simply places the cart in the machine and lets it cue itself, because the tape stops automatically whenever it reaches a cue tone; the advertiser's message, therefore, always begins clean.)

Fig. 11.2. Audio console. (Courtesy of K59 Radio, Honolulu)

At least one standard reel-to-reel recorder per station provides a back-up in case cartridge gear is ever inoperative; also, it is used consistently for another purpose. Carts are enclosed in cases, so any needed editing must be done on a reel-to-reel machine that allows easy access to the tape. Copies of the cart messages are recorded reel-to-reel, and after necessary cutting and splicing operations, the finished message is again dubbed onto a cart for airing. There is, necessarily, a loss in recording quality as material is copied and recopied, but even experts admit it is very slight.

The majority of both radio and TV commercials today include some form of music and/or sound effects, even though much of it may be strictly background (not meant to be especially memorable, but used mainly to enhance the continuity, or flow, of a message). Judging the ideal nature, amount, volume, and placement of these elements is an important production task if listeners are to receive the intended impression from the total message; clearly, the job is interpretive as well as mechanical.

Finally, small, battery-operated cassette tape machines have all but revolutionized the task of on-location recording. Many have automatic adjustments for changing sound levels, and, as mentioned previously, come with built-in mikes. Cassette tapes, somewhat smaller than carts, are likewise self-threading, reusable, enclosed in cases, and (unlike videotape) may be recorded on both sides (thus storing a double amount of material for their size).

TELEVISION AUDIO HARDWARE

All of the music, sound effects, and voice combinations used in radio commercials are obviously available in television as well. Most TV control rooms are equipped with turntables, an audio control board, and cart machines, as well as reel-to-reel equipment. Much in-studio TV sound pickup, however, in contrast to that of radio, occurs under less than favorable conditions. Talent may talk to the camera (rather than directly into a mike); move around while speaking; be preoccupied with demonstrating a product; and work with and talk to other talent while addressing the home viewer.

Boom microphones (positioned on the end of larger, longer mechanical arms than those found in radio studios) are sometimes used during TV commercial recording and are attached to rolling pedestals that can follow moving talent; usually they remain slightly overhead, out of camera range. More often, however, the talent simply wear *lavaliere* mikes. These are slender and unobtrusive and can be concealed under clothing or hung around the neck. Sometimes they are even hand-held.

Both boom and lavaliere mikes are used, when convenient, for both in-studio taping and on-location filming.

An audio track may be recorded separately and later dubbed in over the visual action. This procedure is referred to as *recording wild,* and is a problem only when the visual scene calls for a fairly close shot of a talent's face while his or her lines are spoken; in such shots, synchronizing lip movements with the actual sound track can prove to be a tricky editing job.

TELEVISION VIDEO HARDWARE

Television studio production typically employs lead oxide, plumbicon-tube cameras, which can operate at lower light levels than earlier models and still give the cleanest, clearest reproduction of any; of course, almost all work is done in color. Slide and film chains, used to pick up slides and film clips during a taping session, however, usually involve *vidicon* cameras in the station's control or projection room.

Figure 11.3 shows a high-performance, professional EFP (Electronic Field Production) color camera, offering superb capability for both studio and field production. It's well suited for on-board VCR operation, stand-alone camera operation, and multiple camera production. Figure 11.4 shows another field-and-studio camera that offers a number of special effects, including a "dream scene" atmosphere. As many as eight preset effects can be programmed, stored in the camera's memory, and retrieved on command.

A brief word about lenses is in order here, because copywriters on local accounts often must not only specify shot composition, but also work within the confines of a limited number of cameras. Generally, TV cameras are equipped with lenses of various focal lengths, labeled in inches, and usually ranging from one inch for a very wide shot to eight inches for a very tight shot, but copywriters should be aware that lenses cannot be *racked* (changed) while a camera is live or recording, but only when it is setting up or holding for an up-coming take.

If a storyboard, therefore, calls for a long, or establishing, shot of the talent and product, and then a close-up of product demonstration, two cameras will be involved (one for the LS and one for the CU), unless there is enough time allowed in the commercial for the LS camera to move physically (dolly) in on the product, or the LS camera is equipped with a variable focal length, zoomar lens (see Chapter 10).

Fig. 11.3. Electronic field production color camera. (Courtesy of Ikegami Electronics [USA], Inc.)

Fig. 11.4. Automatic field/studio color-TV camera. (Courtesy of Ikegami Electronics [USA], Inc.)

Fortunately, most stations today have cameras with zoomar lenses; but suppose a small station doesn't (or maybe it is not immediately available), and the LS and CU do, in fact, require the services of the only two cameras involved in the production. There is no particular problem here unless the original long shot or the shot following the close-up calls for use of both cameras simultaneously. (Two such shots would involve a split screen effect or a scene with a super appearing on a studio card.) There is simply no way to cut, dissolve, or wipe to or from a two-camera shot to another shot involving one or both cameras when there are only two cameras in the studio. Either one camera (the one on the super card or half of the split screen, for example) must be freed (taken out) while the second one holds (until the first can be set up on the following shot), or a slide, film clip, or previously recorded videotape must intervene between camera shots. If the super in this example, therefore, is on a slide, no camera is involved, and the problem disappears.

Moving from the studio to the control room, we find that the situation need not always be as cumbersome as the above discussion suggests, even if we are restricted to two cameras. The life-savers today are video carts (counterparts of radio's audio carts)—videotapes that are self-threading, self-cueing, automatically rewound, and enclosed in small, protective cases. With a station's acquisition of a cart machine comes the capacity to pretape parts of a commercial that two cameras alone could not cover. Then these scenes or effects can be inserted onto a final cart as the live action takes place in the studio. Since the cart machine can thereby function as one or more separate video sources, even small, limited-facility stations can produce high-quality, competitive commercials with ease.

Video carts also permit local advertisers to produce a series of commercials quite reasonably. A standard commercial open and close for, say, an appliance dealer, can be preserved on carts (both audio and video material). Then, different sets (featuring, for example, washing machines, refrigerators, and electric ranges) may be recorded on separate carts—visual action only, without sound. Now the cart machine becomes an editing device, as selected sequences are assembled into a series of individual commercials; each uses the stock open and close, while an off-camera announcer reads a new piece of copy when the advertiser feels it is time for a change.

As is true in radio, most TV stations still maintain one or more reel-to-reel videotape machines and reel-to-reel copies of commercials for use as backup in an emergency. Quadruplex machines record on two-inch videotape (reel-to-reel only), a size traditionally considered to provide the highest level of broadcast quality reproduction. Helical Scan equipment, on the other hand, records on one-inch, half-inch, and even quarter-inch tape (either reel-to-reel or cassette). Figure 11.5 shows a recently introduced one-inch videotape recorder available in a full studio console. It can be complemented by a wide range of monitors, loudspeakers, and editing equipment. On the horizon, according to experts, is the widespread use of film carts.

TV control rooms also have equipment for switching each of the studio cameras into the line fed ultimately to the on-air transmitter, for controlling certain picture characteristics (such as contrast and picture intensity), and for mixing the output of various video sources. Such equipment also makes possible the achievement of optical effects discussed in Chapter 10, and special controls may permit other, more complex combinations and transitions.

One popular effect—alternately blurring and sharpening a picture (perhaps before and after a dream sequence or a flash-back scene)—is achieved by the camera operator who manipulates the camera's focal adjustment. A more recent development permits the alternate focus and defocus of different parts of a scene for emphasis; hence, a couple conversing near the camera may blur to shift viewer attention to another couple behind them. Sometimes scenes seem to shrink or to balloon to several times their original size.

A *multiplexer* is an arrangement of mirrors whereby pictures shown by two different projectors can be picked up by one camera. A *telestrator* is a character-generating machine, using computer technology, that allows an operator to compose full color pictures on its drawing-board TV screen with a special stylus. The machine itself can also draw pictures and can make images spin, whirl, and move in a multitude of other ways.[3]

To prevent commercialitis from moving in here, we must caution production personnel against getting bogged down with mechanical and electronic gimmicks. A careful check of current on-air commercials will reveal a relatively limited use of fancy devices compared with the more standard, reliable, and still very effective cuts and dissolves. Special effects can play an important communication role, but only if they are clearly motivated by the sales message.

Before moving into a discussion of software, we need to examine the basic differences between TV's two major recording vehicles.

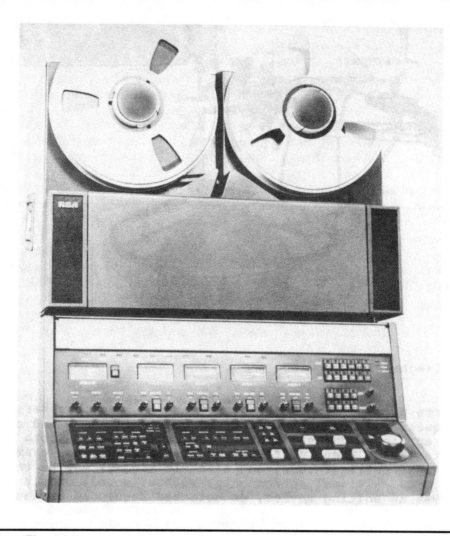

Fig. 11.5. Full-feature videotape recorder introduced in 1980. (Courtesy of RCA)

VIDEOTAPE VERSUS FILM

Few prepared commercials today for radio or TV are presented live. Granted, when radio personalities deliver a sales message for a product, it is usually somewhat spontaneous; a short fact sheet or brief outline of important product benefit information may be supplied, but the production here is extremely simple. Likewise, TV talk show hosts and hostesses have no trouble saying a few words about a sponsor's product (with the help of cue cards), and there is rarely much demonstration involved.

For the most part, however, TV spots produced locally are recorded on videotape—that marvelous material designed especially for television, which years ago freed talent and crew from the worries and problems of live performance mistakes, logistics and time scheduling conflicts, and equipment failure or prop malfunction.

On the other hand, the vast majority of national commercials are still shot on film—a medium of the cinematic arts produced (even in the world of advertising) by fairly conventional motion picture methods developed long before the advent of TV. Now let us compare the separate advantages of videotape and film.

Videotape

Perhaps videotape's most obvious value is its capacity for immediate playback. Did the camera pick up the product behind the mixing bowl? Could the super be read clearly? Was there a shadow across the set? There's no need to ponder questions such as these when a videotape recording can reveal the answers in seconds. With film, processing must be done in a laboratory, and sometimes a lost scene is gone forever (for example, a volcanic eruption or solar eclipse), or at least difficult to restage (depending on time, cost, weather, and talent-commitment situations).

Closely related is videotape's instant editing ability. If errors are detected in a scene, part or all of it may be re-recorded on top of the unwanted portion (thereby erasing the mistakes). The tape rewinds rapidly and also can be moved ahead at a normal or fast speed. In film, lab technicians must handle editing after the development process has been completed; if a dozen different scene takes are recorded, selecting and matching the ideal bits and pieces can be a laborious task. (Although videotape may be cut and spliced together as a unit or edited electronically, the sound track on a finished piece of film always precedes the picture by a number of frames. Most commercial filming today, therefore, records the sound on tape or on a film separate from the one holding the photography; otherwise, editing can be very tricky indeed.)

Ever since its first commercial appearance, videotape has been heralded for its clear, sharp images that can scarcely be distinguished from those presented before a live camera. Film cannot match this realistic look and the feeling of immediacy that accompanies it.

Finally, the quality of videotape is more consistent than that of film, in terms of transmission from station to station. A packaged-desserts advertiser whose videotaped demonstration commercials are shown nationally can rest assured that viewers in Honolulu will see the same rich ingredients, the same fluffy cake texture, and the same moist, creamy frosting as their fellow constituents in New York or Miami.

Film

One of film's key benefits is the portability of its cameras. There are no attached wires and no bulky apparatus to hinder filming operations in the cramped quarters or on the perilous perches sometimes encountered by production crews. True, videotape gear is becoming lighter and more mobile, but it still cannot match the convenience or space-saving features of film equipment (see Figure 11.6). In Omaha recently, a production crew dangled from a helicopter to film a crowd scene on top of a skyscraper.[4]

Film has a unique flexibility and versatility. Pictures can be enlarged or reduced and selected elements of scenes can be frozen or defocused. The whole field of animation is a highly developed art form.

Videotape's stark pictures cannot compete with the soft cinematic properties of film. Many advertisers find this more "gentle" visual quality appealing. Also, a number of optical effects (some of them achieved through use of special lenses and filters) are possible only with film.

Sixteen mm prints (copies) of filmed commercials often cost about half what duplicate videotape recordings cost. Further, it costs less to ship film prints of commercials to stations because they are not as bulky as videotapes.

Both videotape and film have strengths and weaknesses as far as commercial production is concerned and, fortunately, it need not always be a one-or-the-other choice. Numerous possibilities exist for effective combinations of the two. For example, suppose the owner of a local Swiss clock outlet has on hand two film clips, one showing the interior of his shop and all his merchandise, and the other

Fig. 11.6. Ampex VR-3000 portable videotape recorder, mounted on a backpack frame. (Courtesy of Ampex Corporation)

showing master craftsmen at work designing and assembling clocks at the main factory (or even in Switzerland). Either or both could easily be incorporated into a commercial videotaped in a local TV studio. That way a current promotion or sale, a seasonal activity, or expanded shop hours could be presented around the "quality and selection" story that would probably (realistically) remain unchanged for relatively long periods of time.

Recent years have seen development of a *chromakeyer* device, now in use at many stations and hailed as a successor to in-studio rear-screen projection. The chromakey effect represents a matting of people, products, or other items against a selected background. Let us assume that our clock shop owner wants to deliver his own commercials and wants viewers to see him in his store-and-product environment (or maybe he wishes to appear with the craftsmen as they work). By deleting one element from the in-studio scene (such as a color—usually blue), the chromakeyer makes room for a new element to take its place (the desired film clip). The result is a high-quality blending of Mr. Owner, who is actually in the studio, and the filmed interior scenes he asked to be part of—a much cleaner, crisper image than that provided by rear-screen projection.

Animation

Another popular video insert is the animated clip, though some commercials consist entirely of animated sequences. Undoubtedly, cartoons are the best-known form of animation, involving characters (human and animal) who began entertaining many of today's consumers when they were still preschoolers. Those who appreciate the complex production operation behind this photographic technique, however, are relatively few in number.

In cartoon animation, each individual drawing—different in only minute details from the one preceding—is photographed as one film frame. In today's standard 30-second commercials, there are 720 frames of film (24 per second). Hence, in a fully animated one-minute spot, there are 1,440 frames and 1,440 separate drawings and camera exposures. Sometimes when identical drawings are repeated, a technical procedure known as *cycling* can save some time; still, it should be obvious that animated production is a rather laborious process.

When the complete set of pictures is projected at normal film speed, the characters come to life for viewers. Then, as we noted in Chapter 10, these entertaining spokescharacters can go to bat for a commercial's product or service and sales key by endorsing, demonstrating, or dramatizing. The challenge is to persuade through the frivolity and to keep the brand name prominent while the fantasy unfolds on the screen.

Two other forms of animation are known as stop-motion photography and photo animation. Product boxes, bottles, and cans acquire the ability to talk and act, sing and dance, demonstrate and sell. Kitchen appliances work by themselves, tools build, and pieces of sports equipment go into action. In all these instances, the tedious shooting of single-frame exposures is again required. This time, however, the actual objects (not drawings) must be set up in such a way that the difference in position from shot to shot is very slight; otherwise, when the final film is run at normal speed, the movements will appear jerky.

All forms of animation move, but if the action involved is only partial movement, the technique is called *limited animation*. On the other hand, *full animation* is a very refined type of action, often including lip movements. Animation also may be combined with live action in any commercial to provide yet another kind of motion. In this instance, animated elements are usually superimposed over scenes in which regular talent appears.

All of the preceding examples have involved film; we should also note that experiments with computerized animation on videotape are very much in evidence today. For example, IBM punch cards containing information on a planned sequence of scenes can instruct a computer to create and develop, expand and contract, examine and reveal characters or objects in specific ways: backwards or forwards, in slow motion or fast, in miniature or giant size. The process is extremely expensive, but does produce results in a matter of minutes. (Although filmed animation is a highly polished art, its videotaped counterpart is considerably less refined.)

Another recent development is the disc tape machine, which provides still a different form of staccato-like animation. These machines run at several different speeds and in reverse without losing picture quality.

Editing

Despite the existence of a brilliant commercial idea, an expert writing job, superb acting talent, and masterful camera work or recording, nearly all filmed and some taped radio and TV commercials are really made in the editing labs, long after the actual recording process has been completed. Radio involves the simplest procedures, so we will consider this medium first.

Audiotape. Recall that radio commercial elements come in three basic forms: voices, music, and sound effects. Any or all may be picked up live by microphones, or lifted from records or tape recordings. The editing job here consists of physically splicing together, or electronically mixing onto a final tape, all of the desired components (singly and in combination) to form the completed message.

Film. A total of 45 feet of 35mm film is all that is needed to fill 30 seconds of time. It's not unusual, however, for commercial film producers to shoot more than 2,500 feet (up to 30 *minutes*) of film, including numerous takes of the same scene; each may show a little different lighting or background effect, product position, facial expression on the part of talent, or pace of demonstration. Camera angles may also be varied, especially if the same basic scene appears more than once.

The name Moviola has become synonymous with film editing. Figure 11.7 shows an editing machine that has been the workhorse of the motion picture industry for more than half a century. It has both 16mm and 35mm components, and an editor can convert from 16 to 35. Both magnetic and optical sound can be reproduced. A newly designed Videola system transfers 16mm or 35mm film to broadcast-quality videotape (see Figure 11.8).

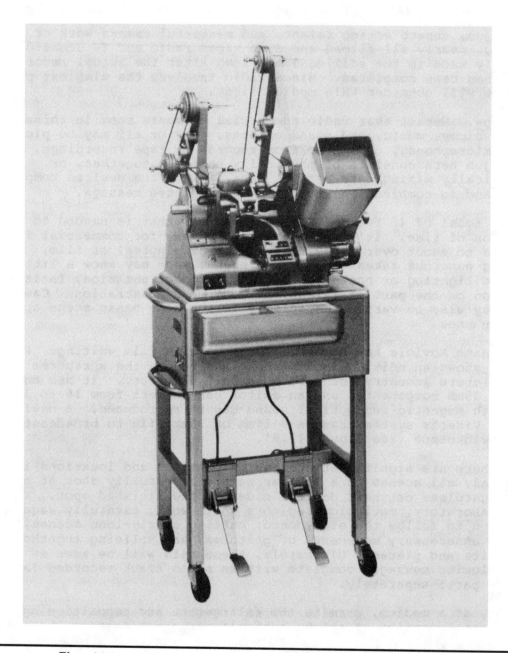

Fig. 11.7. Moviola Series 20 upright editor. (Courtesy of Magnasync/Moviola Corporation)

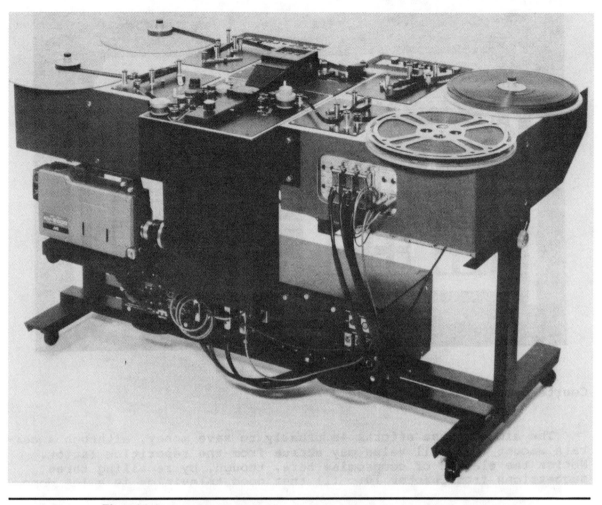

Fig. 11.8. Videola V-1000 film-to-tape transfer system. (Courtesy of Magna-sync/Moviola Corporation)

If there are significant changes in costumes and locations in a commercial, all scenes of a similar nature are usually shot at one time, regardless of their desired order in the finished spot. Then meticulous editors go to work in the laboratory, carefully sequencing the action to follow the storyboard, cutting overly long scenes, deleting unnecessary movements or gestures, and splicing together the choice bits and pieces. Ultimately, these bits will be seen as one smooth-flowing message, complete with an audio track recorded (at least in part) separately.

Film, as a medium, permits the enlargement and repositioning of scenes, the insertion of tricky opticals and stock footage shots from a film library, and the addition of zooms and dissolves to the finished product even if no zoomar lens is used on location and only one camera is present.

Videotape. Although it is true that an immediate playback deemed unsatisfactory may be erased and rerecorded on the spot, some of the more elaborate videotaped commercials still require editing (most all of which today is done electronically). Granted, simple productions staged in a studio, with only minor (if any) cast and set changes, are taped pretty much from start to finish with one, two, or more cameras. Cuts and dissolves between scenes, however, may be edited in after the fact, and taped or filmed inserts (footage borrowed from libraries or shot before or after the in-studio session) may be added, along with certain optical effects.

If all of the above materials are assembled at the time of the in-studio videotaping, they may be recorded on a single master tape. When cutting and splicing of videotape is required, the process isn't much more complicated than it is for audio tape, except that standard videotape size is one or two inches, to allow for storage of visual material; audio tape is only one-quarter of an inch wide.

The process of electronic editing involves selecting sequences from several reels of videotape and combining these pieces in a desired pattern onto a final master tape—all electronically. Figure 11.9 shows a computer-based system that both cues and synchronizes any three audio/video signals.

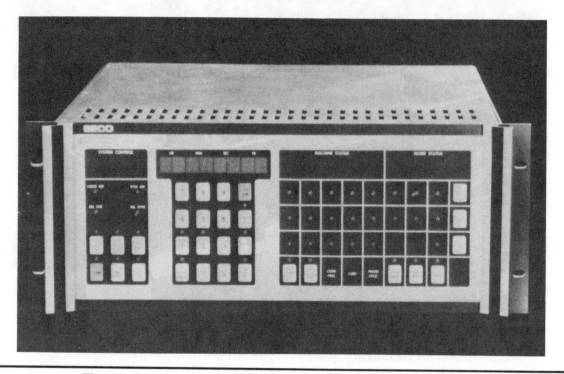

Fig. 11.9. EECO's MQS-100A Series multi-cue synchronizer. (Courtesy of EECO Incorporated)

One final editing note we should mention concerns commercial length. Sometimes a 60- or 30-second commercial (radio or TV, film or videotape) may be edited down to form a shorter spot for use at specified times on specified stations. These new commercials are referred to as *lifts,* and sometimes even apply across media (when the audio track, or part of it, from a TV commercial is used on radio).

The aim of these efforts is usually to save money, although a certain amount of recall value may accrue from the repetition factor. Notice the element of compromise here, though, by recalling three suggestions from Chapter 10: that good television is a lot more than pictures matched to an audio track; that a sales message that can stand alone aurally is not capitalizing on TV's potential as a medium; and that, ideally, every commercial deserves individual attention and as much originality as the copywriter can muster.

TV viewers' increasing demands for realism in commercials often force advertising teams to stretch their creative imaginations. Rest assured, however, that efforts that don't pay off to the client's satisfaction are not repeated.

SOFTWARE

In the early days of radio, all sound effects were produced live before a microphone. Today, radio announcers may occasionally dress up commercials through use of comparable software, but they rely for the most part on prerecorded effects; hence, our discussion here will focus on television.

Sets and Props

Large TV studios normally have several sets suitable for table-top presentations (appliance demonstrations and food preparation, for example) and a certain amount of floor scrubbing, carpet cleaning, and the like. Small studios are often specially designed for commercials requiring a kitchen, laundry, or bathroom setting, and a few simple pieces of furniture, such as a dressing table, easy chair, coffee table, and playpen are often all that are required to establish locale as far as viewers are concerned (especially in commercials utilizing mainly close-ups).

Some sets are built to order from a series of flats similar to those used in theater productions, with all manner of trim and backdrops. Also, murals can be used to enhance communication. If it is important to a store manager, for instance, that a commercial appear against part of the city skyline, a specific residential view, or a country setting, artists can produce murals that correspond exactly to photographs of the selected scenes.

Large studios generally have huge double doors opening into parking lots or other easy-access areas. Automobiles, boats, or even heavy farm machinery may thus be featured in commercials, though some of these spots may best be shot at least partly on location.

Props are usually portable objects such as pots and pans, tools and typewriters, luggage and lamps. Sometimes it's hard to draw the line between items that are actually part of a set (for example, certain pieces of furniture) and those that fall into the movable properties category; although the distinction is not of particular concern to copywriters, union contracts are very strict when it comes to job descriptions.

Productions that require the services of several different unions may be more expensive than those that do not. Even though these people may not work more than a small portion of each production hour or day, they are required to be present to handle the materials that fall within their respective jurisdictions. In short, beginning copywriters should learn early the involvements they may unwittingly write into their storyboards and come to appreciate the crucial behind-the-scenes teamwork involved in commercial production.

Graphics

TV stations usually are equipped to do some commercial artwork for local advertisers. The design of advertiser logotypes and various studio cards (for, say, a company's name and address, store hours, or special sale prices) is handled easily and often converted to 35mm slides; film processing facilities and editing equipment sometimes even permit stations to develop filmed inserts the day they are shot.

It is important to differentiate here, with regard to terminology, between projected TV graphics (slides, film, and videotaped inserts) and nonprojected visuals (various hand-held and manipulated devices). Both film and videotape have been discussed in detail, and as far as slides are concerned, the best advice is: when possible, go easy on them. Though inexpensive and easy to produce, they are static; they cannot take advantage of the dynamic nature of television. Supers make ideal slides because they don't tie up an in-studio camera and are used over other scenes anyway (so interest is enhanced).

Nonprojected visuals may assume dozens of forms, but common ones include *hand cards* (cardboard graphics usually placed on easels or hods); *flip charts* (series of sheets flexible enough to be folded back or flipped over); *zip charts* (sets of cards, one behind the other, seen through windows and moved left to right or up and down); *strip teases* (letters or drawings that are uncovered one part at a time); and *pan strips* (stationary strips of information across which the camera moves). In all of these cases, the following guidelines apply:

1.   *Size.* Although cards are often a convenient 11" × 14", there is no one correct size for visuals. The crucial thing is proportion; all material designed for camera pickup must be in a 3:4 aspect ratio (three units high by four units wide—the same as home TV receivers). Otherwise, either the edges of the cards will be seen (plus some extraneous material beyond the edges) or important material will be cut off at the screen's edges.

On the other hand, given a proper 3:4 aspect ratio, TV cameras still see more information than home sets do; graphic designers, therefore, must leave a blank margin of safety around all critical information (about one-sixth of the area on all sides of printed or other visual material intended for home viewing). That way no vital material is lost during transmission.

If several cards are to be used in succession—without an intervening scene or change of camera—it is a good idea to keep them all the same size. The camera operator is thereby freed from having to refocus on the air (an awkward move). Even though the 3:4 aspect ratio is maintained, refocusing will be necessary if, for example, a 6" × 8" card follows a 15" × 20" card or vice versa.

2.   *Contrast.* As the percentage of color TV receivers in American homes approaches 100 percent, the old black-and-white worry that certain colors would blend together in gray tones is fast diminishing. Still, color contrast is important if all elements in a scene are to show up clearly and attractively. Art directors advise against using any color combination on TV that you wouldn't want in your own living room.

The sharpest contrast possible is pure white against pure black and should be avoided in all cases except one because of possible damage to sensitive television cameras and a blooming effect on the screen around the letters or pictures involved. Words *supered* over a scene should be white, and unless the background card is black, it will not completely disappear in the process of superimposition. In non-supered situations, light letters on dark backgrounds generally show up better than dark-on-light.

3.   *Type.* Usually, minimum type size should be 1/4 inch, though 1/2 inch and larger type faces are preferable. For good readability, spacing is important, too. The areas between letters should appear equal; letters as high as they are wide usually work best. Also, bold type is easier to read than light type or type with frills.

Most TV stations now have character generators—typewriters that electronically insert letters onto the TV screen (and the letters can then be stored in a computer for future use). Hence, hand-set transfer-lettering and manual stenciling activities are not often called for.

Finally, it should be obvious that the number of words per line and the number of lines per visual should be kept to a minimum. A certain amount of creative judgment is called for here, but copywriters must remember the short amount of time each storyboard frame actually remains on camera.

4.   *Other considerations.* A few other guidelines will help insure quality in TV graphics. Illustrations and designs, like copy, should be kept simple; the camera won't pick up intricate details, and viewers cannot be expected to work to figure them out. The surface texture of a visual seldom appears on television as it does to the naked eye. Coarse, open-weave fabrics (or photographs) reflect light and make reproduction unreliable. Dull, matte finishes are ideal. Motion, or the suggestion of it, attracts attention and helps maintain interest. If a static visual must be used, it should be combined whenever possible with others that involve some sort of action.

Lighting and Wearing Apparel

Before moving on, we should mention two other on-camera considerations. Copywriters working on local accounts are probably more directly involved with these than are their national agency counterparts, but the value of sheer awareness cannot be overemphasized.

The first concern is lighting—not the level of footcandles needed for effective operation of TV cameras (a technical consideration), but the use of illumination to enhance sales-message communication (a creative consideration). Examples might be a tiny spot of light on a new product discovery; the flash of light from a photographer's camera; starlight and firelight; or searchlights and flickering lights. Lighting can be used in television (usually in network or other national productions) to achieve some of the same effects provided by sounds and music in radio commercials.

Setting studio lights does require valuable time and energy, and many locally produced commercials involve no elaborate sets or actions, so a standard, flat lighting plan is generally followed. Scenes are broadly lit and often remain at the same level throughout the spot. It is always possible, though, to dim or brighten a scene; a local optical company, for example, might demonstrate quite effectively the problem of trying to read in a poorly lighted room.

When possible, lights should be set at different angles to help achieve visual clarity without distortion. Three lighting terms encountered in even simple productions may be *back lights, key lights,* and *fill lights*. A copywriter need not specify these when preparing storyboards, but if he or she is familiar with them, it is often easier to communicate a desired effect to the eventual production crew.

A back light outlines the general shape of a subject by lighting it from behind. A key light is a strong, major light source in a scene, used to help model the acting talent and the area in which they perform. Often it creates shadows and highlights. But it must be balanced by a softer fill light from the opposite direction if the effect created is to be pleasing to viewers' eyes.

We also need to look briefly at talent attire. Granted, unless we are staging a circus, or major theatrical commercial, it hardly seems appropriate to classify this discussion as costuming; with today's emphasis on the natural look, many commercials (especially those featuring at-home or on-the-street talent) don't involve much make-up either. Still, the rules of color and contrast that were discussed for TV visuals apply in much the same way here. Jet-black pants and skirts coupled with snow-white shirts and blouses may cause blooming effects; likewise, shiny noses or foreheads and glittering jewelry can prove very troublesome when the lights hit them (the old sunshine-on-a-mirror effect). Then, too, unusually eye-catching outfits can steal attention just as overly attractive talent can. Commercial production teams may be brilliant artists in their own right, but effective advertising is sales communication first and theatrical back-up only a distant second.

Now, keeping both hardware and software in mind, it is time to examine the crucial element of cost. Unfortunately, cost frequently dictates the path a commercial will follow; discovering ways to bring disciplined creativity to life under the restrictions imposed by budgets can be the greatest challenge commercial producers ever face.

Costs

Commercial production costs vary widely, depending on such things as production methods utilized, talent involved, location and duration of shooting, and special effects called for during the editing process. We will not attempt, therefore, to discuss dollar figures for specific commercials; rather we will point out some general budget considerations and possible hidden costs, some important cost comparisons, and a few money-saving tips.

First, it is vitally important to remember that commercial production and media time costs are kept completely separate; and, at least in the case of national campaigns, production charges are usually much lower than those for air time. Whether this relationship is as it should be is a matter for debate, the standing argument being that broadcast time is both a highly perishable commodity and a powerful commercial vehicle (regardless of the number of dollars poured into the actual production of spots). As it is, 30 seconds of prime commercial time in a national network program today can range from less than $50,000 to more than $350,000. Production costs for national commercials in the early 1990s average well over $100,000, but, of course, there are extremes. Timex spent $1 million to sink a giant watch off the coast of Israel for a TV spot used for Super Bowl XX (1986), but Pat Cunningham, executive vice president of the N.W. Ayer advertising agency, noted that it was still possible in that year to produce an effective commercial for $36,000.

On the local level, spots usually cost between $1,000 and $15,000 to produce. And costs can double in five years' time, as TV advertisers increase both their use of elaborate sets, special effects, and contemporary music and the time and effort they expend in shooting, and as inflation continues to mount.[5]

Of course, all of these figures are one-time costs. Additional airings cost approximately the same amount in terms of time, and there are talent residuals and tape and film duplication costs to consider in the area of production.

With the exception of certain specified union wages, there are very few fixed production costs; most can be negotiated, and advertisers or their agencies are free to shop around for the best values. Most major agencies today, for example, operate on what is known as the competitive bid system in commercial production. Three or more studios or film production houses might be contacted for production estimates (bids) on a given storyboard. The agency may choose to take the lowest bid, although (as is often the case with low-cost merchandise) the cheapest way may not be the best. In the end, advertisers can wind up paying much more than necessary if entire productions have to be redone because of inferior workmanship the first time through. Under this system, the bidder absorbs original production costs that go beyond those listed on estimate sheets (cost overages); in other words, the estimate figures are fixed for the agency (firm bid).

A second system is a cost-plus arrangement wherein the bidding firm lists cost estimates and adds a certain percentage markup (a kind of profit commission). If additional costs are incurred, the advertiser must pay them. When the base figure increases, the dollar amount of the commission goes up, too.

The third plan frequently encountered is a cost-plus-fixed-fee contract that combines aspects of both of the others. Costs are estimated by the bidding studio or production house, and a fixed dollar sum (not a percentage) is added for profit. If there are overages, the advertiser pays them, but the fixed fee remains fixed.

Commercial production experts recommend several procedures for stretching limited commercial production budgets to their fullest. They place a premium on advance planning. Shooting a scene a number of different ways, waiting to pick the best one until the film is in the editing lab, can prove very expensive in time and talent. And even top quality production cannot make up for a weak sales key—any more than a highly creative ad campaign can sell an unacceptable product.

They note that long shots, revealing costly sets, may not be needed at all if the commercial focuses mainly on a table-top product demonstration.[6]

It also is considerably cheaper to produce a pool of on-location commercials all at once—in the same general areas—than it is to schedule separate shoots at different times. (A seven-scene, 30-second spot normally takes between two and three hours to shoot, but five or six hours are usually scheduled.) If additional in-studio sessions are needed to individualize certain commercials, they are relatively inexpensive.[7]

Finally, a recently developed light pen permits almost instantaneous editing of either commercial film or tape. Separate scene takes are placed in a computer-based device that reads out scene compositions and descriptions. Then selected versions are marked with the light pen; in a simple, straightforward editing job, a 30-second spot can be assembled in less than an hour.[8]

UNION CONSIDERATIONS

Now let us look at some production specifics such as union wages. Both AFTRA and SAG have local chapters in some cities that often are willing to negotiate local talent rates. At least it is a point worth checking, especially if large numbers of talent are involved.

Given that talent is needed in a particular commercial, there are some considerable cost differences between SAG and SEG. If, for example, a talent's hands could fulfill all required commercial actions effectively without any on-camera facial exposure, the savings could be hundreds, even thousands of dollars, because a SEG player instead of a SAG player could be used. Also, an off-camera announcer's rates are lower than those of an on-camera presenter delivering the same lines.

Then again, celebrities and highly talented crews demand and get premium payments; it is not unusual for top-level directors to draw thousands of dollars a day, and star spokespersons can make many times more.

In noncelebrity instances, live-action performances are generally less expensive than animated ones, at least in terms of original production costs. Animation, however, does not involve residuals that mount up quickly if there are a lot of talent and a large number of repeated showings in major markets. (Talent agents earn a fee, too—often 10 percent of their clients' earnings—but payment comes out of the performers' checks rather than the advertisers' pockets.)

MATERIALS

Lifts from both radio and TV commercials can prove very economical because original production costs are incurred just once for the several resulting spots. Or new spots can be built from extra film or tape footage that was shot but not used in a specific, budgeted commercial.

Stations normally receive 16mm prints of filmed commercials (which are cheaper than 35mm), but networks get both 16mm and 35mm. Some stations order several copies; others transfer the filmed spots to videotape carts (that later can be erased and reused). Potential dollar savings here may be difficult to determine, but are worth investigating if budgeting is tight.

In local productions, slides are often more economically obtained than visual cards, murals, or taped or filmed inserts. Once again, however, the cheapest is not necessarily the best in terms of sales message communication.

COMMERCIAL FRILLS

TV commercials can be dressed in elaborate choreography, fancy costuming, and special lighting effects. Radio commercials can be dressed in electronic synthesizers and sound created with painstaking effort. Both TV and radio spots may sport original jingles and accompaniment, and both media may find commercial production costs running way over budget. Are all of these dressings merely frills—gimmicks to hold attention? The answer is, as usual, "It all depends." If one or more of these devices can communicate a sales key more effectively than any other method and can be justified financially on that basis, consideration is certainly warranted.

STATION-ADVERTISER-AGENCY RELATIONSHIPS

Some stations provide certain advertising services free of charge to local advertisers. Examples might include simple copywriting, live or tape-recorded delivery (possibly with a musical background) in radio, and off-camera announcing over slides in TV. Plugs given nationally advertised products (for example, by TV talk-show hosts and hostesses) are also free. The cost of production materials is increasing, though, and station personnel's time is valuable. Advertisers must be cautioned, therefore, against expecting too much without charge.

We noted earlier that stations may rent vacant studios to advertising agencies. Fees vary, but they are much lower than those involved if specialized production houses are hired.

TECHNOLOGY

New production equipment is often labeled expensive at first glance, but over the long haul, savings can be monumental. The chromakeyer discussed previously can save many on-location shooting costs, and audio and video carts and cassettes have changed the whole complexion of the business in terms of speed and efficiency of operation.

On the horizon is a system involving two cameras—one of which will shoot miniature sets while the other handles talent actions. The two images can then be combined electronically, saving costly (life-size) set construction. Other technological advancements will keep commercial production a very dynamic operation for the foreseeable future.

The cost-conscious advertiser may well ask, however, just how much it is all worth in terms of genuine communication of a sales message. Unfortunately, there is no easy answer. But research in the creative area can shed some valuable light, as we shall see in the next chapter.

Study Questions

1. For an assigned local client, not currently using the broadcast media, explain what you would look for in the casting of radio and TV personalities for a new broadcast advertising campaign. Consider your client's needs and personality and those of competitors.

2. Explain clearly the relationship between talent unions and talent buys.

3. For an assigned client's campaign, assume you have been asked to hire a music production firm. Further, assume several such companies are eager for the job, and all have agreed to compose a trial score for you. What kinds of criteria would you use to judge the pieces? Consider both what the music should do and what it shouldn't do.

4. Discuss the advantages and disadvantages of film and videotape for several different assigned advertisers and campaigns.

5. Once a radio or TV commercial is ready for airing, who, from among the following, do you believe deserves the major portion of the credit (in the case of a success) or blame (in the case of a failure): the person or persons responsible for (a) the original idea, (b) the actual writing, (c) the technical direction and execution, or (d) the final editing? Why?

6. Differentiate clearly between an aspect ratio and a margin of safety.

7. For a given commercial, what tips would you give to the production team to help them save money?

ASSIGNMENT 11-A

Watch an hour of programming on a commercial TV station and log the following information for the commercials you see. Write in each advertised item, the length of each spot, and the format employed; then, check all other relevant columns. Finally, summarize what you have learned from the exercise, and include any comments you deem appropriate regarding general message content.

Advertised Item	Length of Spot	Format	Music	On Cam Talent	Animation	Humor	Male	Female	Wipe	Zoom	Celebrity Presenter	Hard Sell	Soft Sell

Summary and Comments

ASSIGNMENT 11-B

Select and list one local and one national commercial. Compare and contrast the commercial production techniques utilized and include the reasons that you think lie behind the differences.

ASSIGNMENT 11-C

Design appropriate in-studio visuals for an assigned TV commercial or for one you've written. List the specific details you considered, along with your rationale for decisions made.

ASSIGNMENT 11-D

Given an assigned TV commercial, make a list of the ways you might cut down on production costs for the players involved. Then do the same thing for crew members.

ASSIGNMENT 11-E

Visit a local TV station and observe production of a commercial (or visit a commercial studio). Include notes and comments on: (a) equipment used, (b) time and personnel involved, (c) problems encountered, (d) sets and props, (e) graphics, and (f) audio track.

ASSIGNMENT 11-F

Given a commercial designed for multicamera production, rewrite it around a two-camera limitation. Use script form, indicating audio and video.

ASSIGNMENT 11-G

For an assigned commercial, list all the tasks that you think would be involved in seeing the spot through its production stages—beginning with completion of the script or storyboard and ending with the finished tape or film.

ASSIGNMENT 11-H

Assume that an assigned commercial is about to be filmed on location. List all of the possible production problems that would increase filming time and costs. Indicate what differences there would be in your list if the shooting were done on videotape.

Notes

1. See "Association of Independent Commercial Producers—A National Philosophy and Perspective" (New York: Nation AICP, 1981).
2. *Advertising Age* (September 22, 1986):61.
3. See *Advertising Age* (July 21, 1980):S2, section 2.
4. *Advertising Age* (June 30, 1986):44.
5. "TV Week," *The Honolulu Advertiser and Star-Bulletin* (May 4, 1986):17.
6. See *Advertising Age* (August 11, 1980):45.
7. See *Advertising Age* (July 21, 1980):S1, section 2.
8. *Advertising Age* (October 20, 1980):66.

Suggested Readings

Bellaire, Arthur. *Controlling Your TV Commercial Costs.* Chicago: Crain Books, 1977.

Burrows, Thomas D., and Donald N. Wood. *Television Production: Disciplines and Techniques.* Dubuque, Iowa: Wm. C. Brown, 1978.

Busch, H. Ted, and Terry Landeck. *The Making of a Television Commercial.* New York: Macmillan, 1980.

Ewing, Sam, and R. W. Abolin. *Professional Filmmaking.* Blue Ridge Summit, Pa.: Tab Books, 1974.

White, Hooper. *How To Produce Effective TV Commercials,* 2d ed. Lincolnwood, Ill.: Crain Books.

Wurtzel, Alan. *Television Production.* New York: McGraw-Hill, 1979.

Zettl, Herbert. *Television Production Handbook.* Belmont, Calif.: Wadsworth, 1977.

ALSO: Check recent issues of *Advertising Age, Broadcasting,* the *Journal of Advertising,* and the *Journal of Broadcasting.*

12

Commercial Copy Testing

oday, both commercial writers and producers are increasingly realizing that a certain amount of scientific input from their partners in research can enhance communication effectiveness in numerous ways. It can assist the creative team in choosing, among other things which overall message theme (of several proposed) is the most credible, important, and relevant to a given audience; which combination of words, sound effects, music, and/or visual actions expresses a specific theme most clearly and memorably; and which commercial presenter, product setting, and jingle or camera technique does the best job attracting attention, differentiating one brand from another, and stimulating action.

In short, any of the creative principles and techniques discussed in Chapters 9, 10, and 11 are subject to test, and the more feedback a creative team gets from intended audiences, the better it can provide those listeners and viewers with the kinds of messages they need to help them answer questions, make decisions, and solve many of the problems they face every day.

There are many different types of research of value to broadcast advertisers, some of which were discussed in Chapter 7. This chapter will deal specifically with copy testing—examination of complete commercial messages and of specific elements therein (before, during, and after airing) and determination of their effectiveness as sales communication vehicles. Broadcast advertising today is too complex, too competitive, and too costly a business to allow for snap judgments in terms of commercial messages (which may play, ultimately, to millions of people on dozens, even hundreds, of different occasions). Educated hunches still determine which directions some commercials take because there is not enough time or money available to test every message. Still, advertisers who can afford it are realizing improved commercial effectiveness from repeated research efforts.

Copy tests are designed primarily for diagnostic purposes—to determine how healthy a commercial message is or to indicate why its health is good or poor. Unfortunately, no test yet devised can predict the right formula for effective commercials time after time. Steps are being taken, however, to determine not only what works, but some of the conditions under which certain appeals and techniques prove successful. Copy research is gradually building a storehouse of knowledge that even experts find very useful; it can prove invaluable to a broadcast advertising neophyte.

Defining the Problem

The first, most important, and frequently most difficult task involved in determining commercial effectiveness is defining effectiveness in communication terms that can be measured. Or, in scientific jargon, effectiveness must be defined operationally. Recall from Chapter 9 that the objective in a commercial's copy platform is a communication objective that, if achieved, should help sell the product or service involved. This objective tells the research team how to set criteria for effectiveness.

218

If a commercial's objective is to convince an audience that product A is stronger than product B, the message is effective if it does just that. On the other hand, if the objective is to associate a new slogan with a specific brand of product (to achieve, for example, a 25-percent slogan-playback figure among current users of a competitive brand), the extent of recall becomes the criterion. Note that memorability per se is not necessarily related to commercial effectiveness; you undoubtedly can repeat phrases, claims, jingles, or even dialogue from radio and TV commercials whose products you would never consider buying. The same is true of credibility, product awareness, and overall message interest; each may be central to or completely alienated from a commercial's original objective. The news that nonbeer drinkers were bored, angered, or even offended by a particular beer commercial would scarcely raise the advertiser's eyebrows (unless the commercial's unlikely objective were to convince these people to try the product, buy the product, or influence others to do so).

On the flip side of this coin, we find that highly favorable reactions to a commercial on the part of nonusers are, likewise, all but worthless to the advertisers involved. Unfortunately, this kind of research data (strictly because of its positive nature) is sometimes used to bolster creative egos, to justify decisions made with respect to commercial production, and to prove competitive superiority. Still, some advertising practitioners maintain that every commercial performs a public relations task for its company, even among listeners and viewers who do not use the product or service advertised. It should be clear by now that both commercial objectives and commercial effects are primarily attitudinal, even though the ultimate objective (the reason for the communication and the intended result of the attitudinal influence) is behavioral: the sale/purchase of the item advertised.

The list of possible mental and emotional responses is practically endless, but commercial effects are often measured in terms of improved brand image, information or knowledge gained (recalled), perceived credibility, and purchasing intent. Hence, defining a research problem in communication terms need not be a difficult task. Completing the job, however, using terms that can be measured (remembering that attitudinal effects are intangible) can be a major endeavor. For example, how does one go about measuring believability? In steps? By degrees? How much recall makes a commercial memorable? What level of memorability is considered good? Somehow decisions have to be made. And before copy testing can begin, exact operations for measurement must be spelled out.

Proceeding in Stages

Only one message factor or effect should be tested at a time so that findings obtained can clearly be linked to the elements under investigation. If a 60-second demonstration commercial, complete with jingle, animated characters, and live talent, proves more informative or persuasive than a 30-second, voice-over, narrative spot (with no demonstration, jingle, or animation), there is no way to tell which message variation, or combination of variations, made the difference.

A *benchmark* study, indicating the accumulated effects of past advertising, should precede any new copy research activity. Otherwise results may be *confounded* by variables not currently being examined.

We also would do well to note three different stages of commercial testing; each is concerned with a different type of response, and unless we are aware of the specific level involved, our interpretation of research findings can be seriously misleading. First, questions calling for mere recognition of commercials (for example, "Did you see this TV commercial last night?" and "Have you heard any radio commercials recently for soft drinks?") are measuring message exposure only. Second, questions that tap the degree of attention paid to or interest generated by a commercial—a respondent's conscious awareness of commercial elements—are testing perception (and often involve some form of aided recall). Third, questions designed to test message communication concern themselves with impressions made (of the manufacturer, brand, or advertised claim), reactions (in terms of credibility or desire to buy), and overall attitude change.[1]

Validity and Reliability

All research studies must face standards of validity and reliability, two very different scientific qualities that are often misunderstood and misused. A test is valid if it measures what it purports to measure. A properly adjusted scale can be used to assess weights, heights, temperature, or distances traveled, but not appreciation or love. Similarly, although item recall is considered a good test of memory, it cannot determine credibility or buying intent.

A test is reliable if, given the same stimulus and type of respondent, its measurements are approximately the same (within statistical tolerance limits) time after time, in situation after situation. Referring to the analogy above, if the temperature is 70 degrees, a thermometer will so indicate, whether outdoors or indoors; north, south, east, or west; in the air or under water. A reliable intelligence test will hold up across regional and cultural differences; a reliable measure of interest in a commercial message should hold up across groups tested if exposure patterns and audience characteristics are held constant. Of course, building a scale to measure ounces and pounds is a much simpler task than constructing an attitude-measurement scale; still, validity and reliability must be checked carefully if results are to be useful to commercial creative teams.

Surveys, Experiments, and Observations

Most advertising research studies can be categorized as either surveys or experiments or, occasionally, as observational activities. Each classification has important traits that must be considered before launching a commercial copy test. One easy way to pinpoint the difference between surveys and experiments is through this little couplet:

> While surveys check the *what is* trend,
> Experiments say, *let's pretend.*

A survey might measure existing attitudes toward specific radio or TV commercials, current related brand preferences and shopping habits, or behavioral intentions at the time the survey is conducted. There's no attempt to vary message elements from group to group, to alter listening or viewing environments, or otherwise to influence responses. The goal, in short, is to determine what is.

In an experiment, however, there is deliberate manipulation of message variables (for example, word choice, repetition, choice of music or talent); systematic variation of listening or viewing conditions (for example, background noises, viewer/listener distances from the screen, speaker, or other audience members, and activities conducted concurrent with reception of the messages); or some other change affecting audience response to the stimuli presented. Here the purpose is to query, "What if" something were true, then to follow the pretense through with physical treatments, and to measure results of the experimental actions, which are often compared with results obtained from a control group that receives no manipulated treatments whatsoever.

EXPERIMENTAL HARDWARE

Experiments often involve a certain amount of mechanical or electronic equipment. For instance, although designed originally for the testing of printed material, such laboratory apparatus as the eye camera and psychogalvanometer have been used to a limited extent in TV commercial tests. Both place respondents in rather uncomfortable positions, make the viewing or listening experience highly artificial, and can only be used with one individual at a time. In terms of true experimentation, however, they probably will remain popular facilities in copy testing labs.

Eye cameras chart on film the exact paths respondents' eyes follow during the viewing of TV commercials. Successful eye camera operation, however, generally requires that a participant's head remain absolutely motionless while each commercial is running. The viewer may be asked to place his forehead against a curved bar, bite on a cushioned bite bar, and endure a somewhat annoying beam of light that shines in one eye throughout the filming process. Results, however, do show copywriters exactly which visual items captured and held viewers' perceptual attention and interest. Limited research in this area has found that eyes are attracted to movement on the screen and that the extent of item recall is not necessarily correlated with the amount of time eyes fixate on objects shown.[2]

The psychogalvanometer measures people's *galvanic skin responses* (sweat gland activity) during the time they view or listen to test commercials. Each respondent is wired to the device in much the same way a patient is connected to an electrocardiograph. Resultant readings reveal which parts of test radio or TV commercials excited respondents (though not any reasons why).

One research organization that works with this equipment today is California's Walt Wesley Company, and staff members justify its use through this rationale: the function of emotion is to prepare a person for action; when someone receives a stimulus (for example, sees a commercial), his or her nervous system immediately prepares the body for possible needed exertion, and the person responds; experience has shown that a change in skin resistance is the fastest, most sensitive indicator of nervous system activity. The company also notes a close relationship between galvanic skin response and commercial effectiveness in the marketplace (often determined from sales or coupon tests).[3]

THE NATURAL SCENE

Some copy testing goes on under such natural conditions that research personnel simply observe (surreptitiously) commercial reception by an audience (and often the activity occurring simultaneously). Common tactics here include two-way mirrors, hidden cameras, and research personnel "plants" in respondents' midsts. Sometimes personal observation is assisted by mechanical devices similar to those described above. In fact, such equipment may itself be thought of in a kind of observational role.

A SCIENTIFIC COMPARISON OF PROCEDURES

Surveys almost always involve much larger sample sizes than do experiments and groups under personal observation. If stimulus materials are easily presented and if identical questions are asked of all respondents, several hundred people may be involved (rarely more in copy testing, although media tests of audience size and composition and occasional national surveys of commercial recall do include as many as several thousand respondents).

Experiments, which are more popular for copy tests, often use tightly controlled laboratory conditions. Meticulous planning may be involved, as well as precise timing, carefully staged exposure patterns, and precisely designed manipulations of variables being tested. Large groups would prove unwieldy under such circumstances, and numbers are often kept well below 100. Likewise, observers generally work with small groups at a time so behavioral responses can be recorded accurately.

From a technical standpoint, the major difference between the survey and the experiment or observational situation is that the survey often involves a randomly drawn, representative sample that (though relatively small) meets the scientific requirements necessary for projection of findings to a much larger population. Assume, for instance, that a sample of a few hundred dog owners truly represents the dog-food-buying public in a particular area. Findings obtained from a survey of this group's reactions to specific dog-food commercials could be projected (or "said to apply") to the entire dog-food-buying population from which the sample was drawn.

Experiments and observation groups, however, do not involve representative samples. The people selected to participate are often those who are conveniently available at the time of the test. Sometimes consumers' responses are solicited outside supermarkets, or passersby can be recruited at shopping centers. Experiments may take place inside research vans in parking lots, or participants may agree to meet elsewhere later (often at a research laboratory or theater). Then, too, TV viewers watching display models in a store might be unobtrusively observed during commercials. Before specific research questions are asked, a screening question may filter out those persons who are not in the market for the products advertised.

Most commercial testing is accomplished in face-to-face (personal or group) interview situations involving at least one interviewer or moderator. Although this procedure generally requires more time, money, and training (as well as interpretation expertise) than do telephone interviews and mailed questionnaires, the advantages far outweigh the disadvantages. The possibilities for demonstration, in-depth questioning, and overall flexibility in the presentation of both test materials and measurement devices are almost infinite; thus the opportunities for detailed scientific findings are maximal.

When to Test

Radio and TV commercials may be tested before they are actually aired (the *pretest)* or after listeners or viewers have heard or seen them on the air (the *posttest).* Pretests are generally the most valuable and the most difficult to conduct effectively. Communication problems detected at this early stage, of course, can save an advertiser vast amounts of time and money and can protect a company image that might otherwise be tarnished. Because they usually involve commercials in a less-than-finished form, however, pretests force respondents to imagine how the polished versions would sound and look; also, interviewees must pretend they are in a normal listening or viewing situation, another assumption that may seriously affect the validity and reliability of findings. Both pretests and posttests merit further discussion.

PRETESTS

Pretests may feature commercials in any degree of finish, from mere ideas on paper to films complete with audio tracks. Depending on the stage, research teams may study basic themes (key ideas, major claims, even slogans); creative and production elements (words, music, camera angles, talent, and the like); or entire commercials, compared with one another on the basis of interest, credibility, memorability, or other effects.

Because there are no absolute standards for commercials, it is usually relative (comparative) effects that are measured, such as an automotive features-versus-performance theme, a demonstration-versus-testimonial format, or animated-versus-live action. The Ralston-Purina Company pretested more than 100 TV commercials one year (about double the number that were actually aired nationally). Local UHF stations aired the spots in rough forms for prerecruited audiences who were then tested for recall. The commercials that proved most memorable were produced in finished form and tested further; when the winners were aired nationally, day-after recall scores correlated highly with those obtained in the pretests.

The three basic types of rough commercial forms used by Ralston-Purina are worthy of note. The least expensive and probably most common is the *animatic* commercial—an artwork storyboard on 16mm film or videotape, shot normally in a still-frame sequence. The audio track is usually on tape. The second form is a *photomatic* commercial—animation made from actual photographs. These commercials are more realistic and involve actual production sets as well as (sometimes) acting talent. Costs are generally 50 percent higher than they are for animatic spots. *Live-action talent commercials,* the third form, are usually the most expensive (although they may not cost as much as elaborate photomatic productions).

Concept testing might feature a number of statements about a product class, which respondents would be asked to compare or otherwise evaluate. For instance, a kitchen appliance manufacturer might consider the following possible commercial themes:

Easy to operate—no batteries to wear out.
Handles a variety of tasks without changing attachments.
Durable—even stands up to tough cutting jobs.
Lightweight, easy to clean and store.
Available in a variety of types and colors to match kitchen decor.

Respondents may either react individually to the proposed claims or participate in a group discussion led by a carefully trained moderator. Groups of seven to ten people, called *focus groups,* give advertisers valuable direction in terms of acceptable product positioning. Sessions last between 30 minutes and an hour and may provide interesting comparative data if group compositions are varied (for example, current brand users in one session, users of a competitive brand in another, and product nonusers in a third).

QUBE, a two-way (pay) cable service now operating in Columbus, Cincinnati, Houston, and Pittsburgh, helps advertisers decide between various commercial appeals and offers. Consoles with numerous response buttons on them allow direct viewer interaction with TV programming; thus the system provides for a type of public opinion polling with regard to advertising messages and overall product and promotional ideas.

Types of Questions

Respondents participating in a pretest or a posttest may be shown several versions of a commercial or prospective commercial and asked to react in any of numerous ways. A few common ones are:

Through *direct questions* (also called structured, or close-ended), involving simple dichotomies or multiple-choice sets. For example:

"The Party-Time commercial mentioned that the product costs $1.59."
TRUE _____   FALSE _____

"Which commercial gave you the most information about the product?"
PARTY-TIME _____   SHOPPING TRIP _____   FAMILY ROOM _____
QUIET NIGHT _____

Through *indirect questions* (unstructured, or open-ended). For example:

"In your opinion, what did the child contribute to the commercial you just saw?"

"Explain briefly which of the commercials you just saw was the most believable to you and why."

Through *ranking* comparatively. For example:

"Rank the commercials you just heard according to your degree of interest in listening to them."
CAR RIDE _____   BUSY DAY _____   AFTER SCHOOL _____   VISITORS _____

"The commercials you just heard were delivered by several different people. Rank these spokespersons in terms of their believability."
MAN _____   WOMAN _____   CHILD _____   SINGER _____   FAMOUS ATHLETE _____

Through *rating* (scales). For example:

"Rate the three commercials you just saw according to how valuable they would be to you if you were about to try the product advertised."

	Very Valuable	Somewhat Valuable	Neutral	Somewhat Worthless	Very Worthless
SPRING DAY	____	____	____	____	____
EATING OUT	____	____	____	____	____
CLEAN HOUSE	____	____	____	____	____

Rating scales measure both the direction (generally positive or negative) and the intensity of reactions in varying degrees. Sometimes they follow a conventional format, borrowed from social psychology, and sometimes they are constructed solely for one particular measurement situation. They are so widely used that they warrant further discussion.

All attitudinal scales must cope with the problem of unequal intervals. For measurement purposes, copy research teams generally make the assumption of equal intervals between scaled steps, but actually there is no proof that respondents perceive such clear-cut divisions. Consider the following example:

COMMERCIAL X IS
Very Good ____ Good ____ So-So ____ Poor ____ Very Poor ____

Who is to say that everyone asked to fill in this scale will feel that good is as far below very good as so-so is below good?

A scale that has no neutral point is another example:

COMMERCIAL X IS
Very Pleasing ____ Slightly Pleasing ____
Slightly Annoying ____ Very Annoying ____

Some people may sense a disproportionate drop between the first two or last two positions; others may feel uncomfortable with the gap between the second and third.

Scales may be set up with as few as three steps:

COMPARED WITH OTHERS, THIS RADIO JINGLE IS
Above Average ____ Average ____ Below Average ____

or as many as 100:

THE CLAIM, "KEEPS YOU FEELING CONFIDENT ALL DAY" IS
_____ 100 Completely Believable
____
____
____
_____ 80 Quite Believable
____
____
____
_____ 60 Believable
____
____
____

_____ 40 Somewhat Believable

_____

_____

_____

_____ 20 Unbelievable

_____

_____

_____ 0 Completely Unbelievable

In the first example, respondents are unable to indicate separate feelings for a superior jingle and one that is good (better than average, but not outstanding). In the second instance, we can seriously question respondents' abilities to differentiate twenty shades of feeling between each of the labeled levels. A related difficulty here is the concept of true zero—the minimum point below which the claim being evaluated would never fall. In other words, some people would not ever award copy lines a zero degree of anything.

Five-, six-, and seven-step scales are especially popular in commercial testing. Two widely used instruments are the Likert scale, which asks respondents to indicate the extent of their agreement with given statements:

"THE USE OF ATHLETES IN THE COMMERCIAL MADE ME ANXIOUS TO TRY THE PRODUCT."

Strongly Agree ___	Agree ___	Neither Agree Nor Disagree ___	Disagree ___	Strongly Disagree ___

and Osgood's Semantic Differential, which calls for evaluation of items on seven-point scales bounded by polar (opposite) adjectives:

"COMMERCIAL X WAS . . ."

Interesting	___ ___ ___ ___ ___ ___ ___	Dull
Powerful	___ ___ ___ ___ ___ ___ ___	Weak
Valuable	___ ___ ___ ___ ___ ___ ___	Worthless

Other scales may be related to product purchase:

"AFTER SEEING THIS COMMERCIAL, HOW APT WOULD YOU BE TO BUY THE ADVERTISED PRODUCT?"

_____ Definitely Would Buy
_____ Probably Would Buy
_____ Might Buy
_____ Might Not Buy
_____ Probably Would Not Buy
_____ Definitely Would Not Buy

A novel approach for use in telephone interviews asks respondents to look at the numbers of their telephone buttons or dials (1 through 10) and to rate a particular message, theme, slogan, or the like, on the 10-point scale.

How Often to Pretest

Raymond Tortolani, vice-president of the Rumrill-Hoyt advertising agency in New York, maintains that it takes time for TV spots to grow on an audience; therefore commercials should be pretested more than once. The procedure has proven particularly valuable in musical commercials; tunes deemed enjoyable have grown more so in repeated tests (increasingly hummable and pleasant to live with). On the other hand, commercials initially faring poorly in terms of interest and recall have improved over time until they have surpassed spots that scored higher originally.

Two different approaches to multiple testing are the *vertical frequency* and the *horizontal frequency* procedures. Each requires that one given audience see the same commercial several times; in the former, it all happens on one day, and in the latter, several days are involved.[4]

POSTTESTS

Posttests are often concerned with recall and attitude change. Ideally, if we are interested in measuring the true results of messages, we need to include a control group in each research plan; we must measure the amount of knowledge held or the degree of attitude change on the part of people who do not see or hear the commercials under study. Otherwise, behavioral scientists argue, we cannot be sure that certain changes would not have occurred by themselves—without any message exposure—just because people are creatures who change their minds, learn and forget, and react differently to the same stimulus at different times. The control group helps ensure the validity of results.

But time and money do not always permit inclusion of a control group in a research study; many advertisers proceed with posttests anyway, convinced that even an indication of commercial effects is better than no research at all.

A Pencil-and-Paper Test

One simple recall test was developed by Henry C. Link and named the Triple Associates Test. It asks respondents for brand names of products, given appropriate product classes and slogans or theme lines expressed in radio and TV commercials. For example, an audience might be asked: "TV commercials for which major appliance manufacturer claim 'The quality goes in before the name goes on'?" A triple association is required here—between the slogan ("The quality . . ."), the product class (major appliances), and the brand name (Zenith).

An adaptation of this technique asks respondents for both product class and brand name (giving them only the slogan): "What television advertiser claims: 'The single most favorite double in the world'?" (Answer: Doublemint Gum.) Sometimes bogus slogans are buried in a test of genuine ones; when respondents go right ahead and attribute these outsiders to specific brands on the market, both advertisers and copywriters appreciate anew the real communication barriers with which they must deal every day.

Using the Telephone

Telephone calls within two hours of the airing of selected TV spots can also tap memorability factors; experience has shown, however, that respondents have a very difficult time remembering the brand names of televised products, let alone actual message details. It is amazing to beginning copywriters to learn how quickly audiences forget and how little attention they pay in the first place; it is the look-but-don't-really-see phenomenon in action (or, in radio, hear-but-don't-really-listen). Again, though, on-the-spot recall alone need not be considered proof of commercial message registry; in the store, familiar packages and displays can easily trigger consumers' memories and work with commercials in determining brand preference and ultimate sales.

Personal Interviews

Some advertisers send out interviewers the day after commercials have been aired. Armed with either storyboards or, sometimes actual films or tapes plus viewing equipment, these research personnel give at-home respondents more cues than is possible over the telephone; hence, they often obtain higher recall scores. But the more aid interviewees receive, the easier it is to claim viewership (whether or not it actually occurred the previous day).

Radio commercials generally run more often than do their TV counterparts. Although it is a simple matter to play a recording of a radio spot for a respondent, it is much more difficult to tie acknowledged message recognition to a specific air time.

Relying on Inquiries

Finally, both radio and TV advertisers may borrow a research method used widely in the print media. Commercials calling for some kind of respondent inquiry ("Write or call for more information" or "Send in for a sample, coupon, or refund") can key addresses or telephone numbers to measure the drawing power of individual messages. For example, a musical food spot might offer a free recipe book through a BOX M address, while a demonstration commercial made the same offer through BOX D.

Pitfalls in Question Structuring

Entire textbooks have been written on the do's and don'ts of proper questionnaire development, but we should mention five common pitfalls in question structuring:

Ambiguous terms. Words and phrases that can be interpreted in several ways, and thereby prove confusing to respondents, will result in biased findings. The question "Do you like inexpensive dishes?" would probably raise additional questions before it could be answered (for example: What do you mean by inexpensive? How inexpensive? What kind of dishes—food or actual place settings? Cheap, shoddy merchandise or expensive items currently on sale?).

The biggest problem here is that some respondents can't or won't ask the interviewer for clarification (can't because they are filling out questionnaires privately or won't because they are shy or embarrassed). The question is, therefore, left to individual interpretation and answered accordingly, and the results cannot indicate which slants the interpretations may have taken.

Double-barreled questions. When two separate questions are asked together as one, the respondent who does not wish to answer both sides the same way has a problem. One example might be "Do you sometimes get tired of hearing the same radio commercials over and over, and wish more of them had musical jingles?" The options are two—give the answer that pertains either to the first half of the question or to the second half (without indicating which) or simply reply with a confused, "I don't know" (and no information is obtained).

Entrapment. Overlapping questions, or parts of questions, can trap respondents by forcing them into unfair choices: "Do you like commercials with male or female speakers you can see, or do you prefer off-camera announcers?" To get an idea of just how confusing this question really is, check a few of the possible bewilderments it can cause: What if males and females are equally appealing (or equally unappealing, in favor of, say, children or animated characters)? What if a respondent's on-camera/off-camera preference depends on the distinction between male and female (or on the product advertised)? What if a respondent does not like commercials with announcers at all, but prefers spots that feature songs or jingles throughout or ones in which slice-of-life dialogue prevails? And, of course, there is always the "what do you mean by like/prefer" quandary: like from an entertaining point of view or prefer from an informative standpoint?

Although it is only one of many questions that could appropriately be asked, notice that another example avoids all four of the previous problems: "If a commercial with news about your favorite detergent could show you either a popular male presenter on camera or a popular female presenter on camera, which would you prefer?"

Leading questions. Questions that suggest a particular answer because of the way they are worded are known as leading questions; here the bias is even more obvious. Examples are "You do watch the commercials in TV news programs, don't you?" "Of course, you've seen some of those award-winning car commercials, haven't you?" "Wouldn't it be nice if someone did away with all of those TV deodorant commercials?" If copy research is going to be valuable, it must measure audience reactions as objectively as possible. If questions wind up leading respondents to predetermined answers, results can only be classified as worthless.

Loaded questions. Specific words are sometimes used to *load* (weight or slant) questions in favor of or against a particular response. The result may be considered another type of leading, but the problem of biased findings remains the same. For example, rather than asking interviewees for their reactions to commercials, a loaded question might query: "Do you like or dislike dull, boring commercials?" Or: "Which do you think is more valuable—an interesting, informative commercial message, or one that's loud and pushy?"

No matter what form questions take in the field of copy testing, they must be checked for these five biasing agents if answers are to provide a true picture of respondents' feelings.

National Commercial Testing Organizations

Some advertisers spend hundreds of thousands of dollars per year for commercial research conducted by national copy-testing organizations. A few of these companies deserve mention.

Burke Marketing Research. Burke measures recall of TV commercials by telephone the day after they have been aired. Selected cues aid respondents in remembering, but each acknowledged viewer is asked to play back both sales messages and visual details. In addition, Burke plays radio commercials over the telephone in groups of five, with the test message placed in the middle. Different respondents hear different versions of the commercial under study, but all are asked a series of like/dislike questions at the end. The following day, follow-up calls establish levels of 24-hour recall.

Burke's *Ad Tel* division attempts to bridge the gap between advertising and sales by correlating TV commercial viewing with purchase diaries kept by audience members. Cable TV systems are used in selected markets, and special test commercials are cut in at desired times. As advertisers vary commercial message themes and elements, diaries can be checked for changes in purchasing habits. The service is valuable, but expensive. A one-market test run every month for a year can cost an advertiser more than $100,000.

Communicus, Inc. Communicus takes recorded radio commercials to shopping centers and plays them for samples of 100 people. An advertiser's test commercial is stopped at intervals, and respondents are asked for feedback in terms of advertiser perception, message comprehension and importance, and overall persuasion.

Gallup & Robinson. The Gallup & Robinson corporation provides advertisers with Proved Commercial Registration (PCR) scores, on the basis of the number of telephoned respondents who prove they saw certain commercials by describing message content (see Figure 12.1).

1. YOU MAY BE FAMILIAR WITH OTHER COMMERCIALS FOR

   _____,

   BUT THINKING ONLY OF LAST NIGHT'S COMMERCIAL, PLEASE TELL ME EVERYTHING YOU REMEMBER ABOUT IT.

   WHAT DID THEY SHOW AND TALK ABOUT?

   Suggested Probes:
     HOW DID THEY SHOW THAT?
     HOW DID THEY GET THAT ACROSS?
     WHAT ELSE DO YOU RECALL ABOUT THAT?

2. WHAT SALES POINTS OR ARGUMENTS FOR BUYING DID THEY SHOW OR TALK ABOUT LAST NIGHT?

   Suggested Probes::
     HOW DID THEY SHOW THAT?
     HOW DID THEY GET THAT ACROSS?
     WHAT ELSE DO YOU RECALL ABOUT THAT?

3. WHAT DID YOU LEARN ABOUT THE (product/service) FROM THIS COMMERCIAL?

4. WHAT WENT THROUGH YOUR MIND AS YOU WATCHED THIS COMMERCIAL?

5. THE ADVERTISER TRIED TO INCREASE YOUR INTEREST IN BUYING HIS (product/service). DID HE SUCCEED, OR NOT?

   ☐ Yes
   ☐ No
   ☐ DK

6. WHAT WAS IN THE COMMERCIAL THAT MAKES YOU SAY THAT?

7. WHAT BRAND OF THIS TYPE OF PRODUCT DID YOU BUY LAST?

   OR

   WHAT COMPANY'S SERVICE DID YOU USE LAST?

   ☐ Doesn't use

   ☐ Doesn't use

   Code Number   **BRAND AND PRODUCT**   *(Only one product to a page)*

Fig. 12.1. Page from the Gallup & Robinson IN-VIEW questionnaire (TV commercials study). (Courtesy of Gallup & Robinson, Inc.)

In-Home Testing Service. The In-Home Testing Service also uses cable TV systems to air test commercials. Telephone interviews conducted the day after commercials have been aired measure aided (cued) recall of advertisers' names as well as unaided (uncued) recall of message content.

Radio Recall Research, Inc. This New Jersey company asks shopping-center customers across the country to fill out shopping-activity questionnaires in a mobile test unit while taped radio spots play in the background. The next day, participants are telephoned and asked for playback of the commercials. Figure 12.2 shows the questionnaire used for this recall study.

Tele-Research, Inc. This company shows TV commercials inside mobile vans parked at supermarkets. Shoppers are invited to view spots for five noncompeting products before entering the store. Afterwards, they are given booklets of cents-off coupons, some of which are for products featured in the test commercials. Because the time span between message exposure and actual purchase (or failure to purchase) is very short, researchers believe they can relate commercial content to buying behavior. Figure 12.3 diagrams the entire Tele-Research design for TV commercial pretesting, and the procedure used for radio spots is essentially the same. Figures 12.4 and 12.5 show the post-commercial viewing questionnaire and the delayed (telephone) recall questionnaire, respectively.

Costs for these research services vary widely, but advertisers can generally count on figures ranging from $1,000 to $5,000 for one test commercial. Sample sizes usually run from 100 to 250.

In all of these tests, the advertisers and their agencies must interpret the significance of actual copy variables to the various scores obtained. The face values of individual test results are rather meaningless by themselves; when they are compared over time with others, however, scores that are relatively high or low may prove very revealing. It is at this point that the specific messages involved should be checked and compared for similarities and differences in content, style, and production technique. Remember, though, that none of the tests described in this chapter can ever prove conclusively that any sales key, message treatment, or combination of variables is better or worse than any other, except, perhaps, as related (very narrowly) to one set of commercials.

Some commercial testing takes place in theaters and often involves both mechanical devices and pencil-and-paper activity. Probably the most famous test theater was the one set up by Horace Schwerin in New York. Though his particular establishments are no longer functional, the same operational procedure is very much alive in cities throughout the country.

SCHWERIN'S SYSTEM

Schwerin's specific routine involves, first, written questionnaires at the beginning of each session (mainly an indication of brand preferences in product categories later to be represented in commercials; respondents are informed that door prizes, awarded to lucky ticket-holders at the end of the session, will consist of the product choices that winners make at the outset). Next comes a bogus TV program screening session. Respondents are never informed that the research is being conducted for advertising purposes; they are merely invited to participate in a program preview session (supposedly to furnish reactions to a proposed new TV series; in actuality, pilot shows already rejected by the networks are used to house-test commercials, so research participants see them within a program context, much as they would at home).

At various times during commercial viewing, a flash of light on the screen cues respondents to indicate on a printed sheet in front of them their instantaneous reactions to the material being seen (positive, neutral, or negative). Then, just to keep everyone believing that it is the show they are really evaluating, the light flashes during the actual program also, although reactions recorded here are later simply discarded.

CALLBACK INTERVIEWER'S NAME _____
PHONE #: _____   PROGRAM 1A   1B
DATE: _____

RADIO TEST CALLBACK INTERVIEW

Hello, I'm _____ of Triple R Research calling (name of person) about the research interview she took part in yesterday. Is she at home? I'd like to speak to her for a moment. (IF NOT AT HOME, ASK:) When would be a good time to reach her today? (YOU MUST REACH RESPONDENT THE DAY AFTER EXPOSURE).

(CALLBACK) I___ II ____ III ____

1. Hello, so that I can be sure I'm speaking to the right person, please tell me the type of questionnaire you filled out yesterday?

    _____

2. During the time you were in the interviewing center, do you remember hearing or listening to a radio playing or background music?

    ( ) Yes   (   ) No

3. What products were advertised on that radio program you heard yesterday in the center? What others? (FOR EACH PRODUCT MENTIONED, ASK:) What brand was that?

    PRODUCT   BRAND
    _____   _____
    _____   _____

    (GO ON, EVEN IF "NONE" TO Q. 3)

4. (ASK Q. 4 FOR EACH PRODUCT NOT MENTIONED ABOVE). Do you remember hearing any advertising yesterday for ... (ROTATE ORDER).

    A. Sloppy Joe Product   ( ) Yes - What Brand? _____ ( ) No
    B. Snack Food   ( ) Yes - What Brand? _____ ( ) No
    C. Chewing Gum   ( ) Yes - What Brand? _____ ( ) No

5. (ASK FOR EACH BRAND LISTED BELOW, REGARDLESS OF WHETHER MENTIONED ABOVE). You may have already mentioned this before, but in the interviewing center yesterday, do you remember hearing any radio advertising for: (ROTATE ORDER).

    A. Hunt's Manwich   ( ) Yes - (ASK Q. 6)   ( ) No
    B. Cheetos   ( ) Yes - (ASK Q. 6)   ( ) No
    C. Trident   ( ) Yes - (ASK Q. 6)   ( ) No

    (ASK FOLLOWING RECALL QUESTIONS FOR ANY OF THE ABOVE 3 BRANDS MENTIONED VOLUNTARILY IN Q. 3 AND Q. 4 OR IN RESPONSE TO DIRECT QUESTION IN Q. 5).

Fig. 12.2. Radio Recall's "Day After Communications Recall Test." (Courtesy of Radio Recall Research, Inc.)

NOTE: REPEAT THE EXACT WORDING OF THE APPROPRIATE BRAND. PROMPT FOR
      EACH OF THE PROBE QUESTIONS (6a -- 6d).

6a. You said you remember hearing a commercial for _____
    on the radio program yesterday. Please describe what you heard
    during that commercial. What else? Anything else?

    _____   38-_____

    _____   _____

    _____   39-_____

    _____   _____

    _____   _____

6b. What did the commercial say about _____? What else?

    _____   40-_____

    _____   _____

    _____   41-_____

    _____   _____

6c. What ideas about _____ did you get from that
    commercial? Any others?

    _____   _____

    _____   _____

    _____   _____

    _____   _____

6d. What thoughts went through your mind when you heard that commer-
    cial for _____?

    _____   _____

    _____   _____

    _____   _____

    _____   _____

6e. Have you ever heard this commercial for _____ before?

          42-1 ( ) Yes   -2 ( ) No

Fig. 12.2. (*continued*)

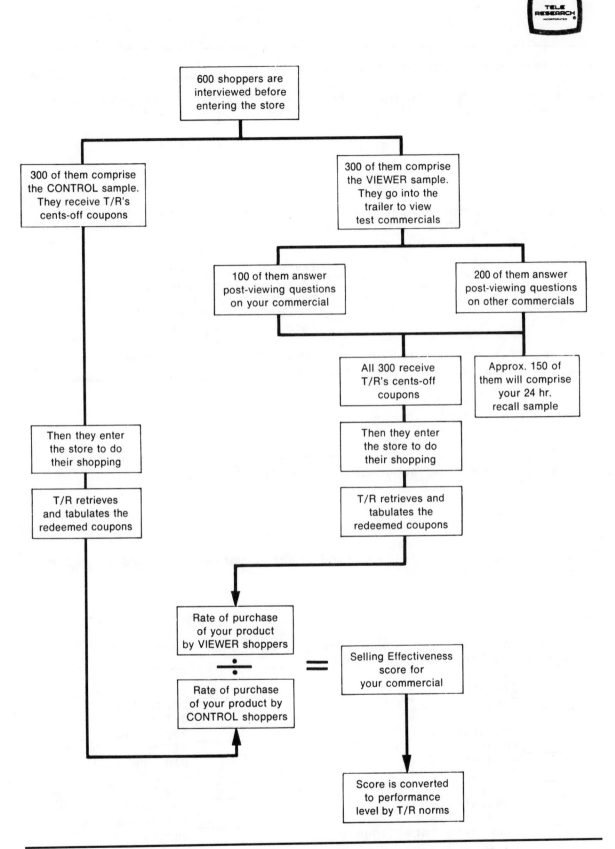

Fig. 12.3. How Tele-Research pretests advertising. (Courtesy of Tele-Research, Inc.)

One of the commercials you have just seen was for _____.

1. Aside from trying to persuade you to buy the product, what <u>main point</u> or idea did this commercial try to get across?

2. How did this commercial affect your opinion of the _____
   _____? Would you say that your interest in using the product was: <u>CHECK ONE</u>

   _____ Increased very much
   _____ Increased somewhat
   _____ Not affected
   _____ Decreased somewhat
   _____ Decreased very much

3. What, if anything, did you particularly <u>like</u> or find especially appealing about the commercial for _____?

4. What, if anything, did you particularly <u>dislike</u> or find especially unappealing about that commercial?

5. What, if anything, did you find unreal, untrue, or <u>hard to believe</u> about that commercial?

6. Please check all the words that you feel come closest to describing the commercial for _____.

   _____ Clever   _____ Interesting
   _____ Convincing   _____ Offensive
   _____ Dull   _____ Original
   _____ Educational   _____ Repetitious
   _____ Entertaining   _____ Silly
   _____ Exaggerated   _____ Sincere
   _____ Friendly   _____ Slow
   _____ Happy   _____ Stale
   _____ Imaginative   _____ Too Long
   _____ Informative   _____ Uninteresting
   _____ Insulting Intelligence   _____ Untrue

Fig. 12.4. Postviewing questionnaire. (Courtesy of Tele-Research, Inc.)

Hello, I'm _____ from Marketing Studies. As you recall
we are conducting a survey at _____. I would like to
ask you a few questions about the commercials you saw yesterday.

1. Please tell me all the products you remember seeing advertised in
   the trailer yesterday. What others? Any others? (ACCEPT ANY
   REFERENCE TO TEST PRODUCT, PROCEED AND CHECK ONE)

   _____ BRAND AND PRODUCT   (GO TO #4)

   _____ BRAND ONLY   (GO TO #3)

   _____ PRODUCT ONLY   (GO TO #2)

   _____ BRAND AND _____   (TERMINATE)
                      wrong product-SPECIFY

   _____ _____ AND PRODUCT (TERMINATE)
           wrong brand-SPECIFY

   _____ NEITHER   (TERMINATE)

2. What brand of PRODUCT was advertised?

   _____ Correct brand   (ASK #4)

   _____ Incorrect product _____   (TERMINATE)
                             SPECIFY

   _____ Don't know   (TERMINATE)

3. Which BRAND product was that advertised?

   _____ Correct product   (ASK #4)

   _____ Incorrect product _____   (TERMINATE)
                             SPECIFY

   _____ Don't know   (TERMINATE)

4. Aside from trying to persuade you to buy the product, what main
   point or idea did this BRAND commercial try to get across?

Thank you very much for helping us in this study.

Fig. 12.5. Telephone recall questionnaire. (Courtesy of Tele-Research, Inc.)

After the viewing period, two additional written activities occur. Respondents are asked to recall the commercials they saw (brand names and message details), and to fill out another brand preference questionnaire similar to the one completed earlier. The excuse offered for this latter exercise centers around an (actually nonexistent) error just discovered in the original questionnaire form, which was collected and supposedly checked over while respondents were watching the program. For example, the moderator might tell the audience that a page was left out of the first questionnaire, two separate forms were mixed together, or some such. At any rate, respondents are told that all original questionnaires will be destroyed, and the brand preferences indicated on the new one will be used to determine door prizes. In reality, of course, both sets of questionnaires are analyzed very carefully. Changes observed in brand preferences before and after commercial viewing are attributed to the messages delivered.

Although one-time commercial impact findings here can be encouraging to advertisers (or discouraging, as the case may be), the only way to compare alternative message themes or treatments is to run different commercials with different (but similarly composed) audiences. Again, much of the value of this kind of copy testing lies in the comparison of findings across repeated test situations.

ASI MARKET RESEARCH

Audience Studies, Inc., in Los Angeles, tests both programs and commercials and works with both radio and TV in on-air and pretest situations. Even commercials in less-than-finished form (for example, a storyboard-on-filmstrip) can be tested. Theater seats are actually wired, so audiences can indicate individual responses electronically, by manipulating various dials, levers, and buttons. Auditorium seating plans are such that reactions from various demographic subgroups can be measured separately. Here, all research participants are fully aware of what is being tested, although the door prize incentive and excuse for filling out a second questionnaire remain much the same as they are under the Schwerin system.

Four basic ASI scores for each commercial tested are:

1. *Interest.* Presented electronically in the form of a *profile curve* graph, interest scores are laid out in points or degrees. As they watch a given commercial, audience members turn special *interest dials* to indicate reactions from very positive to very negative. Then the average scores at each point along the graph are determined and presented in printed graphic form. Each commercial's average is compared with ASI norms for the appropriate product class.

2. *Involvement.* Determined from results of *adjective check lists* administered after commercials have been seen, involvement measures require that viewers indicate adjectives that they feel apply to each message. Both positive (interesting, friendly) and negative (boring, amateurish) adjective lists are included, and, after the percentage of respondents choosing each adjective is determined, one average percentage is computed for the positive category only. This score is regarded as the commercial's involvement image.

3. *Communication.* A commercial's communication value is assessed according to respondents' ability to recall: (a) the brand names of products they have just seen, (b) one selling point from each commercial, and (c) multiple selling points.

4. *Effectiveness.* Effectiveness is presented as a change score, indicating the difference between respondents' selection of desired door prizes before and after commercial viewing. On the first questionnaire, administered at the outset of the session, participants merely name their choices; on the second one, however, five-point scales measure the extent to which the commercials affected viewers' desires to buy (or win as door prizes) the products involved. Effectiveness scores are determined by the number of respondents who indicate an increase in desire.

ASI can also measure degrees of understanding, levels of credibility, or similar effects by utilizing various combinations of buttons, levers, and other electronic controls. Of course, each added piece of information contributes to the overall cost of ASI reports, which may normally run several thousand dollars per commercial tested.

If advertisers or agencies have the time, examination of test commercials scoring both high and low in one or more of the above tests may prove an enlightening experience. The test procedures measure the what of reactions, but not the why. A special study would have to be designed to tap the reasons behind this dimension, but a careful analysis of content and production similarities and differences across test messages (sometimes called *content analysis)* may at least shed some light on the matter. For instance, if the most frequently recalled commercials in a number of test situations all featured on-camera, male presenters and product demonstration, and those least frequently recalled all contained off-camera, female announcers and no action on the part of the product, surely there would be a "message" for creative teams.

Using Test Results

However we define effectiveness, and whatever method we use to determine it, we must remember that the same caveat that applies to media (audience) measurement is vitally important in copy research as well. Neither broadcasting nor advertising is an exact science; both are heavily involved with attitudes and behaviors that operate purely in accord with individual wants and needs. Research in these areas can assist broadcast advertisers in creative and media efforts, but cannot prove conclusively that any one method or plan is right or wrong beyond one specific set of circumstances. It should not be used in place of professional judgment. Looked upon as a counselor, it can stimulate ideas; leaned on as a crutch, it often stifles them.

Also, although social psychologists maintain that attitudes and behavior are related, advertisers who expect dramatic results from every copy test are sure to be disappointed, regardless of how well their products are selling. For example, even when ASI interest, involvement, and communication scores are extremely impressive, experience has proven that actual changes in brand preference as a result of commercial viewing are apt to be around the 5-percent level.

As we have noted repeatedly, advertising is an invisible force whose specific effects are almost always intangible; hence broadcast advertising research teams usually measure commercial results in terms of *attitudinal correlates* of sales, rather than sales themselves. Individual commercials may each contribute only a minuscule amount of the persuasive effort exerted by an entire campaign; in other words, measurements may be made soon after commercials are heard or seen (short-run), but their real value may be in a long-term investment (toward an eventual purchase).

A last major problem plaguing the whole area of copy testing is that of response influencers outside of, but related to, the commercials being studied. First and foremost is the product or service itself; attitudes toward it may have serious effects on reactions to messages about it. There also is the influence of the media position in which the commercial ultimately finds itself—within a popular program, during a cluttered station break, in the midst of a serious newscast or exciting sportscast, and so on. The mood of the audience at the instant a commercial begins may be quite different from the one experienced during an unnatural testing situation.

Given an almost inevitable exposure to a large number of advertising messages every day, respondents participating in a test of commercial copy can hardly be expected to forget associations they have with previously seen and heard commercials for the same product or for competing brands, and similar ads run in print and other media. A four-week test of 1,800 TV commercials in Atlanta, Georgia, found that only one viewer in six could remember the sponsor of a selected message. Thirty-two percent could successfully describe a given commercial, but only half of them correctly named the advertiser. The remaining half was split between "don't know" responses and incorrect advertiser associations.[5]

Still, research techniques for the measurement of commercial effects have advanced steadily over the years. Likewise, those in the area of audience measurement have become increasingly sophisticated. Audience ratings generally play a major role in the determination of rates, so we will consider audience measurement first and then move into the actual purchase of commercial time.

Study Questions

1. Name three ways you might measure the credibility of a given commercial, and three ways you might measure its memorability.
2. Differentiate clearly between validity and reliability. Can any one test be valid but unreliable? Reliable but invalid? How would you determine the validity and reliability of the latest test or quiz you took?
3. Assume you've been asked to test the interest value of a commercial. Explain three different ways you might do it: one in terms of a survey, one in terms of an experiment, and one in terms of observation.
4. Explain the difference between ranking and rating.
5. Make up some of your own examples of (a) ambiguous questions, (b) double-barreled questions, (c) entrapping questions, (d) leading questions, and (e) loaded questions.
6. Differentiate between the testing procedures used by Burke Marketing Research and Tele-Research, Inc.

ASSIGNMENT 12-A

Select a series of radio and/or TV commercials or obtain tapes, films, or scripts from local stations. Decide what you think the objective of each one is and what specific audience each is designed for; include both demographics and psychographics in your discussion. Finally, suggest how you would determine whether the commercials are effective.

ASSIGNMENT 12-B

For an assigned radio and/or TV commercial, prepare a list of important message variables that might be manipulated in an experiment designed to test message effects. Predict the outcomes of such tests, and include rationale for your judgment.

ASSIGNMENT 12-C

Design and list a set of questions that could be asked to measure the exposure, perception, and communication of a selected commercial.

ASSIGNMENT 12-D

Prepare a Triple Associates Test, based on your personal listening and viewing experiences using current commericals only. Administer it to the rest of your class, and provide an analysis of results.

COMMERCIAL THEME	PRODUCT CLASS	BRAND NAME
1.		
2.		
3.		
4.		
5.		
6.		
7.		
8.		
9.		
10.		

Notes

1.   See *Toward Better Media Comparisons* (New York: American Research Foundation, 1961).

2.   Sherilyn K. Zeigler, "Attention Factors in Televised Messages: Effects on Looking Behavior and Recall," *Journal of Broadcasting* 14, no. 3 (summer 1970):307–14.

3.   "Summary of the Wesley 'Arousal' Method" and "Validation Studies Involving the Wesley 'Arousal' Method and Sales" (Mimeographed, The Walt Wesley Company, Sierra Madre, Calif.).

4.   *Advertising Age* (November 15, 1976):52.

5.   *Advertising Age* (December 1, 1980):54.

Suggested Readings

Fletcher, Alan D. *Fundamentals of Advertising Research.* Columbus, Ohio: Grid Publishing, 1979.

Holbert, Neil. *Advertising Research,* Monograph Series no. 1. Chicago: American Marketing Association, 1975.

Lovell, Mark. *Assessing the Effectiveness of Advertising.* London: Business Books, 1975.

Sargent, Hugh W., ed. *Frontiers of Advertising Theory and Research.* Palo Alto, Calif.: Pacific Books, 1972.

ALSO: Check recent issues of *Advertising Age,* the *Journal of Advertising,* and the *Journal of Advertising Research.*

13

Audience Research

The need for high quality, definitive research into audience behavior and program preferences has increased dramatically in recent years. Today, vast numbers of radio listeners and TV viewers represent billions of dollars worth of sales opportunities for advertisers, their advertising agencies, networks and stations, program producers, and other organizations; knowing the size and composition of audiences throughout the broadcast day is vitally important to all of these groups.

Present-day research bears little resemblance to the earliest attempts at analyzing radio listenership that, during the late 1920s and early 1930s, generally consisted of counting fan mail attracted by various programs. Contemporary audience measurement has been elevated to scientific levels and relies on widely accepted procedures of statistical sampling, data collection, and processing. Practical marketing situations require that advertisers deliver their selling messages to potential customers rather than to nebulous mass audiences, so research identifies prospective purchasers as specific *target audiences*.

Program ratings are gathered and published regularly by a number of research organizations. The three most prominent are the A. C. Nielsen Company, Arbitron Ratings Company, and Birch Radio, Inc. Nielsen produces both national television network and individual TV market audience studies, but Arbitron concentrates on market-by-market studies for both TV and radio. Birch Radio, a relatively new organization, conducts market-by-market radio studies throughout the United States. A number of lesser-known firms and many university-related communications research centers offer "on demand" audience measurement and public opinion studies, including surveys of nonmetropolitan radio markets.

The fact that program ratings play such a prominent role in the scheduling of programs and advertising is a testimonial to the acceptance of audience research by broadcasting and advertising industries. Ideally, however, ratings should be regarded as but one of several helpful indicators for analyzing the media. Other valuable considerations include sales results, station images, and advertiser rosters of competing stations.

Audience Measurement Techniques

Modern audience research is based on the concept of statistical inference, which permits the estimation of characteristics of "populations" (such as all TV-equipped households in a given area) from information obtained through sampling. Although methods vary somewhat among research organizations, all audience measurement involves three distinct steps: (1) selecting the sample, (2) gathering the data, and (3) processing results.

SAMPLING PROCEDURES
An ideal research study would solicit detailed information on viewing and listening from every household in a broadcast market. But economic and logistical constraints prohibit such a universal

240

census. Instead, audience research firms obtain data from sample households selected scientifically to represent the entire population being measured.

Although broadcast ratings are sometimes criticized for projecting from relatively small samples, evidence overwhelmingly supports the usefulness and reliability of sampling techniques. For example, statistical projections on voting intentions produced by public opinion polls almost always compare favorably with actual vote tabulations. In many less-sophisticated ways, too, we all base everyday decisions on sampling procedures. What homemaker, for example, doesn't taste a sample of food being prepared to see if additional seasoning is needed? Likewise, farmers test the nutrients in their fields through soil sampling, and physicians take samples of body fluids for diagnostic purposes.

To permit the projection of data to larger populations, a sample must reflect with a high degree of accuracy the universe it represents. Such representativeness is determined by the sources of information on populations and the methods used to draw samples from such listings. Commonly used population catalogs include telephone directories, the U.S. Census data on housing, and household mailing lists prepared by direct-mail firms. The adequacy of any catalog depends on how accurately and completely it lists the population it purports to include. The telephone directory is, therefore, a limited source, inasmuch as it excludes both homes without phones and households with unlisted numbers. The latter deficiency may be overcome, however, by choosing a sample through random digit dialing rather than from the directory itself. Tables of random numbers are frequently used to facilitate access to all telephone households rather than only to those published in directories.

The selection of respondents may be accomplished through a process of random choice or by means of structured quota samples. In random choice, each household within a universe has an equal and independent chance of being selected. Quota samples, in contrast, prescribe representative proportions of persons in such categories as age, sex, education, urban/rural residency, and socioeconomic status. Specific respondents within such quotas, however, still may be selected through random processes. The principal advantage of using the quota approach is the assurance that all significant elements within a population are represented in proportion to their numbers.

Whereas sample representation is a function mainly of sampling procedure, the precision of results depends largely on sample size. The more precision that is required, the larger the sample must be.

Below a certain size, however, results become highly subject to error, and above a certain point, it becomes fruitless to increase the number of respondents. For example, with a sample of 300, the 95-percent confidence interval is plus or minus 5.8 percent above or below the indicated percentage value. (Chances are such that 19 out of 20 times, the true value would fall within the confidence interval.) If the sample is increased to 500, the confidence interval is reduced to 4.5 percent, and a sample of 1,000 results in a confidence interval of plus or minus 3.2 percent. With each increase in sample size, increased precision in results is obtained. Researchers, however, must decide how much sampling error they are willing to tolerate in view of the costs of conducting research surveys and the need for precision in obtained results.

DATA GATHERING

Methods used to obtain viewing and listening information for sample households are among the most critical factors in producing reliable audience research. Four techniques are commonly employed: telephone surveys, the diary method, personal interviews, and metering devices. A fifth approach, mail surveys, is used in rare instances. Each method claims advantages and disadvantages; because none is perfect, two or more techniques sometimes are combined.

The Telephone Survey

The telephone survey method, pioneered during the 1930s by the C. E. Hooper Company and employed today by Birch Radio, Inc., is particularly useful for obtaining data on viewing and listening at the time calls are made. Telephone surveys also maybe used to obtain recalled information about viewing or listening during a recent period, usually the past 24 hours. It is presumed that coincidental data are less likely to contain errors than information collected on a delayed recall basis.

Because telephone interviewing is handled easily from one central location, this technique is faster and less expensive than in-person interviewing; even when long-distance calling is involved, costs can be minimized through the use of WATS (wide area telephone service) lines. In effect, telephone surveys can be used as a substitute for face-to-face questioning, subject to certain limitations. In addition to basic tuning information that may be used for computing ratings, shares, and the like, this method may provide information on audience composition and program sponsor identification.

The telephone-survey approach, however, has certain weaknesses. Many individuals hesitate to answer questions asked over the telephone by an unknown interviewer, especially if he or she probes into such matters as family characteristics and program preferences. The telephone method also should not be used for obtaining coincidental listening or viewing information during early morning and late evening hours.

And not everyone has a telephone. Thus, the sampling may under-report certain types of families, including rural residents, lower income urban dwellers, and, sometimes, members of ethnic groups.

The Diary Method

The diary system places one or more diaries (viewing/listening logs) in a sample of households in which family members have agreed to keep track of all TV or radio use. Diaries are especially helpful in obtaining data on audience composition, as well as raw information needed to compute program ratings, shares of audience, and the total size of media audiences. The diary method is also reasonably fast and economical.

On the negative side, diary research is only as reliable as the respondents who record their set usage. One criticism of this method is that persons failing to record program notations immediately may later be unable to recall accurately their listening or viewing times and the stations or programs to which they tuned.

Another problem is that family members may become extremely conscious of their media behavior and, consequently, may not follow their usual patterns of usage. Program selections may become artificial, and viewing or listening levels may inflate. Hence, some research firms disregard data from the first week or weeks of a family's diary and use only later information, after respondents have become accustomed to the routine.

Personal Interview

Face-to-face interviews, usually conducted in homes, are especially valuable for obtaining detailed information on viewing and listening, including the out-of-home use of receiving sets. This method offers the greatest flexibility because it permits interviewers to probe in some depth for opinions and other qualitative information on programs and commercials.

As with telephone recall interviews, callers ask respondents to recall their viewing or listening within a recent period of time. To assist them, listings of shows broadcast during the period under study are provided; this *aided recall* method has become a standard approach in face-to-face interviewing.

Personal interviewing has an added advantage in that samples can be checked personally for representativeness of audience subsets (such as age, sex, racial, ethnic, or income/educational groups). But the cost of personal interviewing and the difficulty of providing for the security of interviewers in many residential areas have deterred this form of research in recent years. No major audience research firms currently are known to use the personal interview technique in residential areas. *Focus group research*, in which individuals are interviewed together in group settings, is an alternative approach that permits in-depth probing for qualitative information.

Metering Devices

Metering devices are monitoring instruments attached to TV or radio receivers to record set usage. Such devices silently and automatically measure the usage of television sets in a constant sample of homes.

Early mechanical recorders produced film or punched-tape records of viewing information, which respondents had to mail to the research firm's offices. Modern monitoring devices, however, are connected by special telephone circuits to a central computer that dials each unit periodically, retrieves the stored information, and tabulates results.

Although metering devices have advantages, they also have certain limitations. The data yielded are more costly than those obtainable by other methods. For this reason, they have been used mainly for national TV research and for *overnight reports* in a few large cities. Although such devices measure *tuning* (sets on), they do not measure *viewing* (sets watched). And metered devices connected to television sets cannot provide audience composition data. Research services that use automatic recorders for basic set usage data, therefore, generally supplement that information with demographic data obtained by another method, usually from viewer-kept diaries.

Because of the problems noted above, the A. C. Nielsen Company began to experiment with individual metering devices, or "people meters," in 1978. Both Nielsen and Arbitron now use such devices for audience research in certain large markets; eventually viewing in most of the country likely will be measured by these meters.

The heart of Nielsen's people meter system is a device smaller than a cigar box, placed on each TV set in a sample household. An accompanying remote control unit also enables individuals to make electronic entries from anywhere in the room. Each member of the sample household is assigned a personal viewing button on the people meter. Additional buttons are labeled for visitors in the home. Other buttons are used for viewers to record their age and sex. People meters record when the set is turned on, which channel is viewed, when the channel is changed, and when the set is turned off, in addition to information on who is viewing. All of the data are stored in the in-home metering system until they are retrieved by the company's computer. Through this system, more accurate viewing information is said to be available for various demographic groups.

An illustration of the A. C. Nielsen Company's people meter is shown in Figure 13.1.

DATA PROCESSING

The final step in producing quality audience research involves careful tabulation and processing of raw viewing and listening data to its final, usually printed, form. Data contained in diaries and interview forms first must be scrutinized for authenticity and procedural accuracy; then the information is coded by editors for computer processing. Data obtained by mechanical means must be checked for technical malfunctions, but once entered into the computer, they may be tabulated and analyzed in many different ways to discover patterns of audience behavior.

The major audience research services work with industry representatives on a continuing basis to improve their methodologies. Minimum standards for broadcast research have been established by the Broadcast Rating Council in New York, which audits and accredits rating services.

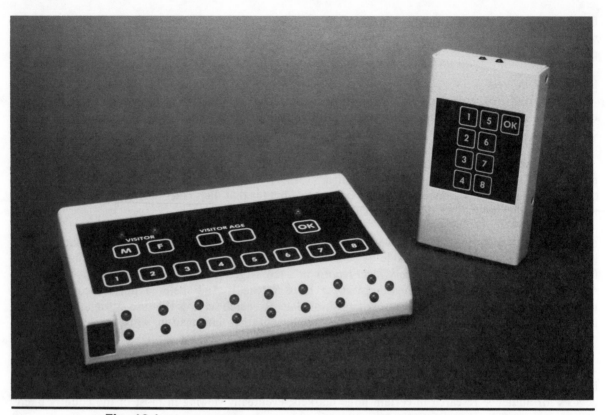

Fig. 13.1. Nielsen people meter. (Courtesy of Nielsen Media Research)

Terminology

Basic to interpreting audience research is an understanding of the terms used in viewing and listening studies. Each rating service has its own terminology, and there are slight variations from one organization to another; we can work, however, with general definitions used in the broadcast industry as a whole. Distinct categories to consider are terms that define survey areas geographically; terms that express audience size; and terms that are used in computations for analytical purposes.

SURVEY AREA TERMINOLOGY

Audience measurement studies are conducted both nationally and on an individual market basis. National program ratings such as those produced for network television by the Nielsen NTI Service are based on sampling throughout the 48 contiguous states. Three geographical designations are commonly used with respect to local broadcast markets: metropolitan statistical areas (MSA), television market areas—ADI and DMA; and total survey areas (TSA).

Metropolitan (Metro) Areas

As defined by the U.S. Government's Office of Management and Budget, a metropolitan area consists of a central city and the urban area that surrounds it. Officially known as a Metropolitan Statistical Area (MSA), such an urban concentration consists of at least one city of 50,000 population or more, or two or more nearby cities with at least 25,000 population each. The MSA also includes the entire county in which the major city (or cities) is located, plus adjacent counties that are integrated with the central community into an urban complex. Markets with at least one million population that contain two or more primary MSAs are designated as Consolidated Metropolitan Statistical Areas (CMSAs).

Because most TV stations and many of the largest radio outlets are located in the nation's approximately 150 metropolitan (MSA) areas, the Metro area takes on considerable significance as the heart of a broadcast market. It is an important geographical area for broadcast advertising purposes because the clientele of many businesses are concentrated within the core urban zones. For those reasons, audience studies usually include Metro viewing or listening data *breakouts*. Figure 13.2 depicts the Metro area of a major television market. For many purposes, however, Metro area information is too restrictive; hence, data on two larger zones, television market areas and total survey areas, may also be provided in rating reports.

Television Market Areas

Television stations, as explained in Chapter 2, normally provide regional coverage, with signals capable of being received at distances approaching 100 airline miles from transmitters. These signals usually reach far beyond urban centers into the surrounding countryside, so the Metro area is inherently an inadequate definition of television markets.

Although there are slight differences between their criteria, the two major TV research services, Nielsen and Arbitron, have developed techniques for defining television market areas exclusive of one another. In essence, both identify each of the country's TV markets geographically on the basis of preponderance of viewing. Thus, under Nielsen's Designated Market Area (DMA) or Arbitron's Area of Dominant Influence (ADI), each TV market is specified as an area that consists of all counties in which viewership is predominately directed toward stations of the home market. This concept is illustrated in Figure 13.2 for the Columbus, Ohio, market (Eastville), for which sixteen counties are included in the DMA; in all of those counties, the Columbus stations are viewed more than those of any other city.

Because each county in the 48 contiguous states is designated as part of some television market, the country may be mapped to show TV market patterns.

Arbitron also uses its television ADI markets as geographical areas for measuring radio listenership. In addition to radio data based on Metro area listening, these reports provide listenership information for larger regions whose parameters are synchronized with television market boundaries. Although the standardization of radio and TV markets facilitates market planning for advertisers, this technique clearly favors large-area radio stations over those with lesser coverage.

Total Survey Area

Under the ADI and DMA plans, each U.S. county is included in one particular television market because most viewing is directed toward stations of a specific city. But how about the viewing of stations in other cities? Arbitron and Nielsen have satisfactorily delineated arbitrary boundaries between TV communities, but shouldn't stations get credit for all of their viewership, even in counties where it's minor? Obviously, the answer is yes.

To provide total information on audience size, the major rating services, in addition to providing *rating* and *share* data for Metro and ADI/DMA areas, include numerical estimates of total viewership for stations regardless of where it takes place. Total Survey Area (TSA) data, found in both Arbitron and Nielsen studies, incorporate total households reached, total persons reached, and estimates for each program on the basis of age and sex.

AUDIENCE DATA TERMINOLOGY

A second group of audience measurement terms indicates the size of audiences for various stations and programs. These terms include *potential audience, households using television* (HUT) and *persons using radio* (PUR), *share of audience*, and *program (station) rating*. TV and radio station audiences also

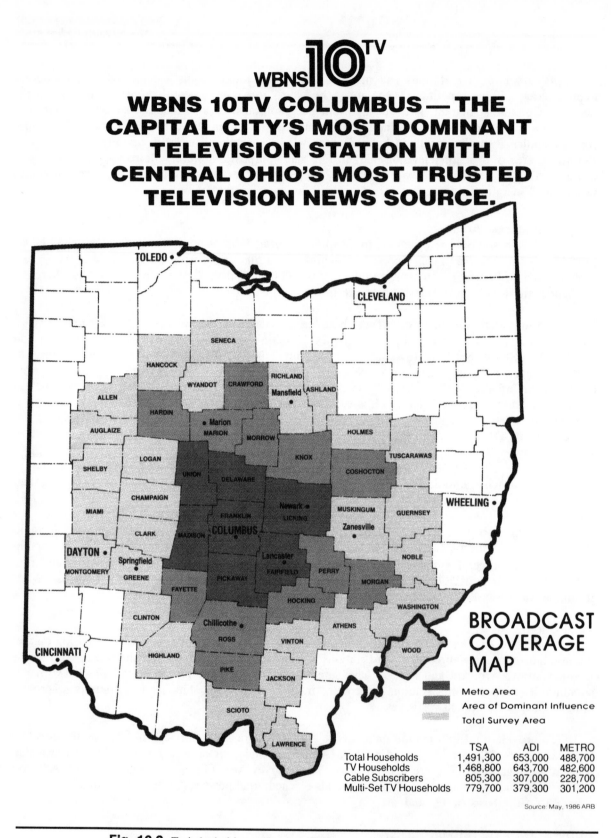

WBNS 10TV COLUMBUS — THE CAPITAL CITY'S MOST DOMINANT TELEVISION STATION WITH CENTRAL OHIO'S MOST TRUSTED TELEVISION NEWS SOURCE.

BROADCAST COVERAGE MAP

Metro Area
Area of Dominant Influence
Total Survey Area

	TSA	ADI	METRO
Total Households	1,491,300	653,000	488,700
TV Households	1,468,800	643,700	482,600
Cable Subscribers	805,300	307,000	228,700
Multi-Set TV Households	779,700	379,300	301,200

Source: May, 1986 ARB

Fig. 13.2. Typical television market area. This coverage map of the Columbus, Ohio, television market is coded to show the three tiers of a broadcast market: the standard metropolitan area (metro), the area of dominant influence (ADI) or designated market area (DMA), and the total survey area (TSA). (Reprinted with permission from WBNS-TV, Inc., Columbus)

are frequently analyzed in terms of demographic composition and demographic ratings, as well as cumulative (unduplicated) ratings and reach. Commonly used radio terms include *average quarter-hour* (AQH) *persons*, *ratings*, and *share*. Note that all terms that include the words share and rating are percentages.

Potential Audience

The potential audience for any program or station consists of all households equipped with either television or radio receiving sets in the sampling area. Estimates of the potential audience for national network television are revised annually by the Nielsen organization. For the 1989-90 season, the national audience potential was estimated at 92.1 million households.

Potential audiences for local markets, of course, vary with their populations and the extent of set penetration. The New York City ADI alone accounts for 7.7 percent of all U.S. television households, and the top-10 markets combined include 31.4 percent of all of the country's homes. A few other examples are given in Table 13.1, including the value of one rating point (1 percent of the market's TV households) for each market.

Table 13.1. Sample percentages of U.S. TV Households (TVHH), 1988-1989

Market	Market Rank	TVHH	Percentage of U.S. TVHH	TVHH per Rating Point
New York	1	6,944,400	7.72	69,444
Los Angeles	2	4,807,700	5.34	48,077
Chicago	3	3,068,600	3.41	30,686
Boston	6	2,045,100	2.27	20,451
Atlanta	12	1,315,900	1.46	13,159
Phoenix	20	959,700	1.07	9,597
Kansas City	30	731,500	.81	7,315
West Palm Beach	50	490,100	.54	4,901
Knoxville	60	426,700	.47	4,267
Roanoke-Lynchburg	70	353,300	.39	3,533
Sioux Falls-Mitchell	100	227,800	.25	2,278

Source: *Arbitron Ratings/Television: 1988-1989 Universe Estimates Summary*, New York: Arbitron Ratings Company, 1988 (used with permission).

Households Using Television

Households using television is an estimate of the number of different households with one or more sets turned on during any specific time period. Thus, HUT represents the total available audience at any point in time.

HUT is expressed as a percentage of the total number of television households (TVHH) in a survey area, which may be the nation, an MSA area, or an ADI or DMA television market area. The concept of households using television is illustrated in Figure 13.3. In this example, with 500 of a possible 1,000 receivers in use, the HUT figure is 50 percent.

Persons Using Radio

The term *persons using radio* (PUR), sometimes expressed as *sets in use* (SIU), is used in radio surveys precisely as HUT is used for television. Persons using radio represents the estimated total number of persons listening to radio for five or more minutes in an *average quarter-hour* in any given *daypart*. PUR and HUT provide indications of how popular radio and TV are at a given time in a given market. If the PUR figure is consistently low in a particular area, another medium, such as TV or newspapers, might prove a better buy for advertisers. Conversely, if the PUR figure is unusually high,

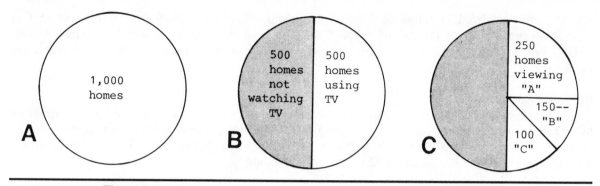

Fig. 13.3. Audience measurement concepts: HUT, share, and rating. A. Potential audience = 1,000 homes. B. Actual audience of 500 homes = 50 percent HUT. C. Station "A" is being watched in 250 homes, which equals a 50 percent share of the audience and a rating of 25. Station "B" is watched in 150 homes and has a share of 30 percent and a rating of 15. Station "C" is watched in 100 homes and has a share of 20 percent and a rating of 10.

advertisers might consider increasing the frequency of their commercial announcements or the duration of their radio campaigns.

Share of Audience

In understanding *share of audience*, it is important to remember that, at any given time, the audience consists of precisely those persons or homes actually using their TV or radio sets. Consequently, a share of audience represents the percentage of those homes or persons (HUT or PUR) that are tuned to a given program or station.

Referring again to Figure 13.3, if half of the households using television (1/2 × 500) are watching Station A, this station has a 50-percent share of the audience. Stations B and C have 30- and 20-percent shares, respectively. But how large an audience share should TV stations really expect? That depends upon the number of stations that can be received well in the market and their program popularity. In major markets such as New York, Los Angeles, and Chicago, network stations generally achieve sign-on to sign-off shares of 18 to 19 percent, while major independent stations average about 10 to 11 percent in the same markets. In contrast, the leading radio stations in those markets usually attain overall average quarter-hour shares (listeners age 12 or older) ranging from 4 to 9 percent.

When it comes to early-morning network programs such as "Today" and "Good Morning America," audience shares usually range from a low of 16 to a high of 29. Other daytime program shares are similar—generally between 16 and 32. Conversely, the top ten primetime programs draw average shares between 30 and 40 percent over the course of six months.

Share-of-audience percentages permit comparison of the popularity of all programs broadcast at the same time. However, a serious problem arises with the need to compare audiences of programs broadcast at different times, because the size of the available audience (HUT or PUR) fluctuates widely throughout the day.

To illustrate this problem, assume that in a market of 500,000 TVHH, the HUT figure for 9 P.M. is 60 percent. The available audience, as simple multiplication reveals, consists of 300,000 households (500,000 × .60). If Station A has a 50 percent share, its reach is an estimated 150,000 homes (300,000 × .50). Now assume that the same station has an identical 50 percent share of the audience at 6 A.M. when the typical HUT is about 2 percent. In this instance, Station A attracts 50 percent of an available audience of only 10,000 households (500,000 × .02), or a mere 5,000 homes. Although share-of-audience data are useful within a specific time frame, a better measure is needed for comparison of programs across time periods.

Program Ratings

By definition, a *program rating* is the estimated percentage of the total potential audience (all homes equipped with TV or radio sets in the market area) that are tuned to a specific program or station. Because the potential audience remains relatively constant, there is comparability between ratings for programs regardless of time of broadcast, so long as the ratings are taken from the same survey. For example, suppose two network shows both attracted ratings of 20. Assuming a projectable sample, the conclusion follows that twenty out of every one hundred households nationwide viewed each program. Their respective shares and audience compositions might have differed, but the numerical size of the audiences for the two programs was identical.

A convenient formula used to compute ratings is

$$\text{RATING} = \text{SHARE} \times \text{HUT}$$

Using this formula, in the example given in Figure 13.3, Station A's 50-percent share during a HUT period of 50 percent results in a 25.0 rating. It can be verified readily from the illustration that Station A indeed reaches 25 percent of its potential audience.

Each national rating point has a stated value in terms of households, equaling one percent of the potential audience. The national television potential for the 1989-90 season was estimated at 92.1 million households, so one national rating for that season equaled 921,000 TV households (1 percent × 92,100,000). The number of households that equal one rating point in a local market is determined by multiplying 1 percent times the potential audience in the market area. See Table 13.1.

Rating points within various demographic groups can be calculated similarly for TV and radio stations. For example, a demographic rating of 5 within the 18-to-34 age group—male, female, or both—indicates that 5 percent of that demographic group's total number were included in the program's audience. The value of demographic ratings lies in their focus on target groups instead of the general population that is measured by overall ratings.

Although both ratings and share-of-audience figures give advertisers comparative data on program appeal, ratings have another more important function. Because they take into account the potential audience, too, they are used to determine rates—the cost of commercial time. Although rates are generally negotiable, stations in each market area set their own asking cost per rating point (based primarily on population), and advertisers respond. Once a deal is made, the advertiser pays that cost times the number of purchased gross rating points, which will be discussed in detail shortly.

Television rating and share data are provided by Nielsen and Arbitron in their audience studies for both MSA and DMA/ADI markets for all time periods of the broadcast week. In addition, rating and share averages are summarized for various *dayparts*.

Rating and share data for radio listening are tabulated on an average-quarter-hour basis. Arbitron and Birch radio reports also provide *average person* estimates, indicating the likely number of persons listening to a radio station during an average quarter-hour within each daypart (for example, 6 to 10 A.M., 10 A.M. to 2 P.M., or 2 to 7 P.M.)

Audience Composition

Broadcast advertisers vitally need information on the make-up of audiences attracted to various programs to schedule commercial messages when they'll reach desired target groups. The major rating services provide a full range of demographic information for network and local television programs and, in major markets, for radio stations as well. Demographic ratings frequently are given for age, sex, and other factors; those ratings represent a percentage of the total number of persons within each category.

Cumulative Audiences

Cumulative audience data (*cumes*) indicate the number of different households or persons who tuned to a program at least once during a stated period of time. TV cumes, for example, estimate how many different households watched a five-day-a-week program at least once during the week. In radio, *cume persons* is used to indicate the number of different people who listened to a station at least once during the time period of interest. Cume ratings express the number of cumulative persons (unduplicated audience) as a percentage of the population in the surveyed area and are particularly useful when reach and frequency are important considerations in an advertiser's strategy. For example, if a radio station has a reach of 100,000 cume persons out of an audience potential of 250,000, its cume rating is 40.

ANALYTICAL TERMS

In addition to the terms already discussed, other concepts are important for decision making in campaigns and for measuring the extent and efficiency of advertising exposures across a campaign. These factors include gross audience, gross rating points, reach, frequency, cost per thousand, and cost per point; these are especially useful in analyzing the progress of a campaign as it develops.

Gross Audience

Gross audience is the total number of households (or persons) reached over a period of time, counting each one every time it is included in the audience. Whereas the cumulative audience counts each viewing or listening unit only once (unduplicated reach), the gross audience indicates the total number of impressions delivered, including duplication.

The gross audience of a TV campaign may be tabulated by adding the estimated audiences for each program used, every time it appears in the schedule. For example, if a schedule includes one commercial each day in a Monday through Friday newscast, the gross audience becomes five times the average audience. The following computation illustrates this point:

Average household audience of WXXX-TV "Evening News"	224,000
Number of weekly commercials	× 5
Gross weekly audience (households)	1,120,000

Similarly, if a schedule includes a number of different programs within a period of time, the procedure is to add the total audience figures together to obtain the gross audience for the campaign:

Average household audience	
for program 1	210,000
for program 2	180,000
for program 3	230,000
for program 4	175,000
Weekly gross audience (households)	795,000

Gross impressions also may be calculated for particular demographic audiences as subsets of a total program audience. This method involves extracting the number of viewers from the appropriate demographic column (for instance, 18- to 34-year-old women) for each program, and adding them together.

Because audience measurement for radio focuses on dayparts rather than particular programs, the gross audience for a radio station is determined by multiplying the average quarter-hour audience by the number of commercials broadcast. The following is a typical computation:

Average quarter-hour audience, 6 to 10 A.M.	45,000
Number of weekly spots during 6 to 10 A.M.	× 20
Weekly gross audience (persons)	900,000

Gross Rating Points

Because each rating point represents 1 percent of the potential audience, gross rating points (GRP) indicate the total reach of a campaign. A schedule consisting of 100 GRPs delivers an audience equivalent in number to the total population of the area surveyed. The audience delivered, however, is not 100 percent of the population because some persons are reached more than once and others are not reached at all.

The GRPs for a campaign are calculated on the same basis as gross audience, with the number of rating points for all programs counted each time commercials are scheduled:

Average household rating for WXXX-TV "Evening News"	18
Number of weekly commercials	× 5
Weekly GRPs	90

If four different programs are used in an advertiser's weekly schedule, with respective ratings of 15, 22, 19, and 27, the weekly GRP becomes the sum of the four ratings, or 83 gross rating points.

To determine GRPs in radio, the procedure involves multiplying the average quarter-hour rating by the number of spots used per week, as follows:

Average quarter-hour rating, 6 to 10 A.M.	4.6
Number of weekly spots during 6 to 10 A.M.	× 20
Weekly GRPs (persons)	92.0

Gross rating points for demographic groups are calculated in the same manner. For example, assume that radio station WXXX has an average demographic rating (adults 25 to 59) of 3.5 during morning drivetime. A schedule of 10 spots per week during this daypart would generate 35 target-group GRPs.

GRP, like gross audience, is an analytical measure used to indicate the extent to which a campaign blankets a broadcast market. Often the number of commercials purchased is based on a predetermined number of gross rating points needed to provide a desired advertising exposure. Generally speaking, at least 100 GRPs per week are required for a low-level saturation campaign, such as one intended to maintain brand awareness. About 200 GRPs per week are needed for a high-level saturation schedule, such as one helping to launch a new product. Broadcast campaigns involving 5,000 GRPs over a year's time may run 250 some weeks, 100 some weeks, and other weeks none at all. At the 7,500 GRP level, popular weekly averages are between 150 and 300 (again, with some "dead weeks"); with 10,000 GRPs to work with, many weeks carry between 200 and 400.

Reach and Frequency

Reach is used in broadcast advertising to indicate the number of different households or persons exposed to campaign messages. A viewer needs to watch only once to be included in the estimated reach; thus the term is synonymous with cume or cumulative audience.

Frequency is the average number of times each viewer or listener is reached or exposed to an advertiser's commercials within a given period of time. The procedure for computing frequency is

Average household audience for WXXX-TV "Evening News"	224,000
Cumulative audience/reach	440,000
Spot schedule	5 messages
Gross HH impressions (5 × 224,000) or	1,120,000

$$\text{frequency} = \frac{\text{gross impressions}}{\text{reach}} = \frac{1,120,000}{440,000}$$

$$\text{frequency} = 2.5$$

The significance of reach and frequency lies in the fact that advertising needs vary from one situation to another. Some products require high levels of repetition (frequency) as constant reminders of brand names and images. Other advertisers need less repetition but require broad audience exposure. Campaigns may be strategically planned to emphasize either reach or frequency within a given number of rating points and a specified budget.

Cost per Thousand (CPM)

Advertisers who place their budgets in the broadcast media do so with the expectation of attaining maximum sales results as efficiently as possible. The most common measure of cost efficiency is the expenditure to reach 1,000 households or persons with an advertising message or an entire campaign:

$$\text{CPM} = \frac{\text{cost of advertising } (\times\ 1,000)}{\text{average audience}}$$

For example, if WXXX-TV's "Evening News" delivers an average household audience of 225,000 and the price for a 30-second spot is $1,125, the household CPM may be computed

$$\text{CPM} = 1,125,000 \div 225,000 = \$5.00$$

A shortened version of the computation is to divide the cost of the spot by the number of thousands of homes, or persons, reached (as given in Arbitron or Nielsen books):

$$\text{CPM} = \$1,125 \div 225 = \$5.00$$

For an advertiser who places commercial messages in a number of different programs, the CPM may be determined on the basis of household reach, total audience, or target audience. The CPM is determined by dividing the total cost of advertising time by the gross households reached, the number of gross impressions, or the gross impressions within the specified target group, by using either CPM formula. For example, let's assume that the cost for the schedule of three spots shown in Table 13.2 is $2,500.00. The CPM calculations for households, total persons, and target persons are $8.33, $6.76, and $9.62, respectively.

One should be aware that the cost per thousand for target audiences varies greatly with the breadth of the audience selected. The narrower the target, the higher the CPM becomes. For example, suppose a manufacturer of men's toiletries seeks comparative CPM data on two programs to reach males 18 to 49 years old. The CPM for this target audience would always be higher than one for all men over 18, or all adults between 18 and 49. For this reason, astute media buyers focus sharply on target demographic numbers, seeking programs that attract a high concentration of the desired group, with a minimum of reach outside the target audience.

Table 13.2. Cost-per-thousand projections

	Households Reached	Persons Reached	Target Audience Reached
Program A	50,000	85,000	45,000
Program B	120,000	150,000	105,000
Program C	130,000	135,000	110,000
Totals:	300,000	370,000	260,000

Cost per thousand–households: CPM = $2500/300 = $8.33.
Cost per thousand–total persons: CPM = $2500/370 = $6.76.
Cost per thousand–target persons: CPM = $2500/260 = $9.62.

Advertising CPMs, Chapter 14 will note, relate closely to the supply-and-demand situation in advertising. Thirty-second network primetime commercials during recent years have ranged from $6 to $10, averaging about $8, on a household cost per thousand basis. CPMs for local and regional advertising vary, depending upon specific circumstances, but tend to be slightly less than network CPMs.

(The student wondering why the measure isn't cost per person should recompute the problems above on that basis; figures of .00833, .00676, and .00962 would prove unwieldy and difficult to compare in terms of value. Besides, what advertiser has any interest in reaching just one person?)

Cost Per Point (CPP)

Just as efficiency-oriented advertisers evaluate broadcast time on a CPM basis, they also consider the cost for reaching each rating point in their commercial schedules. In computing cost per point (CPP), media buyers/sellers must remember that comparisons are valid only within a given market because the value of one rating point differs from market to market. Here is the formula for arriving at cost per point:

$$CPP = cost \div number\ of\ rating\ points$$

Like the CPM, the cost per point can be calculated on the basis of household ratings or on a demographic rating point basis.

$$CPP = \$1,125 \div 12\ rating\ points = \$93.75$$

Adweek's *Marketer's Guide to Media* is a convenient source of prevalent CPP data for all of the broadcast media—network TV, spot TV, and radio. For example, the cost per point for primetime network TV spots averaged about $8,300 during the peak of the 1987-88 season. CPPs for 30-second primetime TV spots and 60-second drivetime radio spots (women 25-54) for selected markets for the first quarter of 1988 are shown in Table 13.3.

Table 13.3. Cost-per-point data for selected markets

ADI Rank	Market	CPP/TV ($)	CPP/Radio ($)
1	New York	838	284
10	Houston	358	162
19	Denver	196	101
32	Nashville	104	53
49	Birmingham	81	44
67	Syracuse	74	55
82	Jackson, Miss.	53	13
94	Las Vegas	37	27

Source: *Adweek's Marketer's Guide to Media*, First Quarter 88 (January-March), New York: A/S/M Communications, Inc., 1988.

Audience Measurement Services

Radio audience measurement began on a systematic basis during the 1930s through efforts of the Cooperative Analysis of Broadcasting (CAB) and Clark-Hooper, Inc. (now C. E. Hooper, Inc.). The CAB was formed by the American Association of Advertising Agencies and the Association of National Advertisers as an industry-supported organization; the famed "Hooperatings," which employed the telephone-coincidental technique, were widely used in radio advertising during the 1930s and 1940s. The CAB discontinued its operation in 1946, but the Hooper organization continues to function today.

As noted, three major firms produce program ratings on a regular basis. In addition to the Arbitron, Nielsen, and Birch organizations, a number of other organizations specialize in customized, rather than regular, research work. Several prominent firms are listed near the end of this chapter. The formats and types of data contained in program rating reports for all of these companies are changed periodically to improve audience measurement services to an ever-changing industry.

A. C. NIELSEN COMPANY

The broadcast division of the A. C. Nielsen Company in Northbrook, Illinois, consists of two units: the Nielsen Television Index (NTI) and the Nielsen Station Index (NSI). The former uses electronic monitoring devices, including people meters, to produce network program ratings and a variety of other national audience data; the latter computes ratings, shares, and audience demographics for local TV markets by using a combination of metering devices and diaries. Nielsen also monitors viewing of pay cable television and in-home use of VCRs.

Data for Nielsen Television Index household audience estimates are gathered by the Storage Instantaneous Audimeter (SIA), a monitoring instrument that silently records all TV set usage in sample homes on a minute-by-minute basis. Its electronic memory stores information about when each television set is turned on, how long it remains on the channel tuned, and what manner of channel switching occurs. Every Audimeter is connected to a special telephone line exclusive to Nielsen; each home is dialed at least twice a day by a computer that retrieves the recorded information. The data are recorrelated with program schedules to produce household program ratings. The entire process is automatic and requires no work by members of the sample household.

Because such monitoring devices as the Audimeter can only obtain data on set usage, Nielsen's NTI reports are augmented with audience composition estimates from the Nielsen People-Meter Service, based on a separate Nielsen sample of U.S. television households. By September 1988, at least 4,000 households were equipped with people meters. Additional households in NTI's network studies continued to use the *Audilog*, a personal viewing diary for each member of sample households, in conjunction with a *Recordimeter*. This device records the time sample TV sets are in use as an aid for diary keepers and provides an audiovisual reminder signal every half hour to encourage timely recording of log entries. NTI's audience studies blend the data from the SIA and the people meters/Audilog diaries, leaning on the latter mainly for information that is not obtainable from the Audimeter.

In selecting households, NTI works with the area probability sampling technique, by using U.S. Census listings of all households in the country as a base. Following scientific sampling procedures, Nielsen's statisticians predesignate neighborhoods and housing units that are to provide audience information. These samples include all types of households and neighborhoods in cities, towns, and rural areas, with and without telephones, geographically dispersed in more than 600 counties. The SIA's operational sample consists of about 1,400 households. Each cooperating home is replaced over a 2-year period, remaining in the sample long enough to provide continuity of information.

The *Nielsen Station Index* uses a random selection of sample households from telephone directories, except in certain of the largest markets where the total telephone frame (all phones, listed and unlisted) is used as a base. In addition, NSI uses the NTI area probability samples in the 18 largest cities where the data gathering is accomplished by a combination of monitoring devices and diary. In the other markets, cooperating households are asked to keep a TV viewing diary for one week.

After basic information from sample homes reaches Nielsen's central office, diaries and data tapes are scrutinized to preserve the accuracy of the data through the processing and production operation. Then diary data are keyed directly into computers that already contain the Audimeter data through a direct-entry system, followed by a final inspection of completed data for internal consistency and any unusual trends. After processing, the information is released in reports for each market. The entire process—from receipt of raw data to finished tabulations and reports—is almost completely automatic.

Nielsen Television Index Data

Commercially launched in 1950, NTI assists subscribers in the use of TV as a national advertising medium. Its best-known published report is the *Nielsen National TV Ratings* (usually called "The Pocketpiece"). Sample information from "The Pocketpiece" is reproduced in Figure 13.4. This biweekly publication, which fits neatly into a pocket, provides the following information about the national TV audience:

1. Household audience estimates and rankings for sponsored network programs
2. Audience composition estimates for a large array of age/sex categories
3. Season-to-date averages of program audiences
4. Average audience estimates for major categories of programs
5. Overall television set usage data on a comparison basis with the previous year
6. Television set usage by time periods

Other program ratings available from NTI include daily national ratings; fast weekly household ratings for all sponsored network programs; fast evening persons audiences; daily 70-market ratings for each network in the seventy markets where there is multinetwork competition; fast multinetwork area ratings, which are weekly recaps of the daily 70-market ratings; and households and persons ranking report, showing the ranking, rating, and estimated audience of each network program in terms of households and 15 demographic categories.

NTI also issues a number of analysis reports that probe other dimensions of television. These include the *NTI/NAC Audience Demographics Report* (NAD); the *Market Section Audiences* (MSA), which provides estimates of audiences among particular categories of households; the *Brand Cumulative Audiences Report* (BCA), which provides estimates of the number of households each brand reaches in four weeks, including frequency distribution and cost efficiency comparisons; the *Program Cumulative Audiences Report* (PCA), which provides estimates of each network program's four-week reach and frequency; and the *NAC Cost Supplement,* which examines the cost of audience reach in estimated cost per thousand commercial minutes delivered.

Nielsen Station Index Data

NSI was launched in 1954 to provide individual stations and time buyers with a local audience measurement service comparable to NTI's national services. NSI currently surveys television audiences in 147 markets, providing at least three (and up to eight) studies per year, depending on specific market needs. These reports, called *Viewers in Profile,* include metro-area and DMA-area ratings, station total audiences, cumulative audiences, and estimates of viewing, over a wide range of demographic categories. Data tabulations are given in terms of time period and program average audiences, as well as by daypart summaries.

As noted earlier, NSI is essentially diary-based, except in about 18 of the nation's largest markets in which a combination of metered and diary-gathered data is used. For those cities, NSI also provides

ABC TV

TOTAL AUDIENCE (Households (000) & %) {	17,650 20.2								21,850 25.0								

DISNEY SUNDAY MOVIE — THE PARENT TRAP (R)(SD)   ABC SUNDAY NIGHT MOVIE — DADDY (SD)

AVERAGE AUDIENCE (Households (000) & %) {	10,140							14,950								
SHARE OF AUDIENCE %	11.6	9.5*	11.0*	12.4*	13.3*	17.1	16.4*	16.6*	17.6*	17.7*
	19	17 *	18 *	19 *	20 *	25	24 *	24 *	25 *	27 *
AVG. AUD. BY ¼ HR. %	8.9	10.1	10.5	11.6	12.3	12.5	12.9	13.7	16.0	16.8	16.5	16.7	17.6	17.7	17.7	17.6

CBS TV

TOTAL AUDIENCE (Households (000) & %) {	26,740 30.6			25,520 29.2			24,820 28.4		

60 MINUTES — MURDER, SHE WROTE (SD) — CBS SUNDAY MOVIE — STILL CRAZY LIKE A FOX (SD)

AVERAGE AUDIENCE (Households (000) & %) {	19,840			21,760			18,530			
SHARE OF AUDIENCE %	22.7	21.3*	24.1*	24.9	24.5*	25.3*	21.2	21.4*	21.3*	21.3*	20.6*
	39	38 *	40 *	37	38 *	37 *	31	31 *	31 *	31 *	31 *
AVG. AUD. BY ¼ HR. %	20.7	21.8	23.3	24.9	24.0	24.9	25.4	25.2	21.4	21.3	21.3	21.4	21.2	21.3	19.8

NBC TV

TOTAL AUDIENCE (Households (000) & %) {	11,100 12.7			15,560 17.8			27,710 31.7		

OUR HOUSE (R) — RAGS TO RICHES — NBC SUNDAY NIGHT MOVIE — TRADING PLACES (9:00-11:30PM)(R)

AVERAGE AUDIENCE (Households (000) & %) {	8,480			11,190			15,990			
SHARE OF AUDIENCE %	9.7	8.9*	10.5*	12.8	12.0*	13.6*	18.3	15.9*	17.5*	18.7*	19.4*
	16	16 *	17 *	19	18 *	20 *	28	23 *	25 *	27 *	30 *
AVG. AUD. BY ¼ HR. %	8.5	9.3	10.2	10.8	11.6	12.3	13.2	14.0	15.5	16.3	17.3	17.7	18.6	18.8	19.3	19.6

TV HOUSEHOLDS USING TV WK. 1 (See Def. 1)	58.7	60.7	63.4	64.9	65.5	66.5	67.8	68.0	66.1	65.7	65.5	64.3	62.9	60.2	58.5	56.9
WK. 2	55.4	57.8	59.9	62.1	63.8	66.1	67.5	68.8	68.4	69.4	69.3	69.4	68.5	66.7	64.6

U.S. TV Households: 87,400,000

For explanation of symbols, See page A.

A-17

EVE.SUN. APR.5, 1987

---

18 ## PROGRAM AUDIENCE ESTIMATES (Alphabetic)   1ST APR. 1987 REPORT

AUDIENCE COMPOSITION
VIEWERS PER 1000 VIEWING HOUSEHOLDS BY SPECIFIED CATEGORIES

PROGRAM NAME WK # DAY START TIME DUR NET TYPE	KEY	HOUSEHOLD AUDIENCES AVG. AUD. % / SHARE % / AVG. AUD. (0,000)	TOTAL PERSONS (2+)	LADY OF HOUSE	WORKING WOM.	WOMEN TOTAL	18-34	18-49	25-54	35-64	55+	MEN TOTAL	18-34	18-49	25-54	35-64	55+	TEENS (12-17) TOTAL / FÉM.	CHILDREN (2-11) TOTAL / 6-11

EVENING CONT'D

HIGHWAY TO HEAVEN — 22 / 211 / 99
2 WED. 8.00P 60 NBC GD
KEY	AUD	SHARE	(0,000)	TOTAL	LADY	WORK	TOTAL	18-34	18-49	25-54	35-64	55+	TOTAL	18-34	18-49	25-54	35-64	55+	T.F	C
A	18.5	29	1617	1832	754	241	832	229	408	378	352	381	567	114^	321	329	324	228	172 61^	261 133^
8.00 - 8.30 B	17.7	27	1547	1681	748	301	857	217	400	388	376	400	521	132	272	272	271	212	129 68	174 112
8.30 - 9.00 A	17.9	28	1564	1783	732	222	816	212	376	346	333	401	555	121^	305	305	305	230	156^ 56^	256 130^
A	19.1	29	1669	1872	772	257	844	242	438	408	368	361	577	105^	333	352	342	225	188 66^	263 136^

HILL STREET BLUES — 4 / 207 / 99
2 TUE. 10.00P 60 NBC OP
A	12.5	21	1093	1388	701	303	753	232^	439	422	378	269	627	179^	405	370	339	199^	8v LT	LT LT
B	13.8	24	1206	1449	672	278	725	233	399	410	351	255	656	208	397	397	341	203	38 12	30 17
10.00 - 10.30 A	12.2	20	1066	1401	701	315	753	230^	417	412	363	290	631	173^	410	378	345	196^	17v LT	LT LT
10.30 - 11.00 A	12.8	22	1119	1369	699	288	749	235^	459	432	386	247^	620	185^	399	358	330	203^	LT LT	LT LT

HOUSTON KNIGHTS — 4 / 206 208 / 99 99
WED. 10.00P 60 CBS OP
A	13.9	25	1215	1492	717	348	802	224	452	441	394	314	636	179	324	331	333	251	37^ 21v	17v 17v
B	15.5	27	1355	1488	704	282	792	244	465	445	389	275	609	165	344	335	323	220	52 24	35 23
10.00 - 10.30 A	14.0	24	1224	1503	725	355	814	240	468	445	388	317	633	181	316	323	327	259	31^ 16v	25v 25v
10.30 - 11.00 A	13.8	26	1206	1478	707	337	787	208	434	438	398	309	640	180	334	337	335	246	43^ 26v	8v 8v

HUNTER — 19 196 / 98
1 SAT. 10.00P 60 NBC OP
A	16.2	31	1416	1586	775	308	835	248	460	417	401	314	460	124^	266	271	201	164^	206 100^	85^ 69^
B	16.8	30	1468	1654	739	287	833	246	443	418	369	332	548	156	303	289	276	209	148 85	125 99
10.00 - 10.30 A	16.1	30	1407	1574	778	299	820	230	433	411	401	327	445	113^	249	260	200	163^	213 101^	96^ 77^
10.30 - 11.00 A	16.4	31	1433	1581	763	313	841	262	484	422	400	297	469	132^	279	276	201	163^	197 97^	74^ 61^

JACK & MIKE — 20 200 / 98
1 TUE. 10.00P 60 ABC A
A	13.4	24	1171	1610	848	476	895	345	586	539	423	256	575	174^	377	367	293	129^	89^ 55v	51v 51v
B	13.4	23	1171	1513	736	356	839	326	547	517	393	226	509	217	363	323	236	115	97 53	68 40
10.00 - 10.30 A	14.0	24	1224	1612	825	464	882	353	585	526	408	250	579	177^	387	383	302	120^	89^ 62^	62^ 62^
10.30 - 11.00 A	12.8	24	1119	1594	869	485	904	333	583	555	438	260	568	172^	365	346	281	137^	83^ 47v	39v 39v

Fig. 13.4. Sample national audience data from Nielsen's *Pocketpiece*. (Courtesy of Nielsen Media Research)

---

continuous year-round metered measurements under the title of *Metered Market Service*. This report provides daily overnight reports on viewing, obtained via computer terminals in clients' offices; weekly printed reports; monthly VIP reports, issued eight times a year; and program audience average weekly reports, issued through computer printout.

Other NSI reports include *DMA Test Market Profiles; Network Programs by DMA; Report on Syndicated Programs; DMA TV Trends by Season;* and *DMA-CATV Audience Distribution Report.*

THE ARBITRON COMPANY

The Arbitron Ratings Company provides network and local market audience research for both TV and radio. A subsidiary of Control Data Corporation, the firm is headquartered in New York with its operational center at Beltsville, Maryland. Arbitron is best known for its regular ratings *sweeps* conducted simultaneously several times a year in more than 200 markets. Arbitron uses diaries for local market reports and an electronic monitoring device for overnight ratings of network primetime programs in more than a dozen major U.S. markets. In addition, the company offers a variety of other audience reports and customized services, including telephone coincidental surveys. Arbitron announced plans to start its ScanAmerica people meter service in 1989 in five cities, with expansion to a national sample to follow later.

To conduct its local market studies, Arbitron has divided the entire country into geographic sampling units, each of which normally consists of one county. Diaries are placed in each sampling unit on a quota basis determined by population and the expected rate of return of diaries on the basis of previous experience. Following an interval-selection process, Arbitron's sample households are computer selected from tapes obtained from the Metro-Mail Advertising Company. These computer tapes are updated frequently and contain the telephone listings of all U.S. telephone directories.

Separate samples are generated for each week of a ratings period, usually four weeks, and each cooperating family keeps its diary for seven days. Special interviewing techniques are used in some markets to aid in obtaining viewing and listening information from households whose members may have language or literacy problems and who otherwise might not be fully represented in the sample. Average weekly rating and share data are computed from the combined multiweekly samples.

When a household has been selected for use in a survey, Arbitron initially notifies the family by mail. The letter is followed by a telephone call soliciting cooperation, thus paving the way for diary mailing. Diaries are sent directly from Beltsville and, to stimulate participation, cash incentives are included. An individual diary is sent for each TV receiver in known multiset households, and all families in the sample are called the day before the survey begins to be sure that diaries have arrived and to clarify log-keeping procedures. A final "thank you" call is made about midweek to encourage respondents to return diaries promptly.

Back at Arbitron headquarters, diaries are screened for accuracy and edited for data processing; they may be rejected if they are postmarked before the last day of the survey week, fewer than seven days are included, or they arrive after the cutoff date. Information is keyed onto computer tapes.

Arbitron TV Market Reports are produced for more than 200 U.S. markets. Each is surveyed at least three and as many as eight times per year. Reports include rating and share information for both the MSA and the ADI; audience totals and demographic data are provided for the Total Survey Area (TSA), which includes viewership both inside and outside the ADI area.

The following major categories are included in *Arbitron TV Market Reports*: ADI market data; daypart audience summary; network program averages; weekly program and time-period averages; program audiences; program title index; and ADI ratings trend. The formats for the *Arbitron TV Market Report* and Nielsen's *Viewers in Profile* local market reports are quite similar. A sample page from an *Arbitron TV Market Report* is shown in Figure 13.5.

In addition to its basic market ratings, Arbitron TV produces other reports: *News Barometer; Significant Viewing Studies; Overnight Coincidental Studies; Tele-Poll Surveys; Network Program Analysis; Syndicated Program Analysis; Syndicated Program Ranking Report; Television Markets and Rankings Guide; Seasonal Variation Index;* and *Spot Activity—Post-Evaluation Reports.*

A majority of commercial TV stations now use "Arbitron Information on Demand" (AID), too. It provides computer access to all diary information obtained during every TV survey conducted during a given year in each market. Station personnel may examine figures on reach, frequency, and audience

Weekly Program Estimates

Time Period Average Estimates

DAY AND TIME / STATION	PROGRAM	WEEK-BY-WEEK ADI TV HH RATINGS WK 1	WK 2	WK 3	WK 4	ADI TV HH RTG	ADI TV HH SHR	ADI TV HH SHARE/HUT TRENDS OCT '87	MAY '87	FEB '87	NOV '86	METRO TV HH RTG	METRO TV HH SHR	TV HH	PERSONS 18+	PERSONS 12-24	PERSONS 12-34	WOMEN TOT 18+	WOMEN 18-49	WOMEN 12-24	WOMEN 18-34	WOMEN 25-49	WOMEN 25-54	WKG WMN 18+	MEN TOT 18+	MEN 18-49	MEN 18-34	MEN 25-49	MEN 25-54
		10/28	11/4	11/11	11/18									TOTAL SURVEY AREA, IN THOUSANDS (000's)															
		1	2	3	4	5	6	58	59	60	61	8	9	11	13	15	16	18	19	20	21	22	23	24	25	26	27	28	29
▲ RELATIVE STD-ERR THRESHOLDS (1 σ)	25%	3	3	4	3	3						3		36	25	29	28	18	19	26	21	18	18	19	20	22	26	19	19
	50%	1	1	1	1	-						-		9	6	7	7	4	4	6	5	4	4	4	5	5	6	4	4
WEDNESDAY																													
10:00P-10:15P																													
KPRC	CH2 NW AT 10	10	9	7	9	9	15	24	21	21	20	9	16	129	196	26	68	103	60	18	28	51	60	30	93	63	30	57	61
KHOU	CH11 NEWS-10	7	7	7	9	8	13	18	15	17	20	8	13	113	178	27	69	88	56	7	26	49	58	24	89	67	39	51	56
KTRK	EYWT NEWS 10	21	21	24	24	22	39	39	33	34	33	23	39	332	513	84	209	277	179	43	97	148	167	83	236	167	87	139	155
KTXH	TALES DARKSD	2	3	2	3	2	4	4	8	8	7	3	4	37	42	22	38	15	14	4	11	12	12	2	26	26	23	10	10
KRIV	PRIME MOVIE	8				8	13					8	13	115	79	37	49	54	44	24	23	32	37	11	25	14		14	14
	THE JEFERSNS		3	3	5	4	6					4	7	55	62	12	31	37	19	9	12	15	19	7	25	18	12	18	20
	--4 WK AVG--					5	8	4	7	7	5	5	8	70	66	18	35	41	26	13	15	19	23	8	25	17	9	17	19
KHTV	GLSTR DB FTR	5				5	8					5	8	68	68		47	11	11		11	11	11	11	57	48	36	48	48
	GOLDSTAR MOV		6			6	11					6	11	88	103	22	95	72	69	22	69	47	47		31	26	26	26	26
	BARNEY MILER			3	2	3	5					3	5	44	37	7	21	17	14	4	7	10	12	9	20	15	14	13	14
	--4 WK AVG--					4	7	7	9	8	8	4	7	61	61	9	46	29	27	8	24	19	20	7	32	26	22	25	26
KXLN	NCHE A NOCHE	1	1	2	2	1	3	**	**	**	**	2	3	22	19	4	18	10	10	4	9	6	6	2	9	9	9	9	9
KUHT	PTV	2	1	3	2	2	3	3	3	3	1	2	3	27	59	20	36	21	12	2	10	10	10	4	38	32	27	15	16
HUT/TOTAL		59	56	54	57	57		59	61	60	61	58		791	1134	210	519	584	384	99	220	314	356	160	548	407	246	323	352
10:15P-10:30P																													
KPRC	CH2 NW AT 10	10	9	8	10	9	17	21	20	21	20	9	17	136	206	25	69	109	66	17	28	59	70	29	97	68	31	60	66
KHOU	CH11 NEWS-10	7	8	8	8	8	14	17	16	16	20	8	14	114	171	20	64	87	50	5	25	45	55	25	84	62	36	50	55
KTRK	EYWT NEWS 10	17	17	21	20	19	35	39	34	31	30	19	35	279	435	72	175	235	154	35	81	128	143	70	200	144	73	119	132
KTXH	TALES DARKSD	2	2	2	3	2	4	5	8	8	6	2	4	35	42	16	31	18	14	3	11	12	12	2	24	21	17	10	10
KRIV	PRIME MOVIE	8				8	14					8	14	113	94	53	64	71	59	40	39	32	37	11	23	14		14	14
	THE JEFERSNS		3	3	4	3	6					4	7	51	66	11	30	37	18	8	12	15	19	7	29	20	11	20	23
	--4 WK AVG--					4	8	5	7	7	7	5	9	67	73	21	39	45	28	16	18	19	23	8	28	19	8	19	21
KHTV	GLSTR DB FTR	4				4	8					4	8	64	66		47	11	11		11	11	11	11	54	48	36	48	48
	GOLDSTAR MOV		6			6	12					7	12	89	108	11	99	52	49	10	49	39	39		56	51	51	50	50
	BARNEY MILER			4	2	3	5					3	5	42	34	5	21	14	13	3	6	9	10	7	20	15	15	14	16
	--4 WK AVG--					4	7	7	9	9	9	4	8	59	61	5	47	23	21	4	18	17	17	6	38	33	29	32	33
KXLN	NCHE A NOCHE	1	2	2	2	2	3	**	**	**	**	2	3	25	24	5	23	13	13	5	12	7	7	2	11	11	11	11	11
KUHT	PTV	2	1	2	2	2	3	3	3	2	2	2	3	23	39	7	14	13	8		3	8	8	3	26	21	11	14	15
HUT/TOTAL		55	52	52	53	53		55	57	56	58	55		738	1051	171	462	543	354	85	196	295	335	145	508	379	216	315	343
10:30P-10:45P																													
KPRC	TONIGHT SHOW	6	5	3	7	5	12	18	14	16	16	6	12	79	112	16	50	64	40	12	26	34	37	13	49	34	18	30	33
KHOU	MASH-S	8	10	8		9	20					8	19	125	190	35	107	100	66	19	42	55	64	32	90	69	54	55	62
	CBS NEWS SP				8	8	18					8	18	114	211	65	90	112	84	41	50	43	45	31	100	61	32	45	55
	--4 WK AVG--					8	19	20	25	27	26	8	18	123	195	43	103	103	71	25	44	52	59	32	93	67	49	52	60
KTRK	ABC NW NGTLN	13	12	13		13	30					13	30	192	285	44	89	151	89	21	35	75	88	36	133	90	41	72	81
	ABC NEWS SPC				10	10	22					10	21	144	215	47	83	123	84	19	37	66	68	49	92	62	33	47	52
	--4 WK AVG--					12	28	27	29	24	26	12	28	180	267	45	87	144	88	20	36	72	83	39	123	83	39	66	74
KTXH	QUINCY-S	1	2	2	2	2	5	7	10	6	6	2	4	30	32	3	15	14	10		5	9	11	5	18	16	10	14	15
KRIV	LT SHOW-FOX	4	5	3	4	4	9	8	8	8	9	4	10	60	91	18	64	57	49	15	38	36	39	24	34	30	23	28	29
KHTV	GLSTR DB FTR	5				5	11					5	11	76	76	2	51	20	20		11	20	20	10	56	50	38	50	50
	BENNY HILL		5	4	4	4	10					4	10	63	84	24	60	31	25	9	18	20	20	13	54	46	35	33	33
	--4 WK AVG--					4	10	10	10	10	9	5	10	66	82	19	58	28	24	7	17	20	20	12	54	47	36	37	37
KXLN	NCHE A NOCHE	1	1	2	1	1	3	**	**	**	**	1	3	19	18	5	18	9	9	5	9	4	4	2	9	9	9	9	9
KUHT	PTV	2	1	2	2	1	3	2	3	3	1	1	3	21	34	7	12	13	8		3	8	8	2	21	16	10	10	11
HUT/TOTAL		45	43	41	44	43		47	51	47	51	45		578	831	156	407	432	299	84	178	235	261	129	401	302	194	246	268
10:45P-11:00P																													
KPRC	TONIGHT SHOW	5	4	4	5	4	12	18	14	16	16	5	11	66	96	15	42	53	33	11	22	26	28	9	42	29	15	26	28
KHOU	MASH-S	8	10	8		9	22					9	21	129	182	31	111	100	71	24	49	58	64	32	81	62	48	58	64
	CBS NEWS SP				6	6	15					6	15	83	139	43	63	66	53	29	36	24	25	28	73	53	26	39	40
	--4 WK AVG--					8	20	23	26	29	28	8	20	117	171	34	99	92	67	26	46	49	54	31	79	60	43	54	58
KTRK	ABC NW NGTLN	11	8	9		9	23					10	24	137	198	17	47	103	59	11	21	48	56	25	95	64	26	58	62
	ABC NEWS SPC				7	7	18					7	18	98	148	31	55	88	55	11	21	44	47	24	60	39	28	26	32
	--4 WK AVG--					9	22	22	24	21	21	9	22	127	185	21	49	99	58	11	21	47	54	24	86	58	27	50	55
KTXH	QUINCY-S	2	2	3	3	3	6	8	10	6	7	3	7	37	31	3	16	15	11	1	5	11	12	7	16	14	10	11	12
KRIV	LT SHOW-FOX	4	5	4	4	4	11	7	7	7	9	4	11	62	92	21	62	60	51	18	38	37	39	24	31	27	19	25	26
KHTV	GLSTR DB FTR	6				6	14					6	14	87	87	2	60	22	22		12	22	22	10	65	59	47	59	59
	BENNY HILL		4	4	4	4	11					4	10	61	86	26	62	32	27	9	20	21	21	15	54	46	35	32	32
	--4 WK AVG--					5	12	11	11	9	10	4	11	68	86	20	62	29	25	7	18	22	22	14	57	49	38	39	39
KXLN	NCHE A NOCHE	1	1	2	2	2	4	**	**	**	**	2	4	25	25	7	24	13	13	7	12	6	6	2	12	12	12	12	12
KUHT	PTV	1	1	1	1	1	3	1	2	3	1	1	3	16	22	7	11	7	4		2	4	4	2	15	13	10	6	6
HUT/TOTAL		42	39	38	37	39		41	47	42	47	40		518	708	128	365	368	262	81	164	202	219	113	338	262	174	223	236
11:00P-11:15P																													
KPRC	TONIGHT SHOW	4	4	5	4	4	13	19	17	20	18	4	12	61	89	15	42	49	30	11	21	22	23	15	39	27	17	24	26
KHOU	BRNABY JONES	5	5	4		5	15					5	14	70	108	17	32	72	36	13	19	23	37	22	36	26	11	25	26
	MASH-S				6	6	17					6	17	87	128	30	40	58	38	16	16	22	26	13	70	20	10	20	40
	--4 WK AVG--					5	15	14	18	24	23	5	15	74	113	20	34	68	36	14	18	23	34	20	44	25	11	23	30
KTRK	NIGHTLNE-WED	9				9	27					9	26	131	165	11	43	110	86	11	27	75	75	16	55	42	16	42	42
	1100 LATE SH		7	8		8	24					8	23	113	146	3	45	83	48	1	19	47	48	29	63	48	26	47	47
	ABC NEWS SPC				6	6	19					7	19	92	105	10	18	68	44			44	44	31	36	26	18	16	16
	--4 WK AVG--					8	23	22	27	24	22	8	23	112	141	7	38	86	56	3	16	53	54	26	54	41	22	38	38
KTXH	QUINCY-S	3	3	3	3	3	9	9	7	7	8	3	9	43	35	3	22	20	17		10	17	17	9	15	13	12	11	12
KRIV	LT SHOW-FOX	3	5	5	3	4	13	9	10	6	9	4	13	61	87	23	48	54	47	21	30	35	39	23	33	29	8	28	29
KHTV	MAGNUM PI-S	2	3	1	3	2	7	12	9	7	8	2	7	35	28	9	19	6	1	3	1	1	1		21	18	15	12	12
KXLN	NCHE A NOCHE	1	1	2	1	1	4	**	**	**	**	1	4	20	25	7	25	13	13	7	12	6	6	3	12	12	12	12	12
KUHT	PTV	1	-	1	1	1	2		2	2		1	2	11	17	5	8	6	2		2	2	2		11	11	6	6	6
HUT/TOTAL		33	32	31	33	32		35	40	35	40	34		417	535	89	236	302	202	59	110	159	176	96	229	176	103	154	165
11:15P-11:30P																													
KPRC	TONIGHT SHOW	3	4	4	3	4	12	18	18	19	16	4	12	52	72	14	34	39	24	10	16	18	19	10	33	24	12	22	23
KHOU	BRNABY JONES	5	4	4		4	15					4	13	63	96	15	27	64	29	11	16	18	28	20	32	23	10	21	24
	MASH-S				6	6	19					6	18	87	131	33	45	61	40	18	18	23	26	12	70	19	11	19	40
	--4 WK AVG--					5	16	14	13	14	21	4	14	69	105	19	32	63	32	13	16	19	28	18	41	22	10	21	28
KTRK	NIGHTLNE-WED	6				6	22					7	22	89	115	8	32	75	58	8	20	50	50	12	40	30	13	30	30
	1100 LATE SH		6	7		7	23					7	22	99	136	3	42	77	42	1	20	41	44	26	59	46	22	45	45
	ABC NEWS SPC				6	6	19					6	19	88	101	10	18	64	40			40	40	28	36	26	18	16	16
	--4 WK AVG--					6	22	20	26	23	22	6	21	94	122	6	34	73	45	2	15	43	44	23	49	37	19	34	34
KTXH	QUINCY-S	3	3	3	3	3	10	10	6	8	9	3	10	43	45	3	32	26	24		16	24	24	10	19	18	16	15	16
KRIV	LT SHOW-FOX	4	5	4	4	4	15	12	10	7	9	5	15	63	84	28	53	52	47	25	29	36	39	25	31	27	10	25	27
KHTV	MAGNUM PI-S	2	2	1	3	2	8	12	8	8	7	2	7	34	24	8	9	7	1	1	1	1	1		17	13	8	6	6
KXLN	NCHE A NOCHE	1	-	2	1	1	3	**	**	**	**	1	3	14	28	7	26	15	15	7	13	9	9	4	13	13	13	13	13
KUHT	PTV	1	-	1	-	1	2		2	3		1	2	9	14	5	7	2	1		1	1	1		11	11	6	6	6
HUT/TOTAL		28	28	29	31	29		31	35	31	35	30		378	494	90	227	277	189	58	107	151	165	90	214	165	94	142	153

HOUSTON 45 WEDNESDAY NOVEMBER 1987 TIME PERIOD AVERAGES

- * SAMPLE BELOW MINIMUM FOR WEEKLY REPORTING
- ** SHARE/HUT TRENDS NOT AVAILABLE
- \- DID NOT ACHIEVE A REPORTABLE WEEKLY RATING
- ‡ TECHNICAL DIFFICULTY
- \+ COMBINED PARENT/SATELLITE
- ▲ SEE TABLE ON PAGE v

Fig. 13.5. Sample page of local TV audience data from Arbitron Television. (Courtesy of Arbitron Ratings)

flow in any selected market combinations (ones that they are considering for purchase).

Arbitron Radio conducts audience surveys up to three times annually in some 160 markets throughout the country. These surveys are conducted during a 12-week period and are reported for an "average week" of the period covered. According to Arbitron, the use of average week estimates tends to decrease the effect of atypical programming that may arise during an individual week of a survey. In an effort to provide comparable information for radio and TV, Arbitron Radio bases its area listening data on the television ADIs. Arbitron reports also include MSA listening information.

Arbitron radio estimates can be classified into two basic categories: *average quarter-hour listening* indicates the estimated number of persons of a given demographic listening to a station in an average quarter hour of a particular daypart, and *cume listening* is an estimate of the number of different persons who listened to a station for at least five minutes within a quarter hour in a given daypart.

Specific types of audience estimates found in *Arbitron Radio Reports* include:

1. Average quarter-hour persons (Metro, ADI, TSA)
2. Average quarter-hour ratings (Metro, ADI)
3. Cume persons (Metro, ADI, TSA)
4. Cume ratings (Metro)
5. Exclusive cume persons (Metro)
6. Percent of listening at home, in-car, and other (Metro)
7. Time spent listening (Metro)
8. AM-FM totals (Metro; ADI; TSA)

Arbitron Radio also conducts a nationwide radio network survey to provide national audience information for both the traditional wired networks and the sales rep networks. Also, Arbitron's special *ethnic reports* detail radio listening habits of the Black and Hispanic segments of the population in several large metropolitan markets.

BIRCH RADIO

Birch Radio, Inc., based in Coral Springs, Florida, has become an important source of radio audience information during recent years. Birch produces spring and fall summary reports on nearly 250 radio markets. In addition to media usage information, Birch reports also include qualitative, product, and service information on listeners to radio stations in markets surveyed.

Birch research uses the telephone recall technique, with each respondent asked a battery of extended demographic questions (household size, household income, respondent's occupation), as well as product, service, and radio listening information.

A Birch Radio *Quarterly Summary Report* typically includes sections on listening trends, target demographics, station "rankers," daypart listening estimates, hour-by-hour listening estimates, location of listening, county-by-county listening estimates, audience composition, weekly cume listenership, exclusive cumes, and quality/product usage estimates. A sample Birch listening report, which also is similar in format to Arbitron Radio, is shown in Figure 13.6.

To illustrate the benefit to be obtained from Birch qualitative data, a station account executive could obtain and use in presentations information about which of the station's listeners eat frequently at fast-food restaurants, travel on airlines, consume diet soft drinks, or plan to buy a new car within the next year. The executive also could present information on the educational or income levels of the station's listeners. Such qualitative information, as shown in Figure 13.7, can be extremely valuable to stations and their advertising clients.

KNOXVILLE TN MSA
MARCH - MAY 1987

AVERAGE QUARTER HOUR SHARE TRENDS - READ ACROSS **

	MON - SUN 6:00AM-MIDNIGHT					MON - FRI 6:00AM-10:00AM					MON - FRI 10:00AM-3:00PM					MON - FRI 3:00PM-7:00PM					MON - FRI 7:00PM-MIDNIGHT				
	SPR 86	SUM 86	FAL 86	WIN 87	SPR 87	SPR 86	SUM 86	FAL 86	WIN 87	SPR 87	SPR 86	SUM 86	FAL 86	WIN 87	SPR 87	SPR 86	SUM 86	FAL 86	WIN 87	SPR 87	SPR 86	SUM 86	FAL 86	WIN 87	SPR 87
WEZK-FM	6.7	11.2	10.1	5.4	6.7	7.5	11.9	10.6	5.1	5.3	6.7	14.7	7.4	4.3	7.8	9.7	10.8	9.1	4.6	5.1	6.2	4.0	21.1	9.3	5.7
WGAP	.7	.3	.5	.8	.3	.2	.9	.2	2.9	1.4	.2	.4	.2	.5	.2	.4	.6								
WIMZ	.4	.3	1.0		.8	1.3		1.0	.2	.4	1.0		.2		.2	.2	.2	2.7		1.9			1.0		2.2
WIMZ-FM	21.5	26.7	15.2	24.5	23.7	19.9	27.2	9.8	22.5	25.5	22.2	27.4	14.0	28.2	19.5	18.8	28.5	15.9	28.3	26.2	22.5	27.5	14.4	30.1	28.9
WITA	.2	.3		.5	.3				.2	.2	1.0			.7	1.0			1.0		.5					
WIVK*	4.5	4.3	8.3	4.0	3.0	4.7	4.6	7.9	3.7	3.7	5.0	5.5	7.2	3.1	1.4	3.8	5.2	5.3	3.1	6.0	1.3	1.1			.4
WIVK-FM	28.0	24.4	31.3	32.9	35.0	31.8	30.5	32.8	40.5	38.5	23.4	24.7	37.0	30.4	41.8	25.7	21.4	25.9	31.0	33.9	35.9	24.5	17.5	25.4	26.8
WJFC*		.3	.8					.6					1.5					.7							
WKGN	6.1	2.8	2.3	3.2	1.1	3.2	2.4	2.7	1.4	1.0	10.5	5.0	.8	3.1	1.9	10.3	4.5	1.8	1.5	1.9	9.5	3.3	3.1		.9
WKNF*																									
WKNF-FM	.7	1.3	1.0	.3	1.1	.9	1.5	.4		1.0	1.7	2.2	.2				1.9	2.4		.2			2.1		.9
WKXV	.7	.3		.3	.5	2.0	.2			.2	.4	.2			.2	.2	.2			.5				1.0	.4
WMYU-FM	9.2	9.7	11.6	8.9	11.1	9.9	6.4	11.5	8.6	9.5	11.3	8.1	13.1	11.5	9.3	6.5	9.9	15.7	8.5	9.0	3.9	14.3	18.6	3.1	7.0
WNOX	2.5	1.8	1.6	2.7	2.2	2.0	.4	1.3	1.2	2.1	1.7	1.3	1.5	3.8	.2	3.0	1.1	2.7	2.1	.5	2.3	.4	4.6	3.6	3.5
WOKI-FM	4.5	5.1	4.9	5.4	3.2	3.6	2.2	5.6	2.5	1.8	2.1	2.6	4.7	5.7	1.9	2.6	6.3	4.2	8.1	2.1	1.6	12.8	12.4	10.9	6.6
WRJZ*	1.1	1.0	2.8	.3	1.3	1.1	.4	4.6	.2	2.7		.4	1.9		2.6	1.0	.6	2.4		.7	1.6	2.6	1.5		
WSEV*		.5	1.0				1.5	.4			.2	.4	1.1					.7							
WTNZ-FM	2.5	1.0	.3	2.7	2.2	1.3	1.1		2.5	1.0	1.7	.4		3.3	3.3	1.4	1.5		2.3	.7	1.6	.4	.5	6.7	4.4
WUOT-FM	4.0	2.3	2.1	3.0	2.7	5.2	2.2	2.3	2.2	2.9	3.1	.7	2.7	.5	1.7	7.7	1.3	3.5	4.2	4.9	3.9	1.5	1.0	5.2	6.1
WUTK-FM	1.1	.5	.3	.8	.3		.2	1.0	1.4	.2	.6	.4		1.7		1.6	.2	1.1	.6	.7	2.0	.4			
WYSH	.2	.3	.5	1.6	.3	.7	.2	2.3	1.4				1.5	.5	1.4		.6		3.1						2.1
PUR	20.9	18.4	17.8	17.1	17.1	26.1	21.2	24.0	22.5	23.7	22.4	21.4	21.8	19.3	19.4	23.2	21.7	20.8	22.2	19.9	14.3	12.8	8.9	8.9	10.5

* ESTIMATES ADJUSTED FOR ACTUAL BROADCAST SCHEDULE
** THE RIGHT MOST COLUMN WITHIN EACH DAYPART CONTAINS THE CURRENT ESTIMATES.

BIRCH RADIO
COPYRIGHT 1987 BIRCH RESEARCH CORP.

PAGE 5

Fig. 13.6. Sample page of radio market data from Birch Radio. (Reprinted with permission from Birch Radio Research, Spring 1987 Quarterly Summary Report)

COMPUTER ACCESS AND COMPUTERIZED RATINGS ANALYSIS

Traditionally, radio and TV audience reports from Arbitron, Birch, Nielsen, and other organizations have been provided to subscribers in printed booklet form, with numerous pages of data similar to the illustrations shown in this chapter. Computers are used extensively in the processing and tabulation of the data obtained from diaries, metering devices, and telephone interviews. Because computerization also allows users of research information to analyze station data quickly, the major research companies also make their reports available on computer tape and diskettes for use with personal computers.

Most leading radio and TV stations, advertising agencies, and sales rep firms now use computers routinely in planning broadcast advertising campaigns. Several companies have copyrighted software programs that permit facile retrieval and analysis of audience data, including quick computations of such important items as average persons reached, cume persons, cume and demographic ratings, cost per thousand, cost per point, and reach and frequency analyses. In addition to their timely benefits for

KNOXVILLE TN MSA
DECEMBER 1986 - MAY 1987 -

TOTAL SAMPLE/AIRLINE TRAVEL
ADULTS 18+
SAMPLE = 2108

QUALITATIVE COMPONENTS OF AUDIENCE

	TOTAL WEEKLY AUDIENCE		COMPARATIVE VALUES - READ DOWN						COMPOSITIONAL VALUES - READ ACROSS						
			NONE		LIGHT		FREQ		AQH COMPOSITION %			CUME COMPOSITION %			
	AQH	CUME	% IND	% PEN	% IND	% PEN	% IND	% PEN	NONE	LIGHT	FREQ	NONE	LIGHT	FREQ	
WEZK-FM	64	727	81	12.6	139	22.7	158	25.9	57.6	24.2	18.2	56.4	28.8	14.8	WEZK-FM
WGAP	10	203	124	5.4	64	2.9	*	*	87.9	12.2	*	86.8	13.2	*	WGAP
WIMZ	3	72	*	*	*	*	*	*	*	*	*	*	*	*	WIMZ
WIMZ-FM	140	1381	95	28.1	113	35.1	112	34.8	72.7	17.8	9.6	66.1	23.4	10.5	WIMZ-FM
WITA	4	56	91	1.1	95	1.2	178	2.2	49.7	42.0	8.3	63.7	19.6	16.7	WITA
WIVK*	22	321	118	8.1	54	3.9	72	5.2	90.2	5.1	4.8	82.1	11.1	6.7	WIVK*
WIVK-FM	292	2379	111	56.5	80	42.7	67	35.7	77.7	16.2	6.1	77.2	16.5	6.2	WIVK-FM
WJFC*		56	*	*	*	*	*	*	*	*	*	*	*	*	WJFC*
WKGN	23	261	106	6.0	94	5.5	66	3.9	85.2	13.6	1.2	74.4	19.4	6.2	WKGN
WKNF*			*	*	*	*	*	*	*	*	*	*	*	*	WKNF*
WKNF-FM	11	183	72	2.8	104	4.3	302	12.4	48.9	27.3	23.8	50.1	21.5	28.3	WKNF-FM
WKXV	7	89	138	2.6	16				100.0			96.6	3.4		WKXV
WMYU-FM	86	1046	90	20.1	107	25.2	163	38.4	64.7	20.4	14.8	62.5	22.2	15.3	WMYU-FM
WNOX	17	357	118	9.0	74	6.0	26	2.1	85.3	12.8	1.9	82.1	15.4	2.5	WNOX
WOKI-FM	34	593	93	11.9	127	17.0	91	12.1	56.6	33.4	10.0	65.1	26.4	8.5	WOKI-FM
WRJZ	12	187	89	3.6	161	6.8	47	2.0	65.6	29.4	5.0	62.1	33.4	4.5	WRJZ
WSEV*	3	90	131	2.5	42	0.8			91.1	8.9		91.3	8.7		WSEV*
WTNZ-FM	11	187	116	4.7	90	3.8			80.2	19.8		81.4	18.6		WTNZ-FM
WUOT-FM	15	331	59	4.2	179	13.4	234	17.5	43.0	27.8	29.2	40.9	37.2	22.0	WUOT-FM
WUTK-FM	2	77	53	0.9	210	3.6	211	3.7	37.0	28.6	34.4	36.7	43.5	19.8	WUTK-FM
WYSH	5	67	128	1.8	50	0.8			99.0	1.0		89.7	10.3		WYSH
PUR	793	4221	99	90.6	104	95.2	103	95.1	71.8	19.5	8.7	69.9	20.8	9.4	PUR

CATEGORY DEFINITIONS	ESTIMATED POPULATION (00)
NONE - HAVE NOT TRAVELLED ROUND TRIP ON AN AIRLINE IN PAST YEAR	3253
LIGHT - TAKEN 1 OR 2 ROUND TRIPS ON AN AIRLINE IN PAST YEAR	921
FREQ - FREQUENT/TAKEN 3 OR MORE ROUND TRIPS ON AN AIRLINE IN PAST YEAR	416

BIRCH RADIO

COPYRIGHT 1987 BIRCH RESEARCH CORP.

PAGE 242

Fig. 13.7. Sample page of qualitative data from radio market. (Reprinted with permission from Birch Radio Research, Spring 1987 Quarterly Summary Report)

generating availability information, such computer programs also are capable of producing attractive, graphically illustrated sales promotion pieces for use by account executives.

Three prominent software packages are "Broadcast Management Plus," "Tapscan," and "$elect-a-Vi$ion." A sample campaign plan using such a package is shown in Figure 13.8.

OTHER AUDIENCE MEASUREMENT SERVICES

Numerous firms engage in audience measurements on a smaller scale in specialized forms. They generally perform custom research assignments for clients on an individual contract basis. Some of the more prominent of these secondary organizations, with their basic services, are listed in Table 13.4.

LIMITATIONS

Whatever ratings research we undertake, we must remember that, at best, it is only one of many tools that can aid broadcast advertisers in making decisions. Human beings are not puppets who behave the same way every time certain strings are pulled. Given various times, moods, and circumstances, they may react very differently to identical program types and to the same kind of scheduling techniques.

TAPSCAN REACH AND FREQUENCY ANALYSIS
ADULTS 25-54
GENERIC CLIENT
TEST SCHEDULE
CITYNAME METRO SURVEY AREA
SPRING 1989 ARBITRON

WEEKLY SPOT DISTRIBUTION   (WEEKS IN SCHEDULE: 4)

STATION	MONDAY-FRIDAY 6-10	10-3	3-7P	7-MID	SATURDAY 6-10	10-3	3-7P	7-MID	SUNDAY 6-10	10-3	3-7P	7-MID	M-FRI AM+PM	M-FRI 6A-7P	M-FRI 6A-MD	WKEND 6A-MD	M-SUN 6A-MD
KCCC A-F	7	6	5	----	1	2	----	----	----	----	----	----	----	----	----	----	----
KHHH	4	4	4	----	1	2	----	----	----	----	----	----	----	----	----	----	----
KJJJ	6	7	8	----	2	----	----	----	----	----	----	----	----	----	----	----	----
KMMM	5	8	5	----	1	2	----	----	----	----	----	----	----	----	----	----	----
KZZZ	5	8	5	----	----	2	----	----	----	----	----	----	----	----	----	----	----
KQQQ	5	6	5	----	1	2	----	----	----	----	----	----	----	----	----	----	----
TOT SPOTS:	32	39	32	----	6	10	----	----	----	----	----	----	----	----	----	----	----
TOT GRP'S:	67.9	74.4	43.3	----	6.3	16.6	----	----	----	----	----	----	----	----	----	----	----

NOTE: "AM+PM" DAYPART IS 6AM-10AM + 3PM-7PM. SPOTS SHOWN IN COMBINATION DAYPARTS ARE ASSUMED TO BE PROPORTIONALLY DISTRIBUTED.

SCHEDULE COMPUTATIONS
ADULTS 25-54   (POPULATION -   894,800)

STATION	SPOTS WKLY	SPOTS TOT	GROSS IMP	GRP'S	REACH	% REACH	FREQ	% EFF RCH	% OF CUME	--CPM--	--CPP--	TOTAL COST
KCCC A-F	21	84	1,769,200	197.7	154,869	17.3%	11.4	14.7%	90.1%	$4.67	$41.78	$8,260
KHHH	15	60	313,200	35.0	27,454	3.1%	11.4	2.6%	91.8%	$5.75	$51.43	$1,800
KJJJ	23	92	1,087,200	121.5	98,268	11.0%	11.1	9.3%	87.3%	$5.43	$48.56	$5,900
KMMM	21	84	2,059,200	230.1	187,972	21.0%	11.0	17.7%	87.8%	$4.90	$43.80	$10,080
KZZZ	20	80	1,332,800	148.9	130,753	14.6%	10.2	12.1%	86.2%	$4.62	$41.36	$6,160
KQQQ	19	76	897,600	100.3	114,735	12.8%	7.8	10.1%	83.3%	$4.88	$43.66	$4,380
TOTALS:	119	476	7,459,200	833.6	519,377	58.0%	14.4	51.0%		$4.90	$43.88	$36,580

NOTE: THE EFFECTIVE REACH COMPUTATIONS REFLECT THE PERCENTAGE OF THE POPULATION EXPOSED TO THE MESSAGE 3 OR MORE TIMES.

REPORT CONTINUES NEXT PAGE ----->

Fig. 13.8. Radio media plan developed with "Tapscan" computer program. (Courtesy of Tapscan, Inc.)

Some practitioners maintain that most TV ratings measure the competitive environment as much as they measure individual program appeals. In other words, what appears to be a vote for one show may really be a vote against the others aired at the same time. Then, again, if a viewer finds three favorite programs on at the same time, he or she can only watch one (the one that would show up if a research tally were taken), though the other two would also be considered very deserving. Yet, if ratings were the sole criterion for keeping programs on the air, these later two would be cancelled. (A lead of just one rating point during a TV network season produced $33 million in extra profits in 1982, according to CBS research.)

Table 13.4. Audience measurement services

Firm	Services
R. H. Bruskin Associates 303 George St. New Brunswick, NJ 08903	Radio-TV station image studies, diary listening studies, program evaluation research
Crossley Survey, Inc. 275 Madison Avenue New York, NY 10016	Marketing, opinion, and media research services
Hamilton & Staff, Inc. 5454 Wisconsin Avenue Suite 1345 Chevy Chase, MD 20815	Radio-TV station images, program preferences, and audience-flow studies; news research
Starch Inra Hooper, Inc. 566 Boston Post Road Mamaroneck, NY 10543	Telephone coincidental radio audience measurement; station image and program evaluation
Frank N. Magid Associates One Research Center Marion, IA 52302	News consulting; opinion polls and focus groups
TVQ, Inc. 14 Vanderventer Avenue Port Washington, NY 11050	Ratings of broadcast personalities
Edward J. Noonan Marketing 1239 Ocean Shore Blvd. Ormond Beach, FL 32074	Radio and TV audience studies; market and opinion research
Sindlinger & Co., Inc. Box E Wallingford, PA 19086	Daily polling of media exposure, consumer attitudes
Videodex, Inc. 342 Madison Avenue New York, NY 10017	Local television audience; test-market penetration research and evaluation

Ratings can only describe listening and viewing behavior at a given point in time; they do not and cannot explain why the behavior occurred or predict that it will occur again. Ideally, therefore, ratings should be supplemented with additional forms of research.

Radio and television ratings provide subscribing broadcasters and advertisers with a very valuable selling tool—and a highly privileged one. Copyright laws prohibit nonsubscribers from using any of these research results in sales and promotional efforts or activities. Violators face the possibility of stiff fines, imprisonment, or both.

PSYCHOGRAPHIC RESEARCH

A new approach toward understanding audiences has recently emerged in the form of psychographic research. Traditional measurement studies reveal the estimated size and demographic composition of audiences, but psychographic research recognizes the presence of social and cultural variations within audience segments. This form of research seeks to discern prevailing life-styles of users of various products—knowledge that may be extremely valuable in the development of commercials and media schedules. Perhaps the most valuable source of psychographic information on a broad range of product users is the *Simmons Target Group Index,* published by Simmons Market Research Bureau, Inc., New York.

Time and budget constraints generally make the procurement of all desired audience information an impossible dream. Armed with whatever data they have been able to obtain, however, TV and radio time buyers make the purchases that determine which commercials are seen before, during, and after selected programs or time segments.

Study Questions

1. In which ADI or DMA television market is your county located? Can you justify its placement on the basis of observed viewing preferences?

2. Newspapers frequently publish articles indicating the most popular national network TV programs and their ratings. Find a recent listing of leading programs and explain the meaning of the audience data given.

3. Explain the difference between gross and cume audiences. Why is a program's gross audience always greater than its cume?

4. Find a published account of a successful broadcast advertising campaign. Do your best to determine the criteria used for measuring success, including gross ratings points, gross audience and cumulative reach data, and delivered audience demographics.

5. Explain how psychographic data can assist an advertiser in media buying.

ASSIGNMENT 13-A
Working with classmates, design and conduct a survey to tap at least one dimension of the popularity of radio stations in your area. List suggested questions, and compare with those of other students before trying to refine and polish.

ASSIGNMENT 13-B
For an assigned broadcast advertiser and research topic, list appropriate question areas. Word your questions in three separate ways—one suited to a face-to-face interview, one to a telephone interview, and one to a mail survey.

ASSIGNMENT 13-C
For given sets of research data, perform the following indicated computations. Summarize your mathematical procedures and give a rule a neophyte could follow if asked to perform a similar task.

If the reach is _____ (given), and the frequency is _____ (given), the gross audience is _____.

If the frequency is _____ (given), and the gross audience is _____ (given), the reach is _____.

If the gross audience is _____ (given), and the reach is _____ (given), the frequency is _____.

Summary:

Rule:

ASSIGNMENT 13-D

For given sets of research data, perform the following indicated computations.

If an area has _____ (given) TV homes, and _____ (given) of them have sets on: _____ (given) tuned to channel 2; _____ (given) tuned to channel 6; _____ (given) tuned to channel 9; _____ (given) tuned to channel 12, then the homes-using-television figure is _____.

The ratings are _____ for channel 2; _____ for channel 6; _____ for channel 9; and _____ for channel 12; and the share-of-audience figures are: _____ for channel 2; _____ for channel 6; _____ for channel 9; and _____ for channel 12.

If, however, _____ (given) sets are tuned to channel 7, producing a _____ (given) rating and a _____ (given) share-of-audience, the number of TV homes in the area is _____, and _____ of them are on.

Suggested Readings

A Guide to Understanding and Using Radio Audience Estimates. New York: Arbitron, 1987.

A Guide to Understanding and Using TV Audience Estimates. New York: Arbitron, 1987.

Banks, James Mark. "A History of Broadcast Audience Research in the United States 1920–1980 With an Emphasis on the Rating Services." Ph.D. diss., University of Tennessee, Knoxville, 1981.

Beville, Hugh M., Jr. *Audience Ratings: Radio, Television, and Cable*. Hillsdale, N.J.: Lawrence Erlbaum Associates, 1985.

Beyond the Ratings. New York: Arbitron, 1978–present. Published monthly.

Christiansen, Mark, and Cameron Stauth. *The Sweeps: Behind the Scenes in Network TV.* New York: William Morrow, 1984.

Duncan, James H., Jr. *American Radio.* Kalamazoo, Mich.: Duncan's American Radio. Published twice yearly.

Everything You've Always Wanted to Know About TV Ratings. Northbrook, Ill.: A. C. Nielsen.

Fletcher, James E., ed. *Handbook of Radio and TV Broadcasting: Research Procedures in Audience, Program, and Revenues.* New York: Van Nostrand Reinhold, 1981.

Lichty, Lawrence W. *Broadcast Program and Audience Analysis.* Madison, Wis.: American Printing and Publishing, 1973.

Nielsen Report on Television. Northbrook, Ill.: A. C. Nielsen. Published annually.

Rubin, Rebecca B., et. al. *Communication Research: Strategies and Sources.* Belmont, Calif.: Wadsworth, 1986.

Wimmer, Roger D., and Joseph R. Dominick. *Mass Media Research: An Introduction.* 2d ed. Belmont, Calif.: Wadsworth, 1987.

ALSO: Check recent issues of *Advertising Age, Television/Radio Age, Journal of Advertising, Journal of Advertising Research, Journal of Broadcasting & Electronic Media,* and *Journalism Quarterly.*

14

Time Buying

As Chapter 13 suggested, the effectiveness of any radio or television advertising campaign depends not so much on its face cost as on the appropriateness of the media schedule for reaching potential customers.

Most large advertisers employ advertising agencies, so time buying is normally handled by media experts there or in specialized media-buying organizations. Sophisticated market and media research gives time buyers the information needed to design media plans for TV and radio, and stations and networks implement them.

In local advertising, time-buying practices vary somewhat with market size. Large market retail establishments may utilize the services of agencies, but in small and medium markets many firms deal directly with radio and TV stations. A key difference between national and local sales at the station level, therefore, is the involvement of the station itself in the development of media strategy. The agency time buyer may be responsible for purchasing schedules on hundreds of stations or on national networks; the local advertiser buys time in a single market.

Account executives sell time for broadcast networks and stations, cable networks and CATV systems, and sales representative firms. They assist media buyers in planning the schedules that are likely to attain positive results for clients. Effective time buying depends on analysis of advertiser goals and needs and on a thorough understanding of the product, its marketing pattern, and the characteristics of its potential customers. A basic knowledge of marketing and advertising processes is mandatory, along with an appreciation for the capabilities and limitations of the broadcast media.

The challenge of time buying is to plan and purchase schedules that will deliver the appropriate target audience, with as little waste circulation as possible, at the desired frequency of exposure, all at the lowest possible cost. The task requires evaluation of all available time periods on networks and individual stations in selected markets; it is complicated by the fact that stations vary considerably in power, coverage, network affiliation, programming, audience acceptance, and advertising rates. Time buyers must be familiar with such media characteristics and, after campaigns begin, must follow their progress, keeping alert to problems that arise and to possibilities for improving clients' schedules whenever more desirable time slots become available.

Sources of Information

The basic source of information on broadcast advertising rates is the *Standard Rate and Data Service* (SRDS). Separate *SRDS Spot TV and Spot Radio* volumes are published monthly, in addition to the *SRDS Network Rates and Data.* These issues contain national advertising rates, as well as information on station facilities, hours of operation, ownership, network affiliation, closing dates for copy and other materials, commission policies, and special features. SRDS books also include market data sections that provide valuable material for the analysis of broadcast markets. Figure 14.1 shows a trade ad indicating the importance of this widely used publication to advertisers (namely, stations themselves and specific broadcast advertising services).

Somebody's looking you up in Spot Television Rates and Data right now.

The environment in which television time is bought, sold and negotiated has undergone a transformation over the years.

New factors are constantly coming into play. Ever-evolving techniques for defining target audiences; more sophisticated approaches to arriving at the right media mix; new dynamics between buyer and seller are but a few!

Some basic things don't change — even in the midst of change. According to recent research, one element of planning and buying television advertising remains stalwartly the same — decision-makers' reliance on SRDS Spot Television Rates and Data.

Wouldn't you feel more confident knowing you had a high-impact, fact-filled advertising message in Spot Television Rates and Data — where more of the people who count can take advantage of it?

Spot Television Rates and Data

Standard Rate & Data Service, Inc.
5201 Old Orchard Road, Skokie, IL 60077
(312) 470-3100

For a copy of a new research report outlining current station and market selection practices at advertising agencies, or for more information on how you can maximize the impact of your station's identification in SRDS, contact your SRDS District Manager or call Rick Botthof, Sales Manager, today.

Fig. 14.1. SRDS trade ad. (Courtesy of Standard Rate & Data Service, Inc.)

Although SRDS attempts to provide up-to-date rate information for all stations, that task has become increasingly difficult because of the extent of rate negotiations throughout the industry and the frequency with which rates are revised. Published rates in *SRDS Spot TV and Spot Radio* provide an excellent starting point, though, for estimating and comparing the cost of time on various stations. The time buyer ultimately must query stations or their national sales reps for both availabilities and rates.

A second source of rate information is *Television & Cable Factbook*. Published annually by Warren Publishing, Inc., Washington, D.C., this two-volume reference lists all U.S. and Canadian commercial television stations, including their facilities, key personnel, coverage/circulation data, and, in many instances, the station's highest 30-second national spot rate. A second volume of the *Factbook* contains information on broadcast networks, cable networks and systems, program producers, trade associations, regulatory bodies, and market characteristics.

A typical station listing from *Television & Cable Factbook* appears in Figure 14.2.

American Radio, a twice-yearly publication, lists the highest 60-second spot rates for radio stations in all U.S. metropolitan areas. Published by Duncan's American Radio, Indianapolis, Indiana, *American Radio* also includes a vast amount of statistical data on radio listening on a market-by-market basis. This reference also lists and ranks leading radio stations across the country by various formats. A typical radio market profile from *American Radio* appears in Figure 14.3.

Broadcasting/Cable Yearbook, published annually by *Broadcasting* magazine, also contains information on agencies and station sales reps, program and equipment suppliers, and other services used by the broadcasting industry. Another valuable aid is *Sales and Marketing Management's Survey of Buying Power*, which provides an annual compilation of population, income, and retail sales for all U.S. metropolitan areas. The *Survey* includes an index of buying power for individual markets. Time buyers may also find trade magazine advertisements and station-produced materials to be of value in familiarizing them with station profiles, personalities, account lists, and other pertinent information.

A most significant development in broadcast data retrieval has been the introduction of computerized availability and scheduling systems. Major TV and radio stations now automate much of their sales operation, an action that permits control over the entire process of order entry, trafficking, and billing. Computer data systems also provide station management with daily analyses of inventory sold and available, revenue projections by salesmen, advertisers, and agencies, and many other useful reports that help determine how well a station is performing in relation to revenue goals. Computers in advertising agencies and station rep firms may be interfaced to talk directly to computers containing station information. Thus, agency media buyers may assess data on availabilities (times, audience sizes and compositions, and cost per thousand) instantly and, in a few seconds, place schedules on stations throughout the country.

The *Broadcast Advertisers Reports* (BAR) provide media buyers and sales reps with comprehensive information on network TV advertising by national clients, showing product and parent company expenditures by dollar volume, time used, and networks and programs scheduled. The companion *BARcume Service* reports advertising activity in spot television on an individual market basis. The same organization also publishes a *BAR Network Radio Service,* and the *Radio Expenditure Reports* publication covers spot radio advertising.

Three trade associations—the Television Bureau of Advertising (TVB), the Radio Advertising Bureau (RAB), and the Cabletelevision Advertising Bureau (CAB)—also offer valuable information and assistance to advertisers and agencies that relates to the use of their respective media. A number of trade magazines also assist by covering current developments in the broadcasting and advertising

WDAF-TV

Ch. 4

Network Service: NBC.

Licensee: Taft Television & Radio Co. Inc., Signal Hill, Kansas City, MO 64108.

Studio: Signal Hill, Kansas City, MO 64108.

Telephone: 816-753-4567. **TWX:** 910-771-2047.

Technical Facilities: Channel No. 4 (66-72 MHz). Authorized power: 100-kw visual, 20-kw aural. Antenna: 1130-ft. above av. terrain, 1163-ft. above ground, 2049-ft. above sea level.

Latitude	39°	04'	20"
Longitude	94°	35'	45"

Transmitter: Signal Hill.

Multichannel TV Sound: Stereo only.

Satellite Earth Stations: Transmit/receive 2 Harris, 9.2-meter; Harris receivers.

AM Affiliate: WDAF, 5-kw, 610 kHz.

FM Affiliate: KYYS, 100-kw, 102.1 MHz (No. 271), 940-ft.

News Services: AP, UPI, NIWS.

Ownership: Taft Broadcasting Co., 100%. See Group Ownership of Television Stations.

Began Operation: October 16, 1949. Sale to present owner by Transcontinent Television Corp. approved Feb. 19, 1964 by FCC (**Television Digest,** Vol. 3:15, 16, 31; 4:8). Sale to Transcontinent by National-Missouri T.V. Inc. (wholly owned by National Theatres & Television Inc.) approved July 13, 1960 (Vol. 16:29). Sale to National Missouri TV Inc. by founding Kansas City Star in compliance with govt. anti-trust consent decree approved April 23, 1958 (Vol. 13:47, 48; 14:17).

Represented (sales): TeleRep Inc.

Represented (legal): Koteen & Naftalin.

Personnel:
EARL BEALL, vice president & general manager.
CHERYL KERNS, general sales manager.
MIKE McDONALD, news & broadcast operations manager.
BUD TURNER, teleport manager.
ED FULGINITI, program director.
CATHY SNYDER, national sales manager.
THERMAL STEWART, business manager.
JACK WINTER, chief engineer.

Highest 30 Sec. Rate: $5000.

NETWORK BASE HOURLY RATE: $1920.

City of License: Kansas City. **ADI:** Kansas City. **Rank:** 29.

Total Households: © MSI Consumer Market Data as of 1/1/87. TV Homes, TV% and Circulation © 1987 Arbitron. County coverage based on Arbitron study.

Net Weekly Circulation	State County	Total Households	TV Households Households	%
	KANSAS			
50% & Over	Anderson	3,400	3,300	97
	Atchison	6,500	6,400	98
	Brown	4,800	4,700	98
	Cloud	4,700	4,600	98
	Doniphan	3,400	3,300	97
	Douglas	25,600	25,200	98
	Franklin	8,900	8,800	99
	Geary	10,400	10,300	99
	Jefferson	5,800	5,700	98
	Johnson	116,400	115,800	99
	Leavenworth	18,600	18,400	99

WDAF-TV   BMPCT-6552 Granted 7/7/67   © American Map Corp., 14244

Net Weekly Circulation	State County	Total Households	TV Households Households	%
50% & Over	Linn	3,500	3,400	97
	Miami	8,300	8,200	99
	Wyandotte	63,600	63,000	99
	MISSOURI			
	Andrew	5,300	5,200	98
	Bates	6,100	6,000	98
	Buchanan	32,000	31,600	99
	Caldwell	3,200	3,200	100
	Carroll	4,600	4,500	98
	Cass	19,300	19,100	99
	Clay	53,000	52,600	99
	Clinton	6,000	5,900	98
	Daviess	3,400	3,300	97
	De Kalb	3,100	3,000	97
	Gentry	3,100	3,000	97
	Grundy	4,700	4,600	98
	Harrison	4,200	4,100	98
	Henry	7,900	7,800	99
	Holt	2,700	2,600	96
	Jackson	243,900	240,900	99
	Johnson	12,800	12,600	98
	Lafayette	11,400	11,300	99
	Linn	6,300	6,200	98
	Livingston	6,100	6,000	98
	Nodaway	7,800	7,700	99
	Pettis	13,800	13,500	98
	Platte	18,900	18,700	99
	Ray	8,100	8,000	99
	Saline	9,400	9,200	98
	Worth	1,100	1,100	100

(Continued on page A-633)

Station Totals	1,028,100	1,014,800	98
Net Weekly Circulation (1987)			779,800
Average Daily Circulation (1987)			462,700

Fig. 14.2. Typical station listing in *Television & Cable Factbook.* (Courtesy of Television Digest, Inc. Copyright American Map Corporation, New York, No. 18256-C)

Arbitron Rank/Pop (12+): 110/318,700

MSA Rank/Pop: 120/378,600
ADI # 67
Average Person Ratings: 16.3
Market TSL: 21.8 hours

Stations: 14/14
Diaries: 778/410:1/55.0%
Sample Target: 710
% Below Line: 0
% Not Listed: 7.9

1986 Revenue: $11,400,000
HH Inc.: $32,599
Retail $: 2.7 Bil
Pop per Station: 22,764
#1 Biller: WHO $3,400,000

12+ METRO	1/4/SHARE	FAL 86	SPG 86	FAL 85	SPG 85	4 Book Avg.	Birch Share	12+ TSA	1/4/CUME	12+ METRO CUME/ METRO CUME RATING		FAL 86	SPG 86
1. KGGO-F	103/19.8	20.7	18.2	17.2	18.0		25.4	1. KGGO-F	177/1756	1. KGGO-F	949/29.8	31.1	29.1
2. KLYF-F	55/10.6	7.5	5.4	6.3	7.5		9.5	2. WHO	150/2265	2. KRNQ-F	781/24.5	25.1	36.8
3. KRNQ-F	43/ 8.3	10.8	20.1	15.5	15.9		8.9	3. KLYF-F	134/1593	3. KLYF-F	677/21.2	18.1	14.7
KSO	43/ 8.3	10.2	9.7	12.3	12.9		7.4	4. KIOA	88/1162	4. WHO	620/19.5	24.8	19.6
WHO	43/ 8.3	10.2	8.3	13.3	12.3		8.5	5. KRNQ-F	85/1629	5. KDWZ-F	585/18.4	10.1	5.3
6. KIOA	37/ 7.1	5.4	4.5	5.1	4.8		5.5	6. KSO	73/ 968	6. KSO	563/17.7	21.0	18.5
7. KDWZ-F	36/ 6.9	3.7	2.0	2.2	2.3		6.8	7. KDWZ-F	46/ 766	7. KIOA	497/15.6	14.3	11.9
8. KJJY-F	27/ 5.2	5.4	5.8	3.1	3.6		5.3	8. KFMD-F	41/ 618	8. KRNT	469/14.7	15.1	14.2
9. KRNT	23/ 4.4	4.8	5.2	6.1	4.6		3.8	9. KEZT-F	32/ 426	9. KJJY-F	383/12.0	14.1	13.3
10. KMRY	22/ 4.2	3.9	6.0	4.5	4.2		3.0	10. KJJY-F	30/ 498	10. KFMD-F	291/ 9.1	11.5	8.1
11. KFMD-F	19/ 3.7	3.9	2.6	1.8	---		4.0	11. KRNT	26/ 538	11. KMRY	257/ 8.1	7.6	9.8
12. KEZT-F	15/ 2.9	1.5	2.4	1.2	2.1		.8	12. KMRY	22/ 266	12. KEZT-F	193/ 6.1	5.0	4.2

12+ FM SHARE (METRO): 62.84% (301 of 479) (SPG 86: 62.32%)

TEENS	18-34	18-49	25-49	25-54	35+	12+ AMD	12+ MID	12+ PMD	12+ EVE	SAT MID
1. KDWZ-F	1. KGGO-F>	1. KGGO-F>	1. KGGO-F	1. KGGO-F	1. WHO	1. KGGO-F	1. KGGO-F>	1. KGGO-F>	1. KGGO-F>	1. KGGO-F>
2. KGGO-F	2. KLYF-F	2. KLYF-F	2. KLYF-F	2. KSO	2. KSO	2. WHO	2. KLYF-F>	2. KLYF-F	2. WHO	2. KLYF-F
3. KRNQ-F	3. KRNQ-F	3. KIOA	3. KIOA >	3. KIOA	3. KIOA	3. KLYF-F	3. KIOA	3. KIOA	3. KRNQ-F	3. KIOA
4.	4. KDWZ-F	4. KRNQ-F	4. KSO	4. KSO >	4. KLYF-F	4. KSO >	4. KRNQ-F	4. KRNQ-F	4. KDWZ-F>	4. KRNQ-F
5.	5.	5. KSO	5. KRNQ-F	5.	5. KMRY	5.	5. KSO	5. KDWZ-F	5. KSO	5. KDWZ-F

WOM 18-24	WOM 18-34	WOM 25-34	WOM 18-49	WOM 25-54	MEN 18-24	MEN 18-34	MEN 25-34	MEN 18-49	MEN 25-54
1. KGGO-F>	1. KGGO-F>	1. KGGO-F	1. KGGO-F	1. KLYF-F>	1. KGGO-F>	1. KGGO-F>	1. KGGO-F>	1. KGGO-F>	1. KGGO-F
2. KDWZ-F	2. KLYF-F	2. KLYF-F	2. KLYF-F	2. KGGO-F	2.	2.	2. KLYF-F	2. KIOA	2. KIOA >
3. KRNQ-F	3. KDWZ-F	3. KRNQ-F	3. KRNQ-F	3. KSO	3.	3.	3.	3. KLYF-F>	3. KLYF-F
4. KLYF-F	KRNQ-F	4. KFMD-F	4. KDWZ-F	4. KRNQ-F	4.	4.	4.	4.	4. KSO >
5.	5.	5. KDWZ-F	5. KSO	5. KIOA	5.	5.	5.	5.	5. KJJY-F
		KJJY-F		KJJY-F					

FORMATS	AM	FM	TOTAL	%	SPG 86 %		OTHER RATED STATIONS/METRO SHARE & CUME RATING		
TOP 40/CHR/CONTEMP		79 (2)	79 (2)	16.5	22.0		KDMI-F	97.3 Des Moines	.6/3.4
AOR/CLASSIC		103 (1)	103 (1)	21.5	20.0		KWKY	1150 Des Moines	1.9/5.1
AC/OLDIES/SOFT ROCK	37 (1)	74 (2)	111 (3)	23.2	13.6				
MOR/VARIETY/FULL	23 (1)		23 (1)	4.8	5.7				
COUNTRY	43 (1)	27 (1)	70 (2)	14.6	19.1				
BLACK/URBAN									
BTFL MUSIC/EZ		15 (1)	15 (1)	3.1	2.6				
NEWS/TALK	43 (1)		43 (1)	9.0	9.0				
NOSTALGIA	22 (1)		22 (1)	4.6	6.5				
RELIGION/GOSPEL	13 (2)		13 (2)	2.7	1.4				
SPANISH									
CLASSICAL									
JAZZ/NEW AGE/ECLECTIC									
UNKNOWN/OTHERS									
			479 (14)						

FORMATS

RADIO STATIONS

KIOA,	949,	10 KW/5 KW (DA-2)	, AC	ABC-E,$ 40.00*	(Banner)	Midwest		Miles Knuteson
KMRY,	1390,	1 KW (DA-1)	, NOSTALGIA	ABC-D,$ 17.00*	(Mc-Guild)	Fuller-Jeffrey		J. Spangler
KRNT,	1350,	5 KW (DA-N)	, MOR	CBS,$ 31.00*	(Katz)	Stauffer		Don Tool
KSO,	1460,	5 KW (DA-N)	, COUNTRY	ABC-I,$ 44.00*	(Eastman)	Stoner		Bill Wells
WHO,	1040,	50 KW	, NEWS/VARIETY	NBC,$ 62.00*	(Christal)	Palmer		Steve Shannon
KDMI-F,	97.3,	115 KW @ 500,	RELIGION	MBS,$ 6.00	(---)			M. Bruinekool
KDWZ-F,	93.3,	100 KW @ 1063,	CHR	,$ 35.00*	(Banner)	Midwest		Miles Knuteson
KEZT-F,	104.1,	100 KW @ 1026,	BTFL/EZ	,$ 20.00*	(---)		(AMES)	Bob Bunce
KFMD-F,	103.3,	100 KW @ 745,	AC	MBS,$ 21.00*	(Masla)	Beasley	(PELLA)	Jim Gregori
KGGO-F,	94.9,	100 KW @ 1066,	AOR/CHR	Source,$ 64.00*	(Eastman)	Stoner		Bill Wells
KJJY-F,	106.3,	3 KW @ 300,	COUNTRY	,$ 30.00*	(Mc-Guild)	Fuller-Jeffrey	(ANKENY)	J. Spangler
KLYF-F,	100.3,	100 KW @ 1700,	SOFT AC	US 2,$ 40.00*	(Christal)	Palmer		Steve Shannon
KRNQ-F,	102.5,	100 KW @ 1248,	CHR	ABC-F,$ 40.00*	(Katz)	Stauffer		Don Tool

MISCELLANEOUS COMMENTS KDWZ changed from Country to CHR late in 1986... KEZT is now classified as BTFL/EZ...

American Radio Spring 1987, Copyright 1987

Fig. 14.3. Typical listing in *American Radio*. (Reprinted with permission from James H. Duncan, Jr., Duncan's American Radio, Inc., Indianapolis, Indiana)

industries. Such periodicals include *Advertising Age*, a weekly publication covering the entire field of advertising; *Broadcasting*, published weekly as a general news magazine about radio, TV, and cable; *CableVision*, a weekly magazine on cable industry matters; and *Television/Radio Age*, a biweekly publication that emphasizes in-depth articles on broadcast advertising.

Preliminary Client Analysis

Determining the needs of the advertiser is the first step in media buying. Before approaching the task of selecting availabilities, the time buyer must understand the client's situation through a careful analysis of marketing problems and goals; become familiar with the product, the types of establishments through which it is sold, the types of customers who buy the product or service, and the particulars of purchasing (such as time of day, day of the week, seasonal factors, and the frequency of purchase); and be fully aware of budget restrictions and length of the proposed campaign.

At any given time, some products are well established, perhaps even dominant in their fields, but others are engaged in fierce competition and still others are just being introduced into the market. Because the problems of these three types of advertisers differ, the media strategies for each must be tailored specifically to achieve their respective goals. The well-established product may require only a nominal level of reminder advertising to maintain brand awareness; the second type needs a heavier schedule of commercial messages to compete successfully. The client launching a new product often demands a very intensive campaign involving the use of many stations or networks to achieve a saturation level of exposure.

Among the basic scheduling options available to broadcast advertisers are

1. Broad reach—exposure of a client's commercials to a broad, heterogeneous mass audience.
2. Narrow reach—exposure focused on a narrow, specialized target audience, such as 18- to 34-year-old homemakers or metropolitan-area high school students.
3. Low frequency—a low level of repetition of advertising messages. This approach entails 100 or fewer GRPs per week and is useful for reminder or maintenance advertising.
4. High frequency—a high level of message repetition—up to 200 or more weekly GRPs. This approach is more suitable for advertisers engaged in heavy competition.
5. Saturation advertising—a technique that incorporates both broad reach and high frequency to saturate listening and viewing audiences with product messages. This strategy is used to launch new products or to promote special sales.

Attention also centers on the value of *continuity scheduling*, as opposed to *flighting, blinking,* or *pulsing*. With a continuity plan, there is continuous advertising weight throughout a selling season. When continuous periods of advertising (usually a minimum of three weeks) are interrupted by periods of no advertising, the scheduled procedure is known as flighting.

Blinking is a regular and repetitious pattern of advertising followed by no advertising, but it is done on a week-in/week-out basis (or, occasionally, on a two-week-in/two-week-out basis). Pulsing is a modification of blinking; instead of complete withdrawal from advertising during certain periods, the advertiser uses a lower, "sustaining" level of messages so the company name is kept before the public. Unfortunately, no research to date has established any ideal frequency levels (ones that consistently provide a maximum amount of effective advertising impact).[1]

Once familiar with a product and its marketing needs, the time buyer proceeds to plan the most appropriate type of broadcast schedule. In radio, for example, unlike TV, since there are often dozens of different stations to choose from in a given market, some advertisers try a procedure known as *roadblocking*. They use at least two (highly rated) stations in the same quarter hour, in an attempt to maximize audience size.

Built into most radio buying systems today is the "seven-day-interval" assumption. If a station being considered by an advertiser has not reached a target audience group at least once in a week's time (as demonstrated by demographic ratings), it is assumed that the station will not reach that audience (at least not often enough to make the station a profitable buy).

A basic decision for national advertisers is the choice between network and national spot advertising; when the latter is selected, markets must be chosen and stations selected in each of the markets used. Local advertisers, of course, need choose only from stations serving their own areas.

Selecting the Network Schedule

Network broadcasting is undoubtedly the most efficient means of communicating advertising messages to the American public. Both TV and radio networks provide excellent technical control of commercial material as well as simultaneous national coverage with a minimum of administrative detail. Before purchasing a network schedule, however, time buyers must remember that, although all three national networks are roughly equal in number of affiliated stations, some variation is present in the strength of station rosters. There are numerous markets with only one or two VHF outlets; in those markets one or two of the national networks must affiliate with less desirable UHF stations. For this reason, each of the major broadcast networks is relatively weak in some markets. Program popularity notwithstanding, however, the three major networks now compare favorably with each other in the caliber of their affiliates. In contrast, the still-developing Fox Network is composed mainly of UHF stations.

The numerous cable networks also vary widely in coverage of the U.S. television public. A principal advantage lies in their appeal to specialized target audiences across the land—audiences that can be reached easily and conveniently on a network basis. The potential audience for even the highest ranking cable networks, of course, is limited to the nation's cable-wired households, which represent slightly more than half of all U.S. TV homes.

In radio, recall from Chapter 2 that the number of stations affiliated with networks varies considerably, reflecting the presence or absence of a number of high-power stations in the lineup. As a result, radio networks cannot provide uniform national coverage to the same extent that TV networks do. Radio networks also differ in their mixture of AM and FM stations, as well as in formats and demographic orientations of listeners. Their audience reach also varies widely, from 500,000 to more than 3,000,000 listeners during an average quarter-hour.

NETWORK AVAILABILITIES

The use of TV and radio networks as advertising vehicles requires careful examination of a number of factors to assure a schedule compatible with advertiser needs. Such considerations include sponsorship patterns, audience composition and program types, rates, and time periods.

Sponsorship Patterns

The overwhelming proportion of network advertising campaigns today involves the use of spot messages; clients generally place schedules in several different programs to attain broad reach and/or high frequency. For television the basic unit is the 30-second spot, although the 15-second form has become quite common. With their lower rate structures, cable networks frequently sell 60-second positions as well as 30-second ones and will accommodate advertisers who wish to run 2-minute or even longer messages. Network radio commercials usually are 30 seconds or 60 seconds. And, although network advertising is mainly of the announcement variety, it is still possible to sponsor individual programs.

Audience Composition and Program Types

In television buying, program audience characteristics are of prime importance, but in network radio (where programming largely takes the form of newscasts), time of day is a main concern, because audience characteristics vary with dayparts. The major program blocks and audience characteristics shown in Table 14.1 are basic elements of network TV schedules.

Table 14.1. Network program periods

Block	Programming	Predominant Audience
Primetime (evening)	Mass-appeal entertainment	Heterogeneous family audience, usually including more adult woman than men
Early evening	News	Adults
Daytime	Serial dramas, game shows	Homemakers
Early morning	News, talk	Adults
Late night	Talk, variety, movies	Young adults
Saturday daytime	Cartoons, dramas	Children and teenagers
Weekend sports	Sports	Adult males

An audience composed entirely of a client's prospective customers would be ideal. Except for universally sold products, however, such availabilities do not exist because audiences are mixtures of both sexes and various age classifications. It is possible, however, to secure availabilities in which there are large concentrations of viewers or listeners of desired characteristics. For example, weekend sports broadcasts reach audiences composed largely of adult men, and daytime serial dramas and game shows efficiently reach homemakers. Advertisers usually must tolerate a higher cost per thousand to reach selective target audiences than they do when communicating to more heterogeneous groups.

Network advertisers also are concerned with the viewing environment in which their messages are shown. Some (such as Kraft and Kodak) avoid participating in shows containing excessive violence, because they feel the atmosphere may be incompatible with both their corporate images and their commercial messages.

After a network schedule has begun, media buyers follow the progress of programs they have purchased through, among other things, ratings performance. Complacency with a good network schedule can prove disastrous because of the frequent shifting of audience loyalties from program to program.

Network Rates

The price of network advertising reflects a combination of factors, including the size of the audience attracted at any given time, the demographic composition of the audience, the amount of commercial time available to be sold, the demand for network time by advertisers, and the prevailing cost per thousand (CPM).

CPM, the price an advertiser must pay to reach 1,000 households, is the overriding factor in the pricing of time slots. The networks can command a high CPM during periods of heavy demand when available time is scarce; when demand is light, however, advertisers generally succeed in bargaining for lower rates. During the 1988-89 season, the cost per thousand obtained by the three networks ranged from $6 to $10 for 30-second spot messages aired during their evening primetime schedules. Daytime CPM's for the same season ranged from $2 to $4. CPMs obviously vary with time of day, reflecting the number of viewers who may be reached per set during various dayparts.

On a long-term basis, the trend has been toward higher TV ad rates and, occasionally, higher CPMs. With greater opportunities for advertisers to place schedules of TV commercials on cable networks, new broadcast networks, barter syndication, stronger independent stations, and even public TV outlets, the rate of increase for network advertising has been slowed during recent years.

The formula media buyers use for estimating network or station rates for 30-second commercials is

$$\text{Rate} = \text{CPM (1/2 minute)} \times \text{Number of viewing households (in thousands)}$$

Suppose an advertiser wishes to place a 30-second spot on a network program that, according to audience studies, reaches 15,000,000 households per week. Also assume that the prevailing CPM for primetime network advertising is $8 per half-minute. Plugging these data into the formula, we see that the estimated price should be about $120,000:

$$\text{Rate} = \$8 \times 15,000$$
$$\text{Rate} = \$120,000$$

We must remember, however, that the rate actually agreed upon by the network and the sponsor might be higher or lower than the average CPM dictates, depending upon the demand for time on a particular program. With a CPM range of $6 to $10, as it existed in 1988-89, a spot for the previous example should cost somewhere between $90,000 and $150,000. Certain shows with exceedingly high advertiser demand, such as "The Cosby Show," exceeded this range by a wide margin in 1988-89, and other programs of lesser appeal commanded prices as low as $40,000 per 30-second spot during the same season. The highest priced network spots usually are found on major sports events, such as the World Series or the Super Bowl, where prices for 30-second spots sometimes reach as much as $500,000.

As Table 14.2 indicates, today's media buyers can expect to pay rates ranging from $64,000 to $180,000 for 30-second spots on most network primetime shows. Exceptional programs may cost as much as $325,000 or more.

Naturally, however, not all commercial positions are valued so highly. Daytime network commercials range from $5,000 to $30,000, reflecting the smaller number of households and persons

Table 14.2. Estimated network TV primetime 30-second spot rates

Program Rating	Households[a] (thousands)	$6 CPM	$8 CPM	$10 CPM	$12 CPM
12	10,800	$64,800	$86,400	$108,000	$129,600
15	13,500	81,000	108,000	135,000	162,000
20	18,000	108,000	144,000	180,000	216,000
25	22,500	135,000	180,000	225,000	270,000
30	27,000	162,000	216,000	270,000	324,000

[a]Household estimates are based on the assumption that one national rating point equals approximately 900,000 television households. As this number increases, the cost per commercial message may be expected to rise, even if the CPM remains constant.

reached, as well as lower CPMs. Thirty-second spots during other network program blocks usually are priced within these ranges:

Evening news	$10,000 to $ 50,000
Saturday morning cartoons	$ 5,000 to $ 28,000
Early morning programs (weekdays)	$ 5,000 to $ 13,000
Late night programs	$ 9,000 to $ 35,000
Weekend sports	$ 9,000 to $200,000

Seasonal influences also affect the cost of network and other forms of television advertising. Peak demand for TV time occurs during the fourth quarter; consequently, network rates are highest during that period. The next highest rates are found in the second quarter, followed by the first and third quarters. Interestingly, the viewing audience is at its peak during the first quarter, when advertising demand falls off.

The pricing of commercial spot messages on cable networks follows a pattern similar to broadcast TV. The prices fluctuate with the ratings and with supply-and-demand. In early 1988, *Adweek* estimated ranges for 30-second spots for several of the major cable networks (see Table 14.3).[2]

Table 14.3. Cable network advertising rates, 1989

Cable Network	Spot Cost Range		
Cable News Network	$ 470	to	$ 5,900
ESPN	1,500	to	6,000
Lifetime	200	to	2,000
Music TV	2,000	to	8,000
Nashville Network	250	to	5,000
Univision (Spanish)	800	to	11,000
USA Network	500	to	5,500
TBS (WTBS Superstation)	250	to	9,200

Source: *Adweek's Marketer's Guide to Media.*

As an alternative to network TV, many national advertisers now choose to place commercials in nationally or regionally syndicated programs. Both prices and CPMs tend to be somewhat lower than on network TV, but advertisers must be aware of coverage limitations when following the syndication strategy. In 1988, typical prices for 30-second spots in barter syndicated shows ranged from $30,000 to $60,000 for primetime airing. During other dayparts, prices ranged from a mere $2,500 to $12,000.

Radio advertising time charges, as expected, are much lower than those for TV. Rates on national radio networks range from $500 to about $5,000 per 30-second spot, depending on the network, number of affiliated stations, and time of day. Highest rates generally prevail during morning hours. *Adweek* quoted 1988 spot rates for CBS Radio at $4,000 for morning time, $2,000 for 10 A.M. to 7 P.M., and $500 for time after 7 P.M. ABC's Information and Entertainment Networks charged $3,000 per spot on a run-of-schedule (ROS) basis.[3]

When to Buy

An important question facing time buyers contemplating the use of networks is "When is the best time to buy?" Some advertisers make commitments for schedules far in advance (for example, during the spring quarter for a fall showing). Such up-front buyers normally find more favorable rates than do those who hold off until availabilities are scarce. Advertisers who wait until dates close to desired air times do so in the hope that networks will have unsold time available at distressed-merchandise prices. The latter strategy sometimes pays off during periods of light demand.

Selecting the Broadcast Market

The most attractive feature of national spot advertising is the geographic selectivity it affords. Advertisers may choose specific markets for a variety of reasons:

1. To fit a product distribution pattern.
2. To achieve a desired level of national saturation (by purchasing schedules, for example, in the top-25, top-50, or top-100 markets).
3. To supplement network advertising in markets where additional media support is needed.
4. To supplement network advertising in markets where weak affiliates are located.
5. To test advertising strategies on a small scale before launching a more extensive campaign.

IMPORTANCE OF MARKET RANK

Many national spot advertisers, particularly those with limited budgets, choose to advertise in a small number of high-potential markets. For this reason, stations located in highly ranked broadcast markets are best situated to attract national advertising clients. The rank of a station within its market, of course, also is important. ADI and DMA household rankings become very important in this context, because a considerable number of media plans cut off automatically at such predesignated points as the 10th, 25th, 50th, or 100th ranked market. The largest U.S. markets, which contain about 31 percent of the nation's households, receive about 44 percent of the total national/regional spot advertising dollars, according to John Blair & Company data.

In some instances, stations may increase their national spot advertising billings by stressing qualitative factors related to their market's rank. For example, if a market just outside the top 25 is ranked higher than 25th, say 20th, in the category of automobile sales, the stations there could develop a strong rationale to attract automotive accounts. Data on market rankings in several meaningful categories may be found in *Standard Rate and Data Service* (SRDS) (Television) and other reference sources. When these rankings result in a positive profile for a market, stations should utilize them in national sales efforts.

A sample ADI market profile is shown in Table 14.4.

Table 14.4. ADI market profile for Centerville, USA

Category	National ADI Rank	Deviation from Base Rank
TV households (base rank)	26	NA
Gross household income	24	+2
Total retail sales	25	+1
Food sales	25	+1
Drug sales	22	+3
Automotive sales	20	+6

TEST MARKETS

Test marketing activities allow for the detection of flaws in marketing and media strategies through the placement of test schedules in a small number of markets before full-scale national campaigns get under way. Good test areas are normally

1. Markets of moderate size and, consequently, moderate cost.
2. Markets that are typical of the nation or of a region in such characteristics as age, income, and racial mix.

3. Markets in which media characteristics parallel the national media structure. Markets with three TV stations, all roughly equal in coverage and circulation, are preferred; markets penetrated by outside stations are usually avoided.

4. Markets in which economic characteristics resemble national patterns and averages. Preferred cities have diversified industry, little tourism, and no seasonal employment patterns and should not be producers of the product under test or its competitors.

5. Markets in which retail distribution outlets resemble national patterns. The proportion of retail sales achieved by chain stores should be typical of the United States.

6. Markets with good past experience as test communities, but ones that have not been overused.

Although dozens of moderate-size cities have been used for testing, popular test markets include Atlanta; Columbus, Ohio; Denver; Fort Wayne, Indiana; Hartford; Kansas City; Peoria, Illinois; Phoenix; Rochester; and Syracuse.

Selecting Specific Stations

Selecting a station or stations to carry an advertiser's campaign is much more complicated than purchasing network time, because of the large number of outlets that must be evaluated. Whether a time buyer is dealing with a national or a local client, a set of interrelated factors must be analyzed in terms of the advertiser's particular goals and requirements. Relying on experience and judgment, the media buyer must choose stations that offer the most suitable combination of coverage, circulation, audience reach, programming, cost, availabilities, and services. And, even with the assistance of modern computers, human judgment remains vitally important; no single mathematical formula is appropriate for all advertisers. The following sections will explore critical factors in station evaluation.

COVERAGE

Coverage patterns between stations transmitting from the same city often vary considerably. VHF stations ordinarily cover large geographical areas, but reception areas for UHF stations usually are smaller. Radio station coverage may vary from a few miles to several hundred in all directions. Careful analysis of coverage is important in arriving at a selection of media outlets that match advertisers' marketing areas. Those whose clientele are concentrated in limited parts of a market may incur waste coverage and unnecessary expense when they use large coverage stations; on the other hand, the use of a large station may be indispensable to a small advertiser if it attracts a defined audience better than other stations.

CIRCULATION

Time buyers must also analyze the circulation, or total audience reach, of competing stations, so as to schedule clients' messages on the most compatible outlets. The two principal concerns with respect to circulation are the number of regular listeners or viewers, which establishes an index for comparing stations, and the extent of audience penetration into various counties within an ADI or DMA broadcast market. Figure 14.4 reproduces a station promotion piece that makes such a comparison.

AUDIENCE

Audience ratings play a significant role in time buying, helping media specialists gain knowledge of both size and types of audiences reached by competing stations. Station audience studies, covering metro areas and total broadcast markets (ADIs and DMAs), are available from one to eight rating periods per year, depending on the size and importance of the market.

COST

Another factor involved in the evaluation of stations is the cost of time. It is the buyer's job to develop a schedule that incorporates both appropriate geographic coverage and adequate reach and frequency of the target audience—within a given budget allocation.

RESEARCH

WSOC-TV P.O. Box 34665 / Charlotte, NC 28234 / Phone: (704) 335-4999

CHARLOTTE ADI
NET WEEKLY CIRCULATION
BY STATION - BY COUNTY

WATAUGA
WSOC 56%
WBTV 75
WCCB 30
WPCQ 4

CALDWELL
WSOC 72%
WBTV 93
WCCB 51
WPCQ 40

ALEXANDER
WSOC 75%
WBTV 99
WPCQ 46
WCCB 43

IREDELL
WSOC 83%
WBTV 92
WCCB 60
WPCQ 45

BURKE
WSOC 67%
WBTV 95
WCCB 36
WPCQ 17

CATAWBA
WSOC 87%
WBTV 98
WPCQ 58
WCCB 54

ROWAN
WSOC 85%
WBTV 80
WCCB 51
WPCQ 48

LINCOLN
WSOC 85%
WBTV 99
WPCQ 71
WCCB 54

CABARRUS
WSOC 93%
WBTV 89
WPCQ 81
WCCB 59

STANLY
WSOC 95%
WBTV 81
WPCQ 65
WCCB 46

CLEVELAND
WSOC 73%
WBTV 92
WCCB 41
WPCQ 33

GASTON
WSOC 83%
WBTV 94
WPCQ 72
WCCB 60

MECKLENBURG
WSOC 93%
WBTV 91
WPCQ 85
WCCB 61

RICHMOND
WSOC 88%
WCCB 46
WBTV 37
WPCQ 20

YORK
WSOC 87%
WBTV 88
WPCQ 65
WCCB 60

UNION
WSOC 95%
WBTV 93
WPCQ 83
WCCB 63

ANSON
WSOC 98%
WPCQ 84
WBTV 70
WCCB 68

CHESTER
WSOC 84%
WBTV 93
WCCB 49
WPCQ 40

LANCASTER
WSOC 86%
WBTV 74
WCCB 60
WPCQ 50

CHESTERFIELD
WSOC 70%
WCCB 43
WPCQ 37
WBTV 26

Net Weekly Circulation — % of homes who view station at least once per week

Source — 1987 ARBITRON Coverage Study

Fig. 14.4. Station sales promotion piece using net weekly circulation data. (Courtesy of WSOC-TV, Charlotte, N.C.)

Monetary constraints force time buyers to study competing rates and cost efficiencies reflected in CPM and CPP computations. Low rates, as desirable as they may appear, do not necessarily equate with efficiency. The best buy may well be the station whose rates are highest but whose waste circulation is very low. Also, care must be exercised when comparing cost-per-thousand data. If a station offers a low CPM but reaches a very small audience, its use may not be worth the administrative costs involved. Table 14.5 presents a table of comparative cost and circulation data for television and radio stations in a typical city.

Table 14.5. Broadcast media comparison market: Hometown, USA

Television Stations

Station	Channel	Network	Base Hourly Rate	Highest 30-Second Spot Rate	Net Weekly Circulation	Average Daily Circulation	Sign On/Sign Off Average Share
WAAA-TV	2	ABC	$2000	$ 950	820,000	460,000	21
WCCC-TV	10	CBS	2200	900	860,000	545,000	24
WNNN-TV	6	NBC	2400	1100	890,200	600,400	30
WIII-TV	13	Independent	1400	600	596,000	310,600	10

Principal Radio Stations

Station	Format	Network	Power (watts)	Average Quarter-Hour Share	Persons per Average Quarter Hour	Cume Rating
WAOR (FM)	Album rock	Source (NBC)	100,000	15.9	23,100	26.2
WSRK (FM)	Soft rock	Radio-Radio	100,000	12.1	17,500	27.8
WTEM (FM)	Contemporary	ABC-C	100,000	10.2	14,800	24.6
WNUS	News-talk	CBS	50,000	8.2	12,000	31.3
WEZL (FM)	Easy listening	...	100,000	7.6	11,000	21.0
WCWW	Country	MBS	5,000	6.8	9,900	18.2
WBLK	Ethnic	Sheridan	5,000	6.2	9,000	15.3

AVAILABILITIES

Time avails may be thought of as unsold periods available for purchase by advertisers. On local stations they include openings for both spot announcements and program sponsorships; positions for spot messages occur both within programs and during station breaks between shows. Good avails are often scarce, with those on better stations and those within or adjacent to the strongest shows selling out first. Because availabilities usually are quoted subject to prior sale, media buyers must analyze them promptly and, when desirable ones are found, act quickly to secure them for clients.

STATION FACILITIES, SERVICES, AND POLICIES

Although problems involving production facilities are rare, the time buyer needs to be sure that every station used has adequate facilities to handle each client's production requirements. This matter becomes especially critical when programs or commercials require remote broadcast origination, special effects, or new modes of sound or picture reproduction. During the past decade, for example, many advertisers switched from filmed to videotaped commercials using cartridge VTR units. Until all stations became equipped for cartridge videotape reproduction, time buyers had to determine which stations had the new capability.

They must also be aware of station services to which clients are entitled. Program sponsors, for example, usually receive periodic on-air promotion spots, as well as occasional newspaper advertisements that help establish and maintain audiences. Merchandising services for client advertisers may include direct mailings to dealers and point-of-purchase displays to remind shoppers of products currently being advertised. Through such efforts, many stations assist their clients in obtaining maximum results from broadcast advertising. However, merchandising services, which are usually billable to advertisers at cost, do not substitute for the basic service of effective audience exposure.

Before a time buyer purchases a schedule, he or she should also check station policies. Some stations impose stringent restrictions and others are very lenient. Advertisers of personal products and alcoholic beverages, particularly, need to determine in advance whether their commercials are acceptable to a given station and under what conditions.

Other common policy matters include copy length, delivery of program and commercial material, product protection, maximum length of contracts, discounts, cancellations and preemptions, and production services. Details of station policies are included in the *SRDS Spot Television* and *Spot Radio* directories, along with information on facilities and station services.

INTANGIBLE FACTORS

The media buyer should remain alert to clues of an intangible nature that may prove invaluable in analyzing television and radio stations. These intuitive factors, gained mainly through experience and observation, relate to station image.

Media buyers can assist their clients immeasurably if they have answers to these questions:

1. Does a station enjoy a good reputation and high credibility among the general population of its service area?
2. Is a station used consistently by leading local and national advertisers?
3. What is the extent of a station's commercial load? Stations that permit excessive advertising risk becoming ineffective media through commercial clutter, but stations that carry few commercials may also be ineffective outlets. As a rule of thumb, stations that maintain reasonable commercial limits (such as those recommended by the NAB Codes) and that customarily sell out most of their availabilities usually can be relied on as effective advertising vehicles.
4. What is a station's reputation for the handling of advertising campaigns? Stations that rarely require *make goods* (a later scheduling of a commercial that was missed or defectively presented at its scheduled time), that handle commercial materials well from a technical standpoint, and seldom have billing errors tend to be used more often than stations where problems in these areas persist.
5. What has past personal experience with a station revealed in terms of sales results? Media buyers, like consumers in general, tend to continue doing business with organizations they like.

Television and Radio Station Rates

Although broadcast stations are licensed by the federal government through the FCC, their advertising rates, with one exception (political), are not controlled by regulation.[4] TV and radio stations differ in this important way from common carriers and other regulated industries.

Commercial time rates are set by individual stations and are based on similar factors to those that determine network charges (audience size and demographic composition, the supply and demand for availabilities, prevailing CPMs, etc.). Rate structures also vary from market to market, depending on the size of potential audiences and such market characteristics as effective buying power, total retail sales, and per-capita income. For example, the highest published 30-second spot rates on television stations range from about $30 on small independent stations to more than $10,000 for major New York City outlets. (Thirty-second spots remain the basic unit of sale, but 15-second TV ads now account for a substantial percentage of all time sold.)

The time charges for 60-second radio commercials range from as low as $1 at some small-town stations to $500 or more on major stations in New York and Los Angeles. Approximate highest 60-second radio spots in a few other selected markets include Asheville, North Carolina, $50; Atlanta, $200; Boston, $350; Chicago, $300; Detroit, $230; Houston, $240; Knoxville, $100; Milwaukee, $130; Philadelphia, $325; and Phoenix, $200. Rates differ widely among stations within any given market because of competitive situations and the status of supply and demand.[5]

Another way to look at rates is according to average cost per rating point. One TV primetime rating point in the New York market is valued at around $750, compared with a value of around $50 in the 50th market. In general, spot TV advertisers buying primetime on network affiliates across the country would pay twice as much per household rating point in the top-10 markets as they would in markets 11 through 20. (Recall that one rating point is equal to 1 percent of all TV households in the measurement area.) Markets 21 through 30 cost an average of one-third as much as the top 10, and markets 31 through 50 average one-fifth as much.

RATE CARD INFORMATION

Station rate cards may be obtained from account executives of individual stations or from SRDS directories. Base rates for radio stations are given in *American Radio*, and those for some TV stations are given in *Television and Cable Factbook*. Figures for estimating rates in various markets utilizing cost-per-point projections may be found in *Adweek*'s *Marketer's Guide to Media*.

Station rate cards normally include the prices of every type of availability offered by a station. They also include package plans, preemptions, frequency discounts, and information on station facilities, services, and policies. Some stations maintain two rate cards—one for national advertisers and a second for local firms—on the theory that local advertisers cannot derive benefits from reaching an audience throughout the coverage area of a large station.

A problem confronting most time buyers is the lack of standardization of rate cards within the broadcasting industry. Furthermore, many rate cards are complicated to interpret and may change as often as every month. And as we noted earlier, listed rates may be only starting points for negotiations.

BASE RATES

Although discount policies differ from station to station, the rates of competing stations may be compared rather easily through their base rates, which are one-time, undiscounted rates. For TV stations, the highest one-time, one-hour rate and the highest 30-second spot rate may be used. Radio stations usually are compared in terms of their highest one-minute spot rates.

TYPES OF RATE STRUCTURES

Two types of rate cards are prevalent among broadcast stations: the traditional class type structure and the grid or graded rate card. The *class card,* generally used by radio stations, divides a station's time into large blocks or classes during which it is assumed that audience size remains fairly constant. Therefore, all availabilities of like duration (30-second spots, for instance) falling within a class of time are priced equally. Radio stations typically show three or more classes of time, which they usually designate as Class AAA, Class AA, and Class A (or Class A, Class B, and Class C). The higher the classification alphabetically, the more expensive the time. Morning and afternoon drive times normally carry the highest classification, the midday period between commuting hours comes next, and the evening hours are placed in the lowest-priced category.

Most station rates are subject to frequency discounts with the price per message declining as an advertiser buys an increasing quantity of commercial units. For example, assume that during drive-time hours (roughly from 7 to 9 A.M. and 4 to 6 P.M., Monday through Friday) the base rate of a 60-second commercial is $50. An advertiser who contracts for a number of commercials during a week, month, or year will be charged a lower unit rate because of the earned-frequency discount. Such discounts normally occur in stages, such as with the use of 6 spots, 12, 18, 24, 52, 104, 1,000, etc.

Many radio stations offer other popular discount plans, too, each of which is based on the concept of frequency discounting. These include the *run-of-schedule* (ROS) arrangement, which places a client's ads throughout a station's day or week on a best-available-time basis, and the *total audience plan* (TAP), which places a portion of an advertiser's messages in each time class, thereby providing advertising exposure to the station's total audience. From the station's standpoint, such plans help fill less desirable time classes, while permitting advertisers to gain entry into the most desirable ones.

An example of a radio class rate card is shown in Figure 14.5 (KRVN, Lexington, Nebraska). KRVN, a farm-oriented station, divides its spot announcement rates into three classes: AAA (7 A.M. to 2 P.M.), AA (early morning and 2 P.M. to 8 P.M.), and A (8 P.M. to 6 A.M.). Frequency discounts apply to all classes of time, both for spot announcements and sponsored programs. (For example, during AAA time, the 30-second fixed rate is discounted from $18 to $13 for the advertiser who uses 312 announcements within a calendar year.)

The rate card for WMSI(FM)/WJDX, Jackson, Mississippi, shown in Figure 14.6, typifies a modified grid/class rate card. Classes of time are indicated as AAAA, AAA, AA, and A, with five grid levels shown for each class. For example, any and all 30- or 60-second spot availabilities within AAAA

TIME CLASSIFICATIONS
Class "AAA" 7 a.m.-2 p.m.
Class "AA" 6-7 a.m., 2-8 p.m.
Class "A" 8 p.m.-6 a.m.

RETAIL RATE CARD

30 Second Announcements

	1	104	156	260	312
AAA Fixed	18.00	16.00	15.00	14.00	13.00
AAA AA BTA or Fixed	15.00	13.00	12.00	11.00	10.00
AA A BTA or Fixed	12.00	10.00	9.00	8.50	8.00
A BTA	9.00	7.00	6.00	5.50	5.00

Fig. 14.5. Class rate card, KRVN Radio. (Courtesy of KRVN, Lexington, Nebr.)

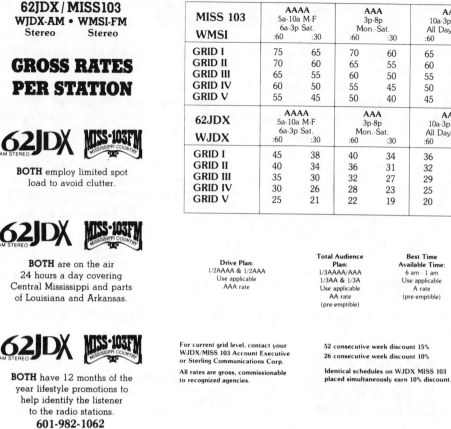

62JDX / MISS103
WJDX-AM • WMSI-FM
Stereo   Stereo

GROSS RATES PER STATION

62JDX **MISS·103FM**
AM STEREO   MISSISSIPPI COUNTRY

BOTH employ limited spot
load to avoid clutter.

62JDX **MISS·103FM**
AM STEREO   MISSISSIPPI COUNTRY

BOTH are on the air
24 hours a day covering
Central Mississippi and parts
of Louisiana and Arkansas.

62JDX **MISS·103FM**
AM STEREO   MISSISSIPPI COUNTRY

BOTH have 12 months of the
year lifestyle promotions to
help identify the listener
to the radio stations.
601-982-1062

MISS 103 WMSI	AAAA 5a-10a M-F 6a-3p Sat. :60	:30	AAA 3p-8p Mon.-Sat. :60	:30	AA 10a-3p M-F All Day Sun. :60	:30	A 8p-1a Mon.-Sun. :60	:30
GRID I	75	65	70	60	65	55	60	50
GRID II	70	60	65	55	60	50	55	45
GRID III	65	55	60	50	55	45	50	40
GRID IV	60	50	55	45	50	40	45	35
GRID V	55	45	50	40	45	35	40	30

62JDX WJDX	AAAA 5a-10a M-F 6a-3p Sat. :60	:30	AAA 3p-8p Mon.-Sat. :60	:30	AA 10a-3p M-F All Day Sun. :60	:30	A 8p-1a Mon.-Sun. :60	:30
GRID I	45	38	40	34	36	31	32	27
GRID II	40	34	36	31	32	28	28	24
GRID III	35	30	32	27	29	24	25	21
GRID IV	30	26	28	23	25	21	22	18
GRID V	25	21	22	19	20	17	18	15

Drive Plan:
1/2AAAA & 1/2AAA
Use applicable
AAA rate

Total Audience Plan:
1/3AAAA/AAA
1/3AA & 1/3A
Use applicable
AA rate
(pre-emptible)

Best Time Available Time:
6 am - 1 am
Use applicable
A rate
(pre-emptible)

Class B:
1 am - 5 am
Mon.-Sun.
.60   .30
$10 $8

For current grid level, contact your
WJDX/MISS 103 Account Executive
or Sterling Communications Corp.

All rates are gross, commissionable
to recognized agencies.

52 consecutive week discount 15%

26 consecutive week discount 10%

Identical schedules on WJDX, MISS 103
placed simultaneously earn 10% discount.

Rates for special packages, and
special program (news, weather,
farm reports, air traffic remotes)
are available on request.

Fig. 14.6. Modified grid/class radio rate card. (Courtesy of Sterling Communications, WJDX/WMSI-FM, Jackson, Miss.)

time are priced at the same grid-level rate while that pricing level is in effect. The five different grid levels allow for variable pricing depending on supply and demand factors, during different seasons and for special events broadcasts.

The grid rate card, widely used by TV stations, prices each availability separately, reflecting the size of the audience normally viewing at each specific time period. Stations using the grid or floating rate system recognize that viewing levels differ noticeably from hour to hour and day to day. For example, because of the variation in program popularity, a station may reach more viewers than any of its competitors at 8 o'clock on Monday evening, but rank as a poor third at the same time the following night. The grid method permits stations to price their availabilities competitively with respect to cost per thousand, regardless of audience size.

Grid cards are revised frequently, generally after each major audience measurement study and on a seasonal basis to take into account variations in viewing levels. Also, TV stations sometimes offer advertisers a choice of fixed position and preemptible rates with the grid structure. Clients who wish to protect their use of certain availabilities pay a somewhat higher rate than those willing to accept the risk of being *bumped* (preempted) from an availability and rescheduled later. Some stations offer as many as three preemption plans—such as three weeks preemptible (preemptible only if the client is given three weeks notice), two weeks preemptible, and one week preemptible—in addition to the *fixed position* (nonpreemptible) rate.

The pricing scheme is such that the shorter the term of protection (freedom from preemptibility), the lower the rate becomes. An advertiser who wants a sale announcement aired at an exact time, or one who is interested in catching a specific audience right before a holiday or special event, is not apt to take the cheapest option; if such spots are preempted, their communication value may be lost entirely (because a later airing would miss the sale or holiday).

Stations in large markets generally have discontinued preempting openly for higher rates because the disadvantages outweigh the advantages. When a preemption occurs, a chain of events takes place. The preempted advertiser must be notified, and a make-good must be found; usually the buyer insists on a substitute position of comparable audience value. A large number of preemptions causes great confusion to all concerned—agency, rep, station, and traffic department—and the gains are mostly illusory. Sometimes invoices become so entangled and difficult to reconcile that payment to the station is held up. Furthermore, heavy preemption creates a bad reputation for the station among buyers. A station that "runs clean" is respected and often is given the edge in a buy, all other factors being equal.

A portion of a television grid rate card for WIS-TV, Columbia, South Carolina, is shown in Figure 14.7. Differences in spot announcement rates appear within each of the evenings shown, and they reflect differing viewership levels throughout the week. Note that the prices for 30-second spots on grid level one (nonpreemptible) range from $1,200 to $4,000 depending upon the ratings of various programs during the week.

RELATIONSHIPS BETWEEN RATES

As a rule, television stations start with 30-second rates and then charge double for 60 seconds. For shorter commercials, TV stations usually charge 80 percent of the 30-second rate for 15-second spots and 70 percent of the 30-second rate for 10-second ads. As noted earlier, the 60-second commercial is much more popular on radio than it is on TV. Thus, radio stations generally establish 60-second rates and then price 30-second spots at 80 percent of those figures. All of these computations are shown in these examples:

	Radio	TV
60 seconds	$200	$2,000
30 seconds	160	1,000
15 seconds	80	800
10 seconds	80	700

The Station Sales Effort

Although most of this chapter has dealt with the role of the time buyer, salespersons representing the media also play a significant role in scheduling successful advertising campaigns. Now, let's focus on the organization and function of the sales department in a broadcast station and trace the steps involved in putting a client's schedule on the air.

During the past quarter century, time selling has evolved into a sophisticated business. As broadcast advertising has grown in importance, so has the demand for a higher grade of management and better informed, more productive salespeople. The sales department of a TV or radio station solicits and services the advertisers who wish to communicate with target audiences; assuming a station does a competent job of serving the public through its programming, its economic success depends on the success of its sales department in assisting clients.

PRIME RATES 87-9

SSU#	PROJ. RTG.			1	2	3	4
			MONDAY:				
	*	7-7:30PM	7 O'Clock Report	1200	950	850	750
	24	8-9PM	ALF/Valerie	1900	1400	1100	900
510	25	9-11PM	NBC Monday Night At The Movies	1900	1400	1200	1000
			TUESDAY:				
		7-7:30PM	7 O'Clock Report	1200	950	850	750
522	35	8-9PM	Matlock	2000	1500	1100	900
523	24	9-10PM	J.J. Starbuck	2000	1500	1200	900
525	24	10-11PM	Crime Story	1400	1200	1000	800
			WEDNESDAY:				
		7-7:30PM	7 O'Clock Report	1200	950	850	750
555	30	8-9PM	Highway to Heaven	1600	1400	1200	1000
561	21	9-10PM	A Year In The Life	1600	1400	1200	1000
571	16	10-11PM	St. Elsewhere	1400	1200	1000	800
			THURSDAY:				
		7-7:30PM	7 O'Clock Report	1200	950	850	750
587	41	8-9PM	The Cosby Show/A Different World	4000	3000	2500	2000
588	28	9-10PM	Cheers/Night Court	3500	3000	2500	2000
595	21	10-11PM	L. A. Law	3000	2500	2000	1500
			FRIDAY:				
		7-7:30PM	7 O'Clock Report	1200	950	850	750
602	18	8-9PM	Rags To Riches	1200	1000	850	700
606	13	9-10PM	Miami Vice	2400	2000	1600	1300
615	24	10-11PM	Private Eye	2400	2000	1600	1300
			SATURDAY:				
625	22	8-9PM	Facts Of Life/227	1400	1200	1000	800
632	22	9-10PM	Golden Girls/Amen	2000	1600	1200	1000
635	17	10-11PM	Hunter	2000	1600	1200	1000
			SUNDAY:				
654	16	7-8PM	Our House	1500	1200	1000	800
662	32	8-9PM	Family Ties/My Two Dads	2500	2000	1500	1000
670	25	9-11PM	NBC Sunday Night at the Movies	1900	1400	1200	1000

87-9 denotes the ninth rate card published.
Discounts available at the discretion of WIS-TV only.
* Prime Time sold in orbits must include M-F 7 O'Clock Report.

9-14-87
P-879

CANCELLATIONS: Contracts firm for first
4 weeks, subject to cancellation upon
4 weeks written notice.

:60 Rate = :30 Rate X 2
:15 Rate = 80% of :30 Rate
:10 Rate = 70% of :30 Rate

WIS TV 10
COLUMBIA

WIS TV 1111 BULL STREET COLUMBIA SC 29202

Fig. 14.7. Television grid rate card. (Courtesy of WIS-TV, Columbia, S.C.)

ORGANIZATION OF THE SALES DEPARTMENT

Because broadcast sales involve both national and local efforts, a typical sales department is divided into national and local sales divisions; a third unit is usually responsible for traffic and operational matters. Figure 14.8 shows the organizational plan of a typical station's sales department.

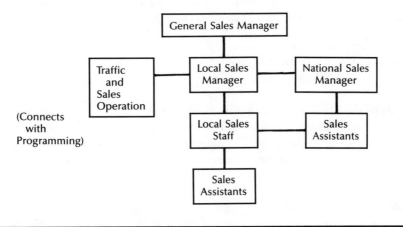

Fig. 14.8. Typical sales department organization.

The proportion of national sales relates closely to the market rank of a station. Television is geared to national selling, accomplished through national sales representation, though local TV advertising is becoming increasingly important. For large market radio stations, national advertising is an important revenue component, but local sales are the principal source of income.

The general sales manager plans and directs the entire station sales effort. Setting goals in dollars for both national and local sales is an essential part of the job, which also includes development of the station's selling strategy and an analysis of prospects. Each sales plan must incorporate a pricing philosophy, an awareness of seasonal demand fluctuations, careful control of commercial inventory availabilities, continual assessment of competitive pricing and programming changes, and alternatives to be followed whenever the station's rating position changes.

At most large stations, the national sales effort is handled by a national sales manager and several assistants who coordinate activities of the national rep firm that handles the station's sales in national markets. In many small and medium-sized stations, national sales are coordinated by the station manager or by the general sales manager.

The task of selling and servicing advertisers in the station's own coverage area is handled by the local sales department; here, the sales force works directly under the local sales manager. An effective sales department resembles a sports team, with sales managers acting as coaches and account executives (salespersons) as players. The local salesperson should be an expert in verbal skills and motivational techniques and be able to win the confidence of prospective clients. Account executives are expected to be well informed about station operations, programs, ratings, and audience characteristics, and they must know the advantages and disadvantages of competitive stations as well as their own. A salesperson also should have a thorough understanding of marketing principles and how they relate to client problems, particularly in the local retailing field.

The effectiveness of a broadcast sales department depends not only on its sales force, but also on the expertise of the traffic and operations staff and the sales assistants who back them up. With more than 1,300 announcements in the daily inventory of an average TV affiliate, the scheduling of announcements and the handling of commercial materials can become complex procedures. An efficient system for matching spots sold with correct commercial instructions is a must. Therefore, the traffic and operations unit generally has the tasks of

1. Coordinating media materials (film, tape, and slides) with broadcast scheduling
2. Cataloging such materials and preparing them for broadcast
3. Ordering spots on the air and cancelling, revising, and rescheduling
4. Preparing reports for sales management
5. Generating sales contracts
6. Preparing the daily broadcast log

In many large stations, sales assistants provide administrative backup to afford salespersons maximum time for selling effectively. Sales assistants must be adept at handling instructional information from agencies and coordinating with agency buyers such things as contracts, make-goods, and other administrative matters relating to orders. Sales assistants also help prepare availabilities and other material for sales presentations.

IMPLEMENTING TIME ORDERS

Each broadcast station must establish procedures and forms for use in implementing time orders. The following chronology of local sales order activity is described by John F. Carpenter, General Sales Manager, WSB-TV, Atlanta.

1. Pre-sell: initiation of the buy. The local sales staff acquires a piece of business in one of two ways: an agency or client on its list calls to request availabilities for a campaign or the sales staff generates the business by convincing a client or agency to use television or radio as part of a media mix or alone.

2. Preparation of the presentation. Based on requested demographic characteristics of the audience, a list of suitable availabilities is prepared for submission to the client. This list normally is computer-generated by using one of numerous software packages. A sample television schedule analysis/proposal form using the "TV Scan" computer program is shown in Figure 14.9. This form indicates day and time that spots are scheduled, rate, program name, rating points (percent), and cost per point (CPP) for each availability used. It also shows totals for the campaign, including cost, gross rating points, CPP, reach and frequency.

3. Selling the station and the availability presentation. A sales call is made, and a complete presentation is given in which the merits of the station are emphasized. If appropriate, a comparison of TV or radio with other media is presented.

4. Getting the order. At this point, the elements of persuasive sales technique come into play as the salesperson solicits the order.

5. Sales order entry. Upon completion of a sale, the account executive places the client's order, using an order entry form.

6. Sales contracts. The next step in processing the order involves preparation of the client's contract or confirmation form.

7. The invoice. The final form is the invoice, in which the station contract is reconciled against performance and the agency or advertiser is billed for the schedule.

8. Post-sell. The salesperson's job isn't over when an account is entered into the station's logs. In fact, the sales job never really ends; the account executive must be available to service the client during the time that advertising messages are aired. Further, he or she is involved in analyzing sales results and in making recommendations for further action after the present campaign has ended.

The increasing complexities of television time sales warrant a special look at the business from the seller's point of view in the next chapter.

```
        TVSCAN AUTO-POST --- TV SCHEDULE ANALYSIS

                 TARGET: METRO HOUSEHOLDS
                    WBBB -- CITYNAME
                    JUL 1985 ARBITRON

                    CLIENT: TV'S R US
                      STEREOS/TV'S
                  SCHEDULE I.D. -- 2005
```

NO.	DATE	DAY	TIME	RATE	PROGRAM NAME	RATING PTS	CPP
1	10/3/85	THU	7:00P	$1800	BILL COSBY	30.9%	$58.25
2	10/4/85	FRI	9:00P	$2000	MIAMI/ML PR	17.8%	$112.36
3	10/8/85	TUE	8:00P	$1500	RIPTIDE	16.5%	$90.91
4	10/10/85	THU	8:00P	$1300	CHEERS	19.5%	$66.67
5	10/12/85	SAT	9:00P	$600	HUNTER	12.3%	$48.78
6	10/14/85	MON	8:00P	$900	NBC MON MOV	15.6%	$57.69
7	10/16/85	WED	7:00P	$1200	HIWAY HEAVEN	25.9%	$46.33
8	10/24/85	THU	9:00P	$1800	HILL ST BLUS	13.4%	$134.33
9	10/25/85	FRI	9:00P	$2000	MIAMI/ML PR	17.8%	$112.36
10	10/27/85	SUN	7:00P	$1500	KNIGHT RIDER	11.1%	$135.14
11	10/29/85	TUE	8:00P	$1500	RIPTIDE	16.5%	$90.91
12	10/31/85	THU	8:00P	$1300	CHEERS	19.5%	$66.67
13	11/1/85	FRI	9:00P	$2000	MIAMI/ML PR	17.8%	$112.36
14	11/4/85	MON	8:00P	$1500	NBC MON MOV	15.6%	$96.15
15	11/6/85	WED	7:00P	$1200	HIWAY HEAVEN	25.9%	$46.33
16	11/9/85	SAT	9:00P	$600	HUNTER	12.3%	$48.78
17	11/12/85	TUE	7:00P	$1200	THE A TEAM	17.6%	$68.18
18	11/15/85	FRI	8:00P	$1100	NBC M/ML PR	11.0%	$100.00

	TOTAL COST	GRP'S	CPP	REACH	FREQ
METRO HOUSEHOLDS					
SCHEDULE TOTALS ...	$25,000	317.0	$78.86	44.6%	7.1

REACH & FREQUENCY PROJECTIONS ARE COMPUTED USING THE BETA-BINOMIAL STATISTICAL EXTENSION FORMULA.
NOTE: AUDIENCE ESTIMATES ARE FOUR-WEEK AVERAGES

PREPARED BY THE TAPSCAN RATING ANALYSIS SYSTEM. REPORT DESIGN & CONTENTS COPYRIGHT 1985 TAPSCAN, INC. (205) 987-7456
DATA FROM THE JUL 1985 ARBITRON. SUBJECT TO LIMITATIONS AND RESTRICTIONS STATED IN ORIGINAL REPORT.

Fig. 14.9. Sample TV schedule analysis/proposal using "TV scan." (Reprinted with permission from Tapscan, Inc.)

Study Questions

1. Think of at least five reasons why radio and television time rates may be subject to a great deal of negotiation.
2. Name an advertiser who you think would be primarily interested in reaching each of the seven major TV program blocks described in Chapter 14.
3. Name three advertisers who you believe would be more interested in achieving broad reach than high frequency if they could only afford one of the two. Name three who would opt for high frequency rather than broad reach. Explain your choices.
4. List several reasons that could account for the lack of any real standardization in broadcast industry rate cards.
5. Differentiate clearly between class and grid rate cards.
6. Explain the importance of pre-sell and post-sell stages in a station's local sales activity.

ASSIGNMENT 14-A

For an assigned market (ADI or DMA designation), evaluate as many advertising strengths as you can find. Use reference publications (*TV Factbook, Standard Rate and Data Service, Sales Management's Survey of Buying Power,* and *Broadcasting Yearbook,* as well as general encyclopedias and almanacs). Prepare your paper in report form, but outline it, concentrating on (1) a general description of the market (its size, economic activities, societal characteristics, growth trends, and any unique factors that affect advertising potential, and (2) a quantitative analysis. The latter should include significant market rankings that indicate the relative position of the broadcast area among those of the entire country (for instance, ADI/DMA household and TV household rankings, consumer spendable income data, and information on retail sales and the sales of special product categories). Interpret these data to suggest market strengths and weaknesses for national advertisers.

ASSIGNMENT 14-B

List all of the reasons you think the market you examined in assignment 14-A is or is not a good test market.

ASSIGNMENT 14-C

Using the references listed in assignment 14-A, compare the TV stations in your assigned market with respect to coverage, circulation, audience shares, and programming. Use the chart for basic information and then answer the questions listed.

Station	Network	Channel	Base hourly rate	Highest 30-sec. spot rate	Net weekly circulation	Average daily circulation

1. How do the stations rank in weekly circulation? In daily circulation?
2. Is the station that leads in circulation ahead by a significant margin? If so, can you explain why?
3. Which station has the highest hourly base rate? The highest 30-second spot rate?
4. Can the base rates be justified on the basis of circulation?
5. Is there any superiority of facilities among the TV stations with respect to power, channel assignment, antenna height, or any other factor?
6. Is any station noticeably weaker than others? Which network affiliation does it claim? Are its rates competitive?

ASSIGNMENT 14-D

Following the same basic plan as that presented in assignment 14-C, consider the radio stations in your market.

Station	Network	Format	Power	Average quarter-hr. share	Persons per average quarter-hr.	Cume rating

1. Which four stations do you believe are the leading stations in this market? Why?
2. Which three stations would you recommend for use by an advertiser who needs broad reach in the market? Why?
3. Examine the highest 60-second spot rates for the radio stations in SRDS. Can they be justified on the basis of audience reach?

ASSIGNMENT 14-E

Using a current weekly network TV schedule, explain which programs you believe would be most suitable for reaching target audiences of the following advertisers:

1. A new, highly economical automobile.

2. A well-established after-dinner wine.

3.   A trimming tool for lawn care.

4.   A new toy, designed for young girls.

5.   A familiar household detergent.

6.   A new men's deodorant.

7.   A generic campaign for milk.

ASSIGNMENT 14-F

Using this form, compute the cost of an assigned media schedule on the basis of the rate cards shown in Figure 14.7 and 14.8.

Schedule:

Spot description	Cost per time (with discounts)	Times per week	Total cost

Grand total:

Notes

1. *Broadcasting* (July 13, 1981): 15.
2. *Adweek's Marketer's Guide to Media*, (New York: A/S/M Communications, January-March 1988), 35-36.
3. *Ibid.*, 96.
4. Broadcast stations do set their own rates for advertising time. Political advertising, however, must be sold at the lowest allowable rates. This means that candidates for office receive the benefit of the greatest frequency discount, regardless of the amount of time purchased. In effect, short-term political advertisers get the benefit of the "best client" discount by law.
5. *American Radio, Spring 1989* (Kalamazoo, Mich.: Duncan's American Radio, August 1989), 14:1.

Suggested Readings

McCavitt, William E., and Peter K. Pringle. *Electronic Media Management*. Boston: Focal Press, 1986.
McGee, William L. *A Marketing Approach to Building Store Traffic with Broadcast Advertising*. San Francisco: Broadcast Marketing, 1978.

McGee, William L., and Wallace L. Hutchinson. *Management Guide & Sales Training Manual: For Increased Local Sales*. San Francisco: Broadcast Marketing, 1984.

McGee, William L., et al. *The Definitive Sales Guide to Broadcast Co-op: Still the Untapped Goldmine*. Incline Village, N.Y.: Broadcast Marketing, 1987.

Marcus, Norman. *Broadcast and Cable Management*. Englewood Cliffs, N.J.: Prentice-Hall, 1986.

Sissors, Jack E., and E. B. Petray. *Advertising Media Planning*. Chicago: Crain, 1978.

Surmanek, Jim. *Media Planning: A Practical Guide*. Lincolnwood, Ill.: Crain/National Textbook, 1985.

Warner, Charles. *Broadcast and Cable Selling*. Belmont, Calif.: Wadsworth, 1986.

Young, Robert F., and Stephen A. Greyser. *Managing Cooperative Advertising: A Strategic Approach*. Lexington, Mass.: Lexington Books, 1983.

ALSO: Check recent issues of *Advertising Age*, *Broadcasting*, *Standard Rate and Data Service*, *Television/Radio Age*, and publications from the Radio Advertising Bureau and the Television Bureau of Advertising.

15

Selling Television Time

The growth of the local commercial television station's sales staff attests to the vitality and opportunities in the industry. Today, the average television station has approximately seven local salespeople, up almost 20 percent from 1982. In addition, new positions in management and support staff have continued to grow, creating new titles such as vendor/co-op specialist, retail specialist, and director of marketing.

We are all well past the era in which "time salesmen" simply sold the basic numbers of television known as the "spots and dots of avails." Today's TV salespeople are marketing consultants who sell advertising and marketing ideas—creative concepts. They are researchers, providing specialized client-oriented information that will help meet prospective clients' needs in making advertising decisions. They are developers of new business who seek out opportunities and new potential sources of revenue for the television industry as well as for their own stations.

But the station's salesperson's responsibility is still to market the station's audience: to position it and package it effectively, to focus in on sales targets, and to determine where potential dollars lie and how to secure them. And it all must be done within the guidelines of each station's managerial philosophy.

Now it's time to take a look at some of the problems and opportunities that confront the salesperson in meeting this responsibility.

Calling on the Local Advertiser

The first call on a local advertiser is usually a fact-finding one. Certain information must be obtained to pre-sell the buy. Who is the ultimate customer? When does the customer buy? What influences the purchase decision? What lines does the prospective client carry; which are the most profitable; and do any of them assist with advertising? What does the client wish advertising to accomplish?

With answers to these questions, the salesperson can explain the station's position in the marketplace and how its goals can mesh with those of the prospective client. Sometimes a firm can be shown how far its current newspaper advertising budget will go in TV. For example, according to 1986-87 TVB analyses, the $8,000 to $9,000 spent on one full-page newspaper ad in Milwaukee, Wisconsin, or in Rochester, New York, would buy 200 to 300 television GRPs. Instead of reaching fewer

Much of the material for this chapter was supplied by the Television Bureau of Advertising.

than half a million (gross) newspaper homes, the advertiser would be reaching more than a million (gross) TV homes.

Later, when planning a television campaign that will fulfill the client's needs, it's important to prepare a complete presentation including:

1. All station programming that is targeted to the client's ultimate consumer. It may be advisable to list with each program some audience delivery estimates from a local credible rating survey such as Nielsen or Arbitron, one or two sentences of rationale that explains why the program will attract the desired audience, the time the program airs, and an estimate of commercial announcement cost, plus a list of upcoming specials or sponsorship opportunities that might also reach the client's ultimate consumer.

2. A package of programs that will help clients select the most desirable ones. The package should include less expensive, low-rated programs as well as high-rated programs and specials all targeted and scheduled to accomplish the client's goal. A short rationale should accompany the package explaining what it will achieve, how much of the targeted audience will see the message approximately how many times, and the total package cost.

3. Special services and opportunities. If a client will need a commercial produced, a script and cost estimate should be presented. If there is a chance for the client to participate in a station's promotion, if a client has an event later in the year that will require extensive planning, or if there are cross-promotion possibilities with another client, the opportunity should be addressed.

Final incentives may include the possibility of recording an audio track by a popular station personality. Also, some stations provide merchandising assistance through in-store, point-of-purchase displays. "Racer-Lites Are Here," an athletic store poster might proclaim, "As Endorsed by Sportswear Sam on TV Channel 3." Former newspaper-only advertisers might be especially attracted to this kind of TV station proposal because it offers a new look in promotion.

Research projects, sometimes coordinated through local college classes, also make excellent selling ammunition for station reps. Audience surveys provide useful feedback at low cost and are valuable to both participants and end-users. Also, station help may be available to advertisers planning to run contests; assistance might be in entry-form processing, for instance, or announcement and distribution of prizes.

Calling on the Advertising Agency

Much of the business for a television station may be placed through an advertising agency; then it's the TV seller's major responsibility to present information in such a way that he/she convinces the buyer to purchase his/her station. The salesperson stresses the station's programming, audience demographic strengths, history of past rating performance, audience trends, program changes, market conditions, ratings updates, and market research. And because the buyer's time is limited, and proposals for numerous stations may seem repetitious, a creative sales approach is often necessary.

When an actual budget has been approved for a client, the buyer requests station proposals in the form of avails. The preliminary gathering of information for the avails is the first step for the salesperson: client, product, buyer, flight dates, budget, spot length, audience demographics, dayparts, ratings book, cost-per-point goals, points-per-program week, program restrictions, number of weeks, post-analysis, and how many stations will be considered.

The salesperson presents the avails, positioning the station in the strongest light possible in regard to the client's needs and goals. This might be accomplished through information on specific demographic strength, daypart strength, audience delivery, or market research.

This information then sets the stage for a discussion of the station's programming estimates. Because all programming is to be bought in the future, an estimate of each program's performance must be established. Discussions of HUT/PUT level projections, current programming, or competitive programming can aid in the formulation of an estimate. Once an agreement between the buyer and seller is reached on the ratings, the station's rates are presented as close to the buyer's goals as possible. Negotiation results in what is believed to be the best possible schedule for the client and station.

Some local advertisers do not understand the concept of ratings. In such instances, sales reps may provide a genuine service by supplying them with information provided by firms such as A. C. Nielsen. Figure 15.1 shows an example of one type of explanatory booklet.

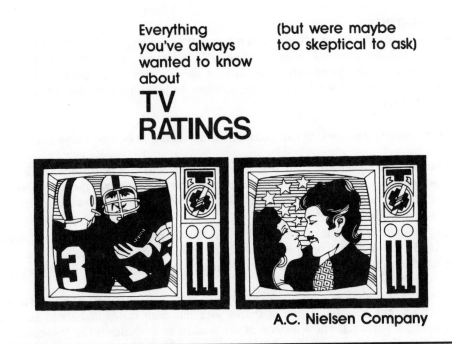

Fig. 15.1. Ratings information booklet. (Courtesy of Nielsen Media Research)

Maintaining Good Relations with Established Accounts

Just as proper pre-sell is important on the first contact, post-sell is vital after the sale. If a good buy is made through an agency, the buyer should be told by letter, with copies to his or her supervisor; or, when appropriate, a letter of thanks signed by the general manager should be sent directly to the advertiser.

Many first-time TV advertisers become nervous about their decisions, especially because they are often bombarded by radio, newspaper, and magazine representatives, as well as those from other media, all telling them how they could have spent their money differently. The television rep, therefore, needs to reinforce the buy just made with additional material and new information about the programs purchased. Perhaps the commercial can be played for the client's sales staff, and they can be given approximate air times so they can watch it as it's run.

What else should reps do? Inform clients of new competitors coming into the marketplace. Let them know of co-op plans or national support being given to products. Bring up new concepts, scripts, or ideas that will reinforce client image. And stay attuned to any objections clients may have about television or specific stations.

Selling the Station and Its Inventory

Whereas years ago most markets had a high-rated station and a low-rated station, television stations are much closer to parity today. Barring coverage problems or a complete lack of aggressive programming acquisition, most stations in a market have both low- and high-rated inventory. The goal, of course, is to maximize the revenue return on both kinds.

LOW-RATED INVENTORY

Low-rated inventory can be an advantage in a national or regional selling situation because buyers are frequently cost-per-point oriented in their thinking. They buy on an efficiency basis, without caring too much about ratings in any given programs, as long as they meet the minimum level. And when inventory is low-rated, stations don't feel as much pressure to maintain rate integrity as they do when selling higher-rated spots.

Some other options that stations can consider when selling low-rated inventory include:

1. Combining with higher-rated and higher-cost inventory to create a package. Thus, the station may get the higher unit rate for the high-rated spot and still be able to move the lower-rated inventory. If the better spot is adjacent to the lesser one, the seller may want to create a broad rotation or an *orbit* to use the best of both positions.
2. Giving the station a special positioning as the "best sports value" or the "best daytime value" in the market. If the station relies on this tactic alone, however, it may either sell the inventory too quickly or find itself in a positioning pigeonhole that hinders general selling ability because the station is identified too closely with that one strategy.
3. Checking rating services (ARB/NSI) computer runs for potential county-by-county success stories. This procedure can help build station shares with franchise stores and some auto dealerships.
4. Positioning a particular show instead of the station as a whole—if the low-rated inventory is local programming (such as news or sports). Many national/regional buyers are interested in purchasing GRPs, whereas many local clients relate better to programs than to rating points. A national/regional buyer buys 10 rating points, but a local store goes after the 6 o'clock news.
5. Combining the lower cost of low-rated inventory with image whenever possible. Most buys on news or sports cable networks are made because of an interest in unique programming or a willingness to experiment—not because of large audience numbers.

HIGH-RATED INVENTORY

Higher-rated inventory brings its own distinct attributes to the selling situation. Station positioning must not only create appeal, but also outline underlying values and intangible reasons to make the buy.

Because the most often heard objection to high-rated inventory is one of price, establishing advertiser benefits becomes the most effective means of overcoming that objection. One example is a station's commitment to on-air promotion, because it not only enhances viewership, but also assures a strong commercial environment for the advertiser. Another example might be the benefit to an advertiser of association with, perhaps, the market's top news personalities.

Positioning also enhances top-of-mind awareness, makes the station appear to be more valuable, makes the buyer feel good about his/her decision, and makes the salesperson appear to be more knowledgeable and professional, thereby laying the groundwork for a sound selling strategy.

Sales materials used should clearly demonstrate a station's superior strength. For example, reach can be a very effective way of showing dominance, as illustrated in Figure 15.2.

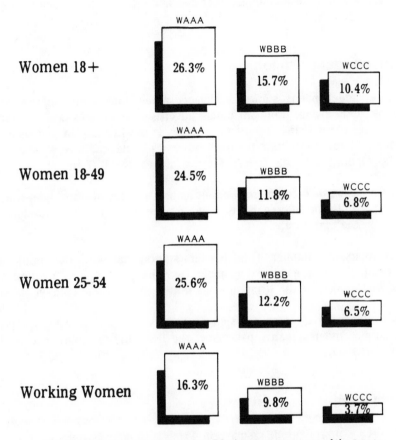

Fig. 15.2. Ratings used as a selling tool. (Courtesy of WVEC-TV, a wholly owned subsidiary of A. H. Belo Corporation, which also consists of WFAA Dallas-Fort Worth, KHOU-TV Houston, KXTV Sacramento, and KOTV Tulsa)

It's important to remember that viewing and ratings are cyclical; no high-rated competitor is invulnerable forever. Successful stations continually and aggressively seek new programming options, especially today, given the large number and types of programming available. Also, all television time should be considered good. Some of it is just better than the rest. And although this statement is true for stations with high-rated inventory as well as for those selling low-rated programs, it has a special significance to the equally rated station.

EQUALLY RATED INVENTORY

In this situation, positioning remains a key focal point. Audience strengths and weaknesses must be carefully analyzed, and packaging must be designed so weak points enhance strong ones. If, however, it remains difficult to find a marketable advantage, the TV rep must dig to find new platforms, new packages, or even a new selling technique. Current customers can be persuaded to buy more while new customers are being approached.

Selling the Independent Station

Although most independent station managers agree that their biggest single problem is programming, along with rising program costs, advertiser prejudices against independents have diminished markedly in recent years. One of the reasons is the increase in audience size now claimed by many independents—thanks, in part, to the availability of popular off-network shows and to successful experiments such as Operation Prime Time, featuring "novels for TV" in the form of miniseries.

Burke research has studied commercial recall among viewers of both independent and network-affiliated stations. No significant difference was found in commercial recall, believability, persuasiveness, or perception between the two groups.

During recent years, the number of independent stations has more than doubled throughout the country. Now, because three or more independents may be present in a market, each one can be marketed and sold on the basis of the strength of its ratings, in the same manner as a network affiliate.

Independents offer many advantages to spot advertisers, too, such as program sponsorships, inside program commercial placements, creative packaging, and flexibility in program scheduling that are not often found on affiliated stations.

Assistance from TVB

Because TVB is a nonprofit trade association which is organized and supported by the television industry, it can be of tremendous value to the local sales executive who has access to the Bureau's services through his station's membership. Its mission, after all, is to generate increased advertising revenue for the television industry.

Here's a sampling of what's available:

- Targeted sales presentations to major national advertisers.
- Platform presentations to groups of advertisers.
- Sales-oriented success stories of TV advertisers.
- Print materials on categories of business/information needed to sell advertisers on the use of TV.
- Videotapes for salespeople and advertisers.
- Sales training seminars.

- Member services consulting.
- Targeted research on TV viewing.
- Competitive information on newspapers, radio, cable television, and other media.
- Pro-television information.
- Creative sales ideas for all categories of business.

In particular, the member services department can brief a salesperson on the status of a sales category, its potential, and its anticipated value in the future; explain how a given advertiser is using television in terms of scheduled dayparts and investments; supply marketing information on a prospect's best customers (who is buying, how much, where, and when); provide advertiser case histories and current articles from the client's own industry trade press; and assist with the handling of co-op dollars, offer tips on whom to contact to get results, and discuss vendor program ideas.

Merchandising ideas and examples of TV commercials for a wide variety of clients also are provided regularly by TVB. Figure 15.3 shows examples of informative brochures distributed to member stations and discussed in detail at sales clinics throughout the nation.

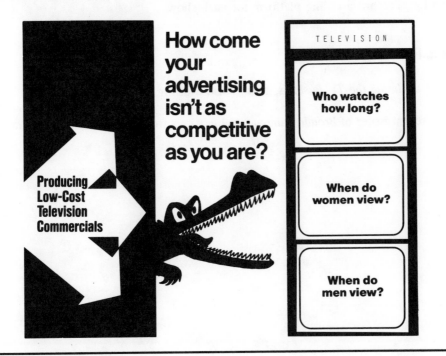

Fig. 15.3. Samples of sales tools available from TVB. (Courtesy of the Television Bureau of Advertising)

Both local and national advertisers are involved with time buying activities, but often their overall objectives are quite different. Although much of our previous discussion in this text has focused on the national scene, the next chapter will examine broadcast advertising specifics solely from the retailer's perspective.

Study Questions

1. Discuss at least two strategic differences between selling TV time to a local advertiser and selling it to an advertising agency.
2. Discuss the differences between pre-sell and post-sell techniques.

3. Discuss some sales approaches appropriate for high-, low-, and equally rated inventory.
4. Why has advertiser reluctance to buying independent stations diminished recently? Do you think this trend will continue? Why?
5. Suggest some merchandising ideas for television stations centered around various holiday or seasonal events.

ASSIGNMENT 15-A

On behalf of an assigned local TV station, prepare a sales kit or presentation suitable for delivery to an identified local advertiser or advertising agency.

ASSIGNMENT 15-B

Prepare a list of TV sales incentives that you think would be appropriate for selected advertisers in your community and include your reasoning.

ASSIGNMENT 15-C

Assume you are trying to sell a (1) very popular and (2) not-so-popular syndicated TV program to a local station. Prepare a selling platform for each show.

Suggested Readings

Klein, Paul, et al. *Inside the TV Business.* New York: Sterling, 1979.

ALSO: Check recent issues of *Broadcasting* and publications from the Television Bureau of Advertising.

16

Broadcast Advertising at the Retail Level

Broadcast advertising at the retail level provides a vital link between national commercials and sales in local stores. Whereas a national manufacturer may be interested primarily in promoting an individual product ("Buy my brand"), the retailer wants to convince customers to purchase at one specific place ("Buy it at my store"). Hence, while each manufacturer's commercials feature the selling point and benefits of particular brands of products, stores aim to attract shoppers through emphasis on large numbers and lines of different products, as well as special store services and other attractive features such as parking facilities, extended business hours, and check-cashing policies. Local area commercials provide the dominant source of advertising for radio stations, and they're making an increasingly significant mark in television.

Functions of Retail Advertising

Before proceeding, we should differentiate between retail advertising and local advertising. Retail advertising normally refers to stores carrying merchandise for sale to the general public; local advertising pertains to establishments providing services, such as banks, restaurants and hotels, dry cleaners, and beauty shops. This chapter will deal specifically with retail broadcast advertising, although some of the discussion may be applied to commercials for local services as well. Figure 16.1 shows leading local categories in TV advertising.

LEADING CATEGORIES OF ANNUAL LOCAL TV SPENDERS
(in alphabetical order)

Amusements and Entertainment
Automobile and Truck Dealers
Banks and Savings & Loans
Department Stores
Discount Department Stores
Food Stores and Supermarkets
Furniture Stores
Leisure Time Activities
Movies
Restaurants and Drive-Ins

Fig. 16.1. Leading local TV spenders. (Courtesy of TvBasics 1987-88, Television Bureau of Advertising, New York)

When all types of local radio revenues are combined, they represent about 75 percent of the annual revenue total for this medium. Not surprisingly, a survey by the National Retail Merchants Association showed that more than 90 percent of American retailers now use radio as an advertising medium. Both AM and FM radio are popular commercial vehicles at the local level, especially because FM, as noted in Chapter 2, is claiming an increasing share of audience. Granted, FM still appeals to a more select audience than AM does, but it can be very well suited, for example, to the advertising needs of stores selling stereo equipment.

Although retail broadcast commercials are designed for a wide variety of purposes, common objectives include:

- Building sales of individual items, lines, or departments.
- Creating general store (or department) traffic.
- Expanding a store's trading area.
- Changing shopping habits (days, frequency, or nature of purchases at a particular type of store).
- Promoting special store services or events (credit and refund policies, contests, charity drives, ecological pursuits).
- Providing information (new store hours or locations, sale prices, availability of merchandise).
- Establishing or reinforcing a given store image or personality.
- Supplementing the retail advertising program in other media, or supporting community activities, sports events, educational and cultural affairs and benefits, or seasonal celebrations.

Music and jingles have proven especially effective in building store image. Events, as well as individual items, can be featured as examples of a store's philosophy or personality. For example, K Mart's long-running theme, "The Saving Place," has been used to promote everything from major appliances to candy bars, and from home beautification days to Halloween parties. In addition, a recording of its musical store ID may be played over a store's public address system during shopping hours.

RETAILERS AND ADVERTISING AGENCIES

Few retailers hire advertising agencies. Notable exceptions are retail chains, but they are really involved in a form of national advertising (though individual outlets personalize messages for their own areas). A few such chains that are heavy users of broadcast media include the Great Atlantic & Pacific Tea Company (A&P), J. C. Penney, Sears, Montgomery Ward, and Woolworth & Woolco, as well as a number of fast-food restaurants.

When we consider the neighborhood jewelry store, however, or the local bakery, we find that several key differences between the retailing business and that of national product manufacturers would make working with an advertising agency a cumbersome task. First, check the number of different items sold in local stores today—dozens in some, hundreds in others, and many thousands in still others—far more than any agency creative team could hope to study and learn as they are used to doing with brand-name product accounts.

What's more, merchandise turnover in many retail establishments is rapid, so the number and type of items available may change by the day or hour. Of course, commercials should never attempt to incorporate these quantities of items in individual messages, but unless they have a genuine familiarity with all the merchandise, copywriters cannot hope to keep up with retailers' daily wishes in terms of promotional tactics.

Turning from separate spots to overall campaigns, let us assume that groups of holiday messages were expected to cover multiple store items or multiple departments within stores. Imagine the headaches agency personnel might have trying to keep a retailer happy when, because of time limitations, commercials wound up slighting even one line or department—especially when it came to a gift-giving theme.

Then again, entire retail campaigns may last only a week or so, but agency-created ones often run for a year or longer. Sudden changes in weather, supplies of goods, competitive ad strategies, or even news events can have an almost immediate effect on sales and, hence, on the need for and the nature of broadcast advertising communication. The retail advertising pace is a lot more hectic than the national one, and if commercials are to keep up with it they require almost constant input from hands close to the information source. That means nearby equipment and facilities, ever-changing copy, and relatively speedy, low-cost productions.

CREATIVITY IN RETAIL COMMERCIALS

National commercials tend to emphasize the soft sell, nonprice emotional approach, but retail spots are mainly hard sell, price-oriented, and rational. National spots frequently stress the "why" behind brand purchase; retail ones are busy developing the "where" with a dash of the "why" thrown in. Also, national messages are more general in terms of price and store location, but at the retail level, copy gets very specific.

Such local area commercials need not be pushy or preachy. Figures 16.2 and 16.3 show two delightful—very different—ways of packaging sales messages for a couple of Tennessee restaurants.

It is important to remember, though, that people shop for benefits. Both national and retail commercials need to stress competitive advantages, not merely spout off superficial descriptions. Of course, neither radio nor television spots are well suited to multiproduct and price information. Still, when this kind of material is paramount to a sales message, the broadcast media can play a valuable reinforcement role; commercial announcers and presenters can effectively advise their audiences to "see ads in today's newspaper for details," or to "check your mailbox for valuable coupons." Some people even feel that such intermedia support enhances the credibility of individual commercials.

Slice-of-life commercials at the retail level can move right to the sales floor or supermarket aisle for on-the-spot confrontation with consumer problems. Testimonials may raise important personal questions and concerns and give listeners and viewers comforting answers and assurances. Dialogue might involve store owners or department managers who are working and planning for the consumer's good.

Finally, some retail spots do not refer to specific city or area stores, but relate a copy line for a chain of stores to a well-known product message. Figure 16.4 provides a radio example and illustrates cooperative advertising, which will be discussed shortly.

Approximately 5 percent of retail TV commercials are only 10 seconds long, and 4 percent are 15 seconds. When it's important to concentrate on just one sale event, one price, or one specific service, though, a short spot can capture quick attention. Then, too, whereas a retailer's small-space newspaper ad may have difficulty reflecting the store's image, even a brief TV message communicates with the same color, motion, and music as its longer counterparts.

Another 5 percent of retail commercials run 60 seconds or longer. If multi-item advertising is involved, added length is essential. We should note, however, that the TV medium should not be asked to perform newspaper's job of providing in-depth explanation of a large number of products and features.

More than 80 percent of retail TV spots are 30 seconds in length—long enough to include specific information about a company, product, store, service, or idea and to relate it to customer benefits. In

```
MUSIC:        BLUEGRASS UP AND UNDER

ANNCR:        (SINGING AND SPEAKING WITH A TENNESSEE DRAWL)

              "When your appetite is hearty

              There's just one thing you should do

              Bring all your friends and hurry down

              To Bobby's Barbecue!"

              Ummm...sweet, spicy barbecue smoked on a hickory pit.

              If there's a barbecue heaven, it just can't be any

              finer than Bobby's when it comes to beef, pork, ribs,

              chicken, and them down-home barbecue beans.  But the

              best part's yet to come.  Bobby's has luncheon specials

              ev'ry week that'll keep you grinnin' and keep your

              wallet happy, too.  So r'member:

              "When your appetite is hearty

              There's just one thing you should do

              Grab all your friends and come on down

              To Bobby's Barbecue!"


LOCAL:        (DEEJAY GIVES THIS WEEK'S SPECIAL PRICES)

MUSIC:        UP TO CLOSE
```

Fig. 16.2. Local radio commercial: Bobby's Barbeque.

a campaign of 30-second commercials, only one or two may be directed to the same target audience. For example, a department store's "Fun in the Sun" campaign might feature clothing, sports equipment, and beach or camping needs in separate messages—and gear particular ones to men, women, teens, and whole families.[1]

PRODUCTION CONCERNS

Advertisers can save money by filming or taping a number of similar commercials at one time, rather than setting aside separate production days and times. Retailers may think in terms of *modulars*—short, interchangeable segments that can be mixed and matched to make each of a series of

SOUND:	CRASHING THUNDER, PELTING RAIN
ANNCR:	Brrr...Tennessee winters can really get you down, but...
SOUND:	HOWLING WIND/BLIZZARD
ANNCR:	...you'll always find a friendly face, a happy smile, and plenty of piping hot food -- at Ponchos! And that's not just for lunch or dinner, but late-night, too, cuz Ponchos stays open every night till 2 a.m. So get out...
SOUND:	ALL EFFECTS OUT; SOFT COUNTRY MUSIC IN BKGD
ANNCR:	...of the storm -- and come in and enjoy. Just listen to these special winter treats: genuine homemade chili, topped with cheese, onions, and peppers, and served with tostados, just the way you like 'em. That's an old Panchos' favorite. Or, try our Nachos Supreme -- a delicious mixture of beef and beans, covered with melted cheese, and topped with jalapeno peppers. Now that's real Mexican flavor! So next time you're fed up with the cold, come feed on some warm homestyle dishes at Ponchos. Open 7 days a week to serve you and your whole family. We'll be looking for you!
MUSIC:	UP TO CLOSE

Fig. 16.3. Local radio commercial: Ponchos.

commercials seem different. For instance, one might provide an introduction to a new store's merchandise, another feature employees as stars, and a third emphasize prices.

Also, detailed sets may not be important to a retailer's message. Sometimes a simple studio set (such as a plain background, one chair, and a desk) will suffice and save money. If an outdoor setting is preferable, both the location and the lighting can be free.

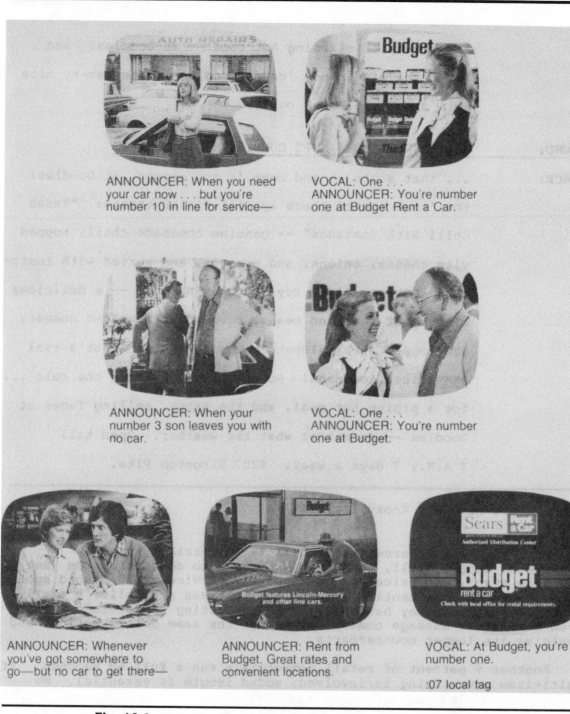

Fig. 16.4. Cooperative TV commercial. (Courtesy of Budget Rent a Car Corp.)

ASSISTANCE FROM TRADE ASSOCIATIONS

Chapter 15 detailed many of the services available to TVB members. In addition, RAB tips for retail promotions have included:

1. Easter egg or Halloween pumpkin hunts (stores hide special eggs or pumpkins all over town—each with a slip that finders bring in for discounts and prizes).

2.   Snowflake sales (for every inch of snow that falls, dealers give 1-percent discounts, or one dollar off the price of selected merchandise; the same idea can apply to a cold-weather sale—temperatures below freezing or zero—and to a hot-weather sale, if temperatures rise above 80 or 90 degrees.

3.   Lucky-Friday-the-13th days (special prices available in combinations of the number 13 and three-for-one buys, plus extra in-store bonuses or prize drawings at 13 minutes after every hour).

4.   Patriotic packages (special give-aways with major purchases around Flag Day or the Fourth of July that may include red-white-and-blue buys as well).

5.   Circus tent or good-old-fashioned-days sales (special prizes and discounts available from appropriately-dressed sales personnel).

6.   Parking lot cookout contests (that may feature specific foods, cooking appliances, wearing apparel, or even related activities in the field of photography).

7.   All kinds of eating contests, build-your-own ice cream sundaes, super sandwiches, or the like, and numerous guess-the-weight or guess-the-number-in-a-container games and contests.

8.   Parades (for which fabric stores or departments selling sewing machines invite anyone who has personally made an outfit to model it for judges; prizes can be set for a multitude of categories, and the idea provides a natural tie-in with Easter, Back-to-School, or seasonal activities; colors can be highlighted around Valentine's Day, St. Patrick's Day, or Christmas).[2]

In each instance, radio announcements can keep listeners posted on the progress of these events almost minute-by-minute, and thereby encourage them to participate. Also, if remote broadcasts emanate from the respective scenes, listeners may be invited to stop by, meet radio personalities, and even get their names on the air.

As is true with TVB, RAB sales clinics and workshops assist local station personnel in selling air time to the retail trade.

TVB has charted two patterns for retail television advertising that help stores plan campaigns designed either to move items or to promote images (see Figure 16.5). Some retailers, worried about potentially high costs in television production, might consider airing actual storyboards, whose artwork or slide-set has been animated (probably for test purposes). The Windsor Total Video company, in New York, suggests that such TV spots often meet broadcast quality standards; retailers running one per week could well find the activity less expensive than procurement of talent, props, and a stage for a spot that would probably only air a handful of times.[3]

Successful Retail Broadcast Campaigns

Some retail establishments, traditionally newspaper and radio oriented, have achieved outstanding success with television. Cunningham drug stores, in Detroit, recently developed a very effective TV creative and media plan. Faced with the proliferation of products carried by different types of stores, Cunningham was competing with supermarkets, discount stores, and department stores, as well as other drug outlets. TV messages changed weekly throughout the campaign but followed a consistent pattern: a strong company identification at the beginning; a "featured event" (such as a back-to-school promotion, a baseball-season salute, or a holiday celebration); sale-item announcements; and a closing logo and positioning line: "Cunningham Drug Stores—the Prescription Experts." Depending on the event, anywhere from 300 to 800 GRPs were purchased each week.[4]

On the other hand, Foley's department stores (a division of Federated), in Houston, ran a spectacular five-week Christmas campaign on four different TV stations. Twenty-two key models and half-a-dozen extras participated in 51 filmed and 18 videotaped commercials—a project involving 6

ITEM advertising requires careful selection of items, commercials, and time periods, and these procedures usually involve

IMAGE advertising usually only requires a

MANY PEOPLE at the store. But item commercials can count on getting manufacturers'

FEW PEOPLE at the store. It is usually paid for by

CO-OP DOLLARS if the store wants them. Different items aim at different

STORE DOLLARS because it doesn't contain manufacturers' items which would entitle the store to co-op dollars. Image spots usually aim at

TARGET AUDIENCES in terms of both demographics and psychographics; therefore,

LARGE HETEROGENEOUS AUDIENCES, but since the number of messages is limited, there need be only a

MANY DIFFERENT COMMERCIALS are needed. If there are going to be many spots, they need to be

FEW COMMERCIALS. Therefore, they can afford to be

LOW COST in production.

EXPENSIVE, and may be produced on

TAPES OR SLIDES are usually the best bet in terms of speed and cost. Then, the TV schedule is tied to sales of individual items, so the store's TV budget and TV schedule can expect to have

FILM. Because image is year-round, the television pattern is

UPS AND DOWNS day by day, week by week, and season by season. Because items were the original emphasis, results should be measured in terms of

STEADY, and doesn't show the ups and downs of item-emphasis advertising. With image as the goal, results should be measured in terms of

ITEMS, although store image may also be affected. Many items, many commercials, and lots of people all add up a pace that's

IMAGE, which could also be reflected in sales of items. With fewer commercials, fewer people involved, and a more steady pattern, the pace is

FAST.

SLOWER.

Fig. 16.5. Two patterns for retail TV advertising. (Courtesy of the Television Bureau of Advertising, New York)

months of planning time (similar to many national campaigns). A monumental buy of 4,000 GRPs per week saw an average weekly airing of 360 30-second spots and the greatest sales record of any Christmas season in the store's history. Foley's, in fact, achieved through television what other advertisers generally expect from newspapers: a kind of instant recognition in terms of image and appeal.

On an entirely different level, the Ace Hardware Corporation had, for years, run its campaign service theme on radio, featuring the Helpful Hardware Man. This dealer/hero idea personalized the friendly Ace image and opened the creative door to some very effective messages (for example, the idea that Ace's Helpful Hardware Man gives consumers high-quality brand-name items, reasonable prices, and special incentives to buy).

In the late 1970s, national network television was added to the Ace media mix to solidify the total advertising effort and give added impact to seasonal promotions. News and sports programming served as primary vehicles for reaching a general audience; drive-time radio added frequency. Overall, the TV schedule reached more than 90 percent of the TV households in Ace marketing areas more than five times on the average, and both radio and TV combined to deliver nearly three billion commercial impressions per year. Examples of recently released spots appear in Figure 16.6.

"Ace is the place with
the Helpful Hardware Man" ™

ACE HARDWARE
:30 TELEVISION COMMERCIAL
"HELPING HAND" OCT/82

VOCAL: ACE IS THE PLACE.
MAN: At Ace, we give you a helping
hand ·

like this Best Buy of the Month — the
Ames Greensweeper lawn rake,

only $3.99! Lightweight, four-foot wood
handle, no metal parts to rust,

and does a real man-sized job!

WOMAN: But don't forget you'll need
these sturdy Kordite bags to finish the
job! Heavy-duty, two-ply bags, with ties,

and another Best Buy at just $2.33!

MAN: And you save up to 40% on each!

WOMAN: Now that's what I call
being helpful!

VOCAL: ACE IS THE PLACE WITH THE
HELPFUL HARDWARE MAN!

...and woman!

TV XDYC 2043
© 1982, ACE HARDWARE CORP.

Fig. 16.6. Two TV spots for Ace Hardware. (Reprinted with permission from Ace
Hardware Corp., Oak Brook, Ill.)

ACE HARDWARE
:30 TELEVISION COMMERCIAL
"HELPING HAND" NOV/82

VOCAL: ACE IS THE PLACE.
MAN: At Ace we give you a helping hand to solve your heating problems

with this Best Buy of the Month — an Arvin portable electric heater

at just $13.99. It puts 850 watts of heat

right where you need it — helps you save energy!

WOMAN: Figure out how much you can save with this Sharp Solar calculator,

only $8.44! Runs on any kind of light, never needs batteries!

Another Ace Best Buy!

MAN: Save up to 35% on each of these Best Buys!

WOMAN: You figured it out!
VOCAL: ACE IS THE PLACE WITH THE HELPFUL HARDWARE MAN!

MAN: . . . and woman!

Fig. 16.6. *(continued)*

Cooperative Broadcast Advertising

When a product manufacturer and a retail store join forces in sales communication, the result is known as vertical cooperative advertising (hereinafter referred to by its industry nickname, co-op). Basically, it's a process of sharing—costs, commercial message time, and company image. For example, a nationally known appliance manufacturer and a neighborhood department store might be featured together in a radio commercial to promote a holiday sale.

Or, come September, local car dealers often team up with automobile manufacturers in a series of TV commercials designed to introduce new models to the public. Time costs usually are divided 50/50, although any mutually agreed-upon split is legal, as long as it remains the same for all parties involved. In other words, national firms can't play favorites among local dealers. Any given manufacturer may choose a 60/40, 75/25, or other split, but once the decision is made it must be offered equally to all interested retailers; otherwise, the activity is in violation of the Robinson-Patman Act, which prohibits price discrimination.

Commercial copy, however, is another matter. Because the national manufacturer often handles the writing and production of all co-op spots (normally through an advertising agency), the major portion of each message is usually devoted to the product. Then a *tag line* at the end of the commercial is provided for the one or more cooperating local outlets. If several dealers are involved, sometimes they are named all together and sometimes separate ones are featured in separate spots.

Some TV advertisers shoot extra (silent) product film footage so retailers can use it with their own voice-overs (giving store details). In these commercials the division of content is more nearly equal. An *integrated* commercial is produced by a manufacturer, but combines the store name into the message in such a way that it seems the spot was produced by the retail outlet. Once in a while, especially in radio, manufacturers let dealers supply their own commercial copy—while retaining ultimate approval of the efforts.[5]

MANUFACTURER BENEFITS

Advantages of co-op to the manufacturer are several. Radio and TV time for co-op commercials is sold at local rates—often a substantial savings (see Chapter 14). The association with neighborhood retailers localizes a national brand message by tying in a familiar store name in each locality (a friendly, personal image) or, perhaps, a local seasonal activity or cultural event. Also, it is a little easier to trace the sales effects of local commercials than national ones, because the buying action generally occurs more rapidly after the commercials run.

And an overall improvement in dealer relations generally results from a healthy co-op program. Because manufacturers pay part of the time costs, more money is actually available; dealers are thus inclined to run more commercials and thereby stimulate more sales. Some manufacturers have even added new outlets to their distribution rosters as a result of co-op offerings. The goodwill generated here tends to offset the negative reactions retailers may have because of the small portion of each commercial actually given to them. Also, dealers take satisfaction in being allowed to choose the stations and air times for their co-op spots. On the other hand, this relative lack of control over the media schedule may be seen as a disadvantage to manufacturers; dealers might choose station outlets for personal, rather than sales, reasons (for example, executive friendships, special discounts, or merely station popularity).

RETAILER BENEFITS

From the retailer's point of view, co-op advantages are as follows: the extra money is an obvious budget-stretcher (especially when several dealers are involved, because they split costs); the national brand association helps boost the retailer's own image; and the relatively high-class free help in creativity and production is very welcome, especially in view of the fact that most retailers don't have advertising agencies.

THE LEGAL SCENE

Three legal concerns, in addition to possible discrimination in payment, involve the use of co-op funds for advertising only, the proof that commercials actually ran as scheduled, and accuracy in billing procedures. Some retailers may try to use the extra money received from manufacturers to grant price discounts to customers on selected merchandise or to finance a store-sponsored contest; the law requires, however, that funds earmarked for commercials be spent entirely on their behalf. Should retailers be granted discounts on the purchase of time, the money saved must be spent for future commercial airings.

Proving that co-op commercials were run on schedule is not nearly so simple in the case of broadcast media as it is in print. Newspaper *tear sheets* (actual dated pages on which ads appear, torn from papers in which they run) are easily provided. When it comes to radio and TV, however, one of four less satisfactory procedures must be followed: advertisers may pay a monitoring service to keep tabs on the stations involved, noting which commercials run and when (a costly endeavor); advertisers may send representatives to visit the stations (unannounced) and examine daily logs to obtain the information (a costly and time-consuming endeavor, although the Young & Rubicam ad agency first undertook such activity in 1984);[6] an electronic verification service may be employed wherein radio and TV signals are monitored and identified;[7] or stations may be asked to supply affidavits—certified statements that designated spots ran at specified times. These latter forms are the closest things to tear sheets that the broadcasting industry has, and this fourth procedure is followed to a large extent. In fact, a statement placed on an actual commercial script, indicating when and at what cost a spot was aired, is known as an "electronic tear sheet."

An illegal procedure known as *double billing* also plagues co-op advertisers but is often difficult to prove. Because retailers actually place co-op spots with local media, the stations send all bills for time charges to these dealers. The dealers, in turn, bill the respective manufacturers for their shares of the cooperative fee arrangement. Retailers are expected to pass along honest bills and not inflated ones or ones for commercials that never ran. As is true in all businesses, however, there are those who choose to ignore the law. Double billing involves a station's preparation of two separate bills—one that is actually paid by the retailer (the smaller of the two), and the other that is sent on to the manufacturer (an inflated one).

The two separate bills may involve a wide range of illegal discrepancies between, for example, national rates and local rates, on-the-books rates and personally discounted rates, 60-second spots that never ran and 30-second spots that did, and high-frequency schedules that never ran and low-frequency schedules that did. The Association of National Advertisers recently advanced a method of validating radio co-op spots that is giving some advertisers greater protection against certain forms of double billing; under this procedure, stations certify on each commercial script the exact times each spot ran. Previously, the certified statements were merely attached to scripts and could be removed and reattached to others. In any circumstances, engaging in a double-billing practice is risky; upon conviction, a number of stations have lost their licenses.

Although vertical cooperative advertising is the most widely used form, the use of retail horizontal co-op is increasing today. Commercials here are mainly institutional in nature and are sponsored by groups of independent businesses, such as pharmaceutical establishments, insurance companies, and real estate agencies. The aim is generally to emphasize a high quality of merchandise and service.

Roughly 75 to 80 percent of American manufacturers make cooperative arrangements available to retailers, and the Radio Advertising Bureau estimates that co-op represents about 30 percent of radio's total volume of business.[8]

Research

The commercial copy tests discussed in Chapter 12 are infrequent at the retail level because of time and budget limitations. Other kinds of research are conducted more often, however, so at least some of the effects of broadcast advertising can be measured on a local basis. For example, suppose a record store decided to run a contest on several different radio stations. Music lovers might vie for free records by sending entries to a specified address. On each competing station, however, the box number in the address would be different—coded so responses collected from various stations could be compared and the relative pulling power of each station assessed. Of course, any demographic information called for on the entry blank could provide useful information to the advertisers as well; the coding idea could also be used for commercials run on radio and TV if the test were between these two media.

Another type of research involves questions asked of customers at the point of purchase (such as "Where did you hear about this particular product?"). An interviewer may be stationed at the store to handle the job (much as an equipment demonstrator or chef displays his or her wares to passing shoppers); or small cards may be handed out by cashiers. Customers might be asked to fill out the cards on the spot while sales are being rung, because many take-home cards either never get that far or are never returned. Questions must be short and simple; often they ask what led shoppers to choose particular stores, products, or both and may provide check lists of various media (or even actual stations) that carried the respective commercials.

Retail stores also can set up test departments or test lines of merchandise, in much the same way test markets are established. For a given period of time, one might receive only radio commercial support, one only TV, one both, and one neither. Sales figures during the period wouldn't prove that the advertising had any particular power, but because outside effects can be controlled more easily in a small area over a short span of time than they can in a national test situation, retailers can get at least a fair idea of the contributions to sales the broadcast media are making.

Now it's time to pull together the many facets of broadcast advertising we have examined thus far to see how they function as a cohesive unit.

Study Questions

1. For a selected local store or service in your area, discuss items that could be stressed in commercials other than merchandise.
2. Come up with your own promotional theme, along RAB lines, and explain how the values of radio would benefit a selected advertiser. Discuss how your theme would fit in with a particular special event.
3. How would you convince an antibroadcast retailer to spend his or her co-op dollars in radio and/or TV?
4. Explain fully what is meant by the term double billing.
5. What product classification do you think will see the greatest local/retail TV expenditures during the next five years? Why?

ASSIGNMENT 16-A
Develop a broad theme for a newly assigned retail campaign. Prepare a 30-second radio commercial that incorporates this theme and recommend possible point-of-purchase tie-ins.

ASSIGNMENT 16-B
Using the theme you developed in assignment 16-A, prepare a second 30-second radio spot, this time adapting your idea to fit an assigned holiday, seasonal, or other promotion.

ASSIGNMENT 16-C

For an assigned store, prepare both an item and an image storyboard for 30-second commercials. Remember the normal production techniques in each and vary your messages accordingly. Prepare a storyboard similar to the one used in assignment 10-B.

ASSIGNMENT 16-D

Prepare 30-second co-op radio and TV commercials for an assigned store and product. Try to use both media to their fullest potentials. Also, design your spots to complement each other without using the same audio track in both. Use a storyboard similar to the one used in assignment 10-B.

ASSIGNMENT 16-E

Given assigned retail campaign objectives and overall campaign length, recommend a local radio and TV media schedule and include rationale for specific audience reach and frequency.

Notes

1. See "Television Commercial Lengths—Who Uses Them and Why?" (New York: Television Bureau of Advertising).
2. Adapted from "Ideas You Can Sell," "Promotion Ideas," and "Salesweek," (New York: Radio Advertising Bureau).
3. *Advertising Age* (January 3, 1977):32.
4. See *Broadcasting* (September 1, 1980):21.
5. *Broadcasting* (September 8, 1980):48.
6. *Broadcasting* (July 30, 1984):56.
7. *Advertising Age* (April 22, 1985):38.
8. *Broadcasting* (September 8, 1980):48.

Suggested Readings

Abrahams, Howard P. *Making TV Pay Off: A Retailer's Guide to Television Advertising.* New York: Fairchild, 1975.

McGee, William. *A Marketing Approach to Building Store Traffic with Broadcast Advertising.* San Francisco: Broadcast Marketing, 1978.

Milton, Shirley F. *Advertising for Modern Retailers.* New York: Fairchild, 1974.

Nielsen, A. C. *The Nielsen Researcher.* Northbrook, Ill.: A. C. Nielsen, published periodically.

Zeigler, Sherilyn K., and J. Douglas Johnson. *Creative Strategy and Tactics in Advertising.* Columbus, Ohio: Grid, 1981.

17

Broadcast Advertising Plans and Campaigns

Throughout this text, we have stressed the value of planning in all phases of broadcast advertising: in writing and production, in the selection and purchase of specific media vehicles and schedules, in the choice of advertising agencies and outside services, in the design and conduct of research studies, and in the coordination of national and retail promotional activities and campaigns. There is far too much at stake today (time and money, brand and corporate images, and many thousands of jobs) to permit operating willy-nilly in this vitally important and potentially powerful branch of marketing and media communication.

Now it's time to consider overall marketing plans from which we can derive more specific advertising plans and the broadcast advertising plans that incorporate all of the specialized subplans we discussed in previous chapters. In a sense, we have moved backwards through this text, because marketing plans precede all others. Without an umbrella plan to guide them, broadcast advertisers cannot be sure their efforts are in line with those of company management; recall from Chapter 1 that although advertising is a communication force, it is also a tool of marketing, utilized to help sell. All elements of the so-called marketing mix, therefore, must work together as separate means toward the achievement of a common end.

The Master Marketing Plan

Some form of master plan must precede the development of every broadcast advertising campaign; fortunately, there is a relatively simple organizational procedure widely used today to facilitate the formulation of such plans. Developed by a leading marketing and advertising executive, Clarence Eldridge, this model has been adopted in one form or another by nearly every major advertising agency and manufacturer in the nation. It is normally set up as an annual plan, but it works just as well for the retailer who employs it on a short-term basis.

The five major parts of the Eldridge Plan are as follows:

1. Statement of facts—generally including a historical perspective of product sales across various target markets and retail outlets, and of packaging, pricing, distribution, and product improvements; competitive efforts; and consumer attitudes toward shopping, buying, advertising and media, product images, and competitive offerings. Merchandising and promotional activities are covered, as well as advertising and personal selling, overall selling expenditures, and profits.
2. Identification of problems and opportunities—apparent after a thorough analysis of the facts and often encompassing many or all of the above marketing concerns.
3. List of objectives—covering all of the categories detailed under part 2; for every problem/opportunity set, at least one objective should be listed and, if possible, both broad, long-term

objectives and specific, short-term ones. Often a distinction is drawn between objectives of increasing existing usage of a product, increasing the uses of a product, and increasing the number and kinds of product users.

4. Recommendations—detailing a complete plan of action consistent with parts 2 and 3; proposals are made about the amount of money to be spent; the ways in which it will be spent; the time periods, geographical areas, and personnel involved; and the procedures that will be utilized to determine results and to assess overall effectiveness.

5. Summary—recapping parts 1 through 4 and including a profit and loss projection.[1]

The Advertising Application

We are making the assumption here that nearly every marketing plan calls for advertising. An ever-timely adage says: "When business is good, it's good business to advertise; when business is bad, advertising is a necessity." With the general marketing parent plan behind us, we can consider its advertising offspring:

Part 1 becomes a statement of advertising facts (creative case histories, media choices, research endeavors, cooperative efforts, legal involvements, audiences sought and acquired, and business conducted with various advertising service organizations).

Part 2 becomes identification of the advertising problems and opportunities revealed through careful study of the material presented in part 1.

Part 3 is now a list of relevant advertising objectives in each category.

Part 4 contains recommended actions for the forthcoming advertising campaign—specifics for creative output, media activities, and so on.

We may omit Part 5 here, unless it is specifically requested.

POSITIONING

Before looking at detailed advertising plans for the broadcast media, we need to examine a very important strategic concept that affects both creative and media planning. To succeed in today's over-communicated society, an advertiser must create a position in prospects' minds, one that takes into account not only its own values, but those of an ever-increasing number of competitors. The annual per capita consumption of advertising in the United States is now more that $400; on a daily basis, thousands of ads and commercials must compete for portions of each consumer's mental set.

The mind may be compared to a memory bank containing a slot or position for each bit of information it retains. Acting also as a defense mechanism, however, the mind filters and rejects much of the overwhelming barrage of information it receives; material accepted is generally that which is in line with existing individual predispositions, and reaches each individual in the place, at the time, and with the degree of frequency that is right for successful sales communication.[2]

Obviously, not all commercial messages—even those that are of interest to a consumer—can get through the mental screening process. The mind could not function at all if it had to deal with every piece of relevant information each time a decision had to be made; even if all data could be processed, consumers are much too busy and preoccupied to spend long hours mulling over each of life's daily problems. So only those messages that are exactly on target in terms of want and need fulfillment are actually taken in.

Successful positioning results in the ranking of products, services, brand names, stores, and even specific selling points and benefits on mental ladders. An advertiser who wants to move up a level in terms of brand acceptance or consumer preference must dislodge the competitor who is already there.

Commercials that do not successfully position their products will either be associated with already established (competing) brands, or merely regarded as clutter and screened out.[3]

A question may arise here with regard to the increasing tendency to name competitors in commercials. Although research studies have found that comparative commercials often confuse audiences and negatively affect credibility, some advertisers feel they aid the positioning effort.[4] It is not necessary, however, for a brand to stand next to competitors to measure up to or surpass them in consumer choice. Commercials can carve out a single, solid niche for a product presented all by itself. For example, Maytag washers are shown as the dependable ones—a position that was personalized through the "lonely repairman" character who served as commercial spokesperson. The image is specific, independent, and memorable.

It is important to differentiate here between a product's share of market and its share of mind. The Scott Paper Company holds about 40 percent of the market for towels, napkins, toilet tissues, and other consumer paper products. As more and more products have been hung on the Scott name, however (ScotTowels, ScotTissues, Scotties, Scotkins, and the like), its position in the consumer's mind becomes less and less distinct. Thus, a few years ago, when Procter & Gamble attacked its competitor with Mr. Whipple and his tissue squeezers, it was no contest; today Charmin is the number-one brand of toilet tissue.

Scott's large share of market did not mean the company owned the share-of-mind position. Shoppers could write Charmin on their shopping lists and know exactly what they were going to buy. Scott, however, had no real meaning, and even actual brand names were confusing. Which brand, for example, is a competitor of Kleenex Tissues—Scotties or ScotTissues? In positioning terms, the name Scott seemed to exist in limbo, but Charmin quickly secured firm footing on the mental product ladder consumers had for toilet tissue.[5]

The Broadcast Advertising Plan

Now we can turn full attention to the offspring of the advertising plan—in effect the grandchild of the marketing parent. Here is an abbreviated, hypothetical broadcast advertising plan for Cruncho Breakfast Cookies, a specific example of the Eldridge Plan applied to a company's interest in radio and TV commercials and in all business operations and activities that surround them. Assume that Cruncho is a two-year-old national cereal company, whose product is competitively packaged, priced, and distributed.

PART 1–BROADCAST ADVERTISING FACTS

1. Cruncho so far has utilized only newspapers and radio for advertising in major markets.
2. The target audience has been mainly single working adults who are nutrition-conscious, but whose lives generally revolve around the clock—men and women who appreciate convenience foods and who are not fussy about home cooking. They are in the middle-income range and are more interested in cost and value than they are in name-brand items.
3. The key idea has been "Good-tasting nutrition travels with you in Cruncho Breakfast Cookies." Research has indicated that it is credible but not particularly stimulating.
4. Thirteen-week newspaper and radio campaigns have featured testimonials from unknown persons employed in a variety of responsible jobs. Attitudinal studies conducted in three different market areas indicated a high level of acceptance and credibility but a low level of recall.
5. A radio jingle was tried and discontinued because although recall of the words and tune was high, 75 percent of those who could identify it claimed it belonged to a Carnation product: "A super way to start your day—the breakfast treat that's quick and neat."
6. Cooperative advertising efforts have been minimal because of low interest on the part of

retailers; competitors' products are more firmly established and, hence, more appealing when it comes to requests for advertising support.

7.   A new advertising agency with outstanding success records in cereal products and use of the broadcast media has just been hired, and management is willing to double the advertising budget if necessary to improve its share of market (currently 1 percent) during the next year.

These facts not only must put all broadcast advertising efforts into perspective, but also should include an indication of the money and manpower plus other resources and facilities available for the new campaign.

PART 2-BROADCAST ADVERTISING PROBLEMS AND OPPORTUNITIES

1.   Limited media efforts have left Cruncho with only a 1-percent market share, and exposure has been limited to a relatively narrow market segment. HOWEVER, an increased budget will permit the addition of television to the media plan, and market segments can be expanded to include students and homemakers, as well as married individuals working full or part time. In addition, radio and TV can work together to reinforce the major sales theme and jingle.

2.   The key creative idea has not proved stimulating or valuable to consumers. HOWEVER, because credibility and recall studies proved favorable, the new agency has the opportunity to combine the key idea and jingle format to breathe life and spark into the former and make the latter much more specific and brand oriented.

3.   Cruncho cookies are often confused with competing brands in consumers' minds. HOWEVER, new creative talent can work on establishing a new identity for this relatively young product—one that lends itself to presentation in the broadcast media.

4.   The testimonial format proved it had merit, but poor memorability indicated low levels of exposure and perception. HOWEVER, unknown product endorsers can be replaced with popular figures or brought to life through television.

5.   The radio jingle was too vague to differentiate its brand from the competition. HOWEVER, a specific, brand-targeted jingle presented in television commercials can be reinforced through radio.

6.   Grocery stores and supermarkets are only lukewarm toward Cruncho cookies and cannot see much value in special promotional efforts on the product's behalf. HOWEVER, with the new positive thrust Cruncho is planning will come increased consumer demand for the product. Retailers can be encouraged to support broadcast efforts at the point of purchase through introduction of a sweepstakes that is tied to the new creative positioning strategy delivered by TV and radio.

7.   Broadcast advertising effects tend to be attitudinal (intangible) and, hence, difficult to measure. HOWEVER, carefully designed research studies can establish benchmarks and then assess progress as the campaign unfolds.

Problems and opportunities are really two sides of the same coin; when we turn a problem over, there is usually an opportunity staring us in the face. Learning to recognize these opportunities, however, is not always easy, and deciding on the best (most effective and efficient) way to exploit them may be harder yet. Still, it is important to remain optimistic; in our culture, problems tend to orient us to the past, while opportunities are future and progress directed. In a sense, we can regard each desired conquest as an experiment in planning. Experiments deal with what-if questions; every time a broadcast advertising problem confronts campaign planners, they'll do well to query: "What if?" and proceed on a positive note.

PART 3-BROADCAST ADVERTISING OBJECTIVES

1.   To increase advertising exposure through the purchase of television time selected to reach a broad segment of working adults.

2.   To position Cruncho cookies as crunchy nutrition in take-along form, with the slogan "A Cruncho treat is breakfast complete."

3.   To utilize new creative talent to increase the visibility of Cruncho cookies.

4. To explore the possibility of obtaining celebrity testimonials for Cruncho commercials and to pretest efforts before making final decisions.

5. To create a jingle for Cruncho cookies that zeros in on the desired mind position for the product.

6. To develop a consumer sweepstakes that will increase store traffic and to convince retailers that their enthusiastic support will pay off at the cash register.

7. To design research studies that will measure the impact of creative and media effects on a continuing basis.

Specific short-term objectives, as opposed to those that are broad and long term, set forth not only the tasks to be done, but the extent to which they will be achieved and the time periods involved.

A comparison between long-term and short-term objectives at four different levels is shown in Table 17.1.

Table 17.1. Broadcast advertising objectives

Level	Long-term Objectives	Short-term Objectives
Corporate	To increase profits/shareholder investment values	To earn 10 percent of capital in the coming year
Marketing	To increase midwestern supermarket sales/market shares	To sell 3 percent more cereal products in designated stores over a 6-month period
Advertising	To improve brand preference	To increase by 3 percent, in the first 6 months of the year, the number of working adults in the Midwest who say they prefer our brand over those of competitors
Broadcast advertising	To associate take-along convenience and good-tasting nutrition with our brand name	To establish awareness and credibility of the "Cruncho treat/breakfast complete" theme among 15 percent of working adults in Chicago, Cincinnati, and Detroit who listen to drive-time radio

Broadcast advertising goals must relate to accomplishments that can be achieved through radio and TV commercials and activities directly related to them such as research, promotional efforts, and cooperative involvements. They may deal with audience reach (both demographic and psychographic) and frequency of exposure, with creative appeals (their interest levels, memorability, degrees of credibility, or persuasive powers), with research attempts (the measurement of creative or media potential or effectiveness), with trade acceptance (improvement of dealer relations and enhancement of promotional support), and with product positioning (strengthening an existing consumer share of mind or establishing a new one).

PART 4-BROADCAST ADVERTISING RECOMMENDATIONS

In this section of the plan are such items as proposed media selections (stations and schedules), specific commercial content ideas, names of potential celebrity spokespersons, examples of proposed sweepstakes terms and retail incentive programs, and detailed research plans. This plan is highly abbreviated. Facts, problems and opportunities, and objectives can actually be drawn from every subject category presented in this book.

Now let us turn to the broadcast advertising budget—methods used to determine specific appropriations and the values of each.

The Broadcast Advertising Budget

The best defined objectives in the world are for naught if no money is available to achieve them. Hence, the appropriation of funds is a crucial managerial task. Before advertisers can decide how much to spend, however, they must first determine what elements will be charged against the broadcast advertising budget. It is generally agreed that costs of radio and TV time, commercial production, copy and media research, and games and contests related directly to broadcast campaigns belong in this category. There is less accord, though, when it comes to coupons, point-of-purchase displays, and premiums packaged with products, even though each of these may be mentioned in commercial copy. It all depends on the individual advertiser's marketing management structure.

Also important in the preliminary stages of budget planning are answers to a number of questions surrounding the product, service, or store involved, the general media mix desired, and the intended audience. For example:

1. Where is the product in its so-called life cycle? If consumers still perceive it as new, greater media reach and frequency may be needed than will be necessary once it has been successfully launched.
2. What type of commercials and media schedules are competitors running? Some advertisers may wish to follow suit, while others want to go one better—depending in part on existing market shares. The introduction or discontinuance of commercial spokespersons (characters) may be considered, new audiences may be sought, and new commercial images may be needed.
3. Does the product lend itself well to television demonstration or is reminder radio particularly appropriate? And are target customers primarily broadcast oriented in their media habits (or more specifically soap opera or late-night movie fans? Sports broadcast enthusiasts? Commuters who drive with rock-music radio as a companion)?

BUDGETARY METHODS

Armed with answers to these and many other media, production, research, and merchandising questions, advertisers can begin looking at dollars and cents. Through the years, they have developed a variety of special methods for establishing ad budgets suited to particular campaign needs. Some employ complex profit-planning systems for budgetary control with the assistance of mathematical models and computers. Others merely arrive at budget allocations arbitrarily (practically on a passing whim or fancy), copy competitors' appropriations for advertising (or deliberately set them above or below the competition), or follow established budgetary procedures in other marketing areas first and allocate to advertising whatever is left (the so-called as-much-as-we-can-afford routine).

By far the two most popular methods for determining advertising budgets, however, are (a) the percentage-of-sales or unit-of-sales approach and (b) the task or objective method.

Percentage (or Unit) of Sales

This procedure traditionally has been a favorite among national and retail advertisers alike. It is an easy one to follow, and allows for simple comparisons from month to month or year to year and between various divisions of a firm or departments of a store. A base sales figure is used as the starting point: a given advertiser's most recently obtained total (for example, last month's or last year's), a predicted total (next month's or next year's), an average of several past totals, or a figure based on showings of a competitor or industry. When the total is a dollar amount, the system is referred to as percentage of sales; when it is a unit amount (for example, the number of automobiles sold), it is called unit of sales.

Then, a percentage of the base figure is computed and the result becomes the new advertising budget. The exact percentage may again be based on a company's own experience or on that of competitors or an entire industry. Percentages vary widely across industries, just as actual dollar expenditures and sales figures do, but a rule-of-thumb average is often around 2 percent. Figure 17.1 shows percentages of total sales figures spent on advertising for selected national advertisers.

Ad rank	Company	Advertising	Sales	Adv. as % of sales
Airlines				
57	Trans World Corp.	$95,235,900	$5,265,500,000	1.8%
75	UAL Inc.	70,585,100	5,141,174,000	1.4
87	Eastern Airlines	54,100,000	3,727,093,000	1.5
89	American Airlines	51,496,900	4,108,699,000	1.2
91	Delta Airlines	44,500,000	3,533,326,000	1.3
Appliances, Tv, Radio				
17	RCA Corp.	208,798,300	8,004,800,000	2.6
35	General Electric Co.	164,696,300	27,240,000,000	0.6
65	North American Philips	83,881,400	3,030,044,000	2.8
Automobiles				
5	General Motors Corp.	401,000,000	62,698,500,000	0.6
11	Ford Motor Co.	286,686,600	38,247,100,000	0.7
24	Chrysler Corp.	193,000,000	10,821,600,000	1.8
51	Toyota Motor Sales	106,186,700	17,014,984,000	6.2
62	Nissan Motor Corp., U.S.A.	87,884,100	15,680,000,000	5.6
67	Volkswagen of America	81,000,000	16,118,505,500	0.5
76	American Motors Corp.	70,000,000	2,588,923,000	2.7
78	American Honda Motor Co.	68,846,800	7,945,401,000	0.9
Chemicals				
44	American Cyanamid Co.	138,000,000	3,649,073,000	3.8
53	E.I. du Pont de Nemours & Co.	105,000,000	22,810,000,000	0.5
58	Union Carbide Corp.	90,000,000	10,168,000,000	0.9
Communications, Entertainment				
37	Warner Communications	159,000,000	3,237,153,000	4.9
43	Time Inc.	141,133,000	3,296,382,000	4.3
46	CBS Inc.	134,010,000	4,125,954,000	3.0
80	MCA Inc.	63,600,000	1,328,988,000	4.8
90	Columbia Pictures Industries	47,500,000	686,600,000	6.9
99	American Broadcasting Cos.	40,000,000	2,443,713,000	1.6
Drugs				
40	Richardson-Vicks	149,000,000	1,088,100,000	13.7
48	Schering-Plough Corp.	119,768,600	1,808,000,000	6.6
59	Sterling Drug	89,700,000	1,792,925,000	5.0
60	SmithKline Corp.	89,265,000	1,985,341,000	4.5
73	Miles Laboratories	72,084,700	767,606,000	9.4
83	Pfizer Inc.	59,000,000	3,249,700,000	1.8
Food				
3	General Foods Corp.	456,800,000	8,351,100,000	5.5
7	Nabisco Brands Inc.	340,983,000	5,819,200,000	5.9
15	McDonald's Corp.	230,248,200	7,129,000,000	3.2
19	General Mills	207,306,100	5,312,100,000	3.9
25	Ralston Purina Co.	192,984,000	5,224,700,000	3.7
30	Dart & Kraft	177,042,100	10,211,000,000	1.7
31	Esmark Inc.	175,065,000	3,132,349,000	5.6
33	Beatrice Foods Co.	170,000,000	9,023,520,000	1.9
34	Consolidated Foods Corp.	166,399,700	5,800,000,000	2.9
36	H.J. Heinz Co.	160,175,000	3,688,500,000	4.3
39	Norton Simon Inc.	149,875,600	3,191,898,000	4.7
47	Pillsbury Co.	131,015,100	3,385,100,000	3.9
54	Kellogg Co.	102,111,300	2,321,300,000	4.4
56	Quaker Oats Co.	95,597,100	2,599,500,000	3.7
61	Nestle Enterprises	88,000,000	2,387,000,000	3.7
63	CPC International	87,000,000	4,343,100,000	2.0
74	Campbell Soup Co.	70,757,000	2,950,000,000	2.4
92	Borden Inc.	44,019,000	4,415,174,000	1.0
94	MortonNorwich Products	42,483,800	957,584,000	4.4
Gum, Candy				
69	Mars Inc.	78,400,000	1,350,000,000	5.8
81	Wm. Wrigley Jr. Co.	63,526,300	607,834,000	10.5
86	Hershey Foods Corp.	56,516,000	1,451,000,000	3.9

Ad rank	Company	Advertising	Sales	Adv. as % of sales
Photographic equipment				
55	Eastman Kodak Co.	$101,000,000	$10,337,500,000	1.0%
88	Polaroid Corp.	51,750,000	1,419,600,000	3.6
100	Canon U.S.A.	36,525,800	705,000,000	5.2
Retail chains				
2	Sears Roebuck & Co.	544,104,500	27,360,000,000	2.0
6	K mart Corp.	349,611,000	16,527,012,000	2.1
18	J.C. Penney Co.	208,600,000	11,860,000,000	1.8
Soaps, Cleaners (and Allied)				
1	Procter & Gamble Co.	671,757,400	11,944,000,000	5.6
13	Colgate-Palmolive Co.	260,000,000	5,261,364,000	4.9
27	Unilever U.S.	188,878,800	2,840,170,000	6.7
68	Clorox Co.	80,761,000	714,023,000	11.3
79	S.C. Johnson & Son	66,560,000	2,000,000,000	3.3
Soft drinks				
14	PepsiCo Inc.	260,000,000	7,027,443,000	3.7
22	Coca-Cola Co.	197,831,700	5,889,035,000	3.4
Telephone service, equipment				
9	American Telephone & Telegraph Co.	297,000,000	58,214,000,000	0.5
38	International Telephone & Telegraph Co.	153,000,000	17,306,189,000	0.9
Tobacco				
4	Philip Morris Inc.	432,971,400	10,885,900,000	4.0
8	R.J. Reynolds Industries	321,279,600	11,691,800,000	2.7
21	B.A.T. Industries PLC	199,301,800	4,592,259,000	4.3
66	American Brands	82,218,900	6,538,161,000	1.3
93	Liggett Group	43,500,000	1,192,481,000	3.6
Toiletries, Cosmetics				
12	Warner-Lambert Co.	270,400,000	3,379,092,000	8.0
16	American Home Products Corp.	209,000,000	4,131,237,000	5.1
20	Bristol-Myers Co.	200,000,000	3,496,700,000	5.7
23	Johnson & Johnson	195,000,000	3,025,900,000	6.4
32	Gillette Co.	171,900,000	2,335,000,000	7.4
42	Loews Corp.	141,384,400	4,776,000,000	3.0
45	Chesebrough-Pond's	136,241,000	1,529,674,000	8.9
50	Revlon Inc.	106,638,750	2,365,938,000	4.5
77	Beecham Group Ltd.	69,123,200	2,947,950,000	2.3
96	Noxell Corp.	41,062,100	233,112,000	17.6
97	Jeffrey Martin Inc.	41,000,000	75,000,000	54.7
Wine, Beer, Liquor				
28	Anheuser-Busch Cos.	187,228,500	4,409,600,000	4.2
29	Heublein Inc.	187,000,000	2,050,121,000	9.1
41	Seagram Co. Ltd.	145,000,000	2,772,733,000	5.2
70	Brown-Forman Distillers Corp.	78,000,000	860,556,000	9.1
85	Jos. E. Schlitz Brewing Co.	56,763,500	881,674,000	6.4
95	Hiram Walker Resources Ltd.	42,283,000	2,945,300,000	1.4
Miscellaneous				
10	Mobil Corp.	293,103,200	68,587,000,000	4.3
26	U.S. Government	189,026,000	—	—
49	Mattel Inc.	110,600,000	1,134,252,000	9.8
52	Gulf & Western Industries	106,140,900	7,409,000,000	1.4
64	Xerox Corp.	84,150,000	8,691,000,000	1.0
71	American Express Co.	76,036,000	7,211,000,000	1.1
72	Greyhound Corp.	75,592,100	5,164,000,000	1.5
82	Kimberly-Clark Corp.	62,440,000	2,900,000,000	2.2
84	Exxon Corp.	58,062,000	115,148,321,000	0.1
98	International Business Machines Corp.	40,700,000	29,070,000,000	0.1

Fig. 17.1. Percentages of total sales spent on advertising. (Reprinted with permission from the September 9, 1982 issue of *Advertising Age*. Copyright 1982, Crain Communications, Inc.)

It is important to note that just because a company's advertising expenditures can always be presented as a percentage of sales, the company does not necessarily follow the percentage-of-sales system in determining its advertising budget. More and more national advertisers are turning to a much more complex but advertising-oriented procedure known as the task, or objective, method (sometimes called the objective-and-task method).

Before discussing this particular system in detail, let us see why the percentage-of-sales procedure is not always satisfactory. By its very nature, this method ties the advertising budget directly to sales, so that "as sales go, so goes advertising." In other words, when sales are up, the advertising budget goes up, and when sales are down, the ad budget drops. From an advertising planning point of view, there are two problems here. The percentage-of-sales system assumes that advertising follows sales—that unless there are sales, there can be no advertising. Management planners who have any faith at all in the power of advertising communication to stimulate sales realize that those expensive commercials may be needed most when sales are down.

This system also assumes that advertising is to blame and, hence, should be curtailed when sales are low. As we have already noted, though, advertising is but one marketing tool that helps sell goods and services; despite elaborately produced commercials, consumers reject products they feel are over-priced, improperly packaged, not conveniently available, or backed by inadequate service policies. And, in the long run, a cut-back in advertising may result in the need for more personal selling or sales promotional efforts at far greater costs than those that an efficiently run advertising campaign would incur. (According to 1988 network pricing patterns, national TV advertisers could expect to reach one U.S. viewer with a minute's worth of advertising for less than a penny; on the other hand, a single postcard mailed to the same person cost 15 cents, and an industrial sales call ran nearly $300.)

Task Method

The task method of budgeting, by far the most scientific system, assumes that advertising leads sales and regards advertising as an investment toward future profits (see Figure 17.2). It is a rigorous, demanding procedure, but it pays off handsomely for the growing number of major firms, most industrial concerns, and even some smaller companies who use it. Under this system, advertising expenditures are guided by management's desire to achieve specific advertising goals, because the budget itself is established on the basis of carefully established objectives in areas of media, creativity, research, and related promotional and cooperative concerns.

The task method uses Part 3 of the broadcast advertising plan as its foundation. Once objectives are clearly defined in terms of people, places, ideas, effects, and time (all detailed as operationally as possible to facilitate later assessment of results), the amount of money needed to achieve each one must be determined. (Anyone who thinks the formulation of goals is challenging should try a hand at pinpointing needed funds!) Now production and research costs, media rates and agency commissions, and the myriad of out-of-pocket expenses incurred during a broadcast advertising campaign must be analyzed so that dollar figures can be attached to stated objectives.

When this monumental task has been completed (often with the help of accounting experts and computers and the involvement of untold hours of human data-gathering operations), the proposed budget is ready for presentation to company management. If it is not accepted because the required amount is deemed too high, the task method does not allow a reversion to some other budgeting procedure. Instead, the budget-planning team goes back to the drawing board and scales down one objective or more, recalculates needed funds, and returns a revised proposal. For example, if an original objective had been to convince 10 percent of Brand X users to switch to Brand Y in the first 6 months of the campaign, perhaps 7 or 8 percent would be a more realistic figure; or, the 10 percent goal might be extended to 12 months. A cutback in media exposure alone could save thousands, even millions, of dollars.

GRIME CREAM HAND CLEANER

	1989 Profit and Loss		Estimated 1990 Profit and Loss	
Sales	$1,000,000	100%	$1,100,000	100%*
Cost of merchandise	800,000	80%	880,000	80%
Gross profit	$ 200,000	20%	$ 220,000	20%

Fixed expenses (do not vary with sales)

Heat, light, water	$ 10,000	1%	No	
Property taxes	10,000	1	changes	
Management salaries	40,000	4	occur	
Rent	20,000	2	here	
Depreciation of equipment	20,000	2		
	$ 100,000	10%	$ 100,000	9.1%

Variable expenses (vary in direct proportion with sales)

Labor	$ 60,000	6%	$ 66,000	6%
Supplies and misc.	10,000	1	11,000	1
Payroll	10,000	1	11,000	1
ADVERTISING	10,000	1	16,500	1.5**
	$ 90,000	9%	$ 104,500	9.5%
Net Profit	$ 10,000	1%	$ 15,500	1.4%

*10% increase
**Up $6,500

Fig. 17.2. Task method of budgeting.

The point is that the broadcast advertising budget is hereby related directly to assigned advertising tasks or objectives and not specifically to sales. Advertising is thus seen as an individual, dynamic entity, capable of performing its own specialized form of marketing service. And, because it demands a thorough job analysis, it opens the door to constant assessment and reassessment of progress. For instance, suppose a 12-month goal calls for reaching 20 percent of new car prospects in the East and Midwest and making them aware of the fuel-saving possibilities of car Z. Three months into the campaign, research should show pretty close to 5 percent of these consumers already aware (or creative and media strategy had better see some fast changes). Six months in, the figure should approach 10 percent, and so on. Again, the performance yardstick is one of communication effects, not sales; awareness may be months, even years, away from purchase, but it's a solid advertising objective.

Figure 17.2 shows a simplified profit-and-loss sheet for Grime Cream Hand Cleaner, comparing the last completed year's figures with those estimated for the next year. We assume favorable economic and competitive conditions ahead and a projected sales increase of 10 percent that will result from an increased broadcast advertising schedule.

We assume that the predicted sales increase will be due, in large part, to an increase in broadcast audience reach and frequency: more stations in the media schedule and additional airings each week. Note that advertising costs will increase about 50 percent, but so will overall profits. Here, advertising can clearly be seen as an investment (relatively long range) toward future profits.

Unfortunately, many retailers, who live on day-to-day (not year-to-year) sales, would have a difficult time with the task method. Long-term benefits of advertising must often take a back seat to instant payoff. Still, these dealers would do well to think through even short-term objectives before allocating advertising funds; although retail advertising can be tied more closely to sales than can most national efforts, the job of advertising as a communication force remains the same.

Before leaving this section, we should note that advertising agency personnel assist their clients in determining ad budgets (advising them, for example, of expected changes in media rates and commercial production choices), though the ultimate decision must lie with company management.

Today advertisers rarely attempt a full-scale national campaign with less than a $10 million advertising budget (though, obviously, regional and local efforts can succeed with considerably less). Table 17.2 shows the advertising investments made by well-known national advertisers.

Table 17.2. Approximate broadcast advertising investments in national campaigns

Advertiser	Spot Radio	Network Radio	Spot TV	Network TV	Cable TV
			(million $)		
Procter & Gamble	...	13	285	489	31
Pepsi Co.	30	5	183	82	5
General Motors	28	9	49	210	5
Anheuser-Busch	40	9	71	155	16
RJR/Nabisco	...	9	82	179	9
Ford Motor	14	7	...	191	6
AT&T	...	25	...	168	4
Beatrice	12	5	53	112	...
Sears	17	21	...	123	4

Source: Adapted from the Sept. 4, 1986 issue of *Advertising Age*.

Ad Campaigns and Program Fare

Returning now to broadcasting's programming environment, as discussed in Chapter 8, we need to reexamine two basic approaches to the scheduling of advertising. The first houses commercials within actual programs; the second places them between shows. When a single advertiser sponsors an entire show, or at least a major portion of one, the strategy is known as a *program campaign*. When multiple sponsors are involved, the program becomes an *announcement carrier* or *spot vehicle*—part of an announcement campaign.

PROGRAM CAMPAIGNS

In the early days of both radio and TV, single advertisers frequently sponsored entire shows; later, cosponsors and alternate-day or alternate-week sponsors were introduced. Today, increased costs, along with the demise of many radio program formats (such as comedy and dramatic shows), have left us with few such sponsorships, though television specials (such as the "Hallmark Hall of Fame," the "Bell System Family Theater," and some musical and variety shows) still fall into this classification. Some advertisers (national and local) also choose to sponsor selected radio and TV newscasts.

A program campaign affords advertisers a closely knit relationship with the show's image and talent. Stations and networks may then include company identification in promotional announcements for the program. (Some corporations are underwriting programs on public television. Although they do not get any commercial time per se, they do receive name recognition; thus, they can promote the shows as vehicles for communication and corporate image.)

Also, program campaign commercials are often longer than those aired under other scheduling plans (even as long as two minutes). And when a sole sponsor takes on responsibility for complete program and commercial production, some of the copywriting guidelines presented in Chapter 10 may not apply. For instance, the need for product name repetition is not nearly so great as it would be if the commercial appeared back-to-back with others for a variety of products; "Hallmark Hall of Fame" viewers obviously know the sponsor's name before the first spot ever begins. On the other hand, such program ties may be seen as a disadvantage to advertisers interested in schedule flexibility. Those choosing to advertise within a given show must, naturally, air commercials at the particular times the program runs, on the stations and in the specific areas where it is scheduled.

ANNOUNCEMENT CAMPAIGNS WITHIN PROGRAMS

Chapter 14 discussed numerous plans through which advertisers may buy participating slots in programs; now it is time to consider some of the reasons why certain announcement advertisers choose a within-program campaign instead of a between-show strategy.

Programs tend to command fairly consistent audiences—people with the same general demographic and psychographic characteristics—from day to day or week to week. And because a loyal audience is also a known audience (one that can be studied), advertisers may tailor commercial messages accordingly.

Research indicates that some of the atmosphere or image claimed by programs does affect reception and perception of commercials therein. Sometimes the effect is simply the result of an audience's state of mind at the exact moment the program fades out and the commercial fades in; the persuasive attempts of a lively Coca Cola spot might benefit greatly from lead-ins such as a comedy show's family picnic, a dramatic trek across a hot desert, or a time-out during a sports event.

At other times the effect is more far-reaching. For example, a nostalgic or otherwise sentimental drama may leave viewers with such a warm glow inside that sponsors such as Kodak film, Kraft Marshmallows, or Nestle's cocoa enjoy a cozy audience association long after the program is over. Later contact with these products at the store may trigger a pleasant program memory and stimulate purchasing behavior.

Unfortunately, negative associations can also operate in either of the above situations. Advertisers and their agencies obviously do their best to select shows that are appropriate to a desired image (within limitations of screening time, cost, and general availability) but cannot always predict episodic script changes or choose specific commercial placement (because of the nature of buying plans).

In addition, with current societal concerns over televised sex and violence have come some sponsor withdrawals from selected series. And, of course, advertisers who do pull out have a ready-made promotional tool; future messages may note that "Company A has voluntarily withdrawn its commercials from all violent TV programs in an effort to show customers we care about you and your family."

A related image-value that a program may give commercials appears in the form of celebrity support: commercials that blend in with a program because they are given by one or more of the program's hosts or stars. For example, some of the commercials on the Tonight Show are delivered by Ed McMahon. Then again, these persons may simply lead into a commercial by announcing the product name and, perhaps, a brief slogan or copy line without actually endorsing the product in any way.

Television and radio programs also can be merchandised both to retailers and to ultimate consumers. Toy manufacturers may convince toy stores or departments to display point-of-purchase promotional materials for Captain Kangaroo, along with the products advertised on the show. "Seen on Captain Kangaroo," a banner might claim, and the good will generated through program association often rubs off on the items displayed, resulting in satisfied customers and happy sales personnel.

Contests and sweepstakes involving products advertised in specific programs provide another popular tie-in. After a kickoff announcement in an RCA-sponsored television special, viewers might receive lucky numbers through the mail. A trip to a participating appliance dealer provides the opportunity to match numbers with a master display board that also promotes the next (and, in a way, all future) RCA TV specials.

ANNOUNCEMENT CAMPAIGNS BETWEEN PROGRAMS

In a between-show strategy, flexibility reigns; advertisers may spot commercials in any place at any hour for any length of time desired (depending on availabilities). The beauty of this plan is that identical commercials or variations may run simultaneously in different places, at different times, and for different schedule durations.

These campaigns, therefore, permit frequent schedule changes if, for example, situations warrant a sudden increase or decrease in advertising emphasis in selected markets. Costs are generally lower when no programs are involved, although it should be obvious that any advertiser can build an elaborate, very expensive announcement campaign (of either type) or a simple, inexpensive program campaign.

Now consider the nature of the time segment between programs—approximately 2 minutes—during which viewers may be changing channels or making snacks. An advertiser who buys a fixed commercial position immediately after or immediately before a program (as opposed to one between these two slots) may capitalize, at least partly, on the program audience that in-program advertisers paid for. For instance, an advertiser striving to reach the audience claimed by an 8:30–9:00 P.M. comedy show, who cannot afford to buy spots within it, might buy the first commercial slot after the program (probably about 8:57:30). The assumption here is that at least part of the audience would not yet have had time to change stations or otherwise become preoccupied. Likewise, the advertiser seeking the audience for an upcoming 9–10 P.M. drama would buy the slot closest to it (about 8:59:30), hoping these viewers would, by then, be assembled and settled enough to catch the preprogram commercial.

We should note that networks can only sell commercial spots within network programs. At the local level, however, stations may attract advertisers to in-program avails and to national spot avails at station-break time (or, as we have referred to it, between-show time).

In Retrospect

As we reflect on campaigns of the future and on the state of broadcast advertising in the years ahead, we find all systems GO for advancement. Exciting new developments in broadcast equipment and transmission facilities, in production techniques and in the measurement of broadcast advertising effects, as well as in program content and scheduling, lie just beyond the boundaries of this text. Every day new ideas, new products, services, and stores, and new human beings enter our progress-oriented society and demand attention. Commercial content—word combinations, musical and staging arrangements, and the like—will remain a demanding, creative challenge. Further experimentation in commercial length and placement is bound to continue.

Consumers and government will maintain a watchful eye on both broadcasting and advertising, and competitors and members of the trade will keep successful media and advertisers ever alert to changes in socioeconomic conditions and life-styles. The job situation in broadcast advertising may remain tight for the foreseeable future, but there is always room for persons with outstanding talent—for those who can work well with both people and ideas, who can cope with daily and hourly problems and pressures, and who never stop striving for excellence.

Study Questions

1. For a selected product class, describe your own mental positioning ladder for particular brands. Why are certain ones ranked above and below others? What do you believe is the influence of radio and TV advertising?
2. Specifically, what do the first four sections of the Eldridge marketing plan develop that those in an advertising plan do not?
3. Differentiate between long-term and short-term objectives at the corporate, marketing, advertising, and broadcast advertising levels. Use a selected product and then a service.
4. Differentiate between the percentage-of-sales and task methods of budgeting. Explain the advantages and disadvantages of both procedures from a broadcast advertiser's point of view.
5. For a given advertiser, cite advantages and disadvantages of a program and an announcement campaign. Explain how they differ for within-program and between-program announcement campaigns.
6. Why do you think there are such wide discrepancies between the percentages of sales figures spent on advertising among major U.S. corporations?

ASSIGNMENT 17-A
Find and list examples of what you consider to be successful positioning efforts in radio and TV commercials. Then relate (compare) each one to major competitive efforts in the field.

ASSIGNMENT 17-B
Given an assigned set of familiar, competing products, rank them according to your own mental ladder. Compare with your classmates. Discuss the role that commercials have played, focusing both on similarities and on differences between your own rankings and those of others.

ASSIGNMENT 17-C
For an assigned product and station, plan a media schedule for a specific campaign, utilizing Arbitron data and SRDS. Include both radio and TV buys as appropriate. List the schedule and include a brief rationale for the choices you make.

ASSIGNMENT 17-D
Select a group of radio and/or TV commercials that you believe are particularly strong. List what you think were the respective advertisers' objectives behind these spots and the exact audiences (demographically and psychographically) to whom you think they were targeted.

Notes

1. Clarence E. Eldridge, "The Role and Importance of the Marketing Plan," in *The Management of the Marketing Function* (New York: Association of National Advertisers, 1966).
2. Jack Trout, and Al Ries, "The Positioning Era" (New York: Ries, Cappiello, Colwell, Inc.), 12.
3. Ibid., 14.
4. *Advertising Age* (October 13, 1975).
5. Trout and Ries, 36–37.

Suggested Readings

Atwan, Robert. *Edsels, Luckies, and Frigidaires: Advertising the American Way.* New York: Dell, 1979.

Buzzell, Robert D. *The Role of Advertising in the Marketing Mix.* Cambridge, Mass.: Marketing Science Institute, 1971.

Coleman, Howard W. *Case Studies in Broadcast Management.* New York: Hastings, 1970.

Hurwood, David L., and James K. Brown. *Some Guidelines for Advertising Budgeting.* New York: The Conference Board, 1972.

ALSO: Check recent issues of *Advertising Age, Broadcasting,* and the *Journal of Marketing.*

GLOSSARY

Account executive: An employee of an advertising agency or broadcast organization who sells and services an advertiser's campaign.

Across-the-board programming: A competitive programming strategy that involves scheduling a given program at the same time every day, usually Monday through Friday.

Advertiser: A business firm (or other organization) that uses the communications media to persuade consumers to buy its products or services, support its activities, or approve its goals.

Advertising: The process of communicating to a defined audience an informative and persuasive message intended to promote buying action; advertising (except for public service messages) is paid for, includes sponsor identification, and is controlled in content, timing, and media placement.

Advertising agency: An organization hired by advertisers to plan and execute advertising campaigns; major responsibilities include media buying, creation and production of advertising messages, and research.

Advisory opinion: A statement of advice from the Federal Trade Commission on request from an individual advertiser in regard to a specific planned course of action.

Animation: A technique for presenting television messages through cartoon characters and other motion sketches as opposed to live action presentation.

Announcement campaign: A campaign relying on the use of short advertising messages known as spot announcements; most commercial TV and radio programs are designed to accommodate clusters of 30- and 60-second advertising messages.

Area of dominant influence (ADI): A television market area designated by the Arbitron Ratings Company, based on predominant viewing patterns to stations of specific cities.

Attention level: The amount of attention viewers and listeners give to broadcast programs and commercials.

Audience composition: The demographic make-up of a television or radio audience at any given time or for any particular program.

Audience flow: The collective behavior of viewers/listeners as they tune in and out of a station's programming.

331

Audience fragmentation: The division of the viewing or listening audience into small segments by large numbers of stations.

Availability: A commercial time position a network or station has available for purchase by an advertiser.

Barter: A system in which a station exchanges broadcast time for an advertiser's products or services.

Barter syndication: A system in which a station exchanges broadcast time for a program supplied by an advertiser or an agency.

Base rate: One-time, undiscounted advertising rates of broadcast stations and networks; typically quoted base rates are the highest hourly and the highest 30-second spot announcement rates.

Blockbuster: A competitive programming technique in which a long program is scheduled directly opposite a competitor's block of shorter programs.

Block programming: A competitive programming strategy that involves scheduling a series of shows with similar audience appeal consecutively over a period of time.

Cable network: A national network organization that provides cable systems and their subscribers with program services, both general and specialized; cable networks obtain revenues from national advertising, payments from affiliated cable systems, and sometimes from subscriber fees.

Cable television: The television industry that delivers programs to household subscribers by cable as opposed to wireless, broadcast transmission.

Circulation: The estimated number of people or households viewing or listening to a station on a regular basis.

Class rate card: A type of rate card that shows a station's time divided into classes during which the audience size is fairly consistent and all like availabilities are equally priced.

Clear-channel station: An AM radio station assigned to operate with 50,000 watts on a clear channel, free from interference by other stations for hundreds of miles, thus permitting reception great distances from the station.

Close up (CU): A television shot that focuses tightly on a small subject, such as the talent's face, a small product, or one feature of a larger product.

Commercial broadcasting: Privately owned, profit-motivated radio and television stations and networks; advertising is their primary source of revenue.

Commission system: A compensation system through which a recognized advertising agency receives (1) a discount, usually 15 percent, on a prevailing quoted time cost for broadcast advertising, (2) a markup on costs incurred outside the agency for production and research, and (3) standard agency rates for services provided within the agency on behalf of its clients.

Communication satellite: A space satellite that relays television and radio signals and other telecommunications messages from a transmission point on earth back to one or more receiving points (earth stations) on earth; communication satellites are used extensively for relaying network programming to broadcast stations and cable systems and for direct satellite broadcasting to individual homes.

Continuity department: The department of a broadcast station that assists advertisers with the writing and preparation of commercials.

Cooperative (co-op) advertising: Advertising jointly paid for by a national advertiser and a local dealer outlet.

Copy platform: The overall strategy and objectives of an advertising campaign, including advertiser, product, and target audience information; competition; and product positioning.

Copywriter: An employee of an advertising agency or broadcast station who interprets sales messages in words and pictures, music and song, sound effects and motion.

Cost per point (CPP): A means of pricing broadcast advertising on the basis of the number of rating points reached; the cost required for reaching one rating point with an advertising message during a campaign.

Cost per thousand (CPM): A measure of cost effectiveness of advertising; the cost required for reaching one thousand households or persons with an advertising message during a campaign.

Counter programming: A competitive programming strategy whereby a broadcast station or network schedules a completely different type of program opposite a competitor's strong program.

Coverage: The geographical area in which a station's signal can be received by viewers or listeners if they wish to tune in.

Cumulative (cume) audience: The number of different households or persons who tuned to a program or station at least once during a stated period of time; the unduplicated audience.

Cut: An instantaneous change from one television shot to another.

Designated market area (DMA): A television market area designation of the A. C. Nielsen Company, based on predominant viewing patterns to stations of specific cities.

Diary method: A research technique in which sample households keep a log of television viewing or radio listening over a period of time.

Dissolve: A blending of one television shot into another until the first is completely replaced by the second.

Dolly: Movement of a television camera toward or away from its subject matter.

Double billing: A form of illegal, fraudulent billing of advertisers by a media outlet in connection with cooperative advertising, in which the local advertiser and the medium deceive the national organization into paying more than necessary to purchase the advertising utilized.

Fade: The appearance of a scene from a totally blank screen (fade in), or the disappearance of a scene into a blank screen (fade out).

Federal Communications Commission (FCC): The federal agency that regulates radio and television broadcasting, including the licensing of stations; the FCC represents the public interest in its broadcast regulation.

Federal Trade Commission (FTC): The federal agency responsible for protecting the public against unfair and deceptive business practices, including false and misleading advertising.

Fee system: A compensation system under which an advertising agency receives fees from its advertiser clients on (1) an hourly basis, (2) a cost-plus-profit basis, (3) a fixed or flat fee basis, or (4) any combination of the first three approaches.

Film recording: A photographic/chemical process for storing visual information on acetate film.

Focus group: A group of seven to ten people participating in a discussion to give reactions to advertising themes and messages; focus groups often provide advertisers with valuable direction in terms of acceptable product positioning.

Freeze frame: A scene held stationary on screen, temporarily frozen in place.

Frequency: The average number of times each viewer or listener is reached by an advertiser's commercials during a given period or during a campaign.

Graphics: Visual material, both pictorial and lettering, used in advertising a product.

Grid rate card: A type of rate card in which each availability is priced individually, reflecting the size of the audience that normally tunes in at that time.

Gross audience: The total number of households or persons reached over a period of time, counting each time a person or household is included in the audience; gross audience is the gross reach of a program or campaign.

Gross rating points (GRP): The total number of rating points delivered by an advertising campaign, usually stated on a weekly basis.

Group (station) ownership: Ownership of two or more broadcast stations by the same firm in different broadcast markets.

Hammock programming: A competitive programming strategy in which the program slot between two successful shows is used to provide exposure to a new program or one that requires additional positive exposure.

Households using television (HUT): An estimate of the percentage of different households with one or more TV sets turned on during any specific time period.

Independent station: A radio or television station with no network affiliation.

Library service: An organization that makes available stock production materials, such as recorded music, sound effects, and visual aids suitable for use in commercials and programs.

Live action: A commercial or program produced with live talent rather than animated presentation.

Local advertiser: A firm engaged in selling products and/or services at the local, retail level.

Local/retail advertising: Advertising placed by local firms on broadcast stations within the market.

Local station: A low-power AM radio station whose coverage is limited to a localized area.

Lottery: Any activity consisting of (1) a prize, (2) the element of chance, and (3) some form of "consideration"; it is illegal to advertise any form of lottery (other than legal state lotteries) over the broadcast media.

Low-power TV station (LPTV): A television station authorized to serve a small community or an urban enclave with low wattage where its operation can be conducted without interference to a full-power TV station.

Make-good: A free commercial provided by a network or station to replace one that did not run or was improperly broadcast for technical or other reasons.

Marketing: The process of selling products, of which advertising is one aspect; marketing includes consumer research, packaging, distributing, displaying, and advertising goods and services.

Market (consumer) research: Research investigating target-market demographics, along with shopping and purchasing habits, product usage patterns, and attitudes toward brands and retail stores.

Master marketing plan: A total plan for marketing a product or service, of which advertising is an important component.

Matte shot: A television shot that blanks out part of the picture.

Media Research: Research that investigates audience preferences and loyalties in media, media outlets, and specific programs.

Medium shot (MS): A television shot showing talent from approximately the waist up.

Merchandising: Station activities beyond the airing of commercial messages that assist advertisers directly with the merchandising of their products.

Message research: Research that investigates the effectiveness of copy appeals, talent credibility, and various production techniques.

Metering device: A monitoring instrument attached to a television or radio receiver to record set usage.

Metropolitan statistical area (MSA): A metropolitan statistical area (MSA) defined by the U.S. Office of Management and Budget as a central city of 50,000 or more population and the urban area surrounding it; ratings information is given for metropolitan areas as well as for other broadcast market areas.

Miniseries: A short series of full-length programs devoted to a single subject of great importance or wide interest.

Narrowcasting: Directing the programming of a station or network to a narrowly defined demographic or special-interest audience.

National advertiser: A marketer whose products or services are available throughout most, if not all, of the United States.

National network: An organization providing programming on a regular basis to affiliated stations throughout the country and selling commercial time slots within these programs to national advertisers.

National/regional spot advertising: Advertising placed directly on individual broadcast stations through national sales representatives by national and regional firms.

Network: Two or more radio or television stations interconnected to carry simultaneous programming.

Network advertising: Advertising distributed via two or more stations simultaneously; national network advertising is the most common form.

Network affiliated station: A radio or television station affiliated with and carrying programming and advertising from a national network.

Packaged show: A complete radio or television program produced by a production company for sale to an advertising agency and its clients.

Pan: Movement of the television camera in a vertical or horizontal plane; a vertical pan is also called a *tilt*.

Personal interview: A technique in which respondents in the research sample are interviewed in person about their media usage.

Persons using radio (PUR): An estimate of the percentage of persons in a market area, usually 12 years of age or older, listening to a radio at a given time.

Photoboard: A storyboard using actual photographs rather than artist's sketches to illustrate every scene in a television commercial.

Piggyback commercials: The practice of placing two separate commercial messages in one commercial position; the practice emerged when multiproduct advertisers began placing two 30-second advertisements into a 60-second commercial slot.

Positioning: The unique niche in the marketplace claimed by a specific product and based on product benefits.

Post-performance analysis: A review of a broadcast campaign after its completion to determine if the actual audience delivered equals the size of the audience projected for a campaign. If the actual audience falls below ratings/audience guarantees, networks and stations must provide additional availabilities to the client at no cost, or reimburse a part of the budget.

Posttest: Testing the effectiveness of a commercial after listeners or viewers have heard or seen the message on the air.

Potential audience: The total number of households (or people) able to receive a usable signal from a broadcast station.

Power programming: A competitive programming strategy placing a strong show of a similar type and appeal against a competitor's entrenched program.

Preemptible rates: In contrast to fixed-position premium advertising rates, lower rates sometimes are available to clients who risk losing favored time slots to higher-paying advertisers—those who pay fixed-position rates.

Pretest: Testing the effectiveness of a commercial with a presentation before a test audience prior to its broadcast.

Production studios: Studio facilities for the production of commercials and programs for radio and/or television; production studios often specialize in such areas as radio, television, film, and animation.

Program campaign: A campaign built around the sponsorship of programs carefully chosen to match audience characteristics needed by the advertiser.

Program distributor: An organization that sells and distributes syndicated programs to individual stations and cable systems.

Program producer: A production organization that creates and produces programs for sale to networks, stations, and cable systems.

Props: Products and other objects used in the on-air presentation of a television commercial.

Public broadcasting: Radio and television stations and networks licensed to nonprofit organizations, usually related to educational interests; financial support is derived from government funds, corporate and foundation grants, donations, and limited advertising.

Public service announcement (PSA): An unpaid advertising message on behalf of a nonprofit organization, promoting its activities, services, or viewpoints.

Rate card: A schedule of rates charged by a station or network for each type of availability offered.

Rating: The estimated percentage of the total potential audience tuned to a specific station or program.

Reach: An estimate of the number of different households or persons exposed to advertising messages during a given period or during a campaign.

Regional advertiser: A marketer whose products or services are available throughout a region, such as a portion of a state, an entire state, or a combination of states.

Regional station: An AM radio station assigned to operate with up to 5,000 watts on a regional frequency, serving a city and its surrounding rural region.

Research organization: An organization that may be hired by advertisers and broadcast firms to determine audience size and demographic composition, to pretest commercial messages, and to measure overall sales effectiveness of broadcast advertising.

Run of schedule (ROS): A media plan that places an advertising client's commercials throughout a station's daily or weekly schedule at the best available times; such plans often provide the advertiser with broad reach at discounted prices.

Sales department: The department of a broadcast network or station that solicits advertising to be carried on its program schedule.

Sampling: A public opinion research technique in which a small number of respondents is selected, usually randomly, to represent the behavior and attitudes of the larger population of which it is a part.

Satellite station: A full-power television station that repeats the programming of a key station to a coverage area beyond the range of its parent station.

Sets in use (SIU): An estimate of the percentage of radio-equipped households with one or more radio receivers turned on.

Share of audience: The estimated percentage of homes with sets turned on that are turned to a specific station or program.

Soft focus: A camera technique in which the picture content is shot slightly out of focus to achieve a hazy effect, as in a dream sequence.

Special: A one-time program, usually sponsored by a single advertiser and heavily promoted to attract a large audience.

Split screen: A technique in which two or more different scenes appear simultaneously, side by side, on the television screen.

Sponsorship identification: Identification of the name of the sponsor or product in a radio or television commercial message as required by the Communications Act of 1934.

Station image: The personality projected by a station through its choice of programs, on-air talent, and the manner in which it produces its programming.

Station (sales) representative: An organization that sells advertising to national and regional firms on behalf of client stations in various markets across the country; often called *national reps*.

Storyboard: An artist's visual rendering of every scene in a television commercial, accompanied with video instructions and audio copy.

Stunting: A competitive programming strategy in which highly unusual tactics are used to draw attention to a program.

Superimposure (super): Showing one scene, character, or graphic lettering over another on the television screen.

Superstations: Large city independent TV stations transmitted via communication satellites to cable systems throughout the country; because of their wide distribution, certain superstations have become important national advertising media.

Talent agency: An agency representing the performers who deliver and/or otherwise participate in commercials and programs.

Talent union: A union organization that represents and negotiates wage schedules for performing talent.

Target audience: The segment of the public, defined in demographic and psychographic terms, to which an advertising campaign is directed.

Telephone survey: A research technique in which respondents in the research sample are interviewed by telephone regarding their media usage.

Television household: Any household unit, such as a family or an individual, living in a house, apartment, or other dwelling equipped with one or more television sets.

Test market: A broadcast market in which an advertiser schedules a test campaign to evaluate marketing and media strategies before launching a full-scale national advertising campaign for its product or service.

Time-buying service: An organization that specializes in negotiating with and purchasing time on networks and stations on behalf of advertisers and/or their agencies.

Total survey area: The entire area from which viewers or listeners report tuning in a given station.

Traffic department: The department of a broadcast station or network that schedules each program, commercial, public service announcement, or other material to be broadcast.

Translator station: A lower-power repeater station used to fill in gaps in the normal coverage area of a television station.

Truck: Movement of the television camera with moving talent and objects in the set, right to left, or left to right.

Videotape recording: An electromagnetic process for recording visual material on magnetic tape.

Wipe: The sweeping of one picture off the television screen as a new picture replaces it.

Zoom: The effect of moving into or away from the subject matter of a television shot through use of a Zoomar lens.

INDEX

Account executive, 267
Account management, 59–60
ACE Hardware Corporation, 310
ADI. *See* Area of Dominant Influence
Advertisers, 12, 17, 18, 19, 214, 252, 274, 276
  broadcast, 14–15
  classification of, 14
  concerns, 40
  expenditures, 11
  noncommercial, 15
  time buying, 267
Advertising, 3–4. *See also* Advertising plans and campaigns; Audience research; Copy testing; Writing radio commercials; Writing television commercials
  advantages of, 17–18
  allowances, 74
  bait and switch, 84
  campaigns, 15, 17, 37, 317–30
  disadvantages of, 37–38
  media percent, 16
  regulatory changes, 11
  research, 117
  revenues, 11
  self-regulation, 82–86
  state regulation, 81–82
Advertising Age, 151–53, 272
Advertising agency, 269, 296–97
  account service, 62
  a la carte services, 68
  billable services, 66
  commercial guidelines, 90–91
  commercial messages, 147–57, 165–66
  commission system, 64, 65, 68
  definition of, 12
  expenditures, 11, 59
  fee system, 64–66
  functions, 58–59
  in-house, 67, 68
  merchandising, 62
  nonbillable services, 66
  payment, 64
  research types, 60
  retailers and, 304–5
  selection, 63–64
  time buying, 267
  TV copywriter, 166
Advertising Council, 93–94

Advertising plans and campaigns
  announcement campaigns, 327–28
  budget, 322–26
  example, 319–22
  master plan, 317–18
  percentage of sales budgeting, 322–24
  positioning, 318–19
  program campaign, 326–27
  task budgeting, 324–26
Advertising rates, 274–76, 281–85
  information sources, 267–69, 272
Adweek, 253, 276
Adweek's Marketer's Guide to Media, 253, 282
Aided recall, 242. *See also* Audience research
Aim toothpaste, 144
"All in the Family," 124
Aloha Week Festival, 95
American Advertising Federation (AAF), 13, 85, 94
American Association of Advertising Agencies (AAAA), 13, 59, 85, 90, 102, 254
American Broadcasting Company (ABC radio and television), 25, 28, 34, 120, 122, 127, 276
American Dairy Association, 184
American Federation of Musicians (AFM), 196
American Federation of TV and Radio Artists (AFTRA), 195, 196, 213
American Marconi Company, 5
American Radio (Duncan's), 29, 51, 112, 269, 282
American Red Cross, 93
American Society of Composers, Authors, Publishers (ASCAP), 195
American Telephone & Telegraph Company (AT&T), 5–6
Amplitude modulation (AM), 24
AM radio, 7, 8, 18, 29, 30, 43, 51, 112, 135
  clear channels, 29
  coverage, 18, 48
  first conference, 107
  frequency and power, 49
  future, 20
  ground-wave signal, 49
  licensing, 25

  local channels, 29, 50
  number of channels, 29
  regional channels, 29, 50
  retail advertising, 304
  station classification, 29, 50
  types of antenna, 49–50
Anacin, 76–77
"The Andy Griffith Show," 124
Anheuser-Busch, 39
Animatic, 222
Animation, 204–5, 213
Announcement campaign, 326, 327–28
Announcement carrier, 326
The Arbitron Company, 27, 30, 112, 240, 243, 245, 249, 252, 256–59
"Arbitron Information on Demand" (AID), 257–59
Arbitron TV Market Reports, 257
"Archie Bunker's Place," 121
Area of Dominant Influence (ADI), 27, 245, 247, 249, 257, 277, 278, 290
Ariyoshi, George, 95
ASI. *See* Audience Studies, Inc.
Association of Independent Commercial Producers, 194
Association of National Advertisers (ANA), 7, 13, 64, 85, 254
Attitudinal correlates of sales, 237
Audience composition, 113–14, 249–50. *See also* Audience research
Audience Demographics Report, NTI/NAC (NAD), 255
Audience flow, 129
Audience fragmentation, 114
Audience measurement techniques, 240–43. *See* Audience research
Audience patterns
  radio, 110–11
  TV, 111
  VCR, 114
Audience research, 240–66
  aided recall, 242–43
  audience selection, 241
  average quarter-hour, 247
  computer access, 257, 260–61
  cost-per-point (CPP), 253
  cost-per-thousand (CPM), 252–53
  data processing, 243
  diary method, 241–42, 254
  focus groups, 243

Audience research (*continued*)
gross audience, 250–51
gross rating points, 251–52
households using television (HUT), 245, 247–48
limitations, 261–63
mail surveys, 241
measurement services, 254–62
metering devices, 243, 254
overnight reports, 243
people meters, 243
personal interviews, 241, 242–43
persons using radio (PUR), 245, 247–48
potential audience, 245
program rating, 249
psychographic, 263
ratings formula, 249
reach and frequency, 251–52
sampling procedures, 240–41
share of audience, 245, 248–49
survey area, 244–45
telephone survey, 241–42
television households (TVHH), 246, 247, 248
terminology, 244–53
tuning, 243
of TV households, 106–7, 247
viewing, 243
Audiences, 18. *See also* Audience research; Radio audience; Television audience
audience composition, 249
cable subscribers, 115, 246
concentration, 114
desirable, 29
flow, 129
fragmentation, 114
life-styles, 116
pay-TV, 115
by radio households, 107
radio sets in use, 108
by TV households, 106–7, 247
Audience Studies, Inc. (ASI), 236–37
Audilog, 254
Audimeter, 254, 255
Audio console, 197
Average Daily Circulation (ADC), 51
Average quarter-hour (AQH), 247, 249. *See also* Audience research
Ayer advertising (N.W.), 212

Banzhaf, John, III, 80
BARcume Service, 269
BAR Network Radio Service, 269
Barter, 5, 35, 69, 70, 123
Barter house, 69
Barter syndication, 69–70
Bell System Family Theater, 15
Benchmark study, 219. *See also* Copy testing
"Benson," 124
Billboards in commercial time standards, 83
Birch Radio, Inc., 240, 241, 259–61
Birch radio report, 249
Blair Television, 66–67

Blinking, 272
Bounty paper towels, 178
Brand Cumulative Audiences Report (BCA), 255
Bravo, 64
Broadcast Advertisers Reports (BAR), 269
Broadcast advertising budgets, 31–32
Broadcast advertising departments, 31–32
Broadcast advertising regulation, 73–88. *See also* Federal Communications Commission; Federal Trade Commission; *specific state and broadcast codes*
Broadcasting magazine, 269, 272
Broadcasting/Cable Yearbook, 269
"Broadcast Management Plus," 261
Broadcast Music, Inc., (BMI), 195
Broadcast Promotion Association (BPA), 13
Broadcast Rating Council, 243
Broadcast signals, 50
Broadcast stations
departments, 31–32
group ownership, 25
independently owned, 26–27
licensing, 24
network owned-and-operated, 25
organization of, 30–32
ownership, 25–27
regulations, 24–25
restrictions, 25
Bumped, 284
Bureaus, FCC. *See also* Federal Trade Commission
Cable Television, 78
Common Carrier, 78
Field Engineering, 78
FTC Bureau of Competition, 73
FTC Bureau of Consumer Protection, 73–74
Mass Media, 78
Safety and Special Services, 78
Burger King, 144
Burke Marketing Research, 228, 300
Ad Tel, 228
Burnett, Leo, 59

Cable advertising revenues, 11
Cable networks, 4, 15
advertiser-supported, 39
advertising, 13, 121
programming, 120
rates, 276
scheduling, 273
subscriber base, 38
Cable News Network (CNN), 127
Cabletelevision Advertising Bureau (CAB), 269
Cable television systems, 38–40, 45, 46, 77, 228, 230, 267
audience concentration and fragmentation, 114
channels, 38
definition of, 12
future, 20–21

programming, 46, 127–28
program types, 38
wired households, 273
CableVision, 272
"Cagney and Lacey," 100
Campbell, Ewald, 59
Campbell Soup Company, 76, 187, 188
Captain Kangaroo, 327
Carpenter, John F., 288
Cartridges, 197
Carts. *See* Cartridges
C. E. Hooper, 7, 241, 254
"Charley's Angels," 121
Charley the Tuna, 178
Charmin, 319
"Cheers," 10
Chevrolet, 14
Chicago Federation of Labor (WCFL), 77
Chicago Tribune, 77
Children and advertising, 11, 84. *See also* Commercials
"Children's Advertising Guidelines," 101
Chromakeyer, 204
Chrysler, 39, 178
Circulation, 43, 50, 51, 52
Clark-Hooper, Inc. (Now C. E. Hooper, Inc.). *See* C. E. Hooper, Inc.
Class rate card, 282–83. *See also* Time buying
Clear-channel station, 50
Close-up (CU), 166, 169. *See also* Video terminology
Coca-Cola, 14, 327
Code authority, 83
Code News, 82, 89
Columbia Broadcasting System, Inc. (CBS radio and television), 6, 7, 25, 28, 93, 95, 120, 122, 127, 262, 276
Columbia Pictures TV, 121
Commercial broadcasting, 4, 7–9. *See also* Cable television systems; Independent station; Local stations; Network; Radio; Regional networks; Television
Commercial copy testing. *See* Copy testing
Commercial production, 192–217. *See also* Advertising agency; Radio broadcast production; Television broadcast production
advance person, 196
advertising agency personnel, 193
animation, 204–5, 213
casting, 194
competitive bid system, 212
copy testing modulars, 306–7
cost overages, 212
costs, 211–14
editing, 205–8
equipment/studio/set procurement, 196
estimate request forms, 193, 194
graphics, 209–10
lighting/wearing apparel, 211
musicians/composers/choreographers,

194–95
noncelebrity use in, 213
nonunionized talent, 196
personnel assistance, 197
players, 195
production equipment, 197–202
radio hardware, 197–98
radio station personnel, 192
residuals, 195
scale, 195
sets/props, 209
software, 209–11
talent agencies, 194
talent unions, 195, 213
television audio hardware, 198–99
television station personnel, 192
television video hardware, 199–202
Commercials, 4, 219. *See also*
    Advertising; Advertising agency;
    Audience research; Copy testing;
    Retail advertising; Writing radio
    commercials; Writing television
    commercials
children's, 11, 101
clutter, 19
consumer confidence in, 92–93
elderly used in, 101
ethics in, 89
ethnic groups used in, 11
flights, 17, 38
forms of, 222
message, 147–57, 165–66
minorities used in, 101
national, 52
persuasion, 92
radio, 138–61
rates, 10, 267–72, 274–76, 281–85
truth in, 91–92
women in, 11, 100–101
Communication satellite, 46
Communicus, Inc., 184, 228
Community Chest, 94
Comparative advertising, guidelines for,
    90
Comparative ranking. *See* Copy testing
Conrad, Frank, 5
Consolidated metropolitan statistical
    areas, 244. *See also* Survey areas
Consumer Protection Act of 1969, 81
Contac cold pills, 188
Content analysis, 237
Continuity scheduling, 272
Control Data Corporation, 256–57
Control rooms, 201
Cooperative (CO-OP) advertising, 14,
    15, 313–14
Cooperative Analysis of Broadcasting
    (CAB), 7, 254
Copy platform, 175
bonuses, 144, 175
client, 142, 175
medium, 142, 175
objective, 142–43, 175
positioning, 144, 175
sales key, 144, 148, 175
strategies, 142–45
style, 143, 175

target audience, 143, 175
technique, 143, 175
Copy testing, 218–39
attitudinal correlates, 237
classifications, 220
content analysis, 237
defining effectiveness, 218–19
effects, 219
experimental hardware, 220–21
experiments, 220, 221, 223
Likert scale, 225
measurement, 219
objectives, 219
Osgood's Semantic Differential Scale,
    225
posttest, 222, 223, 226–27
pretest, 222–23
procedures comparison, 221–22
question types, 223–25
rating, 224–25
reliability, 220
Schwerin's system, 230
stages of, 219
surveys, 220, 221, 222
testing organizations, 228–30, 236–37
using results, 237
validity, 220
Copywriter, 60. *See also* Advertising
    agency
radio, 138
TV, 162–66, 169, 174–75, 176, 184,
    185, 187, 188, 211
Cosby, Bill, 178
"The Cosby Show," 10, 124, 125, 275
Cost per point (CPP), 250, 253, 280,
    282, 288, 298. *See also* Audience
    research
Cost per thousand (CPM), 19, 250,
    252–53, 274–76, 280, 281. *See also*
    Audience research
Council of Better Business Bureaus, 85,
    101
Courtesy announcements, 4, 21
Court of Appeals, and the Fairness
    Doctrine, 80
Coverage, 43, 44, 50
Creative Artists Agency, 121
Crest, 14, 92, 144, 178
Crosley Company, 6
Crossfade, 139. *See also* Video
    terminology
Crossley, Archibald, 7
Cume ratings. *See* Cumulative audiences
Cumes. *See* Cumulative audiences
Cumulative (cume) audiences, 51, 250,
    251. *See also* Audience research
Cunningham, 309
Cunningham, Pat, 212
Custom-made networks, 35–36. *See also*
    Network
Cut, 173. *See also* Video terminology

"The Danny Kaleikini Theater," 125
Data gathering, 241–43. *See* Audience
    research
Data processing, 243. *See* Audience
    research

DeForest, Lee, 4–5
Delta Airlines, 147
Demonstration commercials, 182
Dentyne, 185
Designated Market Area (DMA), 27,
    245, 249, 255, 278
Diary method, 241, 242, 254, 255, 257,
    260. *See also* Audience research
Direct broadcast satellite (DBS), 46
Direct questions, structured, close-
    ended. *See* Copy testing
Direct-response advertising, 21
Dissolve, 173. *See also* Video
    terminology
DMA. *See* Designated Market Area
*DMA-CATV Audience Distribution
    Report,* 256
DMA Test Market Profiles, 256
DMA TV Trends by Season, 256
Dr. Zhivago, 121
Dolly, 172. *See also* Video terminology
"Donahue," 123
Double billing, 314
Doublemint Gum, 226
Dow Chemical Scrubbing Bubbles,
    162–63, 178
Downlink, 34
Duncan, James H., Jr., 29, 51

Effective radiated power (ERP), 29, 48
Eldridge, Clarence, 317
Eldridge plan, 317–18
Electronic field production (EFP), 199
Engineering department, 31
"Entertainment Tonight," 123
Equal Time. *See* Communications Act
ESPN (Sports) Network, 127
Experimental station 8XK, 5

Fade, 173. *See also* Video terminology
Fairness Doctrine, 80
"Family Ties," 124
Family Viewing Time, 100
Federal Communications Act of 1934,
    24, 25, 77–80, 102
Federal Communications Commission
    (FCC), 8, 9, 12, 21, 24, 25, 29, 49,
    50, 73, 77–81, 101, 112, 281
chain broadcasting, 123
channel allocation system, 44, 47–48
channel assignment, 27, 44
cross-media ownership, 25
deregulation, 78
influence over advertising, 25, 77–81
multiple ownership, 25
ownership restrictions, 25–26
power restrictions, 29
primetime access rule, 122
Federal Food, Drug, and Cosmetic Act
    of 1938, 81
Federal Radio Act, 77–78
Federal Radio Commission, 77
Federal Reserve Board, 81
Federal Trade Commission (FTC), 25,
    73–77, 84, 91
Federal Trade Commission Act of 1914,
    73–74

Film, 202, 203-5, 207
Firestone Tire & Rubber Company, 75
Fixed position, 284
Flighting, 272
FM radio, 9, 18, 29, 30, 43, 47-48, 112, 135
  advantages of, 29
  future, 19
  licensing, 25
  number of channels, 29
  retail advertising, 304
  station classifications, 29
Focus group, 223, 243. *See also* Audience research
Foley's, 309-10
Food and Drug Administration, 81
Foote, Cone & Belding, 59, 64
Ford Motor Company, 14
Fox Broadcasting Company, 25, 28, 120
Fraudulent billing, 80. *See also* Federal Communications Commission
Freeze frame, 174. *See also* Video terminology
Frequency modulation (FM), 7, 9, 24

Gallup & Robinson, 228
Galvanic skin responses, 221
General Electric Company, 6
General Mills, 39
General Motors, 64, 100
General office department, 32
"Gilligan's Island," 124
The Godfather, 121
"The Golden Girls," 10, 286
Golden Gridle Syrup, 76
Golf Digest, 178
Gone With The Wind, 121
"Good Morning, America," 122
Goodyear Tire, 14
Graphics, 209-10
Great American Independent Football Network, 35
Great Atlantic & Pacific Tea Company (A&P), 304
Grid rate card, 282, 283-85. *See also* Time buying
Gross audience, 250-51. *See also* Audience research
Gross rating points (GRP), 251-52, 295, 298. *See also* Audience research
Group (station) ownership, 25-26
  radio, 6, 26

Hallmark Greeting Card Company, 127
"Hallmark Hall of Fame," 15, 132, 326, 327
Hare, Ernie, 6
Hawaiian Telephone (GTE), 178
Height above average terrain (HAAT), 44
Helical Scan equipment, 201
High-band stations, 44
Home Box Office, 40
Home Shopping Network, 21, 127-28
"Hooperratings," 7, 254
Households using television (HUT),

109, 245, 297. *See also* Audience research
  definition of, 247-48

Iacocca, Lee, 178
"I Love Lucy," 124
Independently owned station, 25, 26, 27
Independent Network News (INN), 28, 126
Independent representatives, 26
Independent station, 19, 26, 27, 28, 84, 120
  counter programming, 126-27
  general service, 125
  rates, 281-82
  specialty, 125-26
Independent TV Sales, 66, 300
Indirect questions, unstructured, open-ended. *See* Copy testing
Infomercials, 15
In-Home Testing Service, 230
Inouye, Daniel, 97
Interconnect basis, 39
International Alliance of Theatrical Stage Employees (IATSE), 196
International Brotherhood of Electrical Workers (IBEW), 196
International Creative Management (ICM), 121

J. C. Penney Company, 14, 142, 304
Jello, 178
"Jeopardy," 123
John Blair & Company, 66-67
Johnson Wax, 64
Jones, Billy, 6

KABL, 77
Kaleikini, Danny, 95-97, 125, 178
Katz Television, 66-67
KDKA, 5
Keebler cookie elves, 178
Keep America Beautiful, 94
KFBK, 50
KFI, 50
KGBS, 77
KHON-TV, 125
Kilohertz (kHz), 29
KIRO, 50
Kleenex Tissues, 319
K Mart, 14, 304
Kodak, 100, 178, 274, 327
Kool-Aid, 188
Kraft Foods Company, 39, 100, 188, 274, 327
KRVN, 283
KYYS-FM, 270

Landers, Ann, 176
LBS Communications, 70
Lenses, 199
Lever Brothers Company, 67
Library services, definition of, 13
Life cereal, 178
Lifts, 208
Lighting, 211
Likert scale. *See* Copy testing

Link, Henry C., 226
Linton, Bruce, 84-85
Listerine, 76
Live action, 222
Local advertiser, 14, 19, 282, 295-96, 303
  time buying, 267
Local/retail advertising, 13-14
Local station, 9, 19, 120
  self-regulation standards, 85
Lottery, 80, 81
Low-band stations, 44
Low-power television station (LPTV), 9, 24, 44

McCann-Erickson Advertising Agency, 11, 16
McCollum Spielman & Company, 153, 178, 182
McDonald's Corporation, 14, 144, 177
McMahon, Harry, 166-88
Magnasync/Movila Corporation, 206, 207
"Magnum P.I.," 100
Magnuson-Moss Warranty Federal Trade Commission Improvement Act, 74
Mail surveys, 241. *See also* Audience research
Make-good, 281, 285
Malden, Karl, 178
Marconi, Guglielmo, 5
MARKET, 106
Marketing, 3-4, 9, 317-18
Marketing (consumer) research. *See* Advertising agency
Market rank, 27, 28
Marketing Science Institute, 101
Market Section Audiences (MSA), 255
"The Mary Tyler Moore Show," 124
"M*A*S*H," 131
Matte shot, 174
Maytag, 178, 319
MCA, Inc., 59
Media. *See* Advertising agency
Medium shot (MS). *See* Video terminology
Megahertz (mHz), 29
Merchandising, 32. *See also* Advertising agency
Message research. *See* Advertising agency
Metered Market Service, 256
Metering device, 241, 243, 254, 255, 256, 260. *See also* Audience research
Metro-Mail Advertising Company, 257
Metropolitan statistical area (MSA), 112, 244, 246, 249. *See also* Audience research
Michelob, 165
Microphones, 197, 198
Midas Muffler Shops, 59
Mislou Network, 35, 126
MMT Sales, Inc., 67
Motion pictures, 59
Moviola upright editor, 206

MTM Productions, 121
Multi-cue synchronizer, 208
Multimedia, 26
Multiplexer, 201
Music and jingles, 6
Mutual Broadcasting System (MBS), 6

NAC Cost Supplement, 255
Narrowcasting, 4, 77, 115, 135
National advertisers, 14, 17, 282
National Advertising Review Board
  (NARB), 85-86, 100
National Alliance of Businessmen,
  JOBS program, 94
National Association of Broadcasters
  (NAB), 6, 13, 82
  advertising ethics, 89-90, 93-94
  self-regulatory codes, 73, 82-85, 281
National Broadcasting Company (NBC
  radio and television), 6-7, 25, 28,
  107, 120, 122, 125, 127, 256, 270,
  271
National Institute of Mental Health,
  101
National networks, 6
  classification, 34
  radio formation, 6-7
National/regional spot advertising, 13
National Retail Merchants Association,
  30
National Safety Council, 93
The Nestle Company, 142, 327
Net Weekly Circulation (NWC), 51
Network, 24-42, 36
  advertising, 13, 269
  affiliation, 34, 36
  audience concentration, 114-15
  availabilities, 273
  classification of, 34
  commercials, 19
  compensation plan, 36
  contract duration, 37
  custom-made, 35-36
  format, 132
  ownership, 25
  programming, 121-22
  rates, 274-76, 282
  schedules, 121, 122, 273-76
  self-regulation standards, 84
  signal delivery, 34, 37
Network advertising. *See* Network
Network-affiliated station, 28, 36, 282.
  See also Network
Network Program Analysis (Arbitron),
  257
Network Programs by DMA, 256
Networks, 12, 120
Network-station relations, 36. *See also*
  Network
News Barmometer (Arbitron), 257
News department, 31
Newsweek, 178
Nielsen (A. C.) Company, 16, 27, 93,
  106, 107, 109, 112, 114, 240, 243,
  244, 245, 246, 247, 249, 252,
  254-56, 261, 287
Nielsen Station Index (NSI), 254,

255-56, 298. *See also* Nielsen (A.
  C.) Company
Nielsen Television Index (NTI), 114,
  254, 255. *See also* Nielsen (A. C.)
  Company
"Night Court," 10
"Nightline," 122

Office of Child Development, 81
Oglivy & Mather, 90, 140
"Operation Prime Time" (OPT), 28,
  300
"The Oprah Winfrey Show," 123
Orbit, 298
Oscar Mayer, 188
Osgood's Semantic Differential Scale,
  225. *See also* Copy testing
Overnight Coincidental Studies
  (Arbitron), 257
Owned & operated (O&O) stations, 25,
  66, 67

Packaged shows, 7
Palmer, Volney, 58
Paramount Television, 121
Pay TV, 12, 40, 46, 254
  audience, 115
People meter system, 243-44, 254, 257.
  See also Audience research
"People's Court," 123
Pepsi, 14
Personal interview, 241, 242-43. *See*
  also Audience research
Persons using radio (PUR), 245,
  247-48. *See also* Audience research
Persons using television (PUT), 297
Philco Company, 6
Philip Morris, Inc., 39
Photomatic, 222
Piggyback commercials, 9
Pillsbury Doughboy, 162
Pizza Hut, 14
Plugs, 5
"The Pocketpiece" (Nielsen National
  TV Ratings), 255, 256
Political advertising, 80, 101-2. *See also*
  Federal Communications Act of
  1934
Positioning, 144
Post Office regulations, 81
Posttests, 222, 223, 231-32, 234-35
  inquiries, 227
  pencil and paper tests, 226
  personal interviews, 226-27
  telephone, 226
  testing organizations, 228-30
Potential audience, 245, 247. *See also*
  Audience research
Preemptible rates, 284-85
Pretests, 222-23, 233. *See also* Copy
  testing
Procter & Gamble, 39, 64, 183, 323,
  319
Production studios/facilities, 12-13, 52,
  280-81
Product Movers, 62
Program campaign, 326-27

Program Cumulative Audiences Report
  (PCA), 255
Program department, 31
Program distributors, definition of, 12
Program producers, definition of, 12
Program ratings, 245. *See also* Audience
  research, definition of, 249
Program syndication, 69
Promotion department, 31
Proved Commercial Registration (PCR),
  228-29
Prudential Insurance, 14, 187
Psychogalvanometer, 221
Psychographic research, 116, 143, 167
Public broadcasting, 4, 21
Public Broadcasting Act of 1967, 4
Public Broadcasting Service (PBS), 120,
  126
Public service, 94, 95-100
Public service advertising, 4, 15
  campaigns, 93-94
Public Service Advertising Bulletin, 94
Pulsing, 272

Quall, Ward L., 126
Quarterly Summary Report (Birch),
  259-60
QUBE, 223
Questionnaire development, 227-28. *See*
  also Copy testing
Quinn-Martin Productions, 121

Racked, 199
Radio, 10
  advantages, 18
  audience patterns, 110-11, 114
  coverage, 18
  demographic groups, 18
  first conference, 107
  future, 20-21
  home set location, 108-9
  listening, 16, 110
  rate structures, 282-85
  revenue, 19
  set ownership, 10, 16, 107
  sets in automobiles, 108
  sets in households, 107
  sets in use, 16
Radio Act of 1912, 76
Radio advertising, 7. *See also* Radio
  commercial writing; Radio
  programming
  advantages, 18
  clutter, 19
  coast-to-coast, 13
  cost, 18
  effectiveness, 267
  rates, 281-86
  retail, 303-16
  revenue, 7-8, 11
  saturation, 7
  station growth, 7-8
  types, 13
Radio Advertising Bureau (RAB), 32,
  67, 107, 108, 110, 269, 308-9, 314
Radio audience, 106-19, 243-45, 250,
  259-60, 261. *See also* Audience

Radio audience (*continued*)
research; Audiences; Cumulative audiences
composition, 113, 114
average quarter-hour, 247, 249
seasonal variation, 113
set usage, 109–13
Radio Code Board, 82
Radio commercial writing, 138–61. *See also* Copy testing
audio tape, 205
call for action, 156
content specifics, 151–57
copy platform, 142–47
dialogue, 149–50
drama, 151
early selling, 153
elements of, 138–42
graphic spot, 154
humor, 138, 151–53
immediate attention, 15
interview, 151
jingles, 139–41
message, 147
nature of task, 138
personality/ testimonial, 148
"play on words," 156
promise, 151
sound effects, 141–42
straight announcement, 148–49
target audience, 143
tracking, 154
words and voices, 139
Radio Corporation of America (RCA), 6, 202
Radio Expenditure Reports, 269
Radio hardware, 197–98. *See also* Cartridges; Microphones; Reel-to-reel
Radio households, 107–8. *See also* Audiences
Radio networks/program services, 35, 37, 274. *See also* Network commercial costs, 18
Radio programming, 10, 120, 133–36. *See also* Radio advertising; Radio commercial writing
coverage, 17
ethnic, 135
general service, 133
music, 133
policies, 29
schedule, 17
specialty, 135
talk, 133–34
Radio Recall Research, Inc., 230
Radio signals, 49–50
Ralston-Purina Company, 222
Rapid Shave, 76
Rate card, 282–84. *See also* Time buying
Rating, 223–25, 262, 263. *See also* Copy testing
Ratings formula, 249
Raycom Sports, 126
Reach and frequency, 7, 250, 251–52,

288. *See also* Audience research
Recordimeter, 254
Recording wild, 199
Reel-to-reel, 198, 201
Regional feed, 14
Regional networks, 34
Reliability, 220
Rep. *See* Station representative
Report on Syndicated Programs, 256
Research. *See* Audience research; Copy testing
Research department, 32. *See also* Advertising agency
Research organizations, 7, 17. *See also* Audience research; Copy testing; *individual listings by firm*
definition of, 13
Residuals, 195
Retail advertising
benefits, 305, 313–14
campaigns, 309–13
cooperative, 313–14
creativity in, 305–7
functions, 303
legalities, 314
objectives, 304
production, 306–7
research, 315
trade association services, 308–9
Rigged promotions. *See* Federal Communications Commission
RJR Nabisco, 39
Roadblocking, 273
Robinson-Patman Act, 74
Roper Organization, 92
Run of schedule (ROS), 276, 283, 310

Sales and Marketing Management's Survey of Buying Power, 269
Sales department, 31, 287–88
Sales promotion department, 31, 62. *See also* Advertising agency
Sales representative firms (station representative), 12, 14, 34
Salvation Army Kettle Drive, 97, 98, 99
Sarnoff, David, 5
Satellite communication, 12, 34, 45
Satellite station, 44, 45
ScanAmerica, 257
Schwerin, Horace, 230. *See also* Schwerin system
Schwerin system, 236. *See also* Copy testing
Scott Paper Company (Scot Towels, Scot Tissues, Scotties, Scotkins), 319
Screen Actors Guild (SAG), 195, 213
Screen Extras Guild (SEG), 196, 213
Script, 7, 167–68
Sears, 14, 304
Seasonal Variation Index, 257
Segue, 139
Seigle, Schiller, Rolfs, Wood, Inc., 61–63, 193
"$elect-A-Vi$ion," 261
Selling television time

agency calls, 296–97
equally rated inventory, 300
established accounts, 297–98
high-rated inventory, 299–300
independent stations, 300
local advertiser calls, 295–96
low-rated inventory, 298, 300
TVB, 300–301
Seltel, Inc., 67
Sets-in-use (SIU), 247
Shadow areas, 44
Share-of-audience, 245, 248–49. *See also* Audience research
Significant Viewing Studies (Arbitron), 257
Simmons Market Research Bureau, Inc., 18, 110, 263
Simmons Target Group Index, 263
Singer Company, 67
Single-station owner, 26
Soap operas, 7
Soft focus. *See* Video terminology
Sound effects, 7
Spanish International Network (SIN), 127. *See also* Hallmark Greeting Card Company; Univision
Split screen. *See* Video terminology
Sponsorship identification, 4, 6, 9
Sports Illustrated, 178
Spot Activity–Post Evaluation Reports (Arbitron), 257
Spot advertising, 6, 9, 14, 15, 17, 18, 19, 273–74, 276, 280, 305
campaigns, 13
rates, 269, 281, 282
Spot sales, 67
Spot vehicle, 326. *See also* Announcement carrier
SRDS Network Rates and Data, 267
SRDS Spot TV and Radio, 267, 269, 281
Standard Directory of Advertising Agencies, 68
Standard Rate and Data Service, Inc. (SRDS), 267, 268, 269, 277, 282, 290
Standards and Practices department, 84
"Star Trek," 124
State regulation. *See* Advertising
Station (sales) representative, 66, 67, 269, 299
Storage Instantaneous Audimeter (SIA), 254. *See also* Audimeter
Storer, George B., 77
Storyboard, 167, 169, 170–71
Stunting, 338
"Sunday Morning," 122
"Sunday Today," 122
Superimposure (Super). *See* Video terminology
Superstations, 12, 39, 46, 121
Supreme Court, 76, 80
Survey area, 244–45. *See also* Audience research
Sweeps, 257. *See also* Arbitron
Syndicated Program Analysis (Arbitron), 257

Syndicated Program Ranking Report (Arbitron), 257
Syndicated programs, 28, 123–24

Tag line, 313. *See also* Cooperative advertising
Talent, 7, 213
Talent agencies, definition of, 13
Talent buy, 196
Talent union, 213
Talk programming, 31
"Tapscan," 261, 262
Tapscan, Inc., 289
Target audience, 4, 10, 30, 31, 114, 143, 252
Taster's Choice, 142
TAT Productions, 121
"Taxi," 121
Telemundo, 127
Telephone survey, 241, 260. *See also* Audience research
Tele-Poll Surveys (Arbitron), 257
Telerep, Inc., 67
Tele-Research, Inc., 230
Telestrator, 201
Television advertising
  advantages, 17–18
  clutter, 19
  rates, 10, 19
  revenues, 11, 19
  types, 13
Television & Cable Factbook, 8, 36, 44, 54, 269–70, 282
Television and radio networks, 9, 32
Television and radio stations
  coverage maps, 44
  definition of, 12
  future, 20
  growth, 9
  high-definition, 46
  number of employees, 31
  operating log, 33
  propagation pattern, 45
  revenue, 11
  sales department, 287–88
  sets, 16, 108
  signal obstructions, 44
  television (TV) antenna height, 44
  time-based, 16, 17
Television audience, 18, 106–19. *See also* Audience patterns; Audience research
  composition, 113–14
  seasonal variation, 112
  set usage, 109–13
  viewing, 16, 108, 110, 111, 112, 113
Television Bureau of Advertising (TVB), 67, 70, 162, 269, 295, 300–301, 303, 308–9, 310
Television Code, 83
Television Code Review Board, 82
Television commercials, 162–91
  after-use, 167
  children, 188
  communication effect, 187
  frames, 167

graphics, 164
incidentals, 167
in-use, 167
photoboard, 168
players, 163
presenters, 163
product personalities, 162
props, 163
result-of-use, 167
retail, 303–16
script, 167
sequential action, 168
sets, 163
spots, 187–88
storyboard, 167–68
talent, 167
talent's face, 174
Television commercial writing
  animation, 164
  aural elements, 164
  commercial message, 165–66
  content specifics, 184–89
  copy platform, 175
  copywriters, 164
  demonstration, 182, 183
  documentary, 176
  elements of, 162–65
  fantasy land, 182
  formats, 175–84
  humor, 185–87
  message content, 166–67
  nature of task, 162
  personal endorsement, 178, 179
  presentation, 166–69
  product personalities, 162
  recall, 185
  sound effects, 165
  storytelling/slice of life, 175–76, 177
  talent, 163
  video terminology, 169, 172–74
  visual elements, 163–64
  voice over, 164
  words and voices, 164
Television Digest, Inc., 10, 270. See also *Television & Cable Factbook*
Television Factbook, 10, 46, 54, 108
Television households (TVHH), 107, 108, 247, 249. *See also* Audience research
Television Markets and Ranking Guides (Arbitron), 257
Television Program Enterprises, 70
Television programming, 10, 17, 120–32, 274
  affiliates, 121, 123–25
  audience concentration, 114–15
  block, 129
  blockbuster, 129
  cable systems, 120–21, 127–28
  commercial content, 132
  commercials, 132
  comparable-time scheduling, 37
  competitive scheduling, 129
  counter, 126, 129, 130, 131
  coverage, 17
  encounter, 129

Hammock, 131
independent stations, 125–27
long-form, 131
miniseries, 131
network, 121–22
newspaper log, 130
policies, 29, 274
power, 129, 130
regular series, 131
schedules, 17, 121, 122
serialization, 131
specials, 9, 15, 95, 131
spectacular, 131
station image, 128–29
strategies, 128–32
strip (horizontal), 131
stunting, 131
syndicated, 123–25
syndication fees, 124
Television video hardware, 199–201
Testing. *See* Copy testing
Test market, 277–78
Texas State Network, 35
"Three's Company," 124
Time, Inc., 178
Time buying, 267–94
  audience composition, 274–78
  availabilities, 273
  blinking, 272
  circulation, 278
  client analysis, 272–73
  continuity scheduling, 272
  cost, 273
  coverage, 278
  flighting, 272
  information sources, 267–72
  market rank, 277
  market selection, 277
  network rates, 274–76
  network schedule, 273–76
  production requirements, 280–81
  program types, 274
  rate card, 282–84
  rates, 281–86
  rate structures, 282–85
  roadblocking, 273
  run of schedule, 283
  scheduling options, 272
  sponsorship patterns, 273–74
  station selection, 278–81
  test markets, 277–78
  total audience plan, 283
Time-buying services, definition of, 12
Time-shifting, 16, 17, 114
"Today," 122, 248
Toll broadcasting, 5–6
"Tonight Show" (NBC), 122
Total audience plan (TAP), 283
Total Survey Area (TSA), 245
Tracking problem, 185
Trade associations, definition of, 13
Tradeouts, tradeoffs, 69
Traffic department, 32, 287
Translator station, 44, 45
Treviesas, Herminio, 85
Triple Associates Test, 226

Truck. *See* Video terminology
Truth-in-Lending Law, 81
Turner Broadcasting, 28, 39
TV Guide, 32, 136
"TV Scan," 288, 289

UHF television, 24, 27, 39, 43, 44, 45, 48, 127, 222, 278
Ultra high frequency (UHF), 24
United Air Lines, 147
United Independent Broadcasters, 6, 26
United Negro College Fund, 94
U.S. Census, 241, 254
U.S. Criminal Code, 80–81. *See also* Federal Communications Commission
U.S. Office of Management and Budget, 244
U.S. Savings Bonds, 93
United Stations Radio Network, 35
United Way, 94
Universal Television, 121
Univision (formerly Spanish International Network), 126, 127, 131, 276
USA Network, 39, 127
U.S. News, 178

Validity, 220
Vampire video, 185, 187. *See also* Video terminology
Vaseline Intensive Care Lotion, 165
Vermont Maple Industry, 76
Very high frequency (VHF), 24, 278
VHF television, 27, 43, 44, 45, 48
Video carts, 200–201. *See also* Cartridges
Videocassette recorders (VCR), 16, 17, 107, 184, 254
   zap, 16, 184
Videola system, 206–7
Videotape, 200–201, 202, 203, 205, 207
Videotape recording, 13, 52, 202, 280
Video terminology, 169, 172–74
   arc, 172
   background, 174
   belly shot, 169
   boom, 172
   chest shot, 172
   composition terms, 169, 172
   crossfade, 139, 173
   cut, 173
   descriptive terms, 173–74
   dissolve, 173

dolly, 172, 199
extreme-close-up, 169
fade, 173
flashback, 174
follow, 172
foreground, 174
freeze frame, 174
head-and-shoulder shot, 172
headless, 169
lap dissolve, 173
long shot, 169, 199, 200
match dissolve, 173
matte shot, 174
medium-close-up shot, 169, 199, 200
medium-long shot, 169
medium shot, 169
montage, 173
one-shot, 172
pan, 172
pedestal, 172
post-up, 169
reverse motion, 174
ripple dissolve, 173
slow motion, 174
soft focus, 174
speed-up action, 174
split screen, 174
studio camera, 200
super, 174
take, 173
three-shot, 172
tight shot, 169
tilt, 172
titles, 174
top shot, 172
tracking problem, 185
transition terms, 172–73
truck, 172
two-shot, 172
vampire video, 185, 187
waist shot, 172
wide shot, 169
wipe (horizontal, vertical, diagonal, closing doors, iris), 173
zoom, 172
Vidicon, 199
Viewers in Profile, 255, 257
Violence, 100, 327
Visine, 189
VTR. *See* Videotape recording

"The Waltons," 121
Walt Wesley Company, 221
War Advertising Council. *See* Advertising Council
Warner-Lambert Company, 76
Warren Publishing, Inc., 269. See also *Television & Cable Factbook*
Watson, Tom, 178
WBIR-TV, 45
WBNS-TV, 245
WCCO, 50, 133
WCKY, 50
WEAF (WNBC, WFAN), 6
Wendy's, 14, 144
Westinghouse (Group W), 26
Westinghouse Electric and Manufacturing Company, 5–6
WFAN, 5–6
WGN, 50, 77, 133
Wheeler-Lea Amendment, 74
"Wheel of Fortune," 123
Whirlpool, 14
White-Westinghouse, 14
Wide area telephone service (WATS), 242
William Morris Agency, 121
Windsor Total Video Company, 309
Wipe, 173. *See also* Video terminology
WIS-TV, 285–86
WIVK AM-FM, 33, 133
WJDX-AM, 283–84
WJR, 133
WJZ, 6
"WKRP in Cincinnati," 124
WLW, 50
WMC-TV, 128
WMSI-FM, 283–84
WNBC, 6
WNDU AM-FM-TV, 26
Woolworth Woolco, 304
WPIX-TV, 28
WPTF, 133–34
WRVA, 133
WSB, 77, 128, 288
WSM, 50
WTIC, 133
WTTG-TV, 131
WWL AM-FM-TV, 26

Young & Rubicam, 59
YMCA, 94
YWCA, 94

Zapping, 16
Zenith, 226
Zest soap, 187
Zoom, 172. *See also* Video terminology